Endgames

The 2011 Arab Spring tells the story of what happens to autocrats who prepare their militaries to thwart coups but unexpectedly face massive popular uprisings instead. When demonstrators took to the streets during that fateful year, some militaries remained loyal to the powers that be, some defected, while others splintered. The widespread consequences of this military agency ranged from facilitating transition to democracy, to reconfiguring authoritarianism, or triggering civil war. This study aims to explain the military politics of 2011, both in Egypt and Syria, and across Tunisia and Libya. Building on interviews with Arab officers, extensive fieldwork, and archival research, as well as hundreds of memoirs and political accounts, Hicham Bou Nassif shows how divergent combinations of coup-proofing tactics inform military behavior when autocratic regimes face nationwide popular protests.

Hicham Bou Nassif is Assistant Professor of Government at Claremont McKenna College. He is the author of numerous articles in academic journals including *Democratization*, the *International Journal of Middle East Studies*, *Middle East Journal*, *Political Science Quarterly*, and the *Journal of Strategic Studies*.

Endgames

Military Response to Protest in Arab Autocracies

Hicham Bou Nassif

Claremont McKenna College

CAMBRIDGE
UNIVERSITY PRESS

CAMBRIDGE
UNIVERSITY PRESS

University Printing House, Cambridge CB2 8BS, United Kingdom

One Liberty Plaza, 20th Floor, New York, NY 10006, USA

477 Williamstown Road, Port Melbourne, VIC 3207, Australia

314–321, 3rd Floor, Plot 3, Splendor Forum, Jasola District Centre,
New Delhi – 110025, India

79 Anson Road, #06–04/06, Singapore 079906

Cambridge University Press is part of the University of Cambridge.

It furthers the University's mission by disseminating knowledge in the pursuit of
education, learning, and research at the highest international levels of excellence.

www.cambridge.org
Information on this title: www.cambridge.org/9781108841245
DOI: 10.1017/9781108893695

First published 2021

A catalogue record for this publication is available from the British Library.

Library of Congress Cataloging-in-Publication Data
Names: Nassif, Hicham Bou, author.
Title: Endgames : military response to protest in Arab autocracies / Hicham Bou
Nassif.
Description: Cambridge, United Kingdom ; New York, NY : Cambridge
University Press, 2021. | Includes bibliographical references and index.
Identifiers: LCCN 2020011138 (print) | LCCN 2020011139 (ebook) |
ISBN 9781108841245 (hardback) | ISBN 9781108893695 (ebook)
Subjects: LCSH: Civil-military relations – Arab countries. | Arab countries –
Military policy. | Arab countries – Armed Forces – Political activity. | Arab
Spring, 2010– | Protest movements – Arab countries – History – 21st century.
Classification: LCC JQ1850.A38 C586 2021 (print) | LCC JQ1850.A38
(ebook) | DDC 322/.50956–dc23
LC record available at https://lccn.loc.gov/2020011138
LC ebook record available at https://lccn.loc.gov/2020011139

ISBN 978-1-108-84124-5 Hardback
ISBN 978-1-108-81015-9 Paperback

To Yola and Nabil

The Iraqi Army was the only force capable of conspiring against me.
The only power we fear is this army . . . The army is like a pet tiger.
Saddam Hussein

Contents

Tables

Acknowledgments

This book began as a dissertation at Indiana University in 2011. William R. Thompson was my advisor at IU and he remains to this day a source of profound admiration and deep respect. As an advisor, Thompson gave me leeway to work on my own and develop my early ideas on military politics, but was immediately there for me anytime I needed him. I am indebted to him for his support since we met during my first year in graduate school in 2008. As I write these words, we are working on a new research project and I hope we will collaborate further in the future.

I am also very grateful to yet another great scholar, the late Alfred Stepan. We met when I was doing fieldwork in Cairo, in the summer of 2012. At the time, many saw the Muslim Brotherhood as the actor to be watched and studied. Stepan expressed frustration that few researchers were investigating Egyptian military politics and took me immediately under his wing when I told him that I was in Cairo to interview officers. From that moment until he passed away in 2017, Stepan read and commented upon pretty much everything I wrote, served on my doctoral committee, wrote letters of recommendation on my behalf, and invited me to present my findings at Columbia and write a chapter in the last volume he edited. May his soul rest in peace; I will never forget what I owe him.

Kevin Martin taught Middle East history at IU during my time there, and he was invariably supportive and generous with his time. I am not a native speaker of English, which isn't even my first foreign language. When I took my first steps into academic publishing in 2012, Martin patiently read and reread first drafts and improved my work in substance and in form. I am grateful for his kindness, hospitality, and the hours we spent discussing Syria.

My research in Cairo was greatly facilitated by M. K., an Egyptian academic, and M. H., a PhD student whom I met thanks to Alfred Stepan. I will not write their full names because of the nature of the political regime currently holding sway in Cairo, and because of what I have written on the political economy of corruption in the upper echelons of the Egyptian military. But I do wish to acknowledge their help and thank them for it. M. K. asked an influential retired military general to meet me; he, in turn, invited his colleagues to do the same and I snowballed from there. M. H. shared with me his intimate understanding of Egyptian society and patiently answered my questions as I began investigating the politics of his country. My time in Cairo was made far more interesting because of his friendship.

Alissa Strunk, a PhD student at IU, introduced me to several of her friends in Tunis. They, in turn, arranged for me to meet Mukhtar Hishayshi and Boubaker Ben-Kraiem, two retired officers whom I interviewed several times and who agreed to ask their colleagues to meet me. I am grateful to the three of them. I will not name the officer who facilitated my research on Syrian military politics. May he be able to return to Syria one day, and may the bloodshed finally stop in his long-suffering country.

Carleton College gave me my first job after graduation in 2014. I wrote most of this book during my years at Carleton between 2014 and 2018. I couldn't have asked for nicer colleagues or for a more congenial environment in which to begin my academic career. For their humor, kindness, friendship, and support, I wish to thank Alfred Montero, Dev Gupta, Greg Marfleet, Laurence Cooper, Richard Keiser, Tun Myint, and Barbara Allen. Alas, the Minnesota winters proved too much for me and I searched for employment elsewhere; but the presence of this incredible group of fine scholars and fundamentally decent individuals brought warmth to my heart amid the cold and the gray.

I was teaching at Carleton when I published "Generals and Autocrats: How Coup-Proofing Predetermined Military Elite's Behavior in the Arab Spring," *Political Science Quarterly*, vol. 130, no. 2, June 2015. I have spent the last four years essentially developing the arguments I first put on paper in my dissertation, and then in this article. I thank *PSQ*'s editor and the anonymous reviewers who commented on the piece.

My colleagues in Claremont McKenna College have also been very supportive since I joined them in 2018. After I finished writing, several colleagues read the draft and gave me helpful feedback. For their encouragement, I especially wish to thank Hilary Apel, Minxin Pei, William Ascher, Joseph M. Bessette, Andrew Busch, Rodric Camp, Aseema Sinha, Jennifer Taw, Giorgi Areshidze, and Lisa Koch.

Zoltan Barany is perhaps America's foremost scholar in the field of civil–military relations. I benefitted immensely from his comments on a first draft of this book and I wish to thank him for taking the time to read the manuscript carefully. Marc Lynch read the same draft after we met at the 2018 Middle East Studies Association annual conference, in Texas.

His suggestions were very useful in reorganizing the manuscript along new lines. For his impeccable professionalism, warm regards are due to Daniel Brown, my editor at Cambridge University Press. I was lucky I got to work with him and I very much hope to do so again in the future. I also thank Maria Marsh and the two anonymous reviewers at the Press.

Hazem Saghieh, a Lebanese political writer, read and commented on an early draft of Chapters 3 and 4. I thank him for doing so. I also thank Yezid Sayigh for his friendship and support.

I met Julie, my wife, during the last stretch of this work. Her unwavering backing proved instrumental in getting me through the exciting but stressful final miles. Julie is a historian currently finishing a dissertation on the Lebanese Civil War. She plans to transform it into a book soon and I promise to be by her side just as she was by mine since we met.

My mother, Yola, and my father, Nabil, are the shining stars of my life. No words will be enough to describe what they mean to me, and so I won't even try. I will simply say that I owe them everything I am today. This book is dedicated to them in humble acknowledgment of the incredible love they carry in their beautiful hearts.

Introduction

The 2011 uprisings in the Arab world shared similar characteristics and produced radically divergent outcomes. The tens of thousands of protesters who took to the streets in Tunisia, Libya, Egypt, Yemen, Bahrain, and Syria clamored nonviolently for regime change. The urban poor, Westernized elite, Islamists, union activists, liberals, and leftists mobilized along cross-class, cross-regional, and nonpartisan lines. The commonalities in terms of motivations, grievances, protest size, as well as the peaceful nature of the popular mobilization, were unmistakable. And yet the popular movements triggered markedly different military responses. In Syria and Bahrain, the armed forces sanctioned bloodbaths to defend their leaders. In contrast, the military refrained from using violence in Egypt and Tunisia. Meanwhile, troops splintered in Libya and Yemen where some units defected wholesale whereas others stayed loyal and willing to uphold autocracy. In every case, the armed forces sat at the crux of the unfolding cataclysmic events and influenced the fortunes and misfortunes of democracy in the Arab region. But why was the military reaction to these upheavals strikingly dissimilar? This is the central question of this book. I maintain that coup-proofing structures military politics during endgame scenarios.[1] Specifically, I study the historical origins of civil–military relations in Arab autocracies and show that institutional

---

[1] David Pion-Berlin et al. were the first to use the "endgame" metaphor to describe a situation where civilian uprisings threaten autocrats' desperate grip on power, leaving the armed forces as the ultimate defense line of the status quo. See David Pion-Berlin and Harold Trinkunas, "Civilian Praetorianism and Military Shirking During Constitutional Crises in Latin America," *Comparative Politics* 42, no. 4 (July 2010): 398; and David Pion-Berlin, Diego Esparza, and Kevin Grisham, "Staying Quartered: Civilian Uprisings and Military Disobedience in the Twenty-First Century," *Comparative Political Studies* 47, no. 2 (2014): 236. Endgames are typically short and can last for only a few days (e.g., Romania, December 1989) or a few weeks (e.g., Egypt, January/February 2011), or a few months (e.g., East Germany, September 1989/March 1990). In the wake of endgames, dictatorships transition to democracy, consolidate their autocratic order, or plunge into civil strife.

legacies pertaining to coup-proofing informed the agency of officers during the 2011 turning point.

Iron laws in the social sciences are scarce, but the following axiom may qualify as such: no transition from autocracy to democracy is possible if the armed forces remain cohesive and loyal to the powers that be. Put differently, popular uprisings can only trigger autocratic breakdowns when militaries desist from defending the status quo. This, of course, breaks with much of the classical literature on revolutionary transformations. Marx, for example, asserts that proletarian triumph in the struggle pitting the bourgeoisie against the workers is made inevitable by contradictions inherent to capitalism. Increasing economic exploitation heightens class conflict and consciousness, and the ensuing polarization creates conditions favorable to the seizure of power by revolutionary movements. Guevara and Mao agree: revolutionary triumph over the forces of reaction is not only possible, but it is actually made ineluctable by the persecution of the masses, galvanizing popular resistance.[2] Interestingly, the analyses of Lenin and Trotsky are more nuanced in this regard. They maintain, respectively:

No revolution of the masses can triumph without the help of a portion of the armed forces that sustained the old regime.[3]

There is no doubt that the fate of every revolution at a certain point is decided by a break in the disposition of the army. Against a numerous, disciplined, well-armed and ably led military force, unarmed or almost unarmed masses of the people cannot possibly gain victory.[4]

In other words, Marx, Guevara, and Mao seem to imply that once the revolution is set in motion, there is little the status quo can do to uphold it. Lenin and Trotsky, on the other hand, suggest that revolutionary victory is a function of armed forces defection. Academics are also divided over the matter. Some, like Gurr or Hobsbawm, are closer to the Marxist notion of revolutionary triumph as historical inevitability. Others, like Russell, argue that the disloyalty of the armed forces is a necessary condition for autocratic breakdown.[5] The debate is fascinating, but it is also

---

[2] See D. E. H. Russell, *Rebellion, Revolution and Armed Force: A Comparative Study of Fifteen Countries with Special Emphasis on Cuba and South Africa* (New York: Academic Press, 1974), 13.

[3] Cited in Zoltan Barany, "Explaining Military Responses to Revolutions," Arab Center for Research and Policy Studies, Research Paper (July 2013), 1, www.dohainstitute.org/en/lists/ACRPS-PDFDocumentLibrary/Explaining_Military_R esponses_to_Revolutions.pdf (accessed April 5, 2015).

[4] Leon Trotsky, *History of the Russian Revolution* (Chicago, IL: Haymarket Books, 2008), 88.

[5] Russell, *Rebellion, Revolution and Armed Force*, 4 and 80.

largely settled. Russell was right to contend that the "oppression cannot last" argument is empirically unwarranted. Tyranny can and does last for years and decades when the coercive apparatus is committed to the status quo. Nearly a century after the 1917 Russian Revolution, practically every upheaval, violent or nonviolent, has been an occasion to corroborate this rather pessimistic view. In 1979, the triumph of the Islamic Revolution in Iran demonstrated spectacularly how dependent upon military defection revolutionary triumph really is. In contrast, the tragedy of Tiananmen Square, China, in 1989 proved how insufficient the most favorable revolutionary conditions (i.e., divisions within the ruling elite, media-backing, and widespread mobilization) can be in the absence of armed forces defection. From Southern and Eastern Europe to Latin America, South Korea, the Philippines, Burma, Indonesia, and, more recently, Serbia, Georgia, Ukraine, the countries of the Arab Spring, Venezuela, Algeria, and Sudan, each time a new democratic wave challenged authoritarianism, the central question has been the same: Will the military answer the call for repression, or will it be part of a "dissenting alliance"?[6] Like Lenin and Trotsky, modern transitology asserts that in order for transition to be possible, the military, or significant parts of it, at least, should be within the soft-liners' camp.[7]

In brief, it has become increasingly clear that military defection shifts the correlation of forces in favor of widespread civilian uprisings against autocrats, and that protests can quickly reach – and, more importantly, sustain – critical mass only if the military refuses to defend dictatorships. Note that the literature on social movements, revolutions, and civilian uprisings highlights the centrality of political opportunity structures in terms of generating revolutionary outcomes. Still, the literature typically neglects to study the military, despite the fact that the armed forces create, when they defect, the ultimate opening for the expansion and ultimate triumph of contestation. Doug McAdam, one of the few social movement scholars to put the state's capacity (or lack thereof) to repress at the center of his conceptualization of political opportunity structures, finds the tendency to obscure state repression in the related literature "puzzling."[8] Indeed, it is.

---

[6] Schmitter cited in Terence Lee, "The Armed Forces and Transitions from Authoritarian Rule: Explaining the Role of the Military in 1986 Philippines and 1998 Indonesia," *Comparative Political Studies* 42, no. 5 (2009): 641.
[7] Guillermo O'Donnell and Philippe Schmitter, *Transitions from Authoritarian Rule: Tentative Conclusions about Uncertain Democracies* (Baltimore, MD: Johns Hopkins University Press, 1986), 19–20.
[8] Doug McAdam, "Conceptual Origins, Current Problems, Future Directions," in *Comparative Perspectives on Social Movements: Political Opportunities, Mobilizing*

The Arguments in Brief

(1) Civil–military relations in autocracies where leaders fear being overthrown by officers center upon coup-proofing, which is defined as the set of measures governments take to prevent putsches. In such regimes, the military's attitude toward popular uprisings and the prospects of democratic transition is structured by coup prevention tactics. When the tenures of democratic leaders end, they can retreat into private life or remain politically active in one capacity or another. In either case, their lives do not depend upon staying in office. The stakes for remaining in power are higher in nondemocratic regimes, because ousted leaders typically face death, imprisonment, or exile. Historically, autocrats have been far more likely to succumb to putsches than to popular revolutions or foreign invasions as Milan Svolik has shown.[9] In fact, Goemans, Gleditsch, and Chiozza found that a greater number of autocrats lose power to military coups than to civil war, popular protests, and foreign invasions combined. Moreover, they discovered that only 20 percent of deposed autocrats avoid post-tenure punishment, whereas exile, imprisonment, death, or suicide await the others.[10] I develop this issue further in Chapter 1. For now, it is sufficient to pinpoint the implication of such facts, which is straightforward – no other priority supplants the need to avoid or foil coups in autocracies where the political reliability of the military is questionable. Dictators may want their troops to be competent as a fighting force to counter an international menace or, say, a secessionist movement. However, the organizational requirements of battlefield performance, such as devolving authority to field officers and decentralizing command to maximize their tactical leeway, may be deemed threatening politically. The same is true of fostering intra-military trust, which is crucial for cross-unit operations, and of recruiting and promoting officers on the basis of merit rather than loyalty or ascriptive characteristics.[11]

Structures, and Cultural Framings, ed. Doug McAdam, John D. McCarthy, and Mayer N. Zald (Cambridge: Cambridge University Press, 2008), 26.

[9] Milan Svolik, "Power Sharing and Leadership Dynamics in Authoritarian Regimes," *American Journal of Political Science* 53, no. 2 (2009): 478.

[10] Henk E. Goemans, Kristian Skrede Gleditsch, and Giacomo Chiozza, "Introducing Archigos: A Data Set of Political Leaders," *Journal of Peace Research* 46, no. 2 (March 2009): 274–275.

[11] On the trade-off between military performance and coup-proofing, see Caitlin Talmadge, *The Dictator's Army: Battlefield Effectiveness in Authoritarian Regimes* (Ithaca, NY: Cornell University Press, 2015). See also Norvell B. De Atkine, "Why Arabs Lose Wars," *Middle East Quarterly* (December 1999), www.meforum.org/441/why-arabs -lose-wars (accessed September 12, 2018); and Bashir Zein al-'Abidin, *Al-Jaysh wa-l-Siasa fi Suria (1918–2000), Dirasa Naqdiyya* (London: Dar al-Jabia, 2008), 474;

In prioritizing regime security over national defense, autocrats act politically, in the narrow, self-centered sense of the term. To be sure, when countries face major defeats and imminent collapse, autocrats may act in accordance with the objective needs of national security to avoid officers' wrath or loss of power to invaders. For instance, a series of military setbacks in the first years of the Iran–Iraq War (1980–1988) forced Saddam Hussein to reverse the most damaging aspects of coup protection. As a result, the Iraqis performed better after 1986 and nearly collapsed the Iranian armed forces in a run of aggressive campaigns in 1988. Such extreme cases, however, are an exception to the rule. In truth, autocrats can blunder heavily in the strategic realm or lose major international wars and still remain in power. This is especially true of military strongmen and civilian bosses leading weakly institutionalized personalist dictatorships, as Jessica L. P. Weeks has shown.[12] Think of Stalin as a case in point: his Winter War against Finland in 1939 was supposed to deliver a quick victory after a short campaign. Though Finland eventually surrendered, the war proved a disaster for Soviet troops, who lost more than 125,000 to the Fins. Later on, Stalin misjudged Hitler's intentions and failed to anticipate Nazi Germany's attack on the Soviet Union in 1941. The Soviet military initially collapsed because it was taken by surprise and also weakened by previous purges. Stalin had proved strategically inept between 1939 and 1941, and yet he survived, because he had coup-proofed his regime effectively. Similarly, Gamal ʿAbdul Nasser of Egypt lost twice to Israel on the battlefield, in 1956 and 1967. In the Six-Day War, the Egyptian military suffered its biggest defeat in history and was, in essence, wiped out in Sinai. Yet Nasser was still very much in power when he died in 1970. Israel also routed the Syrian armed forces in 1967 and in 1982. The Iraqi military was dealt a heavy blow and forced to retreat from Kuwait by the American-led international coalition in 1991. The Libyan armed forces were expelled from Chad in 1987. Yet the regimes of Hafez al-Asad, Saddam Hussein, and Muʿammar al-Qaddhafi weathered these spectacular debacles. Autocrats can also face armed insurgencies and lead their countries straight into civil war and still remain in office. As I write these words in 2020, strife is still ongoing in Syria yet Bashar al-Asad remains firmly ensconced in Damascus. In contrast to conventional and civil wars, successful putsches are a quick one-way ticket

and Joel Migdal, *Strong Societies and Weak States: State–Society Relations and State Capabilities in the Third World* (Princeton, NJ: Princeton University Press, 1988), 207.
[12] Jessica L. P. Weeks, *Dictators at War and Peace* (Ithaca, NY: Cornell University Press, 2014), 75.

out of power, and coup-plotters are far more dangerous adversaries than foreign powers or insurgents.[13]

It is thus inevitable that coup-proofing structures military politics in dictatorships with a history of civil–military conflict, because it forms the essence of authoritarian survival politics, even when threat environments are multifaceted and dangers stemming from civil war, secession, or conventional war are also lurking. To coup-proof, autocrats seek to either make militaries loyal to the regimes they serve, or unable to challenge them, or both. The loyalty of soldiers is cultivated through material and/or ideational incentives. Incapacity to threaten autocrats' tenure is guaranteed by keeping the armed forces small and ill-equipped; playing divide-and-rule tactics to foster division within military ranks; counterbalancing the military with the police or paramilitary forces; or a combination of these maneuvers in order to render armed forces "coup-proofed to death."[14] All coup-proofing tactics share the same aim: rendering successful putsches unfeasible. However, they shape civil–military relations – and by extension officers' political agency – in fundamentally divergent ways. When coup-proofing centers upon the manipulation of ascriptive loyalties, officers who belong to the autocrat's in-group are likely to be loyalists irrespective of rank, and willing to snuff out the threat of ethnic others. The same is not necessarily true when coup-proofing relies upon the provision of material incentives to the top brass, but not to their subordinates. Put differently, one coup-proofing tactic is more likely than another to foster politically significant, generational cleavages inside the armed forces. In a similar vein, counterbalancing typically fosters unity in officer corps against a backdrop of shared animosity to the police or other institutional rivals. In contrast, divide-and-rule tactics disseminate hostility and mistrust among officers. These are very different dynamics to study as we ponder military politics during popular uprisings. In essence, my argument is this: because these variances mold civil–military relations differently, probing the military's political behavior requires investigation of

---

[13] To quote Talmadge in this regard: "Coups are, in a sense, the ultimate offense-dominant weapon: they occur quickly and afford tremendous and potentially total rewards to first movers. As such, the best defense is prevention, which is exactly what the military organizational practices geared toward coup protection provide. By contrast, other threats, even internal ones, are usually relatively more defense-dominant and do not require the same level of constant vigilance." Talmadge, *The Dictator's Army*, 19.

[14] Florence Gaub, "An Unhappy Marriage: Civil-Military Relations in Post-Saddam Iraq," Carnegie Report, January 13, 2016, http://carnegieendowment.org/2016/01/13/unhapp y-marriage-civil-military-relations-in-post-saddam-iraq/im00 (accessed February 20, 2016).

control mechanisms and what scholars variously refer to as coup-proofing's "unintended effect,"[15] "by-product,"[16] "downside,"[17] "paradox,"[18] "adverse effects,"[19] or "unintended consequences."[20]

The bare-bones reality in this regard is that what works to foil military conspiracies against the status quo may not work when danger stems from the streets. For instance, while counterbalancing is effective from a coup-proofing perspective, it is likely to encourage military defection in times of popular uprising. Sheena Chestnut Greitens argues in an excellent book centered upon East Asia that it is "impossible" for an autocrat to "create a coercive apparatus that is truly optimized to deal with a popular threat and an elite one."[21] According to Greitens, dictators resolve their coercive dilemma by bracing against dangers that seemingly pose the most acute threat to their rule. That, in the Arab world, was putsches. This is not to say that civil society never challenged Arab autocrats; it did. Think, for example, of the massive bread uprising (intifadat al-khubz) in Egypt in 1977, or the confrontation between Hafez al-Asad's regime and the various syndicates in Syria culminating in the general strike that the Syrian Bar Association declared in March 1980. Think also of the nation-wide strike and bread riots in Tunisia, respectively in 1978 and 1983. These and other similar examples show that the Arab street was not invariably dormant or subdued. And yet it is a fact that until 2011, popular mobilization was unable to force regime change in Arab auto-cracies, except during the October Revolution of 1964 in Sudan, which overthrew General Ibrahim Abbud, and the April Intifada of 1985, also in Sudan, which toppled General Jaʿfar al-Numeiri.[22] Historically, the

---

[15] Pion-Berlin, Esparza, and Grisham, "Staying Quartered," 245.

[16] Lee, "The Armed Forces," 642; Risa Brooks, "Political–Military Relations and the Stability of Arab Regimes," Adelphi Paper 324, International Institute for Strategic Studies (London: Oxford University Press, 1998), 40.

[17] Philip Roessler, "The Enemy Within: Personal Rule, Coups, and Civil War in Africa," World Politics 63, no. 2 (2011): 315.

[18] Jonathan M. Powell, "Coups and Conflict: The Paradox of Coup-Proofing" (PhD diss., University of Kentucky, 2012), http://uknowledge.uky.edu/polysci_etds/3 (accessed March 3, 2016).

[19] Terence Lee, "Military Cohesion and Regime Maintenance: Explaining the Role of the Military in 1989 China and 1998 Indonesia," Armed Forces & Society 32, no. 1 (2005): 83.

[20] Aurel Croissant and Tobias Selge, "Should I Stay or Should I Go: Comparing Military (Non-) Cooperation during Authoritarian Regime Crises in the Arab World and Asia," in Armies and Insurgencies in the Arab Spring, ed. Holger Albrecht, Aurel Croissant, and Fred H. Lawson (Philadelphia, PA: University of Pennsylvania Press, 2016), 123.

[21] Sheena Chestnut Greitens, Dictators and Their Secret Police, Coercive Institutions and State Violence (New York: Cambridge University Press, 2016), 32.

[22] Strictly speaking, a coup ousted al-Numeiri in 1985, but the loyalist military leadership acted under extreme pressure from the street. I provide additional information on the 1985 military politics in Sudan further below in this introduction.

survival of Arab dictators depended far more on coup prevention than on optimizing the armed forces to deal with popular threats. To use the words of Milan Svolik, the problem of Arab rulers was essentially that of *authoritarian power-sharing* (i.e., countering the challenge of regime insiders) not of *authoritarian control* (i.e., bracing against popular masses).[23] This changed abruptly in 2011. The ruling elite did indeed face a coercive dilemma that year, albeit one different from what Greitens probes: Arab autocrats needed to convince coercive agents hailing overwhelmingly from the popular and lower middle classes – and thus suffering from the economic repercussions of the post-1990 neoliberal turn – to slaughter fellow countrymen mobilizing against the same policies that they, the coercive agents, were also aching from. Wherever autocrats were able to draw upon shared ideational aversions this challenging task proved possible; the opposite was also true. Contra Greitens, I show in this book that some coup-proofing tactics are versatile in the sense that they can be used effectively against menacing elites *and* popular challenges when the threat environment changes. Other tactics are less adaptable. The fact is fortune does not always serve autocratic whims and events sometimes take unanticipated turns. A strongman becomes vulnerable if, having prepared his coercive apparatus to thwart coups, he is unexpectedly challenged by the streets; or having braced for popular mobilizations he suddenly faces a military putsch. This is where the institutional design of the coercive apparatus comes into play.

(2) Coup-proofing tactics are path-dependent. The scholarship on contemporary civil–military relations often ignores their historical origins.[24] Consequently, the literature on coup-proofing tends to overlook the durability of its patterns. This is problematic, because once mechanisms for surveillance and control of the armed forces have been established, they tend to endure and may shape military politics for years, and sometimes decades, to come. Consider ethnic stacking, for instance. An autocrat who counts on his co-ethnics to uphold his regime alienates other groups and heightens ethnic tensions, within both state institutions and the society at large. Consequently, the autocrat becomes more dependent upon his group, and more likely to reproduce the same patterns of ethnic dominance and exclusion as long as he retains power. Otherwise, he could lose the loyalty of the in-group, having previously

---

[23] Milan Svolik, *The Politics of Authoritarian Rule* (New York: Cambridge University Press, 2012), 2.

[24] Notable exceptions include Zoltan Barany, *Democratic Breakdown and the Decline of the Russian Military* (Princeton, NJ: Princeton University Press, 2007); and Brian Taylor, *Politics and the Russian Army: Civil–Military Relations, 1689–2000* (New York: Cambridge University Press, 2003).

alienated the out-group – a position in which no ruler would want to find himself.

What is true of ethnic stacking is also true of other coup-proofing tactics, such as promoting the material interests of officers or counter-balancing. If the police, or, say, the Republican Guard, functions as an autocratic regime's coercive pillar, then the risk of alienating these institutions would be too great to incur, lest regime survival be at stake. When existing arrangements serve the interests of powerful actors who yield coercive power, they are likely to endure. This is not to say that such arrangements are set in stone. They are not, and autocrats can and do innovate: by adding additional tactics to the coup-proofing system inherited from their predecessors, or by dropping parts of it. Furthermore, a young autocrat who inherited power may purge barons from his father's generation and supplant them with his own cronies. But personnel replacement should not be equated with institutional transformation when the organizational structure of the regime remains untouched. The fact is there is typically more continuity than change in coup-proofing systems. Autocrats tread carefully with coup-proofing, and often lack the incentive and/or capacity to change the configurations upon which they rely for survival. This means that coup-proofing at a specific time and place is the product of current necessities as much as institutional legacies.

In his study of democratic transition in Latin America, Bruce W. Farcau shows how events unfolding in the 1940s, namely, the participation of the Brazilian Expeditionary Force in World War II on the side of the Allies, and its subsequent transformation into a faction known as the "Sorbonne Group," directly influenced military politics and the breakdown of authoritarian regimes in the 1980s.[25] Along similar lines, Hazem Kandil maintains that the legacies of six decades of power struggle pitting the military, security, and civilian wings of the Egyptian power elite against one another structured the collapse of the Mubarak regime in 2011.[26] I show this contention to be true in Egypt and other countries of the Arab Spring as well.

(3) Armed forces are not unified actors and need to be disaggregated along vertical and horizontal lines. To be sure, generals cherish the projection of an image of the armed forces as a hierarchical organization

---

[25] Bruce W. Farcau, *The Transition to Democracy in Latin America: The Role of the Military* (Westport, CT: Praeger, 1996), 87–106.

[26] Hazem Kandil, *Soldiers, Spies, and Statesmen: Egypt's Road to Revolt* (New York: Verso Books, 2012), 220. See also Kevin Koehler, "Officers and Regimes: The Historical Origins of Political–Military Relations in Middle Eastern Republics," in *Armies and Insurgencies in the Arab Spring*, 52.

whose leaders speak for all its members. Behind the facade of discipline and unity, however, officers' relations with superiors, subordinates, and peers are often fraught with tension, if not outright animosity.[27] In this book, I highlight vertical and horizontal differences within officer corps, and analyze the ways in which they structure the agency of the armed forces, during nonviolent revolutions and beyond. Intergenerational (i.e., vertical) friction is particularly important to investigate, for several reasons. First, the moral authority of senior officers (i.e., generals, lieutenant generals, major generals, and brigadier generals) over their subordinates (i.e., colonels, lieutenant colonels, majors, captains, first lieutenants, and second lieutenants) is reduced when the former order the latter to slaughter civilians. Field officers and soldiers may be ready to die to the last man when foreign armed forces invade their country – think of the beleaguered German military facing impossible odds in 1944, and yet fighting on two fronts against the Allies and the Russians until Hitler's surrender and suicide in 1945. Opening fire on women and children is a different matter, however, and senior officers who issue repression orders cannot always assume unconditional obedience from their subordinates.

Lest we forget, generals give directions from afar, but rarely do they lead fighting units operationally. This means that if the military elite decide to resort to force against popular uprisings, mid-ranking and junior officers will have to perform the dirty work of repression, and they may be reluctant to slaughter the countrymen they have sworn to protect.[28] Samuel E. Finer notices, in this regard, that professional militaries chafe at being used for the "sordid purposes"[29] of politicians. Police operations that require killing unarmed fellow nationals symbolize this type of purpose par excellence – hence the severe strain they put upon relations between loyalist generals and not-so-loyalist subordinates. Second, mid-ranking and junior officers are further removed than the top brass from circles of power, and tend to be more sensitive to social grievances and more readily alienated from the ruling elite or welcoming of democratic aspirations. Finally, officers sometimes have professional incentives for supporting change. If successful, civilian uprisings have the potential to drastically reshape the political arena by bringing about the

---

[27] See Alfred McCoy, *Closer than Brothers: Manhood at the Philippine Military Academy* (New Haven, CT: Yale University Press, 1999), 10; and Pion-Berlin, Esparza, and Grisham, "Staying Quartered," 232.

[28] In the words of McCoy, "Whether war, peace, or martial rule, generals keep to their tents while lieutenants form the line and suffer its fate." McCoy, *Closer than Brothers*, 7.

[29] Samuel E. Finer, *The Man on Horseback: The Role of the Military in Politics* (Boulder, CO: Westview Press, 2006), 23.

downfall of one civilian elite and the rise in prominence of another. This political upheaval could have deep implications for the armed forces, especially the officer corps. Consequently, self-centered professional considerations may contribute to shaping officers' attitudes in favor of or against democratic transitions.

As a general rule, autocrats make sure to buy the loyalty of the commandership of the armed forces. Typically, the upper echelons of officer corps are loyalists. Because the top brass are part of the ruling elite, when the latter fall, senior officers may go down with them. This is not always bad news for their colleagues and subordinates in the officer corps. In fact, quite the opposite is often true. The demise of one coalition of military commanders leaves a vacuum at the top that can only be filled by other members of the officer corps. In terms of career perspectives, the breakdown of autocratic regimes, and the ensuing restructuring of both political and military arenas, this creates a window of opportunity for ambitious officers who manage to retain their posts in the armed forces after the fall of an ancien régime. This observation is particularly relevant when specific cohorts maintain a monopoly over the highest military echelons for extended periods, thereby blocking the upward movement of their fellow officers. The domination of command billets by Class 6 in the Indonesian military in 1965 stands as a case in point.[30] Officers in less-privileged cohorts may look favorably upon regime change if it means unblocking their upward mobility in the military hierarchy.

(4) There must exist a distinction between generals' will and their capacity to prevent democratic transition. This follows the classic work of Finer, and, more recently, Jonathan Powell.[31] I argue in this book that the issue of capacity was central to repression during the 2011 upheavals. On paper, Arab generals did, indeed, control enough material and men to suppress the popular movements. Yet this was only true provided their subordinates were ready to carry out orders to repress civilians. Absent such a disposition, the military elite lacked the capacity to uphold the status quo, irrespective of the number of men they commanded. Put differently, although, say, the commander of the Egyptian Armed Forces (EAF), Field Marshal Mohammad Tantawi, had half a million men under his command in 2011, he could only have repressed civilians had his subordinates in the officer corps been willing to slaughter their own countrymen to defend the Mubarak regime. Military capacity is a function of officers' cohesion and loyalty to the powers that be as

---

[30] Siddharth Chandra and Douglas Anton Kammen, "Generating Reforms and Reforming Generations: Military Politics in Indonesia's Democratic Transition and Consolidation," *World Politics* 55, no. 1 (October 2002): 109.

[31] Finer, *The Man on Horseback*, 72 and 229. See also Powell, "Coups and Conflict."

much as it is a question of the armed forces' size and firepower. I argue that *when autocrats lose the loyalty of mid-ranking and junior officers in the armed forces, they can no longer count on the military to defend them against popular uprisings, even if their generals remain committed to the status quo.*

Two sets of relationships involving the officer corps are activated when autocrats call upon their soldiers to repress civilian protests. First, the association between rulers and generals is put to the test. Senior officers owe their positions and corresponding perks to the head of state. If they are closely affiliated with the regime, they have reason to fear its downfall. Beyond self-centered considerations, ideational variables could also be at play. For instance, if an autocrat hails from the armed forces, the military elite may be loath to see him fall out of corporate solidarity. This is especially true if generals perceive the opposition set to benefit from regime change as an ideological nemesis. With that said, top-brass solidarity with beleaguered rulers is not automatic. Some autocrats become exclusivist in their exercise of power, which narrows their support base in the military, including neglected senior officers. Bitterness is particularly acute when officers assume the reins of government collegially after a successful coup, and the regime eventually becomes controlled by one man or a restricted clique. Autocrats who build a personal clientele rather than counting on the armed forces to whom they owe their rise to power (e.g., Peron in Argentina and Suharto in Indonesia) create a wedge between the military as an institution and their regimes. The progressive narrowing of the original coalition that captured power leaves autocrats defenseless when popular mobilizations threaten their tenures.[32]

The second relationship to be put to the test is the one between generals and their subordinates in the officer corps. The former depend on the latter to execute their directives, a classic principal–agent dynamic.[33] But mid-ranking and junior officers charged with slaughtering civilians are frequently resentful of their superiors, who stay away from the carnage. Equally important, colonels, majors, captains, and lieutenants lead combat units on the ground. It is the mid-ranking and junior officers, not their superiors, who are in direct operational control of the troops. If officers occupying middle and lower positions in the military hierarchy oppose

---

[32] Robert Dix, "The Breakdown of Authoritarian Regimes," *The Western Political Science Quarterly* 35, no. 4 (December 1982): 565.

[33] On the principal–agent dynamic in military hierarchies, see Peter D. Feaver, *Armed Servants: Agency, Oversight, and Civil–Military Relations* (Cambridge, MA: Harvard University Press, 2003). See also David Pion-Berlin and Harold Trinkunas, "Civilian Praetorianism and Military Shirking during Constitutional Crisis in Latin America," *Comparative Politics* 42, no. 4 (July 2011): 395–411; and Hicham Bou Nassif, "Generals and Autocrats: How Coup-Proofing Predetermined the Military Elite's Behavior in the Arab Spring," *Political Science Quarterly* 130, no. 2 (2015): 245–275.

opening fire on civilians, the military elite cannot order them to do so, lest they threaten the cohesiveness of – and their control over – the armed forces. The implication is twofold: first, loyalist generals are only useful to the powers that be if they maintain their authority over their subordinates. Second, the imperative of avoiding a mid-ranking and junior officer rebellion supersedes the generals' loyalty to ruling autocrats. This is true not just because the top brass value military unity, but also because they lose control over the armed forces at large when their subordinates reject their authority.

A central question for senior officers considering the repression of popular protests is the following: "What would my subordinates do if I ordered them to open fire on civilians?" If they do not expect their subordinates to be reliable upon the issuance of repression orders, the military elite cannot uphold the status quo even if they want to. This was precisely the dilemma of the Iranian Shah's generals in 1979. Overall, the top brass were loyalists. When the Shah appeared wavering, Iranian generals considered staging a coup, or retreating to the south and waging war against Khomeini's supporters, rather than delivering their country to the Ayatollah. But their subordinates in the officer corps were anti-Shah; clerical leaders were rightly boasting at the time about controlling "everyone below the rank of major."[34] The Iranian monarchy crumbled that year because the generals lacked the capacity – though never the will – to defend it. Ukraine in 2004 is another example in this regard. As popular opposition to the Kuchma regime mounted, mid-ranking officers in the military signaled their refusal to use force against civilians. A retired chief of the Ukrainian air force, General Volodymyr Antonets, had joined the opposition, and began canvassing the officer corps. In his own words:

My people had their own friends, contacts ... many who directly were commanders of military sub-units. For us, it was important to start the movement from the bottom up, so that the leadership would understand that it would not be possible to fulfill the orders of Kuchma, because at the lower levels, they would not support the use of arms.[35]

---

[34] According to Barany, the Iranian military elite refrained from meting out violence to the anti-Shah protesters because they understood that "their odds of successfully rallying the troops against a massively popular uprising were very low." See Zoltan Barany, *How Armies Respond to Revolutions and Why* (Princeton, NJ: Princeton University Press, 2016), 62 and 66. See also Andrew Scott Cooper, *The Fall of Heaven: The Pahlavis and the Final Days of Imperial Iran* (New York: Picador, 2018), 452.
[35] Anika Locke Binnendijk and Ivan Marovic, "Power and Persuasion: Nonviolent Strategies to Influence State Security Forces in Serbia (2000) and Ukraine (2004)," *Communist and Post-Communist Studies* 39, no. 3 (2006): 419. Note that Antonets's efforts proved successful and the intergenerational friction impeded – and indeed restricted – the political leeway of the Ukrainian military elite.

Yet another case in point is Sudan in 1985. Thousands of protesters took to the streets in April that year to challenge then president Jaʿfar al-Numeiri. The loyalist State Security Organization, headed by General ʿOmar al-Tayyib, pressured the military commandership to apply repression. But the army's chief of staff, General ʿAbdul-Rahman Siwar al-Dahab, refused to comply and announced via public broadcast in the early hours of April 6 that the armed forces had "decided to stand with the people." In effect, Siwar al-Dahab sided with the opposition, which immediately triggered regime breakdown. What is less known, however, is that he actually had little sympathy for al-Numeiri's opponents.[36] W. J. Berridge has shown convincingly in a detailed study on Sudan that Siwar al-Dahab remained "reluctant to take the side of the demonstrators until the very end." In fact, in several meetings with his officers, he tried unsuccessfully to convince them that it was the "malign influence" of leftist parties and Libyan interferences that were fueling turmoil in Sudan. The chief of staff also pledged to al-Numeiri that he would defend his regime and support him all the way. And yet, Siwar al-Dahab reneged on his promise shortly afterwards because his subordinates were unwilling to repress civilians. In other words, he lacked the capacity to defend al-Numeiri though he himself did not favor regime breakdown. To quote Berridge:

Did the senior officers "side with the people" during the Intifada? ... In the cases of crucial figures such as Uthman Abdullah, Siwar al-Dahab and probably other members of the army leadership, it seems that political survivalism rather than sympathy with the objectives of the popular uprising provided the real motive. This does not mean they were part of any great conspiracy to preserve the ideologies and institutions of the May Regime, but simply that they decided to abandon Nimeiri and Umar al-Tayyib only when it became clear that the rest of the army would not stand in the way of demonstrations against these two men.[37]

Similarly, General William Kaliman, a loyalist of President Evo Morales, who commanded the armed forces during the 2019 uprising in Bolivia, turned against the embattled Morales due to pressure from the officer corps.[38] Other examples abound and I will show in Chapter 4 that Egypt bore in 2011 a striking resemblance to the 1985 Sudanese case. Simply

---

[36] Nor did Siwar al-Dahab harbor presidential ambitions for that matter. He surrendered power to the government of a civilian politician, Sadiq al-Mahdi, in 1986.

[37] W. J. Berridge, *Civilian Uprisings in Modern Sudan: The "Khartoum Springs" of 1964 and 1985* (New York: Bloomsbury Academic, 2005), 144. See also Aurel Croissant, David Kuehn, and Tanja Eschenauer, "The 'Dictator's Endgame': Explaining Military Behavior in Nonviolent Anti-incumbent Mass Protests," *Democracy and Security* 14, no. 2 (2018): 188–189.

[38] John Otis, "Veteran President's Rift with Bolivian Military Helped Drive His Early Exit," *The Wall Street Journal*, December 5, 2019, www.wsj.com/articles/veteran

put: when the top brass anticipate that their subordinates will disobey orders to fire, they will defect from the embattled elite irrespective of their own preferences in the matter.

Conceptualization and Literature

I conceptualize as defection the military's failure to use violence in order to uphold the status quo after the police or loyal paramilitaries collapse and the armed forces become the last line of defense for embattled autocrats during endgames. Some forms of defection are "hard" – for instance, the military can openly call on the ruling elite to abdicate or remove them by force under pressure from the street. Other forms are softer: this is the case when the military refrains from ousting autocrats, but also refuses to repress demonstrators. From the vantage point of this book, both types of behavior amount to defection – because they inevitably trigger regime breakdown. In contrast, I deem the military to be loyal when it opens fire on behalf of its leaders and actively tries to squelch dissent. It is true, of course, that sometimes the armed forces fail to act in a unified way, which leads me to the second conceptualization needed for this work, namely, that of cohesion.

I consider a military to be cohesive during endgames when it meets the following criteria: (1) An overwhelming majority in the officer corps follows a single course of action throughout the crisis; and (2) Dissenters desert as individuals or in small groups but fail to trigger the defection of units wholesale. From this perspective, I label the Syrian military in this book as "cohesive" though thousands of officers and soldiers joined the opposition after the popular uprising that broke out in March 2011 had escalated into civil war by the end of that year. The information I garnered from Syrian officers whom I interviewed pertaining to this specific issue is the following: (1) Most defections in Syria happened in 2012 and 2013 during wartime.[39] This means that these

-presidents-rift-with-bolivian-military-helped-drive-his-early-exit-11575541801 (accessed December 5, 2019).

[39] Since September 2011, armed opposition members began returning fire at loyalist troops. Until then, violence had been essentially perpetrated by the government forces against civilian demonstrators. The peaceful uprisings had lasted for approximately six months and failed to dislodge Bashar al-Asad from power by the time the spiral of violence escalated into civil war. Throughout this period, the military had remained cohesive. Riad al-As'ad, a Syrian colonel who defected early in July 2011 and co-founded the rebel Free Syrian Army (FSA), claimed that his group would boast 15,000 defectors by mid-October 2011. Observers were skeptical and suggested that only a few thousand soldiers and officers had defected by the end of 2011. But even if we accept al-As'ad's claims, that still means that the Syrian military remained largely cohesive throughout the nonviolent uprising. See Human Rights Watch, "Syria: 'By All Means Necessary!'

defections fall outside the scope of this book, which is interested in military response to nonviolent protests, not military behavior during civil war. (2) Defection in the officer corps remained essentially a Sunni phenomenon; and the ratio of Sunnis in the officer corps prior to 2011 never exceeded 10 percent under Bashar al-Asad. (3) About half of all Sunni officers switched their loyalty; the other half were unable or unwilling to do so. These figures suggest that up to 95 percent of the Syrian officer corps remained loyalist to Bashar al-Asad. Furthermore, those Syrian officers who did desert failed to switch the loyalty of the troops they had led previously. The high-profile defection of Manaf Tlass, the son of longtime defense minister Mustafa Tlass and senior commander in the Republican Guard, is one such example: Tlass joined the opposition in July 2012, but the Republican Guard itself remained loyalist. In contradistinction, when 'Ali Muhsin al-Ahmar defected in Yemen, his First Armored Division (around 30,000 troops) followed him wholesale in March 2011. Similarly, in Libya, when Major General Suleiman Mahmud, the military commander of Tabruk, switched his loyalty in February 2011, the troops under his command did the same. This was also true per the commanders of military forces in al-Jabal al-Akhdar, al-Marj, Misratah, al-Zawiyah, and units they led. Nothing of the sort happened in Syria all through the civil war, let alone during the endgame that preceded it. And so, while acknowledging that thousands of Sunni officers – hailing overwhelmingly from the lower echelons, and from poorly equipped units – and soldiers switched their loyalty after the uprising escalated into civil strife, the Syrian case remains far closer to the "cohesiveness" than "splintering" end of the spectrum. Even more than Syria, the militaries in Egypt, Tunisia, and Bahrain meet the criteria I set for cohesiveness; the armed forces in Libya and Yemen do not. In these two countries, the troops splintered almost immediately, while the endgame was still ongoing.

As I wrestled with the questions of this book, I benefitted immensely from the existing literature on military response to mass protest. A particularly influential scholar in the field is Eva Bellin, who exhibited her nuanced knowledge of Middle East authoritarianism in her oft-cited 2012 article in *Comparative Politics*. Bellin wrote convincingly that the term "coercive apparatus" sometimes used casually in the literature actually "begs for disaggregation";[40] her framework separates the coercive

Individual and Command Responsibility for Crimes against Humanity in Syria," December 2011, 19, www.hrw.org/sites/default/files/reports/syria1211webwcover_0.pdf (accessed June 12, 2014).

[40] Eva Bellin, "Reconsidering the Robustness of Authoritarianism in the Middle East: Lessons from the Arab Spring," *Comparative Politics* 44, no. 2 (2012): 130.

apparatus into its different components, namely, the military, the intelligence agencies, the police, and praetorian guards. Bellin then argued that despite the complex nature of the security archipelago in dictatorships, regime survival in endgames ultimately hinges on the armed forces – she opposes institutionalized militaries to others organized along patrimonial lines – and, primarily, the army.

The work of David Pion-Berlin is also of critical importance. In a *Comparative Politics* article co-authored in 2010 with Harold Trinkunas, Pion-Berlin discerningly uses the principal–agent model to develop a new conceptual approach to military behavior during endgames. The framework begins from the premise that the civilian president, who is also the commander in chief of the armed forces, is the principal; as such, he delegates authority to his subordinates, the military commanders of the armed forces, and expects them to fulfill his orders. But the generals know that if they gamble on the incumbents and lose during endgames, they will suffer the consequences later on. Consequently, the generals' perception of the correlation of forces between the civilian elite and the opposition is central to determining their behavior.[41]

My own interest in breaking up the coercive apparatus into its various components and using insights from the principal–agent model responds to the observations of Bellin, Pion-Berlin, and Trinkunas. To a certain extent, my work extends their frameworks along the following lines: first, I use the analytical disaggregation that Bellin recommends to ponder the army's officer corps, which remains in its own right too complex to be studied as a unified actor. By interrogating the effect of generational differences among officers, I generate a conceptual deviation from Bellin's argument. Bellin maintains that military capacity was not pivotal in determining military response to the 2011 Arab uprisings because commanders such as Hussein Tantawi in Egypt or Rashid 'Ammar in Tunisia wielded enough "supply of tanks, machine guns, or men."[42] By contrast, I contend that senior officers do not have the capacity to repress, irrespective of the number of troops and fire power under their disposition, if their subordinates are not ready to follow orders. Specifically, if the officers occupying the intermediate and lower echelons in the military hierarchy refuse to carry out repression orders, then the military elite lack, in effect, the *capacity* to crush the opposition, even though they might harbor the *will* to do so. Put differently, the capacity to repress should not be strictly conceptualized in terms of troop numbers and fire power.

[41] Pion-Berlin and Trinkunas, "Civilian Praetorianism."
[42] Bellin, "Reconsidering the Robustness of Authoritarianism," 131.

Rather, the convergence of views between senior officers and their subordinates, or lack thereof, sits at the very crux of the matter.

On the other hand, I use the principal–agent model to analyze interactions within the officer corps itself. Put differently, whereas the top brass are the agent in Pion-Berlin and Trinkunas's model, they are the principal in mine, and their subordinates replace them as agent. The same moral hazard potentially at play between autocrats and generals during endgames can also exist between the upper and lower echelons of the officer corps. In effect, then, the game has two rounds: the first plays out between the political and military elite; and the second between the latter and their subordinates. These two rounds are distinct, but not completely autonomous: the mid-ranking and junior officers are more likely to follow orders of the loyalist elite if they themselves support the status quo; and the generals are more likely to uphold embattled autocrats if they know their subordinates will follow repression orders. My model joins the interaction between autocrats, generals, and junior offers in a single framework.

Terence Lee has also advanced our understanding of military behavior during popular uprisings. In *Defect or Defend*, Lee stresses regime type to explain variations in endgame scenarios. More precisely, Lee draws a distinction between personalist and non-personalist forms of authoritarian rule. Personalism, according to Lee, creates "apt condition for the defection of disaffected senior officers seeking to improve their political positions."[43] Lee shows that extreme concentration of power in personalist regimes is correlated with conflicted militaries and divide-and-rule tactics, pitting generals against each other. Strife among the top brass spawns favorable conditions for military disloyalty. The opposite is true in non-personalist regimes where juntas, ruling councils, or political parties enjoy actual power. Under these configurations, the armed forces are cohesive and, by extension, "less likely to back political liberalization." Lee's theorizing makes a step in the right analytical direction, as it highlights the causal relationship between internal military politics and armed forces' response to popular uprisings. Specifically, Lee maintains that "although divide-and-rule policies shore up control and prevent coups, these strategies ferment zero-sum competition within the military leadership," which leads estranged generals to side with protesters during endgames. The opposite is also true as cohesive militaries "are less likely to back political liberalization."[44] In other words, Lee demonstrates that

---

[43] Terence Lee, *Defect or Defend: Military Responses to Popular Protests in Authoritarian Asia* (Baltimore, MD: Johns Hopkins University Press, 2015), 4.
[44] Lee, "The Armed Forces," 662 and 660.

there is a direct causal link between one coup-proofing tactic (i.e., divide-and-rule) and military response to protest; I show this insight to be true for other coup prevention methods as well.

That said, the Arab Spring poses many empirical challenges to Lee's hypotheses. On one hand, Arab autocracies were (and, overall, remain) highly personalist. To be sure, some barons were permitted to acquire wealth or relative influence in regimes run by, say, the al-Qaddafis, al-Asads, or al-Khalifas; but ruling parties or legislatures were in general rubber stamps. Real power lay elsewhere and its practice was typically sultanistic. And yet, military response varied widely in the countries of the Arab Spring. If regime type matters so much and there was little disparity in it among Arab autocracies besieged by uprisings, why the obvious dissimilarity in coercive responses to the protests? In fact, the closest Arab regime to the non-personalist type in 2011 was that of Hosni Mubarak, where the military, and to a lesser extent the judiciary, were permitted some autonomy. And yet the armed forces failed to repress demonstrators on behalf of its leaders in Egypt. This is hardly what we would expect if we follow Lee's argumentation. Furthermore, the upper echelons of the Egyptian and Tunisian militaries in 2011 were not divided by intense rivalries and factionalism and yet the generals did not block transition. By contrast, where the upper echelons of the armed forces were indeed divided by intense competition (e.g., Yemen), the outcome was not peaceful regime breakdown, but the splintering of the armed forces accompanied with severe repression, civil war, and ultimately, state implosion. Again these outcomes can hardly be explained through the prism of Lee's framework. Undeniably, Lee offers a convincing explanation to military behavior during end-games in Asia; to use the jargon of political science, Lee's model has solid internal validity. But its external validity is open to question, certainly in the Arab context.

As for Zoltan Barany, his book *How Armies Respond to Revolutions and Why* is a seminal contribution to the field. Barany's framework centers upon the following six variables: military cohesion; the composition of the military (i.e., volunteer or conscript army); the regime's treatment of the armed forces; the generals' view of the regime legitimacy; as well as the size, composition, and nature of protests; and the potential for foreign intervention. Barany finds that the first of these factors (i.e., cohesion) carries an especially important weight in determining armed forces' response to mass protests whereas the external environment is the least significant in shaping military politics during endgames. The other four variables matter in various degrees according to cases. While conceding the complexity of the topic, Barany ends his book on an optimistic note and maintains that it "*is* quite possible, and in some cases not at all challenging to confidently predict an army's response to a revolution."[45]

My findings in this book corroborate several of Barany's own. I, too, assign particular weight to the cohesion of the armed forces (or lack thereof) in structuring coercive responses to civilian uprisings; and I also find that internal politics matters far more than foreign factors in shaping military politics during endgames. That said, my approach is officer-centric while Barany is critical of the tendency in the literature to neglect the non-officer component of the military. In essence, the debate here centers around one important question: To what extent does it matter whether regiments are manned by conscripts rather than professional soldiers? Barany and other scholars contest the officer corps-centric approach that is pervasive in the subfield of civil–military relations. They argue that the extent to which a military's rank and file reflects the composition of a society matters in times of nonviolent revolution. The lower ranks of a conscripted army are closer to society than those of a country with no compulsory service. Consequently, these scholars posit that a greater identification of the rank and file with society should correlate with a lower likelihood of meting out violence to nonviolent protesters. The opposite is also true.[46]

In contrast, Pion-Berlin argues that there exists no causal relationship between conscription and military behavior toward the civilian opposition. He notes that militaries in Latin America were historically conscripted forces, yet they meted out brutal crackdowns to various oppositions. The Bolivian forces in 2003 were a case in point. The Iranian Republican Guard also opened fire on unarmed citizens during the 2009 popular protests in Iran, though it, too, is a conscripted corps. In contrast, the Argentinian and Ecuadorian militaries declined to suppress popular uprisings in 2001 and 2005, respectively, though both institutions are volunteer forces. According to Pion-Berlin, a conscripted army does not deter repression nor does a volunteer force induce it.[47] Similarly, Farcau maintains that conscripts have neither the time nor the drive to develop a shared sense of corporate identity. Thus, when enlisted men are short-term soldiers, military politics and attitudes are essentially those of the officer corps.[48] These officer-centric positions reflect the dominant

---

[45] Barany, *How Armies Respond*, 177 (italics added).

[46] Denis Prieur, "Defend or Defect: Military Roles in Popular Revolts," SSRN, July 2012, 12, https://papers.ssrn.com/sol3/papers.cfm?abstract_id=2115062 (accessed September 14, 2014).

[47] See Pion-Berlin, Esparza, and Grisham, "Staying Quartered," 237. See also David Pion-Berlin, "Military Relations in Comparative Perspective," in *Armies and Insurgencies in the Arab Spring*, 32.

[48] Farcau, *The Transition to Democracy*, 54.

view in the subfield of civil–military relations studies where officer corps – rather than Non-commissioned Officers (NCOs) or soldiers – have traditionally occupied center stage in terms of scholarly research. In fact, Finer goes so far as to assert that "in most cases, the equation of 'the military = the officer corps' still holds."[49] And along similar lines, Alfred McCoy argued in his study of the officer corps in the Philippines that while over a million civilians took to the streets in 1986 against Marcos, the final outcome of the uprising depended upon the internal dynamics of only two cohorts of officers with less than a hundred men each.[50] Meanwhile, Florence Gaub's recent study of Arab militaries focuses almost entirely upon officer corps.[51]

I agree with Barany that a massive presence of conscripts among the rank and file could be challenging to manage during popular protests. But as I show in this book, the Syrian case study suggests that conscripted armed forces can still obey orders to open fire on civilian mobilizations when officer corps and intelligence agencies are cohesive and overwhelmingly loyal to the powers that be. The fact is officers lead their troops in times of war and peace, supervise training, and maintain discipline. If unhappy with the officers' leadership, NCOs, soldiers, and conscripts can desert on an individual basis, but they typically lack the authority to trigger massive mutinies within the ranks. Consider Shia soldiers in Saddam Hussein's army: they were suffering from discrimination in the military and used as cannon fodder when ordered to fight fellow Shia during the Iran–Iraq War in the 1980s. The Iraqi officer corps was ethnically stacked, with loyalist Sunni officers keeping a watchful eye over Shia recruits, who remained quiescent despite mounting casualties. Decades ago, Majid Khadduri opined that in Arab military politics, it was officers who counted, not soldiers.[52] Eliezer Be'eri also argued in his classic work on Arab militaries that the norm of obedience to officers is deeply internalized by enlisted men, sometimes described as "potters clay in the hands of their commanders."[53] Later events, including the Arab Spring, overall corroborate these statements[54] – hence my focus on officers in this book.

[49] Finer, *The Man on Horseback*, 227.   [50] McCoy, *Closer than Brothers*, 10.
[51] Florence Gaub, *Guardians of the Arab State: When Militaries Intervene in Politics, from Iraq to Mauritania* (London: Hurst & Company, 2017), 11.
[52] Majid Khadduri, "The Role of the Military in Middle East Politics," *The American Political Science Review* 47, no. 2 (June 1953): 517.
[53] Eliezer Be'eri, *Army Officers in Arab Politics and Society* (New York: Praeger, 1970), 260.
[54] In the words of a Western diplomat in Cairo, commenting on the tension between the top brass in the Egyptian Supreme Council of the Armed Forces (SCAF) and their junior subordinates in 2011: "Very senior officials do not want to risk a split, and infantry members mostly follow orders, but the officers are the ones to watch." Patrick Galey,

Sources, Scope, and Structure of the Book

I collected data for this work essentially through interviews, and exploration of primary sources in Arabic. Students of Arab military politics have
long complained about the inaccessibility of Arab officers, and my own
experience after six rounds of research in the field certainly attests to
such grievances. Interviewing active officers did prove daunting; in
contrast, retired officers in Egypt and Tunisia, and Syrian officers who
broke with the al-Asad regime, were generous with their time, and open
to debating military affairs. Indeed, some were eager to discuss their
version of events. Between 2011 and 2016, I conducted ninety interviews with Egyptian, Syrian, and Tunisian officers, in trips that took me
from Cairo, to Beirut, Tunis, and the Turkish–Syrian border. My
Egyptian (34) and Tunisian (32) interviewees were retired senior officers; in contrast, my Syrian (24) interviewees had been active-duty
officers until they defected after the escalation of the civil war in their
country. Also, I interviewed scores of civilians, mainly journalists and
academics, working on military affairs. I had been a journalist myself for
seven years prior to becoming an academic, and former colleagues
helped me in establishing early contacts. Because most of my interviewees have spent decades of their lives in the armed forces and typically
remain enmeshed in informal military networks – e.g., officers' clubs,
veterans' associations, or military-run economic institutions – they have
been well-informed about, and attentive to, military politics and affairs.
Some interviewees allowed me to mention their names, others preferred
to remain anonymous – I respected their wishes scrupulously. In addition, I rummaged national and newspaper archives in Cairo and Tunis,
and used extensively the wealth of memoirs published by Arab officers
throughout the last five decades.

Three clarifications pertaining to the scope of my framework are essen-
tial. First, this study is strictly concerned with military reaction to *inclusive
nonviolent* challenges to autocracies where civil–military relations are
conflictual. When insurgents shoot at soldiers, the latter are likely to
shoot back, if only to save their lives. By contrast, civilian protesters are
unarmed, which makes the decision to open fire on them more problematic. In addition, insurgent groups confine their membership to
a restrained number of activists, for security reasons, whereas participation in nonviolent revolutions is open to all; inevitably, civilian uprisings
project an image more inclusive (i.e., nonpartisan) than ideologically

"Why the Egyptian Military Fears a Captains' Revolt," *Foreign Policy*, February 16, 2012,
http://foreignpolicy.com/2012/02/16/why-the-egyptian-military-fears-a-captains-revolt/
(accessed November 28, 2014).

committed insurgents, which adds a further layer of complication to the always unpleasant task of repression.[55] Second, I am interested in *massive nationwide* protests during moments of potential regime breakdown, not in parochial opposition movements restricted to one city or region. Local nonviolent uprisings usually keep the security forces counterbalancing the military intact. Challenges confined to specific geographic areas – typically, the periphery – do not trigger the collapse of the police nor threaten regime survival. Consequently, militaries have to do the auto- crats' bidding in order to avoid harsh retaliations irrespective of officers' true political predilections. By contrast, massive nationwide popular rebellions that transcend ideology, class, and parochial attachments are more likely to trigger the breakdown of ruling parties, the police, and various security forces under the control of the interior ministry. These endgame scenarios open the door for defection – defined as the military's unwillingness to repress civilians – and liberate the armed forces from the need to falsify their preferences because the correlation of forces shifts drastically in their favor. If the officers genuinely support the status quo, they will use violence to uphold it. Otherwise, military neutrality suffices to pave the way toward regime breakdown. My framework applies to such endgame scenarios activated by nationwide, cross-partisan uprisings. The story I cover begins when popular protest reaches critical mass and threatens the continuity of the status quo; it ends with the breakdown of the autocratic order, its consolidation after repression, or the escalation of nonviolence into insurgency. Finally, I study uprisings aiming to achieve *regime change*, whether this goal was set from the first day of the move- ment, or soon afterwards. These three features – tactics, size, and goal – are limiting conditions for the applicability of my causal model. If the protest was not peaceful, nationwide in scope, and committed to regime change, my framework does not apply to it. The same is true after initially peaceful uprisings escalate toward violence, as sometimes is the case.

I develop my theoretical argument in Chapter 1. My starting point is straightforward: the survival of nondemocratic leaders in coup-prone countries is, above all else, a function of successful coup-proofing. I show how frequently coups have taken place in developing countries in the wake of decolonization, but also how harsh the fates of fallen leaders have typically been following military takeovers, particularly in the Arab world. To coup-proof, autocrats used ideational factors (i.e., shared aversions), material factors (i.e., counterbalancing, promoting the mate- rial interests of senior officers, and divide-and-rule tactics), or

---

[55] See Erica Chenoweth and Maria Stephan, *Why Civil Resistance Works: The Strategic Logic of Nonviolent Conflict* (New York: Columbia University Press, 2011), 34–38.

combinations of both. I demonstrate the ways in which coup-proofing tactics structure civil–military relations differently, but also amplify or reduce vertical and horizontal cleavages in the officer corps. I link these variations to military behavior when popular uprisings challenge the authoritarian status quo.

Chapters 2, 3, and 4 cover Egypt and Syria, my main case studies. Both countries were coup-prone in the decades following independence, and officers-turned-presidents in Cairo and Damascus had good reasons to worry about military interventionism. Counterbalancing became a permanent fixture of coup-proofing combinations in both Egypt and Syria. Institutional competitors of the armed forces were beefed up in order to tilt the correlation of forces between the ruling elite and the military in favor of the former. In addition, Egyptian and Syrian autocrats made sure to promote the material interests of their generals. That said, the autocratic rulers of Syria could ethnically stack their armed forces, whereas Egyptian presidents could not because the societal structure of their country precludes such an option. I examine the historical origins and evolution of these and other coup-proofing tactics with regard to the armed forces and civil–military relations while pondering their effects on military politics and behavior. I pay special attention to the challenges faced by the autocratic status quo as a result of the Arab uprisings. In Chapter 5, I do the same for Tunisia and Libya, my secondary case studies, in order to test my argument additionally and comparatively.

1   Coups, Coup-Proofing, and Military Politics in Endgames

When popular uprisings overwhelm loyalist police or security forces and threaten embattled autocrats, some militaries refrain from upholding the status quo. In some cases, the armed forces actually trigger coups to oust unpopular dictators under the pressure of events. In other cases, the military refuses to deploy in the streets and confines itself to the barracks – in essence the troops remain above the fray and on the sidelines. This is what Pion-Berlin et al. have labeled "staying quartered."[1] In yet other cases, the armed forces deploy to keep public order and safeguard state institutions, but refuse to repress. To be sure, these are divergent sorts of military behavior; active rebellion is hard defection whereas neutrality is a softer form of it. As mentioned previously, however, these different types of agency can functionally be conceptualized as a single category because they trigger the same outcome during endgames: the fall of the powers that be. On the other end of the spectrum, some militaries prove capable of slaughtering thousands in order to prevent change, while yet others splinter into warring factions in the heat of action. The political repercussions of these variations are tremendous and open the door to democratic transition or, alternatively, autocratic consolidation, and civil war. What explains the dissimilarity in military response to nonviolent unrest?

I answer this question through the prism of coup-proofing. Florence Gaub has argued that the reaction of the Libyan armed forces to the 2011 uprising has been shaped by "institutional variables created by the [Mu'ammar al-Qaddhafi] regime."[2] For his part, Noureddine Jebnoun maintained that the heavy-handedness of the security sector in dealing with the military under the former Tunisian president Zein al-'Abidin Ben 'Ali alienated the armed forces and structured their attitude toward

---

[1] See Pion-Berlin, Esparza, and Grisham, "Staying Quartered."
[2] Florence Gaub, "The Libyan Armed Forces between Coup-Proofing and Repression," *Journal of Strategic Studies* 36, no. 2 (2013): 233.

the popular movements in 2010/2011.[3] I show that these insights are also true outside Libya and Tunisia. Ultimately, even the most powerful autocrat is not all-powerful, and past actions have consequences. Earlier choices of coup-proofing tactics spawn direct effects – sometimes undesirable for autocrats – on military loyalty and readiness to uphold the status quo. In this chapter, I present a theoretical framework geared to analyzing the response of the armed forces to nonviolent revolutions. I disaggregate officer corps along vertical and horizontal lines, and link such cleavages to coup-proofing and military behavior in times of popular uprisings. First, however, I dwell briefly on the nature of threats coups pose to autocratic rule.

Keeping Power to Stay Alive: What Frightens Frightening Autocrats

Coups are forceful and illegal seizures of power leading to the replacement of one ruling elite by another. Coups are also the most common form of nonconstitutional exit from power in autocracies, as Table 1.1 shows. From 1950 to 2000, at least one putsch was triggered in 80 percent of countries in sub-Saharan Africa, 76 percent of countries in North Africa and the Middle East, 67 percent of countries in Latin America, and 50 percent of countries in Asia.[4] So endemic were coups that they were frequently described as a "functional equivalent of elections,"[5] a "normal mode of political change,"[6] or just "an ordinary fact of life,"[7] in coup-prone countries.

Beyond their pervasiveness, three characteristics are particularly interesting to note in twentieth-century coups. First, putsches were ruthless affairs. Victors were rarely magnanimous, nor could they afford to be so, lest deposed leaders seek revenge and a return to power. In his study on the manner and consequences of losing office, Goemans found that only 20 percent of leaders deposed by coups suffer no punishment, whereas 41 percent are exiled, 22 percent are imprisoned, and 18 percent are killed. In contrast, only 8 percent of leaders who lose power via regular

---

[3] Noureddine Jebnoun, "In the Shadow of Power: Civil–Military Relations and the Tunisian Popular Uprising," *Journal of North African Studies* 19, no. 3 (2014): 303.

[4] Naunihal Singh, *Seizing Power: The Strategic Logic of Military Coups* (Baltimore, MD: Johns Hopkins University Press, 2014), 2.

[5] Samuel Decalo, *Coups and Army Rule in Africa* (New Haven, CT: Yale University Press, 1990), 2.

[6] Edward Luttwak, *Coup d'Etat: A Practical Handbook* (Cambridge, MA: Harvard University Press, 1990), 9.

[7] Mehran Kamrava, "Military Professionalization and Civil–Military Relations in the Middle East," *Political Science Quarterly* 115, no. 1 (Spring 2000): 77.

Table 1.1 *How autocrats lose power*[8]

Nonconstitutional exit from office of authoritarian leaders	303 autocrats between 1946 and 2008
Coups	205 (68%)
Popular uprisings	32 (11%)
Public pressure to democratize	30 (10%)
Assassination	20 (7%)
Foreign intervention	16 (5%)

norms and procedures suffer similar fates.[9] And while it is generally agreed that autocrats who lose power face a high probability of death, imprisonment, or exile, there is a debate as per the type of autocrats most likely to suffer such fates post-ouster. On the one hand, Debs and Goemans argue that military dictators (and monarchs) face the worst fate if they are overthrown.[10] On the other, Geddes et al. maintain that personalist dictators, i.e., leaders of sultanistic regimes, pay the highest costs should they be ousted.[11] Together, these results suggest that the post-tenure fate of military personalist rulers or "strongmen" is particularly likely to be dark.[12]

These dynamics are perfectly illustrated in the Arab world, where some of the most notorious autocrats have combined military background with personalist regimes – e.g., Muʿammar al-Qaddhafi in Libya, ʿAli ʿAbdullah Saleh in Yemen, ʿUmar al-Bashir in Sudan, Gamal ʿAbdul Nasser in Egypt, or Hafez al-Asad in Syria. Here, victorious coup-plotters have rarely shown leniency toward fallen leaders. When CIA operative Steve Meade pressured military colonel Hosni al-Zaʿim, the general who triggered the first Syrian coup in March 1949, to spare the life of President Shukri al-Quwatli, whom he had just overthrown, al-Zaʿim retorted: "What do they want me to do with him, let him free to plot against me?"[13] Brigadier General Sami al-Hinnawi was probably thinking along

[8] Svolik, *The Politics of Authoritarian Rule*, 4–5.
[9] Henk E. Goemans, "Which Way Out? The Manner and Consequences of Losing Office," *Journal of Conflict Resolution* 52, no. 6 (December 2008): 774 and 781.
[10] See Alexander Debs and Henk E. Goemans, "Regime Type, the Fate of Leaders, and War," *American Political Science Review* 104, no. 3 (August 2010): 440.
[11] Barbara Geddes, Joseph Wright, and Erica Frantz, "Autocratic Breakdowns and Regime Transitions: A New Data Set," *Perspectives on Politics* 12, no. 2 (June 2014): 321.
[12] Barbara Geddes, Erica Frantz, and Joseph Wright, "Military Rule," *Annual Review of Political Science* 17 (May 2014): 158.
[13] Hugh Wilford, *America's Great Game: The CIA's Secret Arabists and the Shaping of the Modern Middle East* (New York: Basic Books, 2013), 104. Al-Zaʿim was originally

similar lines when he had the same al-Za'im and his prime minister executed after seizing power in August 1949. In 1970, when Hafez al-Asad and his associates became leaders of Syria, an ally of al-Asad, General Mustafa Tlass, argued that had victors and vanquished traded places in the intra-Ba'ath Party struggle for power, the latter would have skinned the former alive (*"law kanu fi makanina la-salakhu juludana"*). Al-Asad agreed: he kept his rival Salah Jdid in prison from 1970 till he died in 1995, because he feared Jdid's retaliation should he be freed.[14] King Hussein of Jordan too faced coups, plots, and assassination attempts – the title of his autobiography speaks volumes about his troubles and might have been fitting for other Arab rulers as well, *Uneasy Lies the Head*.[15] That Arab autocrats have appeared terrifying because of the ferocity of their coercive apparatuses should not obscure the fact that they themselves have been terrified of losing power. This insight is central to understanding politics in general (and civil–military relations in particular) under their tenures. In this regard, Roger Owen notes perspicaciously:

[T]here is no reason to suppose that the life of a president was anything but an extremely difficult and often dangerous one in the early years of most of the Arab republics, just as it was in Sub-Saharan Africa and other parts of the newly independent word where the turnover rate at the top due to assassination, imprisonment, and enforced exile was initially very high.[16]

The data I have collected in Table 1.2 sheds additional light on the matter.

The second characteristic of military coups in the twentieth century was that once a successful coup was triggered in a country, the propensity of future coup attempts being staged became high. Coups bred coups, and "coup traps" sometimes extended for years or decades of political instability.[17] Finally, the likelihood of success for skillful coup-plotters was reasonably high. To be sure, nothing guaranteed victory: bad weather, failure to capture a transmitter, or simple miscommunication can and did account for the collapse of otherwise carefully hatched plans. Yet one central factor played to the rebels' advantage: as a general rule, soldiers were reluctant to shed fellow soldiers' blood and forsake the

considering disposing of al-Quwatli by execution or poisoned food. Eventually, he settled for jailing him, and seizing his property before sending him into exile.

[14] Mustafa Tlass, *Mer'at Hayati, al-'Aqd al-Thaleth, 1968–1978* (Damascus: Dar Tlass li-l-Dirasat wa-l-Nashr wa-l-Tawzi', 2003), 462.

[15] King Hussein of Jordan, *Uneasy Lies the Head: The Autobiography of His Majesty King Hussein I of the Hashemite Kingdom of Jordan* (New York: Random House, 1962).

[16] Roger Owen, *The Rise and Fall of Arab Presidents for Life* (Cambridge, MA: Harvard University Press, 2012), 27.

[17] See John B. Londregan and Keith T. Poole, "Poverty, the Coup Trap, and the Seizure of Executive Power," *World Politics* 42, no. 2 (January 1990): 151–183.

Table 1.2 *The post-tenure fate of deposed leaders in the Arab world at the height of military coups (1949–1980)*[18]

Date	Country	Coup leader	Post-tenure fate of deposed leader
30 March 1949	Syria	Husni al-Za'im	**Jail, then exile for 5 years** (Shukri al-Quwatli)
14 August 1949	Syria	Sami al-Hinnawi	**Assassination** (Husni al-Za'im)
19 December 1949	Syria	Adib al-Shishakli	**Jail, followed by exile and assassination** (Sami al-Hinnawi)
29 November 1951	Syria	Adib al-Shishakli	**Jail** (Ma'aruf al-Dawalibi)
23 July 1952	Egypt	Gamal 'Abdul Nasser	**Exile for life** (King Faruq)
25 February 1954	Syria	Hashem al-Atassi	**Exile, then assassination** (Adib al-Shishakli)
26 February 1954	Egypt	Khaled Muhieddin	**No punishment** (Gamal 'Abdul Nasser)
26 March 1954	Egypt	Gamal 'Abdul Nasser	**House arrest for 18 years** (Mohammad Neguib)
14 July 1958	Iraq	'Abdul-Karim Qassem	**Assassination** (King Faisal II)
17 November 1958	Sudan	Ibrahim 'Abbud	**No punishment** ('Abdullah Khalil)
28 September 1961	Syria	'Abdul-Karim al-Nahlawi	**Exile** (Abdul-Hakim 'Amer)
28 March 1962	Syria	'Abdul-Karim al-Nahlawi	**Jail** (Nazim al-Qudsi; released after the 2 April counter-coup)
2 April 1962	Syria	'Abdul-Karim Zahr al-Din	**No punishment** ('Abdul-Karim al-Nahlawi)
26 September 1962	Yemen	'Abdullah al-Sallal	**Exile** (King Muhammad al-Badr)
8 February 1963	Iraq	'Abdul-Salam 'Arif	**Assassination** ('Abdul-Karim Qassem)
8 March 1963	Syria	Ziad al-Hariri	**Exile for life** (Nazim al-Qudsi)
11 November 1963	Iraq	'Abdul-Salam 'Arif	**Exile for life** ('Ali Salih al-Sa'di)
19 June 1965	Algeria	Houari Boumediene	**Jail, then house arrest for 15 years** (Ahmed Ben Bella)
23 February 1966	Syria	Salah Jdid	**Jail, then exile for 36 years** (Amine al-Hafez)

[18] The dates and names of coup leaders in this table are taken from Eliezer Be'eri, "The Waning of the Military Coup in Arab Politics," *Middle Eastern Studies* 18, no. 1 (January 1982): 80–81. I collected the data pertaining to the fate of fallen leaders from the various memoirs of Arab officers I read while researching this book. Note that I restricted this table to *successful* coups because I was interested in probing the fate of Arab autocrats after they were ousted from power by successful putschists.

Table 1.2 *(cont.)*

Date	Country	Coup leader	Post-tenure fate of deposed leader
4 November 1967	Yemen	'Abdul-Rahman al-'Aryani	**Jail, then exile for 14 years** ('Abdullah al-Sallal)
17 July 1968	Iraq	Ahmad Hasan al-Bakr	**Exile for 11 years** ('Abdul-Rahman 'Arif)
30 July 1968	Iraq	Ahmad Hasan al-Bakr	**Exile, then assassination** ('Abdul-Razzaq al-Nayyif)
25 February 1969	Syria	Hafez al-Asad	**Assassination** ('Abdul-Karim al-Jundi)
25 May 1969	Sudan	Ja'far al-Numeiri	**Jail, followed by death in August 1969 while still a prisoner** (Ismail al-Azhari)
1 September 1969	Libya	Mu'ammar al-Qaddhafi	**Exile for life** (King Idris al-Sanusi)
13 November 1970	Syria	Hafez al-Asad	**Jail for life** (Salah Jdid)
19 July 1971	Sudan	Hashem al-'Ata	**Jail, then quick escape** (Ja'far al-Numeyri)
22 July 1971	Sudan	Ja'far al-Numeiri	**Assassination** (Hashem al-'Ata)
13 June 1974	Yemen	Ibrahim al-Hamdi	**Exile for 7 years** ('Abdul-Rahman al-Iryani)
10 July 1978	Mauritania	Mohammad Ould Mohammad Zaliq	**Jail, then exile for 23 years** (Mokhtar Ould Daddah)
6 April 1979	Mauritania	Mohammad Khuna Ould Haidalla	**No punishment, then jail** (Mohammad Ould Mohammad Zaliq)

sacrosanct unity of the armed forces. Thus, when a determined faction seized a presidential palace, or a defense ministry, other factions in the military were not always ready to heed orders to nip the rebellion in the bud. Coup-plotters typically called for intra-military comradeship and for the avoidance of fratricide bloodshed in order to consolidate their grip and prevent backlash. Such calls were frequently effective. These dynamics, too, are exemplified in the Arab world where 56 percent of coups triggered between 1949 and 1980 were successful.[19]

The implication of the data above is threefold. First, even dictators presiding over seemingly stable regimes had ample reasons to dread losing power – theirs were politics of survival in the most literal sense of the

[19] See Be'eri, "The Waning of the Military Coup," 70 and 80–81.

word. To assume that any ideological belief or political priority super-seded their will to stay alive and in control is to misunderstand the threat environments in which these leaders lived. In particular, autocrats end-lessly fretted about hidden enemies in the military, who could do to them what they themselves did to their fallen rivals. For instance, Gamal 'Abdul Nasser was still agonizing in 1969, seventeen years after his successful power grab, lest the Americans be grooming in the officer corps an "Egyptian Suharto" to replace him.[20] Nasser admitted that he had conspired for so long prior to his rise to power that he was unable to "break the habit of suspicion" afterwards.[21] For his part, Saddam Hussein noted that he seized power by plotting against his predecessors, and that it was only normal that others may want to do the same to him. According to the former dictator himself:

I know there are scores of people plotting to kill me, and this is not difficult to understand. After all, did we not seize power by plotting against our predecessors?[22]

Second, trigger-happy mutinous officers challenged the status quo more effectively when regimes were less security conscious. Coup-plotting was easier in the Arab world under civilian regimes in the 1950s than it was later, once officers took over: Be'eri shows that 89 percent of coup attempts triggered between 1949 and 1956 in the Arab world were successful, in opposition to 47 percent between 1957 and 1964, 55 percent between 1965 and 1972, and 43 percent between 1973 and 1980. These figures suggest that the lowest number of coups and the feeblest likelihood of success occurred in the last years that the data covers, i.e., between 1973 and 1980.[23] We know in hindsight that this trend only deepened subse-quently as Arab regimes employed increasingly skillful coup-proofing tech-niques, and systems of keeping the military in check became more complex. According to Powell and Thyne, only thirteen coups were triggered in Arab countries in the three decades between 1980 and 2010, in contradistinction with fifty-two putsches in the three decades from 1950 to 1980.[24] Furthermore, only five of the post-1980 power grabs were triumphant in

---

[20] Mohammad Hasanein Heikal, *Kharif al-Ghadab, Qissat Bidayat wa-Nihayat 'Asr Anwar al-Sadat* (Cairo: Markaz al-Ahram li-l-Tarjama wa-l-Nashr, 1988), 138.

[21] Raymond William Baker, *Egypt's Uncertain Revolution under Nasser and Sadat* (Cambridge, MA: Harvard University Press, 1978), 28.

[22] Talmadge, *The Dictator's Army*, 153.

[23] Be'eri, "The Waning of the Military Coup," 70.

[24] The data on coups collected by Jonathan M. Powell and Clayton L. Thyne is available at: www.uky.edu/~clthyn2/coup_data/powell_thyne_coups final.txt (accessed September 27, 2019). According to this data, Arab countries in which coups unfolded between 1980 and 2010 are the following: Syria (1982); Sudan (1985, 1989); Southern Yemen (1986); Tunisia (1987); the United Arab Emirates

Table 1.3 *The post-tenure fate of deposed leaders in the Arab world after the waning of military coups (1980–2010)*[26]

Date	Country	Coup leader	Post-tenure fate of deposed leader
7 April 1985	Sudan	'Abdul-Rahman Siwar al-Dahab	**Exile for 14 years** (Ja'far al-Numeiri)
7 November 1987	Tunisia	Zein al-'Abidin Ben 'Ali	**House arrest for life** (Al-Habib Bourguiba)
1 July 1989	Sudan	'Omar al-Bashir	**Exile for 12 years** (Ahmad al-Mirghani)
14 January 1992	Algeria	Khaled Nezzar	**House arrest for 7 years** (Al-Shadhli Ben Jedid)
27 June 1995	Qatar	Hamad Ben Khalifa al-Thani	**Exile for 9 years** (Khalifa Ben Hamad al-Thani)

Arab autocracies (see Table 1.3). The decline is stark both in term of numbers and success rate (38 percent). Joseph Sassoon notes correctly in this regard that the waning of military takeovers in the Arab world did not stem from "objective" norms of civil–military relations suddenly prevailing over the forms of old, but from improved coup-proofing capacities.[25] Unsurprisingly, coup prevention was maintained when it proved effective. After all, power grabs had waned but not disappeared altogether, and the post-coup trajectories of deposed leaders after 1980 were hardly desirable. And so the decreasing frequency of putsches did not impact the need to coup-proof: autocrats had to remain vigilant. This means in effect that Arab militaries that faced protesters in 2011 had been structured uninterruptedly by several decades of implacable coup-proofing.

(1987); Iraq (1991, 1992, 1995); Algeria (1992); Libya (1993); and Qatar (1995, 1996). My findings suggest that while additional coup plots may have been hatched in the region during the above period, as I show in Chapters 3 and 5, they do not in any case debunk the notion that coups declined steeply in the Arab world following 1980.

[25] Joseph Sassoon, *Anatomy of Authoritarianism in the Arab Republics* (New York: Cambridge University Press, 2016), 96. Note that Ahmad Hamrush, an early associate of Gamal 'Abdul Nasser, admitted candidly in his memoirs that the Free Officers regime penetrated the Egyptian military and controlled it better than the monarchy ever had. What is true for Egypt is also accurate in other Arab countries. See Ahmad Hamrush, *Thawrat Yulyu* (Cairo: al-Hay'a al-Markaziyya li-l-Kitab, 1992), 147. Note that "objective control" refers to the framework that Samuel Huntington has famously developed in his book *The Soldier and the State: The Theory and Politics of Civil–Military Relations* (New York: Vintage Books, 1957), 83–85.

[26] The dates of coup in this table are taken from the aforementioned dataset by Powell and Thyne. I collected the data pertaining to the fate of ousted leaders from various sources and memoirs I read while researching this book.

Third – and this point is an extension of the previous one – wherever autocrats feared power usurpation by coercive agents, coup-proofing structured the very foundations of civil–military relations. Inevitably, this affected the capacity of autocrats to use the armed forces as tools of internal repression. The fact is some coup-proofing tactics deliver on both levels: they make staging coups more difficult while simultaneously preparing the armed forces for use in internal repression. When the military is ethnically stacked, for instance, the organizational trade-off in designing the coercive apparatus to face coups, on the one hand, and out-group popular unrest, on the other, disappears. Other tactics are not so pliable: they help secure autocrats from their armed forces, but leave them vulnerable to challenges from the streets. This is why studying coup prevention is central to understanding the officer corps, as well as the armed forces at large, in times of popular uprising. What autocrats do to shield their regimes from military putsches has repercussions on their ability to use their armed forces against civilian mobilization. I cultivate this insight further throughout the rest of the chapter.

Factional Divisions in the Officer Corps

The framework I develop in this study rests upon a threefold disaggregation. First, the state's machinery is not to be treated as a unified actor. To be sure, some militaries put such a high stake on the survival of authoritarian regimes that it becomes difficult to treat their agency as autonomous. Yet because armies do not always intervene to save autocratic regimes, we cannot posit a priori that the military agenda will necessarily be concomitant with that of the political leadership. Some officers may be frustrated enough with the status quo, or confident enough about the post-regime order, to lack the will to defend the autocrats in power. Other officers may have the will, but not the capacity, to break popular mobilizations. Either way, the relationship between civilian and military components of authoritarian regimes needs to be problematized, instead of lumping generals and civilians together under all-encompassing rubrics such as "the regime" or "the incumbents." Second, the coercive apparatus itself is to be disaggregated into constituent elements: the military, on the one hand, and the police and other internal security forces, on the other. Each of these organizations tends to develop a distinct set of institutional interests, alliances, and values. The rivalry that structures the relationship between these different components in the coercive apparatus shapes their reaction to popular mobilizations, as does the depth of their attachment to the regime. Finally, the officer corps in the armed forces should also be disaggregated along vertical (i.e., intergenerational) and horizontal (i.e., intra-generational) lines. Both matter, though I show that the former is particularly important to keep in mind, for it should not be assumed a priori that the interests and views of senior officers in the armed forces are always concomitant with those of their subordinates in the hierarchy. In what follows, I ponder intra-officer corps divide lines and their implications for military politics in times of nonviolent uprisings.

Vertical Cleavages: Intergenerational Dynamics in the Officer Corps

In his classic study of military institutions in Third World countries, Morris Janowitz highlighted the pervasiveness of generational friction within the officer corps of newly independent nations:

> The strong pressures toward social cohesion [in the military] based upon uniform training and indoctrination are weakened by sharp intergenerational cleavages of younger versus older officers, a source of cleavage with particular political import. Younger officers with less seniority have fewer interests in the military system. They are less involved in the social and political status quo and more involved in contemporary political currents, with the result that they are inclined toward a more radical outlook.[27]

Janowitz's observation has been widely corroborated since the publication of his study. Friction between senior officers (i.e., generals), on the one hand, and mid-ranking officers (i.e., lieutenant colonels and colonels) and junior officers (i.e., lieutenants through majors), on the other, is globally ubiquitous. The top brass in developing countries frequently turn into members of the ruling elite, with whom ordinary people have "little in common materially or ideologically."[28] In opposition to the typically conservative political attitudes of their commanders, mid-ranking and junior officers have been depicted as more "intensely nationalistic" in Iraq;[29] "radical" in Turkey and Bangladesh;[30] "inclined toward a more

---

[27] Morris Janowitz, *Military Institutions and Coercion in the Developing Nations* (Chicago, IL: The University of Chicago Press, 1964), 147. Note that intergenerational friction in the officer corps is also a fact of military life in advanced industrial democracies. See Lindy Heinecken, "Discontent within the Ranks? Officers' Attitudes toward Military Employment and Representation – A Four-Country Comparative Study," *Armed Forces & Society* 35, no. 3 (April 2009): 477–500.

[28] Kamrava, "Military Professionalization," 81.

[29] Majid Khadduri, "The Coup D'État of 1936: A Study in Iraqi Politics," *Middle East Journal* 2, no. 3 (July 1948): 276.

[30] Tanel Demirel, "Lessons of Military Regimes and Democracy: The Turkish Case in a Comparative Perspective," *Armed Forces & Society* 31, no. 2 (Winter 2005): 250; Croissant and Selge, "Should I Stay or Should I Go," 112.

radical outlook" in South Korea;[31] open to "revolutionary propaganda" in Guatemala;[32] "influenced by the extremist ideas of the Muslim Brotherhood and the Communists" in Sudan;[33] "sympathetic to the social conditions of the shopkeeper, the farmer, and the peasant" in Japan;[34] "idealistic" and "radicalized" in Venezuela;[35] "idealistic" and "antioligarchic" in Brazil;[36] "reformist" in El Salvador;[37] "militant" in Nigeria;[38] "radical leftist" in Portugal;[39] and favoring "populist democracy" in Ecuador.[40] Four pervasive trends are particularly interesting to note in this regard:

First, as previously mentioned, mid-ranking and junior officers tend to be more sensitive to civilian grievances and pervasive political malaise in society at large than the upper echelons of the officer corps. Egypt stands as a case in point here. Radical populism, whether expressed in nationalistic terms (e.g., the Free Officers), religious revivalism (e.g., the Muslim Brotherhood/Islamic Jihad),[41] or class conflict (e.g., the Democratic

---

[31] Jae Souk Sohn, "Political Dominance and Political Failure: The Role of the Military in the Republic of Korea," in *The Military Intervenes: Case Studies in Political Development*, ed. Henry Bienen (New York: Russel Sage Foundation, 1968), 108.

[32] Kenneth J. Grieb, "The Guatemalan Military and the Revolution of 1944," *The Americas* 32, no. 4 (April 1976): 530.

[33] Yusuf Fadl Hasan, "The Sudanese Revolution of October 1964," *Journal of Modern African Studies* 5, no. 4 (1967): 497.

[34] Finer, *The Man on Horseback*, 41.

[35] Paul Zargoski, "Democratic Breakdown in Paraguay and Venezuela: The Shape of Things to Come for Latin America," *Armed Forces & Society* 30, no. 1 (Fall 2003): 93.

[36] Alain Rouquie, *The Military and the State in Latin America* (Berkley, CA: University of California Press, 1982), 106–113.

[37] Philip J. Williams and Knut Walter, *Militarization and Demilitarization in El Salvador's Transition to Democracy* (Pittsburgh, PA: University of Pittsburgh Press, 1997), 10.

[38] Michael Bratton and Nicolas van de Walle, *Democratic Experiments in Africa: Regime Transitions in Comparative Perspective* (New York: Cambridge University Press, 1997), 216.

[39] Zoltan Barany, *The Soldier and the Changing State: Building Democratic Armies in Africa, Asia, Europe, and the Americas* (Princeton, NJ: Princeton University Press, 2012), 127.

[40] Steven Barraca, "Military Coups in the Post-Cold War Era: Pakistan, Ecuador, and Venezuela," *Third World Quarterly* 28, no. 1 (2007): 147.

[41] It is significant that eight of the thirteen officers who formed the Revolutionary Command Council (RCC) in 1952 had, at some point in their lives, been members of the Muslim Brotherhood (i.e., Gamal 'Abdul Nasser, Abdul-Hakim 'Amer, Anwar al-Sadat, Kamal al-Din Hussein, Hussein al-Shafe'i, Khaled Muhieddin, 'Abdul-Latif al-Baghdadi, and Hasan Ibrahim). Decades later, an Egyptian intelligence lieutenant colonel, 'Abbud al-Zumur, became the founder and first emir of the Egyptian Islamic Jihad and recruited Khaled Islambuli, an Egyptian first lieutenant who was tried and executed in 1982 for his role in the 1981 assassination of Egyptian president Anwar al-Sadat. Leftist penetration of the military was more modest, and culminated in the 1940s and 1950s. The most prominent leftist officer in the Egyptian military was Khaled Muhieddin, who was briefly a member of the Muslim Brotherhood's armed wing before joining the communist organization HIDATU. Other left-leaning Free Officers included Ahmad Hamrush, author of

Movement for National Liberation/HADITU) has had a better chance of penetrating the Egyptian officer corps from below rather than from above. It is interesting to note that the first officers' revolt in the modern history of Egypt was led by a mid-ranking officer, Colonel Ahmed 'Urabi. The latter's movement coalesced around young nationalistic officers who harbored deep corporate grievances, and, like most Egyptians, resented the weakness of the monarchy vis-à-vis British imperialism.[42] 'Urabi was defeated by British forces at the battle of Tel el-Kebir in 1882, but the receptiveness of the lower echelons of the officer corps to the societal and political influences unfolding among the public at large proved enduring. During the 1919 revolution against British occupation, junior and mid-ranking officers participated in popular protests, though the military institution per se remained neutral.[43] A few decades later, the Free Officers, who toppled King Farooq in 1952 and continued the nationalist struggle against the British, bore an unmistakable resemblance to the 'Urabi movement. In both instances (i.e., 'Urabi and the Free Officers revolts) the politically conscious lower echelons of the officer class were not insulated from surrounding popular grievances. In 1972, when disillusionment became widespread in Egyptian society due to military inaction vis-à-vis Israel, disaffection was particularly strong among mid-ranking and junior officers.[44] And when popular protests erupted the same year against the regime of Anwar al-Sadat, junior officers joined the demonstrations – but not one of their superiors did.[45] The same phenomenon repeated itself during the 2011 turning point: scores of officers defected to the demonstrators in Tahrir Square, and all of them occupied mid-ranking and junior positions in the military hierarchy. Three constants seem to have been a fixture in the turbulent history of the Egyptian armed forces: (1) The views of the lower ranks of the officer corps did not always correspond with the views of their superiors;

a series of classical accounts of the 1952 coup, and Yussef Siddiq, who played an important operational role in the execution of the Free Officers' coup.

[42] Tareq al-Bushari, *Al-Dimoqratiyya wa-Nizam 23 Yulyu, 1952–1970* (Cairo: Dar al-Shuruq, 2013), 66–67.

[43] Ibid., 70.

[44] Raymond A. Hinnebusch, *Egyptian Politics under Sadat: The Post-populist Development of an Authoritarian-Modernizing State* (Boulder, CO: Lynne Rienner Publishers, 1988), 127. Note that the same is true of the church structure in Catholic countries: opposition to dictators typically begins not among cardinals and bishops, but in the lower-ranking priesthood. H. E. Chehabi and Juan J. Linz, "A Theory of Sultanism 2: Genesis and Demise of Sultanistic Regimes," in *Sultanistic Regimes*, ed. H. E. Chehabi and Juan J. Linz (Baltimore, MD: Johns Hopkins University Press, 1998), 42.

[45] Ahmed S. Hashim, "The Egyptian Military, Part One: From the Ottomans through Sadat," *Middle East Policy* 18, no. 3 (Fall 2011), www.mepc.org/journal/middle-east-policy-archives/egyptian-military-part-one-ottomans-through-sadat (accessed April 16, 2015). See also Hinnebusch, *Egyptian Politics under Sadat*, 51.

(2) Latent intergenerational friction precipitated tremendous political consequences when activated; and (3) Junior and mid-ranking officers have always been more in tune than the top brass with the mood of ordinary Egyptians. An Egyptian king or president could forfeit the kind of political legitimacy stemming from popular acceptance and maintain the loyalty of senior officers – but not of their subordinates. I show later on that these observations are particularly important to a complete understanding of the military politics and behavior prevalent in 2011.

Second, in times of popular mobilization against authoritarian regimes, mid-ranking and junior officers frequently lean toward democratic reforms, while their superiors tend to back ". . . whoever gave them their exalted jobs."[46] Zoltan Barany has argued persuasively that junior officers support uprisings because they have spent less time in the military than their superiors, and are less invested in the status quo.[47] Animosity against the top brass may also explain the political agency of the lower echelons: loyalist senior officers are often perceived by their subordinates as forfeiting corporate and national interests in exchange for private benefits. Revolutionary moments provide an opening to activate these dynamics, and it's unsurprising that cases of intergenerational tension abound in transitional times. For example, in Spain, the lower echelons of the armed forces officer corps were enthusiastic about democratic transition in the 1970s, in opposition to the reluctance of the top brass. Captains organized "tactical committees" in the military to prevent the higher command from blocking the post-Franco democratic process.[48] In 2007 Pakistan, the military high command that had backed Pervez Musharraf's second coup eventually withheld its support. The embattled president was forced to resign in 2008 after losing his top brass power base. In doing so, the Pakistani generals were "responding to pressure from the middle-ranking and junior officers" who backed the popular mobilization against Musharraf.[49] During the last years of the USSR, the Soviet officer corps became divided along generational lines over Gorbachev's *Perestroika*. On one hand, the reform-minded, mid-ranking, and junior officers overwhelmingly supported the democratic opening promoted by the civilian leadership. On the other, the military elite espoused more conservative political views and were united by opposition to Gorbachev.[50] Similarly, while mid-ranking and junior

---

[46] Luttwak, *Coup d'Etat*, 80.   [47] Barany, "Explaining Military Reponses," 8.
[48] Filipe Aguero, *Soldiers, Civilians and Democracy: Post-Franco Spain in a Comparative Perspective* (Baltimore, MD: Johns Hopkins University Press, 1995), 104–105.
[49] Aqil Shah, "Constraining Consolidation: Military Politics and Democracy in Pakistan, 2007–2013," *Democratization* 21, no. 6 (2014): 1014–1015.
[50] Taylor, *Politics and the Russian Army*, 214.

officers in the Indonesian military became alienated from Suharto in the mid-1990s, their superiors were still committed to the status quo, including generals critical of the regime.[51] More recently, in Algeria, young officers of the seventh armored brigade circulated a petition supportive of the 2019 popular uprising, and critical of the alliance between the military commandership and the Bouteflika regime. The support that the junior officers received among their peers in the armed forces alarmed the powerful generals and signaled to the opposition that it has sympathizers in the lower ranks of the military hierarchy.[52] Meanwhile, the same phenomenon was unfolding in Sudan. Indeed, recent journalistic accounts suggest that young Sudanese officers and the lower echelons of the armed forces were sympathetic to the 2019 uprising against ʿOmar al-Bashir and fraternized with protesters irrespective of instructions from above.[53] Similar intergenerational tensions in the armed forces were also reported in 2019 during the ongoing crisis in Venezuela.[54] Other analogous examples abound.

Third, mid-ranking and junior officers are generally more disinclined to open fire on civilian protestors than their superiors in the higher echelons of the military – an attitude consistent with the intergenerational political divergences described above. When senior officers ignore the unwillingness of their subordinates to open fire, the ensuing disaffection among the middle and lower echelons of the officer corps triggers defections and internal divisions. Bolivia in 2003, Thailand in 1992, and Venezuela in 1980 are cases in point.[55] Students of military politics have long highlighted the threat that police-like operations pose to the

---

[51] Marcus Mietzner, *Military Politics, Islam, and the State in Indonesia: From Turbulent Transition to Democratic Consolidation* (Singapore: Institute of Southeast Asian Studies, 2009), 101.

[52] See Hassan Benadad, "Le 'Hirak" Algérien Gagne la Citadelle De L'Armée," *Kiosque 360*, February 18, 2019, http://fr.le360.ma/politique/le-hirak-algerien-gagne-la-citadelle-de-larmee-184362 (accessed March 30, 2019). See also TV interview with Algerian activist Essaid Aknine: www.youtube.com/watch?v=cnGg7I2Ptyc (accessed March 29, 2019).

[53] See Jean-Philille Rémy, "Les manifestants au Sudan appellant désormais à la chute de la junte," *Le Monde*, April 12, 2019, www.lemonde.fr/afrique/article/2019/04/12/les-manifestants-au-soudan-appellent-desormais-a-la-chute-de-la-junte_5449085_3212.html (accessed April 12, 2019).

[54] See Nicholas Casey, "Venezuelan Opposition Leader Steps Up Pressure, but Maduro Holds On," *The New York Times*, April 30, 2019, www.nytimes.com/2019/04/30/world/americas/venezuela-guaido-maduro.html?action=click&module=Top%20Stories&pgtype=Homepage (accessed April 30, 2019).

[55] See Pion-Berlin and Trinkunas, "Civilian Praetorianism," 405; and Wendy Hunter, *Eroding Military Influence in Brazil: Politicians against Soldiers* (Chapel Hill, NC: University of North Carolina Press, 1997), 20.

internal cohesion of the armed forces.[56] The fact is officers and soldiers relish the idea of being the nation's protectors. This self-image is not compatible with missions during which troops are asked to kill their own countrymen – especially when civilians stand for what recruits deem to be legitimate demands.[57] Significantly, in 1962, a Soviet officer committed suicide rather than opening fire on striking workers. By the end of the eighties, when ethnic tension was on the rise in Soviet republics, the interior ministry troops were beefed up because the army refused to be used for internal security operations.[58] The Lebanese armed forces are typically obedient to political authorities, yet they refused to intervene against civilian demonstrators during the 2005 Cedar Revolution – even though they were ordered to do so by the pro-Syrian president and former army commander Emile Lahoud. I will argue later on that coup-proofing tactics based upon ideational links between autocrats and their armed forces are particularly effective in inducing the armed forces to overcome their reservations against killing civilians.[59]

And finally, top brass corruption has been an important reason for friction between senior officers and their subordinates. It is not infrequent that generals amass wealth and power, while their subordinates and ordinary citizens at large struggle to make ends meet. The corruption and self-enrichment at the top fosters resentment among mid-level and junior officers, who do not benefit from the same privileges, but are nonetheless expected to risk their lives when generals order them to do so. In the 1980s, this was precisely the case of lower ranks in the Philippine military who resented being sent to fight regional insurgencies against a backdrop of "cronyism and lack of professionalism of the top loyalist Marcos generals."[60] The same dynamic is frequently at play in

---

[56] Finer notes in this regard that the so-called "mutiny" of the Curragh, which according to him is "the only serious clash between soldiers and the government in recent British history," happened precisely because the soldiers were ordered to fire on civilians. Finer, *The Man on Horseback*, 23. See also Janowitz, *Military Institutions and Coercion*, 46–47.

[57] Bellin, "Reconsidering the Robustness of Authoritarianism," 132.

[58] See Timothy J. Colton, *Commissars, Commanders, and Civilian Authority: The Structure of Soviet Military Politics* (Cambridge, MA: Harvard University Press, 1979), 251. See also Taylor, *Politics and the Russian Army*, 212–213.

[59] Militaries find even counterinsurgency missions distasteful if the enemy is domestic. To avoid putting their internal cohesion under severe strain, some armies opt to outsource internal repression missions to loyalist paramilitary forces. Turkey and Algeria throughout the 1990s stand as an excellent example in this regard. See Yezid Sayigh, "Agencies of Coercion: Armies and Internal Security Forces," *International Journal of Middle East Studies* 43, no. 3 (2011): 404.

[60] Temario Riveria, "The Middle Class and Democratization in the Philippines: From the Asian Crisis to the Ouster of Estrada," in *Southeast Asian Middle Classes: Prospects for Social Change and Democratization*, ed. Embong Abdul Rahman (Bangi: National University of Malaysia, 2001), 237; quoted in Dan Slater, *Ordering Power, Contentious*

Venezuela, where the top brass traditionally benefit from oil booms and overpriced defense purchases to accumulate private wealth.[61] If corruption money is not trickling down, the mid-ranking and junior officers are likely to identify with the suffering of ordinary citizens and to be alienated from the military and civilian power elite.

When, because of intergenerational friction, generals no longer command the loyalty of their subordinates in the officer corps, they lose control over the armed forces. In some cases, this means mid-ranking and junior officers simply cease to obey orders from above. For instance, the Argentinian military elite remained loyal to President Alfonsin in 1987, when mid-ranking and junior officers rebelled against him. That support, however, yielded little benefit. In the words of Alfred Stepan, the generals failed to "deliver a rifle" when their subordinates in the officer corps dissented.[62] Similarly, the king of Greece assumed that his 1967 counter-coup against the junta that had seized power in Athens would be successful because the top brass were on his side. The generals were, indeed, loyalists, but their subordinates were not. When the commanders of the Third Corps and Armored Division issued orders to the mid-ranking and junior officers serving under them, they were detained by the junta's supporters in the officer corps.[63] Other examples abound. Coups labeled "nonhierarchical,"[64] i.e., putsches led by disaffected officers in the middle and lower echelons of the military hierarchy, have been quite recurrent – Thompson established decades ago that most coups are indeed nonhierarchical.[65] More recently, Sing found that of all the coups he studied, 179 were triggered by the mid-ranking and lower echelons of the military hierarchy, and 174 were staged by senior officers.[66]

   Politics and Authoritarian Leviathans in Southeast Asia (Cambridge: Cambridge University Press, 2010), 179.

[61] Harold Trinkunas, *Crafting Civilian Control of the Military in Venezuela: A Comparative Perspective* (Chapel Hill, NC: University of Carolina Press, 2005), 165–166.

[62] Alfred Stepan, *Rethinking Military Politics: Brazil and the Southern Cone* (Princeton, NJ: Princeton University Press, 1988), 115.

[63] Singh, *Seizing Power*, 87.

[64] Juan J. Linz and Alfred Stepan, *Problems of Democratic Transition and Consolidation: Southern Europe, South America, and Post-Communist Europe* (Baltimore, MD: Johns Hopkins University Press, 1996), 130.

[65] William Thompson, "Organizational Cohesion and Military Coup Outcomes," *Comparative Political Studies* 9, no. 3 (October 1976): 259. See also William Thompson, "Regime Vulnerability and the Military Coup," *Comparative Politics* 7, no. 4 (July 1975): 459–487. More recent studies corroborate Thompson's findings, which are, by now, conventional wisdom in the field. See Robin Luckham, "The Military and Democratization in Africa: A Survey of Literature and Issues," *African Studies Review* 37, no. 2 (September 1994): 39.

[66] Singh was unable to identify the origins of another 118 coups. See Singh, *Seizing Power*, 66. Note that the latest young officers' coup unfolded in Gabon, in January 2019. The power grab was unsuccessful, however.

Yet another consequence of generational friction within the officer corps is insubordination in the lower ranks during nonviolent revolutions – or the threat of it. Senior officers with the authority to issue directives depend, for the actual implementation of their orders, upon their subordinates' willingness to execute them. Field marshals and chiefs of staff can order their troops to quell popular uprisings, but they themselves do not open fire upon unarmed civilians demonstrating in public squares.[67] When orders to suppress mobilization are issued, mid-ranking and junior officers become operationally in charge of the slaughter, and because butchering unarmed fellow countrymen is a particularly problematic task to undertake as noted previously, they might refuse to obey. Indeed, they might defect by joining the uprising.[68] Enlisted men are likely to follow orders from their immediate superiors, i.e., mid-ranking and junior officers, even if that entails disobeying the orders of senior officers. According to Nordlinger:

> While the hierarchical principle accords ultimate authority to the senior commanders, the principle also includes the dictate that primary obedience is owed to immediate, face-to-face superiors. Direct orders are always to be obeyed. And it is the middle-level officers – the colonels, majors, and captains – who are the highest-ranking immediate superiors of the men who wield the guns.[69]

Consequently, when the mid-ranking and junior officers signal their refusal to repress protesters, the soldiers under their command follow. This explains why avoiding a large-scale mutiny among mid-ranking and junior officers is paramount to the military elite, whose own influence and prestige – indeed, whose very raison d'être – is dependent upon preserving their authority over the officer corps and the military at large. There is a virtual consensus in the literature that officers typically prioritize the maintenance of hierarchy, discipline, and cohesiveness within the military over any other goal.[70] The risk of undermining the organizational

---

[67] In the words of McCoy, "Whether war, peace, or martial rule, generals keep to their tents while lieutenants form the line and suffer its fate." McCoy, *Closer than Brothers*, 7.

[68] Chenoweth and Stephan have shown that large nonviolent campaigns have about a 60 percent chance of producing loyalty shifts within security forces. See Chenoweth and Stephan, *Why Civil Resistance Works*, 48. The reluctance of soldiers to harm civilians has been identified as one of the main reasons why they defect rather than follow orders to quell unarmed protesters. Sharon Erickson Nepstad, *Nonviolent Revolutions: Civil Resistance in the Late 20th Century* (New York: Oxford University Press, 2011), 122.

[69] Eric A. Nordlinger, *Soldiers in Politics: Military Coups and Governments* (Upper Saddle River, NJ: Prentice Hall, 1977), 102.

[70] See, for instance, Decalo, *Coups and Army Rule*; Barbara Geddes, "What Do We Know about Democratization after Twenty Years?" *Annual Review of Political Science* 2 (June 1999): 115–144; and Pion-Berlin and Trinkunas, "Civilian Praetorianism."

integrity of the officer corps can severely constrain the military elite's leeway and alter their line of action.

Of course, divergence between the military elite and mid-ranking and junior officers in times of nonviolent uprisings is not inevitable; both the top brass and their subordinates might agree on the necessity of suppressing mobilization. Alternatively, they might be resentful of the status quo, and thus unwilling to defend the regime. A convergence of views within the officer corps, or the absence thereof, will depend upon the strength of linkages between each of the following actors: (1) autocratic rulers; (2) military elite; and (3) mid-ranking and junior officers. I show later on that by shaping these linkages into different molds, coup-proofing tactics generate the following outcomes: (1) Some military elite have both the will to defend embattled autocrats and the capacity to protect them without jeopardizing their own authority over the officer corps. (2) Other military elite have the will to save a nondemocratic regime threatened by popular mobilization, but not the capacity to do so, because orders to suppress the protesters, if issued, would be ignored. (3) Still other military elite have neither the will nor the capacity to uphold the status quo.

Horizontal Cleavages: Intra-generational Dynamics in the Officer Corps

Just as vertical splits can divide the officer corps along generational lines, horizontal splits can pit factions of officers occupying the same ranks against one another. Rivalry between different branches of the armed forces over resources and prestige is a common theme in this regard. Whether in democratic nations or dictatorships, officers compete as they lobby the powers that be in favor of their own branch in the military. Each sector in the military is protective of its own field of action, and apprehensive about "encroachments" from other sectors.[71] On the other hand, clientelism often emerges as another feature of horizontal splits. Powerful generals frequently resort to enhancing their position in the

---

[71] Jealousies within the US military that pit the army, the air force, and the navy against one another exemplify these dynamics. For one famous, relevant incident, see Andrew L. Lewis, "The Revolt of the Admirals," Air Command and Staff College/Air University, April 1998, www.au.af.mil/au/awc/awcgate/acsc/98-166.pdf (accessed June 15, 2014). Yet another relevant example is the interservice tension between the army and the navy in Japan throughout the 1930s. The former pushed for land grabbing in China, because ground warfare would increase its budget, whereas the admirals lobbied for expansion in the South Seas, which would have served the corporate interests of the navy. See Weeks, *Dictators at War and Peace*, 122. Similar interservice quarrels are recurrent globally.

military by surrounding themselves with a retinue of loyal subordinates. The top brass expect to count upon their clients' support as they compete with their peers for preeminence in the armed forces. In exchange, patrons are expected to help the careers of their younger followers eager to climb the ranks of military hierarchy. Clientelism, sometimes referred to as the "godfather institution,"[72] divides, in essence, the office corps into warring cliques vying for power and professional advancement within the military institution. With that said, factional splits between officers can also be driven by motivations going beyond career-centered rivalries to include ideological and political considerations (e.g., Islamists vs. secularists; leftists vs. conservatives; soft-liners vs. hard-liners).

From another perspective, competition over promotions frequently divides officer corps horizontally along factional lines. As a general rule, climbing the ladder toward the most prominent positions in the military hierarchy requires political backing, even in professional armed forces. Thus, beyond a certain level of seniority, officers need connections with the powers that be in order to rise even higher in the hierarchy. They frequently compete with each other to ingratiate themselves with those who can further advance their careers. Horizontal factionalism within the officer corps is heightened when the ruling elite play divide and rule to strengthen their positions vis-à-vis the military, a tactic particularly recurrent in authoritarian regimes. Sukarno, for instance, manipulated rivalries among the senior officers of the Indonesian armed forces in order to neutralize the hostility of the military to its policies: namely, the alliance with the Communist Party at home and with communist China abroad.[73] His successor, Suharto, was famous for believing in the need for permanent "creative tension" among the military barons of his regime, and for his skillful instrumentalization of their rivalries to weaken their positions while strengthening his own.[74] In the Philippines, Marcos used similar methods to control the armed forces, though he ultimately paid a heavy price when his tactics backfired. The 1986 and 1998 uprisings that ended Marcos's and Suharto's long tenures in the Philippines and Indonesia, respectively, began as military rebellions staged by senior officers alienated by the dictators' support for their rivals in the armed forces.[75]

---

[72] Bruce W. Farcau, *The Coup Tactics in the Seizure of Power* (Westport, CT: Praeger, 1994), 12.

[73] Harold Crouch, *The Army and Politics in Indonesia* (Singapore: Equinox Publishing, 2007), 54.

[74] David Jenkins, *Suharto and His Generals: Indonesian Military Politics, 1975–1983* (Ithaca, NY: Cornell University Press, 1984), 135–136.

[75] Lee, "The Armed Forces," 650–651. See also Lee, *Defect or Defend.*

As the Philippine and Indonesian examples show, horizontal splits can structure the military's reaction to popular uprisings when hard-line officers plead for a repressive approach, while soft-liners lean toward change. Schmitter and O'Donnell, Przeworski, and Huntington all emphasized the effect upon the transitional process of officers splitting into standpatters and reformers.[76] When some senior officers are ready to take draconian measures against protesters while others call for recognizing the legitimacy of popular grievances, the immediate question becomes: Which faction commands the allegiance of the mid-ranking and junior officers? If one faction within the military elite enjoys the overwhelming support of subordinates, the rival faction can be purged without putting the cohesiveness of the armed forces in jeopardy. For example, when Defense Minister Juan Ponce Enrile and vice-chief of staff of the Armed Forces of the Philippines (AFP) Lieutenant General Fidel Ramos withdrew their support for Marcos in 1986, the cascade of defection that followed left the rival faction, led by chief of staff General Ver, with virtually no support within the ranks of the officer corps. The loyalist faction was quickly purged after the fall of Marcos, and Ver accompanied him to exile. Despite the fragmentation at the top, the AFP remained largely cohesive throughout the 1986 critical juncture.[77]

In contrast, if factionalism among senior officers is replicated in the lower echelons, and if each section at the upper end of the military hierarchy can count upon the support of a clique of subordinates, then the military runs the risk of splintering when crises come to a head. In two countries during the 2011 Arab Spring, Yemen and Libya, this was precisely the case. In Yemen, General ʿAli Muhsin al-Ahmar, the friend and ally of then president ʿAli ʿAbdullah al-Salih and commander of the powerful First Armored Division (al-Firqa), defected to the uprising while keeping the loyalty of the entire officer corps of his regiment. The Yemeni armed forces became divided between the loyalists, headed by Ahmad al-Salih, the president's son and commander of the Republican Guard, and the opponents of President al-Salih, headed by General al-Ahmar.[78] In Libya, Muʿammar al-Qaddhafi lost the loyalty of his interior

---

[76] O'Donnell and Schmitter, *Transitions from Authoritarian Rule*, 35. See also Adam Przeworski, *Democracy and the Market: Political and Economic Reforms in Eastern Europe and Latin America* (New York: Cambridge University Press, 1991), 54; and Samuel Huntington, *The Third Wave: Democratization in the Late Twentieth Century* (Norman, OK: University of Oklahoma Press, 1991), 121.

[77] McCoy, *Closer than Brothers*, 252–253.

[78] See BBC News article "Top Yemeni General, Ali Mohsen, Backs Opposition," March 21, 2011, www.bbc.com/news/world-middle-east-12804552 (accessed March 24, 2014). Note that ʿAli ʿAbdullah al-Salih was allocating four billion Yemeni rials monthly for al-Firqa, and twelve billion for the Republican Guard, though the size of both corps was

minister and veteran regime insider General 'Abdul-Fattah Younes, as well as that of officers stationed in Benghazi almost as soon as the uprising began. The civil war that ensued pitted one section of the armed forces, which was supplanted by mercenaries and paramilitary forces loyal to al-Qaddhafi, against officers and soldiers allied with the insurgents.[79]

Coup-Proofing, Intra-military Cleavages, and Popular Uprisings

How can autocrats coup-proof their regimes when their officers' ethos is interventionist? The answer is straightforward: if officers lack the incentive to challenge the status quo, the capacity to do so, or both, the autocrat's grip on power is secure. Incentive is a function of ideational congruence. Shared worldviews and animosities provide powerful motivations for officers to support the powers that be as long as they last. Material incentives matter, as well. All else being equal, officers satisfied with their lot are less likely to trigger coups than officers who are not. On the other hand, the capacity to stage putsches is a function of the officers' perceptions of the correlation of forces and their ability to build coalitions in the military. Officers who do not believe they stand a chance of defying the established order will refrain from doing so, despite being politically alienated or professionally unhappy. In the same vein, officers separated by entrenched suspicions and animosities are less likely to engage in the kind of coalition-building necessary for coups. Fragmentation in the officer corps magnifies the officers' collective action problem, and reduces their capacity for coalition-building. Ideally for autocrats, officers will lack both the incentive and the capacity to overthrow the status quo.

The routes rulers take to coup-proof typically include one, or several, of the following tactics: (1) wedding the armed forces ideologically to the regime via shared worldviews and aversions to common enemies; (2) promoting the material interests of senior officers; (3) counterbalancing the military through the establishment of parallel armed forces, powerful ruling parties, intelligence services, or some or all of the above; (4) divide-and-rule tactics pitting military factions against one another. These techniques are not mutually exclusive. Autocrats can, and have, integrated

roughly even. See Holger Albrecht and Dorothy Ohl, "Exit, Resistance, Loyalty: Military Behavior during Unrest in Authoritarian Regimes," *Perspectives on Politics* 14, no. 1 (March 2016): 38–52.

[79] See International Crisis Group report "Popular Protest in North Africa and the Middle East (V): Making Sense of Libya," no. 107, June 6, 2011, www.crisisgroup.org/middle-east-north-africa/north-africa/libya/popular-protest-north-africa-and-middle-east-v-ma king-sense-libya (accessed January 5, 2013).

more than one into their arsenals. Yet the above-mentioned methods are divergent in the control mechanisms they install over the armed forces. Consequently, they mold civil–military relations through different means. Whether autocrats manipulate shared aversions, promote material interests, counterbalance, or prey on intra-military tensions, the nature and strength of their links with the top brass, as well as those with mid-ranking and junior officers, is affected. As I show below, these tactics structure fundamentally military responses to popular uprisings.

Ideology and Fostering Shared Aversions

Authority is more likely to elicit obedience when accepted as legitimate, and dissent from below is more frequent in hierarchical relations ungrounded in normative justifications. Autocrats tend to frame their rule in normative terms to garner acceptance, and some succeed. Examples include Hitler, Stalin, Khomeini, Mao, and Castro, all of whom projected an ascetic image of a leader with a mission greater than mere power politics and personal enrichment. Legitimacy is not a given, however, and can, in fact, be reversed when propaganda fails to hide the discrepancy between slogans and the actual practice of power. For instance, an autocrat who raised hopes of liberalization jeopardizes popular goodwill if his regime remains predatory. The same is true if an insensitive display of elite privilege and opulence makes promises of social justice and redistribution appear risible.

The fundamental strength that legitimacy bestows on a leader is this: subordinates obey him not just out of material self-interest, or fear, but because they believe that he has the right to issue orders, and that his directives aim to serve a higher purpose to which they too are committed. But to be credible and wield such power, leaders must appear to be genuinely dedicated to the pursuit of a higher purpose transcending self-serving politics. Autocrats widely perceived to be corrupt stooges of foreign powers, or strictly devoted to the interests of a narrow power circle, are more likely to be vulnerable to political opposition. To be sure, dormant disapproval may take years to become active. But when coup-plotters strike, or when masses take to the streets to clamor for regime change, the ideological vacuity of autocrats no longer wedded ideationally to a power base can generate a quick collapse. Consider the Somozas in Nicaragua, the Duvaliers in Haiti, and Batista in Cuba. They could all originally boast some backing among the mestizos, blacks, and mulattoes of their respective countries. Years of oppressive rule and blatant corruption, however, eroded their initial appeal and discredited their claims as champions of higher impersonal principles. The shrinking of their social bases to their direct clientele heightened their political vulnerability and contributed to their eventual demise.

Juan Linz contends that legitimacy is particularly important for militaries to accept civilian authority because soldiers will not be beneficiaries of decisions that could cost them their lives, and thus need other motivations than self-interest to follow orders.[80] Along similar lines, Ted Gurr maintains that the loyalty of officers is greatest when they feel that the regime they serve is legitimate.[81] I agree. I also add that the turbulent political history and societal structure in the developing countries have provided fertile terrain for autocrats to use ideology, ethnic solidarity, or both in order to wed the armed forces to their regimes ideationally, and cultivate an image of legitimacy. Some autocrats posed as national liberators and legitimatized their rule accordingly. Turkey's Ataturk is a case in point, among others. Autocrats have also used the place and role of religion in the public sphere to frame themselves either as progressives committed to secularization and modernization or as protectors of the faith. This dividing line was particularly salient in the Muslim world, and frequently pitted nationalists against Islamists.

Communism is another illustration following this dynamic. The ruling elite in the former Soviet Union and its sphere of influence in Eastern Europe deployed systematic efforts to achieve ideological congruence between the communist parties and the armed forces. Their aim was to build officers who were simultaneously "red" and "experts."[82] The indoctrination of young recruits in the officer corps into communist ideology was not an easy task to undertake, due to the incompatibility of values widespread within the populations from which the officers hailed, and communist dogma. The Poles, for example, were known for being highly nationalistic, individualistic, staunchly Catholic, and generally anti-Russian. One evident way of resocializing officers into more acceptable norms was to make sure they joined the communist parties of their respective countries. This goal was largely obtained, and party membership of military officers reached extremely high proportions: 99 percent in the National People's Army (East Germany), 90 percent in the Romanian People's Army, 82 percent in the Hungarian People's Army, 80–83 percent in the Bulgarian People's Army, 80 percent in the Polish People's Army, and 75 percent in the Czechoslovakian People's

[80] See Gerardo L. Munck and Richard Snyder, *Passion, Craft, and Method in Comparative Politics* (Baltimore, MD: Johns Hopkins University Press, 2007), 166.

[81] Ted Robert Gurr, *Why Men Rebel* (Princeton, NJ: Princeton University Press, 1970), 252.

[82] Dale R. Herspring and Ivan Volgyes, *Civil–Military Relations in Communist Systems* (Boulder, CO: Westview Press, 1978), 254.

Army.[83] On the other end of the spectrum, anti-communism also served as a powerful ideological reference uniting regime clients behind determined autocrats: think of the Suharto regime in its early years as a case in point.

Fostering shared aversions via ethnic stacking is particularly effective as a coup-proofing tactic. Relying strictly upon material incentives typically puts a coterie of privileged senior officers on the regime's side. By contrast, ideational links based upon shared aversions deliver the loyalty of the ethnically skewed officer corps as a whole, not just the military elite. Lest we forget, officers are commanded by the top brass – but officer corps are not field marshals and generals alone. The allegiance of senior officers serving autocrats is characteristically for sale and rulers buy it when they can. But rarely are the forces of the status quo able to secure the loyalty of officer corps at large – let alone rank and file – strictly via financial incentives. Hence the importance of giving troops ideational motivations to kill on behalf of the ruling elite during popular uprisings. The fact is military defection in times of unrest is negatively correlated with the strength of ideational beliefs in the ranks when civilians challenge autocracy. Furthermore, ideational animosities make the likelihood of extrication pacts between loyalists and the opposition less likely. On the other hand, wedding troops ideationally to the status quo liberates autocrats from dependency on the provision of material incentives, thus shielding their regimes from the negative repercussions of fiscal crises. Shared aversions deliver military loyalty on the cheap. Under such configurations, the relationship between the autocrat and "his" military becomes mired in paternalism as the ruler transmutes into a protector/father figure for his co-ethnics. If anti-regime demonstrators take to the streets, shared aversions facilitate autocratic efforts to frame them as the "others," agents of foreign powers and enemies of the ruling elite's ethnic group per se. This is precisely why identities are laden with tremendous political consequences; not for being primordialist and unmalleable – they are not – but because they can form a solid basis for effectively "othering" opponents in heterogenous societies. In 2011 Egypt, the overwhelming majority of the political elite were Sunni Muslim, of course, just as the military. Joined sectarian identity in itself clearly did not stimulate ideational links in this case. In contrast, Sunni soldiers who defended the Saddam Hussein regime in Iraq when Shia and Kurdish uprisings erupted

[83] Zoltan Barany, "Civil–Military Relations in Comparative Perspective: East-Central and Southeastern Europe," *Political Studies* 41, no. 4 (1993): 594–610. The commissar system was another way of linking the officer corps to the communist parties through bonds of shared ideology. Commissars were political officers entrusted with the task of carrying out party propaganda and indoctrination work in the armed forces.

Table 1.4 *Examples of ethnic stacking in authoritarian regimes*[84]

Country	Time period	Dominant vs. dominated group(s) in the military
Afghanistan	1996–2001	Pashtun (Kandahari) (vs. Tajik; Uzbek; and Hazara)
Algeria	1962–Present	Arabs (vs. Berbers)
Bahrain	1971–Present	Sunni (vs. Shia)
Benin	1960–1972	Fon; and Yoruba (Southerners) (vs. Bariba; and Pila Pila – Northerners)
Cameroon	1960–1982	Peuhl; and Fulani (Northerners) (vs. Bamileke and Bassa – Southerners)
Iraq	1964–2002	Arab Sunnis (Takritis) (vs. Arab Shia; and Kurds)
Jordan	1946–Present	Bedouin-Jordanians (East Bank) (vs. Palestinian-Jordanians/West Bank)
Kenya	1978–2002	Kalenjin (vs. Kikuyu)
Libya	1969–2011	Qadhadhifa; Warfalla; and Maqarha (vs. Easterners)
Nigeria	(January–July) 1966	Igbo (Christian Easterners) (vs. Hausa – Muslim Northerners)
	1966–Present	Hausa (vs. Igbo)
Pakistan	1947–1971	Punjabis (Westerners) (vs. Bengalis – Easterners)
Sierra Leone	1964–1967	Mende (vs. Temne)
South Africa	1946–1993	White (Afrikaner) (vs. Black)
Sudan	1956–2011	Arab Muslims (African Christians/Animists)
Syria	1963–Present	Alawis (vs. Sunnis)

[84] I collected the data in this table from several sources I used in the book. Particularly helpful were Cameron S. Brown, Christopher J. Fariss, and R. Blake McMahon, "Recouping after Coup-Proofing: Compromised Military Effectiveness and Strategic Substitution," *International Interactions* 42, no. 1 (2016): 1–30; and Decalo, *Coups and Army Rule*. For the sake of simplicity, I am subsuming religious, regional, tribal, and sectarian identity traits under the heading of "ethnic stacking" as the literature on coups typically does.

Table 1.4 *(cont.)*

Country	Time period	Dominant vs. dominated group(s) in the military
Uganda	1962–1971	Langi and Acholi (Northerners) (vs. Buganda)
	1971–1979	Kakwa (Northwestern Uganda and South Soudan) (vs. Langi and Acholi)

simultaneously in 1991 thought of the dictator's enemies as theirs as well. The same is true of Alawi loyalists in Syria, who proved ready to kill Sunni civilians well before the rise of ISIS and other fundamentalist organizations. Table 1.4 shows the extent to which ethnic stacking has been prevalent specifically in African and Arab autocracies.

A correlate to ethnic stacking can be found in all-in-the-family tactics. Autocrats in sultanistic regimes have frequently appointed their sons, brothers, in-laws, or cousins to sensitive positions in the armed forces in order to destroy military autonomy. Yemen's ʿAli ʿAbdullah Salih exemplifies this point. His son, Ahmed, led the redoubtable Republican Guard, stacked with men hailing from Salih's Sanhan tribe of the Hashid tribal confederation; another son, Khaled, commanded the Mountain Armored Infantry Division. Salih's nephew, Tariq Muhammad ʿAbdullah Salih, headed the Presidential Guard; and his half-brother, Muhammad Salih ʿAbdullah al-Ahmar, was commander of the air force.[85] A study has found that the chief of staff and commanders of all branches of the Bahraini armed forces, save the navy, belong to the al-Khalifa ruling family.[86] Other autocrats from the Arab world who have appointed family members extensively in the armed forces include Hafez and Bashar al-Asad in Syria, Saddam Hussein in Iraq, and Muʿammar al-Qaddafi in Libya. In Latin America, the Castro, Somoza, Trujillo, and Ortega regimes also appointed family members in leadership positions in the armed forces.[87]

---

[85] For a detailed account of civil–military relations in Yemen, see the International Crisis Group report "Yemen's Military-Security Reform: Seeds of New Conflict?" Middle East/ North Africa Report No. 139, April 4, 2013, https://d2071andvip0wj.cloudfront.net/ye mens-military-security-reform-seeds-of-new-conflict.pdf (accessed June 5, 2015).

[86] See Brown, Fariss, and McMahon, "Recouping after Coup-Proofing," 5.

[87] Sometimes the tactic backfired. Oman's crown prince Qabus al-Saʿid overthrew his father, Saʿid al-Saʿid, in a 1970 palace coup. Qatar's crown prince Sheikh Hamad bin

Promoting the Material Interests of the Military Elite

Authoritarian regimes often tolerate – indeed, encourage – the military elite's involvement in the economy in order to cultivate their loyalty. The subsequent inequality of income sets senior officers so far above their subordinates in the armed forces (and their fellow countrymen at large) that generals may morph into a "military enclave,"[88] separated from society and preying upon it. Officer-run economic fiefdoms comprise ventures aimed at securing the financial autonomy of the armed forces, projects helping civilian agencies to develop the national infrastructure, or both. The sums circulating in these activities can be significant, and thus provide officers-turned-economic managers ample opportunities for personal enrichment. In addition, the generals, eager to benefit from their political connections in exchange for commissions and financial assets, are frequently allowed to form partnerships with private capital. Sometimes, the economic involvement of military leaders morphs into what Rouquie labeled "pure and simple gangsterism." For example, Somoza's generals in Nicaragua imposed protection rackets on bars and gambling halls, or made money from distributing gun permits or collecting fines.[89] Other fast routes to opulence for loyalist generals in nondemocratic countries have included appropriating public lands or sequestering the properties of political opponents. Because monitoring agencies are forbidden from scrutinizing their dealings, corruption becomes rampant among senior officers. Lust for gain and fear of a day of reckoning consolidate the generals' loyalty to authoritarian leaders who promote their material interests and shield them from prosecution. Family members of senior commanders frequently benefit, as well.[90]

Autocrats who count on corruption to cultivate military loyalty can be very generous toward their top generals. Philippe Droz-Vincent notes convincingly that generals in authoritarian regimes are often extremely

Khalifa al-Thani did the same in 1995. Rif`at al-Asad, the commander of the Syrian Defense Brigades, challenged the authority of his brother, President Hafez al-Asad, in 1982. Then again, all of these were intra-elite and intra-group struggles for power. When regimes face out-group challenges, family members and co-ethnics tend to rally around the flag. In fact, they typically can be counted upon to go all the way in order to uphold the status quo.

[88] Steven A. Cook, *Ruling but Not Governing: The Military and Political Development in Egypt, Algeria, and Turkey* (Baltimore, MD: Johns Hopkins University Press, 2007), 14.

[89] Rouquie, *The Military and the State*, 161.

[90] According to an offspring of a Burmese general: "When we knew that we could get business concessions using our father's connections, we tried it. We were also approached by some businesspeople to do business with them. Sometimes, we did not have to do anything. They just used our names, and we received a certain percentage of the profits." Kyaw Yin Hlaing, "Setting Rules for Survival: Why the Burmese Military Regime Survives in an Age of Democratization," *The Pacific Review* 22, no. 3 (July 2009): 284.

loyal to the powers that be and can become the military "creatures" of autocrats.[91] I add that autocrats face a dual challenge in this regard. First, wherever loyalty depends upon the continued provision of private goods to clients in the coercive apparatus, autocratic survival becomes a function of maintaining solid fiscal health. Financial crises may be lethal for the autocrat who relies strictly upon material incentive to link his officers to his rule. Second, even if autocrats avoid dramatic economic meltdowns, they rarely possess sufficient resources to make the mid-ranking and younger officers, let alone the rank and file, affluent, as well. In essence, the lower echelons of the officer corps are supposed to wait their turn, and avoid trouble in the meantime. Struggling to make ends meet for three decades or more, after graduating from military academy, while generals hoard millions, however, is frustrating. And because the private goods lavished on the top brass do not generally trickle down, officers in autocracies frequently become divided into two camps – the "winners" vs. "losers" dichotomy separates in such cases loyalist generals from their not-so-loyalist subordinates.[92] Venezuela was a case in point during the 1980s, when the wages and benefits of officers failed to keep up with the inflation. Four decades later, the dividing line separating the pampered generals in the Venezuelan military from their subordinates in the officer corps remains stark. Quoting Harold Trinkunas, and a recent report in the *New York Times*, respectively:

In the context of declining living standards, the growing corruption in military procurement among both civilian politicians and senior military officers simply infuriated many officers ... Junior officers, who were expected to exhibit exemplary honesty in their own affairs, were offended by the enrichment of senior military officers and civilian politicians at a time when their own families suffered financial hardship and their troops lacked proper uniforms, food, and lodging.[93]

While Mr. Maduro has sought to ensure the loyalty of the military's top brass with promotions and lucrative contracts, middle- and lower-ranking officers and their families are increasingly affected by the crisis. That makes them restless ... "The hunger came to the barracks and the military ranks became infested with dissidence," said Ms. Acosta, the lawyer. "The armed forces are gripped by paranoia, suspicion and division between those that support this government and those who don't."[94]

---

[91] Philippe Droz-Vincent, "From Fighting Formal Wars to Maintaining Civil Peace," *International Journal of Middle East Studies* 43, no. 3 (August 2011): 393.

[92] Lee, "The Armed Forces."   [93] Trinkunas, *Crafting Civilian Control*, 176–177.

[94] See Anatoly Kormanaev and Isayen Herrera, "Venezuela's Maduro Cracks Down on His Own Military in Bid to Retain Power," *The New York Times*, August 13, 2019, www.nytimes.com/2019/08/13/world/americas/venezuela-military-maduro.html (accessed August 13, 2019). See also Nicholas Casey and Anna Vanessa Herrero, "As Maduro's Venezuela Rips Apart, So Does His Military," *The New York Times*, August 8,

This dichotomy in the officer corps informs military responses to popular uprisings because intergenerational friction severely restricts the leeway of the top brass, should a nonviolent revolution threaten the continuity of authoritarian rule. In order to avoid losing control over reluctant mid-ranking and junior officers, the military elite may withdraw support from the embattled political elite – not because generals have an interest in change, but because they fear mutinies within officer corps. The situation in Algeria is still unfolding as I write but analysts are already stressing the distinction between the "extremely corrupt" top brass in the Algerian armed forces, and a new generation of reform-minded professional subordinates. Algeria in 2019 may prove to be yet another case of politically significant generational cleavages restraining the agency of senior officers committed to the status quo.[95]

Counterbalancing

Counterbalancing is a widely used coup-proofing tactic. The essence of counterbalancing lies in the creation of a parallel force that operates as a counterweight to the military. For instance, autocrats can keep the military in check by building intelligence units to monitor political dissent in the armed forces. Infiltrators report malcontents in the officer corps to the powers that be, preempting the translation of their misgivings into coups. On the other hand, loyal Special Forces and militarized police can also be created to counterbalance regular troops.[96] Paramilitaries do not need to be able to defeat the regular armed forces in a full-fledged battle, but they can still make the cost of a putsch prohibitive. Lest we forget, coups do not always involve the entire military. Sometimes, 2 percent of the armed forces or less is all it takes to trigger a successful coup: the 1952 and 1958 putsches in Egypt and Iraq, respectively, stand as cases in point.[97] Swift and bloodless takeovers are more likely to gain the support

---

2017, www.nytimes.com/2017/08/08/world/americas/nicolas-maduro-venezuela-military.html?smid=fb-share&_r=0 (accessed August 10, 2017).

[95] See Carnegie's Amel Boubekeur quoted in Leïla Mignot, "Algérie: Pourquoi l'armée peut changer la donne," *L'Orient Le Jour*, March 9, 2019, www.lorientlejour.com/article/1160857/pourquoi-larmee-peut-changer-la-donne.html?fbclid=IwAR2qsChQtQ1TEOsVoUkJDl8Ea1Q9qbuTfQLsXYBRNKSxc0AL2UyD4xCHcc4 (accessed March 9, 2019).

[96] Quintessential examples include the Waffen SS in Nazi Germany, the Revolutionary Guard Corps in the Islamic Republic of Iran, Hugo Chavez's Bolivarian National Militia, Saddam Hussein's Republican Guard, the Securitate under Ceausescu in communist Romania, Nkrumah's Presidential Guards in Ghana, and the National Guard in Saudi Arabia. Private militias, such as the Duvaliers' Tonton Macoutes in Haiti, can be and have been used for the same purpose.

[97] Gaub, *Guardians of the Arab State*, 12.

of the armed forces at large because they create the impression that the coercive apparatus supports the coup-makers, and that resistance is futile. Loyal police and paramilitaries are effective because their mere presence signals to potential coup-makers that a quick and bloodless takeover is unlikely, which reduces the risk of coups. They also keep an eye on the military on behalf of the ruling elite, and report any suspicious movement of troops. Parallel agencies also liberate regimes from the need to depend on militaries for everyday repression, and thus reduce the political clout of the armed forces. With that said, rulers need to tread carefully with counterbalancing. On the one hand, officers are resentful when resources that could have been spent on the armed forces are actually allocated to their institutional rivals. On the other, officers are characteristically jealous of their monopoly over the legal use of force, and alternate armed forces are perceived as a threat to the corporate identity and mission of the military. Thus, attempts to wrestle this exclusivity away from the armed forces may backfire, and trigger the exact military intervention they were meant to prevent.[98]

Counterbalancing can also include cultivating civilian counterweights to the military. A ruling party with a significant following enhances the position of the powers that be vis-à-vis their officers. Party machineries can be wedded ideationally to autocrats. Apparatchiks may also be committed to the status quo, because they reckon that new rulers may serve a different clientele. Whether because of high-minded commitments or self-centered considerations, party cadres can contribute to deterring coups if they summon the popular masses in support of the status quo. The image of civilian loyalty to the ruling elite signals to the military that a coup is likely to be perceived as illegitimate, and may be actively resisted by the population. This in itself may be enough to deter military interventionism because violence raises the specter of civil strife and possible splits within the armed forces that officers characteristically want to avoid. Demonstrations of support to the powers that be may thus prevent putsches, or at least discourage initially uninvolved units from joining coup-plotters.[99]

---

[98] Coups aiming to disband military rivals have been particularly salient in sub-Saharan Africa. Guatemala in 1954, Algeria in 1965, and Bolivia in 1971 stand as additional examples. The 1960 coup in Ethiopia is an interesting case, because it was triggered by the Imperial Guard that Haile Selassie had used to counterbalance the Ethiopian armed forces. Because of the entrenched animosity between the military and the Imperial Guard, the former crushed the coup, keeping the emperor in power rather than cooperating with its rivals. See William Thompson, "The Grievance of Military Coup-Makers," Sage Professional Papers in Comparative Politics, no. 01-047 (Beverly Hills, CA: Sage Publications, 1973), 15.

[99] For example, the massive civilian mobilization against the 1991 coup in the former Soviet Union clearly contributed to its subsequent unraveling. Indeed, Soviet generals lacked the capacity to clear the large number of protesters without the acquiescence and support

In brief, counterbalancing creates competing institutions with over-lapping (or even redundant) functions that spy on one another and keep the armed forces beleaguered. Erica De Bruin has shown recently that while counterbalancing does not necessarily correlate with fewer coup attempts, it certainly reduces the likelihood of the success of coup plotters by half.[100] The drawback of this technique for autocrats, however, is that military loyalty becomes questionable should a popular uprising challenge the status quo. Though alienated officers may not threaten auto-cratic rule successfully themselves, they will likely refuse to defend it if a massive uprising proves too formidable for the police to handle alone. Officers can facilitate autocratic breakdown simply by staying garrisoned in a context of popular revolution. The military can also signal to parallel forces that they are in a rock-paper-scissors scenario. Should the police or a party militia attempt to suppress the people, the armed forces would turn their firepower on the loyalists. Events leading to the breakdown of the Milošević regime in Serbia illustrate this dynamic. The former Serbian autocrat counted on the police to counterbalance the armed forces and squelch internal dissent. Military personnel struggled finan-cially under Milošević and felt sidelined, whereas the interior ministry thrived. By the time the protestors took to the street in 2000, Milošević had the interior ministry on his side as well as the military top brass, whose loyalty he cultivated. That wasn't enough to save him, though; the lower echelons of the officer corps had long since been alienated. The generals understood that their subordinates were not ready to suppress civilians, and the police reckoned the military would turn against them if they used force against the demonstrators. The interior ministry and military top brass were loyalists, but they had to accept the breakdown of the status quo simply because they were unable to uphold it. Interestingly, a Milošević advisor had adequately predicted the situation months before the autocrat's fall:

... Army is not the top, chief of staff, and few generals. Army is the captains, and they will not shoot at their own people, nor will the police intervene ... when the

---

of their subordinates in the armed forces – which was lacking. In Venezuela, the massive popular mobilization in favor of the late president Hugo Chavez saved him from being overthrown in 2006. See also Barbara Geddes, "Why Parties and Elections in Authoritarian Regimes?" (unpublished manuscript, University of California, Los Angeles, 2006).

[100] Erica De Bruin, "Preventing Coups d'Etat: How Counterbalancing Works," *Journal of Conflict Resolution* 62, no. 7 (March 2017): 1433–1458. See also Erica De Bruin, "Coup-Proofing for Dummies: The Benefits of Following the Maliki Playbook," *Foreign Affairs*, July 7, 2014, www.foreignaffairs.com/articles/iraq/2014-07-27/coup-proofing-dummies (accessed July 7, 2014).

critical mass shows up in the streets, police will not intervene. Technically, it will be impossible for them to intervene.

Divide-and-Rule Tactics

Divide-and-rule tactics resemble counterbalancing in the sense that both imply the manipulation of rivalries in the coercive apparatus. The difference is that counterbalancing pits organizations that are either unaffiliated with the military (e.g., the police), or loosely affiliated with it (e.g., the Republican Guard), against the armed forces. By contrast, divide and rule sets one military corps against another (e.g., army vs. navy and/or air force; Special Forces vs. regular troops; units deployed in the capital vs. units relegated to the periphery). Typically, divide and rule entails manipulating appointments and promotions to reward reliable generals while preventing others from rising in the military hierarchy. Divide and rule could also entail purges and frequent reshuffling of officers. Indeed, both methods heighten intra-military competition to occupy coveted positions that open up when some officers are transferred or dismissed. In these games of musical chairs, the reasons for autocratic preferentialism are variegated. Not infrequently, generals-turned-presidents favor their own branch or specific cohorts (with whom they have personal connections and can secure stronger loyalties) over others.[101] Other times, favoritism is structured by identity politics when autocrats promote the interests of branches dominated by their kinsmen. Intra-military divisions fostered by manipulative autocrats do not necessarily make coup attempts impossible; however, they do make the task of potential coup-plotters more difficult. Putsches are more likely to succeed when a swift move against the nation's capital and symbolic seats of power is followed by the defection of segments of the armed forces not involved in the coup attempt. When opponents of the regime within the military know that significant segments of the armed forces are unlikely to support a move against the incumbents, they will be less likely to challenge them – or, at the very least, less likely to do so successfully. In addition, rival factions keep a keen eye on one another and are quick to report real or imagined acts of disloyalty by their competitors.

Divide and rule has its advantages as a coup-proofing tactic, but it also exhibits significant downsides. If a faction feels permanently slighted by the ruling autocrat, it may look favorably upon regime change. Dan Slater

---

[101] The class of 1971 from the Philippine Military Academy was the pillar of the Marcos regime in the Philippines, and its members benefited greatly from Marcos's generosity in exchange for their loyalty. See McCoy, *Closer than Brothers*, 206–207.

notes in his analysis of civil–military relations in Indonesia that armed forces subjected to divide-and-rule tactics are "only conducive to a dictator's survival when levels of social protest are low."[102] I concur. Sustained popular uprisings activate intra-military fault lines. Officers alienated by divide-and-rule tactics could bank on civil protests to challenge the status quo and their institutional rivals in the armed forces. Three scenarios become possible depending on which combination of coup-proofing tactics is at play: (1) Loyalist military generals keep the bulk of the officer corps under their grip. The marginalized faction remains neutral as the military represses the rebellion, or members defect individually without taking their units with them to the rebellion. (2) The marginalized faction gains the upper hand in the intra-military elite's struggle for the hearts and minds of the officer corps, and the armed forces refuse the autocrat's call for repression. The regime is thus rendered defenseless, and eventually breaks down. The previously marginalized clique in the armed forces moves to center stage of the military institution and purges the hitherto privileged officers. (3) The loyalist faction maintains the loyalty of a sector of the officer corps while the military opposition keeps a grip on another sector. The loyalists may still crack down on the popular mobilization, which leads the regime's opponents in the military to defect to the opposition. The armed forces splinter, typically ushering the way toward internal turmoil. This was true in Yemen during the 2011 uprising when military-on-military clashes occurred a few times in Sanaa despite efforts to avoid them.[103] Alternatively, the loyalists may understand that repression could trigger intra-military fighting, and back down to avoid it. As previously mentioned, Georgia was such a case in 2003.

Combinations

An autocrat can bank on one coup-proofing tactic or more to defend his regime. Because the four tactics explained above are not mutually exclusive, various combinations of them are possible. The amalgamations shape the relationships between the civilian elite, senior officers, and their subordinates differently – hence the variation in the reactions of the officer corps to civilian uprisings as I show in the following chapters.

---

[102] Slater, *Ordering Power*, 205.
[103] For a review of the Yemeni military's response to the 2011 uprising, see Michael Knights, "The Military Role in Yemen's Protest: Civil–Military Relation in the Tribal Republic," *Journal of Strategic Studies* 36, no. 2 (2013): 261–288.

2 Coups, Coup-Proofing, and Regime Formation in Egypt and Syria

I asserted previously that autocrats prioritize coup-proofing over all other considerations, including military performance on the battle-field. Every Egyptian regime from the Free Officers onward stands as a case in point. Consider Gamal 'Abdul Nasser, for instance. Shortly after seizing power in 1952, the Egyptian strongman secured the appointment of his lifelong friend 'Abdul-Hakim 'Amer as com-mander of the armed forces. That 'Amer was not fit to lead and had failed to transform the Egyptian military into an effective fighting force was made blatantly clear by his lackluster performance in the October 1956 Suez War. Throughout the crisis, 'Amer shifted from euphoria to defeatism, and Nasser suspected that his lieutenant's predilection for hashish was affecting his mood and mental capacities.[1] Nasser could have replaced him in the wake of Suez, but that which served Egypt's national security purposes undercut the coup-proofing imperatives of the regime, and these proved over-riding. 'Amer stayed at the top of the military echelon long enough to transform the armed forces into a personal fiefdom, and then he led the Egyptian armed forces into yet another debacle in the Six-Day War of 1967. Significantly, the memoirs of Egyptian Field Marshal Mohammad 'Abdul-Ghani al-Gamasy reveal that intelligence services under Nasser, including Military Intelligence (MI), were more con-cerned with spying on Egyptian officers than on Israel in order to keep the armed forces under control. Egypt headed to the Six-Day War with very little understanding of Israel's military capacity, though the converse was not true.[2] And despite efforts to improve the profes-sional competence of the military in the wake of the war, coup-proofing remained paramount; the memoirs of officers Madkur Abul-'Iz, Amine Huweidi, and Mohammad Fawzi show that even

---

[1] Anthony Nutting, *Nasser* (New York: E. P. Dutton, 1972), 177.
[2] Mohammad 'Abdul-Ghani al-Gamasy, *Mudhakkarat al-Gamasy, Harb October 1973* (San Francisco, CA: Dar Buhuth al-Sharq al-Awsat al-Amirikiyya, 1977), 75–76.

during Egypt's darkest hours, Nasser invariably prioritized regime security (*al-ta'min al-dhati*) over national security (*al-'amn al-qawmi*).[3] The same was true in Syria, where politics were particularly contentious and the country itself especially coup-prone. First, fierce ideological animosities pitted leftists against conservatives, secularists in opposition to Islamists, and supporters of Greater Syria against Arab nationalists. It was perhaps inevitable that a nascent postcolonial entity would struggle to funnel the polarization ensuing from these mutually exclusive views via a tentative democratic order with shallow roots. Second, Syria was severely and negatively affected by the merciless struggle for supremacy in the Arab world, in which Egypt and Iraq – and to a lesser extent Saudi Arabia – vied to control decision-making in Damascus. From independence in 1946 till the rise of Hafez al-Asad to power in 1970, each Arab contender for leadership supported clients willing to do his bidding in Syria. Consequently, regional quarrels reverberated directly in Damascus, further complicating its politics and destabilizing the country.

---

[3] Amine Huweidi was war minister for a brief period after the Six-Day War in 1967. Huweidi maintains in his memoirs that merging the positions of war minister and commander of the armed forces had disastrous consequences on Egypt's civil–military relations, and was particularly deleterious to the principle of military subordination to civilian authority. But Egypt's generals did not want to answer to a civilian minister of defense and Nasser was keen on keeping them loyal. Except for a few months in 1967, the commander of the armed forces served also as war minister throughout Nasser's tenure, though the negative consequences of the arrangement were plain to see.

For his part, Field Marshal Mohammad Fawzi – who followed Huweidi as war minister – notes in his memoirs that the Egyptian leadership actively discouraged educated Egyptians from joining the armed forces, though they were badly needed to absorb the sophisticated weaponry which the Soviet Union had made available to Egypt. The reason again pertained to coup-proofing: graduates from Egypt's schools and universities were more likely to be political than the masses of analphabetic peasants who formed the bulk of Egypt's army – and, thus, potentially more problematic from a political perspective. Fawzi also notes that the Egyptian Special Forces (aka al-Sa'iqa, lit. "the Thunderbolt Unit") were equipped with heavy weaponry, which had little to do with their original mission – to be a light force capable of striking behind enemy lines – because al-Sa'iqa was deemed politically loyal and potentially useful, should a coup be staged. Likewise, anti-tank divisions were deployed to check any bid for power by mechanized brigades, not by potential enemy invasions. As for Madkur Abul-'Iz, Nasser appointed him commander of the Egyptian Air Force after it was largely destroyed by the Israelis in the Six-Day War. Rebuilding the air force became the most indispensable condition for Egypt's military recovery, and Abul-'Iz had a crucial need for new pilots. Yet Abul-'Iz relates that Nasser ordered him to dismiss ten accomplished trainers from the air force when it was discovered that they had relatives who belonged to the Muslim Brotherhood. Such a revelation stained these officers politically, which trumped strict military concerns. See Amine Huweidi, *Al-Foras al-Da'i'a, al-Qararat al-Hasima fi Harbay al-Istinzaf wa-October* (Beirut: al-Sharika al-'Arabiyya li-l-Tawzi' wa-l-Nashr, 1992), 130 and 242; and Mohammad Fawzi, *Harb al-Sanawat al-Thalath, 1967–1970, Mudhakkarat al-Fariq, Mohammad Fawzi Wazir al-Harbiyya al-Asbaq* (Cairo: Dar al-Wihda, 1988), 55–56, 63, and 247–248; and Mohammad al-Gawadi, *Mudhakkarat Qadat al-'Askariyya al-Masriyya, 1967–1972, fi A'qab al-Naksa* (Cairo: Dar al-Khayyal, 2001), 119.

With sectarian and parochial hostilities added to this unstable backdrop, it became difficult to stop military interventionism in politics once the Pandora's box of military coups was opened. From 1949 until 1970, putsches were ubiquitous to the point of becoming an ordinary way of doing politics. The Ba'ath Party coup in 1963 proved to be a turning point of particular importance because it put Hafez al-Asad on the road to power. The roots of the regime still in control of Syria go back to the crucible decade of the 1960s.

In what follows, I dwell briefly on coups under Nasser and the Ba'ath Party, and study the coup-proofing methods of their regimes. The years during which the Free Officers and the Ba'athist Military Committee held sway were transformative for civil–military relations in Egypt and Syria, respectively. Below, I show how the ruling elite fashioned systems of political control with long-term consequences for military politics in both countries.

Coups under Nasser

In his authoritative work on the Free Officers regime, Ahmad Hamrush suggests that Nasser was obsessed with the fate of Hosni al-Za'im and Sami al-Hinnawi, the Syrian military leaders who seized power, only to be overthrown soon afterward and killed. The former was executed by fellow officers, and the latter was assassinated in Beirut.[4] These fears were anything but paranoia. Nasser successfully grabbed power in July 1952, and only a month later, a plot by Non-Commissioned Officers (NCOs) was discovered and crushed, followed in December by an equally unsuccessful conspiracy among air force mechanics. Both were relatively small attempts to challenge the new regime, but they heralded much more serious rebellions that were soon to unfold.[5] Artillery officers plotted against the regime in January 1953, and thirty-five of them were arrested for conspiring against the revolutionary command. The next threat to the new regime came from the armored brigades and escalated against the backdrop of Nasser's power struggle with Mohammad Neguib. Nasser had banked on Neguib's popularity to garner the commitment of the officer corps to the 1952 coup, and his gamble paid off. After the seizure of power, Nasser hoped Neguib would leave decision-making in his hands, but the latter refused to be a figurehead. On February 23, 1954, Neguib resigned, but his supporters in the street and the armed forces

---

[4] Hamrush, *Thawrat Yulyu*, 324.
[5] Owen L. Sirrs, *The Egyptian Intelligence Service: A History of the Mukhabarat, 1910–2009* (London: Routledge, 2010), 35.

brought him back to power. Nasser weathered the storm by promising democratic reform but quickly reneged. His coalition in the armed forces eventually gained the upper hand for several reasons. First, the officers in the revolutionary command council had tasted power, and the majority of them were not ready to give it back; they worked effectively to block democratic transition.[6] Second, officers appointed in civilian positions were benefitting from their plum jobs and were equally unwilling to give up on them; they were ready to fight for their newfound privileges.[7] Whereas Neguib had only ideational links with his supporters (i.e., the promise of democracy), Nasser could muster both ideology (i.e., radical transformation) and material rewards to expand his coalition in the officer corps.[8] Third, officers in the Military Police (MP) had been heavy-handed in their dealings with political opponents and worried about retribution should military rule crumble. They knew they had little to worry about as long as Nasser was in power. Fourth, Nasser had lobbied for his friend 'Amer to become commander of the armed forces. 'Amer used his position to appoint loyalists in strategic positions, which tilted the correlation of forces in the officer corps in favor of military rule, allowing him to quickly secure the loyalty of the military, with the exception of the armored brigades.

On February 26 of the same year, 300 officers in the armored brigades attended a meeting in which they openly called for restoring the parliament and ending military rule. The officers criticized the concentration of power in the hands of an unelected body (i.e., the revolutionary command council) and military interference in politics. Nasser attended the meeting and feared for a moment that a coup was unfolding as the officers debated.[9] Only weeks later in March, Nasser led a counter-coup, after mustering enough support to tame the armored brigades. To do so, however, Nasser was forced to free imprisoned artillery officers to secure the backing of their colleagues against his new opponents. Nasser's supporters in the artillery, infantry, air force, and MP laid siege to the mechanized brigades' headquarters, whose officers braced to defend themselves. Simultaneously, troops stationed in Alexandria declared their support for the mechanized brigades and parliamentary rule. The army came close to splintering and Egypt to civil war before the crisis was

---

[6] Riad Sami, *Shahed 'ala 'Asr al-Ra 'is Mohammad Neguib* (Cairo: al-Maktab al-Masri al-Hadith, 2004), 42–43.
[7] Jamal Hammad, "Qissat al-Sira' 'ala al-Sulta bayna Mohammad Neguib wa-'Abdul Nasser," in *Man Yaktob Tarikh Thawrat Yulyu, al-Qadiyya wal-Shahadat*, ed. Faruq Juaida (Cairo: Dar al-Shuruq, 2009), 207.
[8] Jamal Hammad, *Asrar Thawrat 23 Yulyu*, vol. 2 (Cairo: Dar al-'Ulum, 2011), 1086.
[9] Ibid., 909.

diffused – though not for long. A coup plot by armored brigade officers was discovered on April 26, only a day before the time set for execution. The coup-plotters had decided to attack military headquarters and Nasser's house, dismiss the Revolutionary Command Council (RCC), keep Neguib as president, and restore parliamentary rule. The plot failed, and twenty-six officers in the armored brigades were imprisoned.[10] In the same year, a ring of Muslim Brotherhood supporters in the military was dismantled. Two additional coup plots were nipped in the bud in 1957 and 1958.[11]

The next military conspiracy was more successful. Nasser had scored his major foreign policy success in 1958, when Egypt and Syria merged into the United Arab Republic (UAR). Nasser's prestige in the Arab world reached its zenith, but the experiment was short-lived. In September 1961, Syrian officers staged an anti-unionist putsch, and the UAR quickly crumbled. The blow was severe for Nasser's regime, the legitimacy of which stemmed in part from commitment to unionism and Pan-Arabism. Also, Nasser worried that the success of the coup in Syria might inspire similar attempts in Egypt. As it turned out, his concerns were not idle. Only four months after the Syrian coup, a secret movement was discovered in the Egyptian armed forces, headed by Hasan Rif'at, an army captain. Rif'at was arrested in January 1962, and confessed he had been planning to stage a coup in order to save Egypt from communism – and from Nasser, who had "betrayed the revolution." Rif'at's group had infiltrated the Republican Guard, and decided to use it in its attempt to seize power. In the wake of the trials, twenty-five officers were struck from the lists, including one who belonged to 'Amer's staff. The officers involved in the coup attempt had hoped to replace Nasser with their commander, though the latter was not implicated in their scheme.[12]

The most severe threat to Nasser's authority came from 'Amer, however. Following the breakup of the UAR in 1961, Nasser decided to reshuffle his regime in order to limit 'Amer's influence over the armed forces. In 1962, the latter resigned, in an open challenge to Nasser. The latter was forced to bring him back to commandership of the armed forces and to appoint him vice president under pressure from the top brass, who assembled at the military commandership in Cairo and threatened mutiny.[13] Heikal, Nasser's chief propagandist,

---

[10] Ibid., 108.

[11] The 1957 conspiracy was allegedly supported by the British Secret Intelligence Service (SIS). See Hamrush, *Thawrat Yulyu*, 361 and 496.

[12] 'Abdul-Latif al-Baghdadi, *Mudhakkarat 'Abdul-Latif al-Baghdadi*, vol. 2 (Cairo: Maktab al-Masri al-Hadith, 1977), 171 and 177.

[13] Fawzi, *Harb al-Sanawat al-Thalath*, 34.

Table 2.1 *Major coup plots under Nasser (1952–1970)*

	Date	Leading officer involved	Outcome
(1)	July 1952	Free Officers, led by Gamal 'Abdul Nasser	Success
(2)	January 1953	Artillery officers	Failure
(3)	February 1954	Armored brigades officers, led by Khaled Muhieddin	Success
(4)	March 1954	Gamal 'Abdul Nasser	Success
(5)	April 1954	Armored brigades officers	Failure
(6)	September 1961	Anti-UAR Syrian officers, led by 'Abdul-Karim al-Nahlawi	Success
(7)	January 1962	Hasan Rif'at	Failure
(8)	September 1967	'Abdul-Hakim 'Amer	Failure

labeled the 1962 crisis a "peaceful coup d'état."[14] Indeed, it was, and the event only heightened the mistrust between the military and civilian wings of the ruling elite. After the 1967 debacle, 'Amer again rebelled against Nasser. At the height of this crisis, Nasser revealed to the aforementioned General Abul-'Iz that he was expecting to "be taken away by the armed forces."[15] In reality, the shock of the military debacle and Israeli occupation of Sinai kept Egyptian officers focused upon military affairs, and momentarily distracted from palace intrigue.[16] This, combined with Nasser's skillful maneuvering, tilted the correlation of forces in his favor. The rivalry between Nasser and 'Amer continued until the latter reportedly committed suicide in September 1967.[17] In sum, while never losing power to a competitor, Nasser faced the challenge of military opposition virtually from the first days of his ascendency to the last years of his tenure as Table 2.1 shows.

Coup-Proofing under Nasser

To coup-proof his regime, Nasser combined ideational and material elements with counterbalancing as I show below.

---

[14] Baker, *Egypt's Uncertain Revolution*, 93.   [15] al-Gawadi, *Mudhakkarat*, 117.
[16] Ibid., 316.
[17] On the Nasser–'Amer interaction throughout the Suez Crisis, see al-Baghdadi, *Mudhakkarat*, 351–376. See also the memoirs of Fawzi, *Harb al-Sanawat al-Thalath*, 38–43; and Faruq Fahmi, *I'tirafat Shams Badran wa-Mu'amarat 67* (Cairo: Mu'assasat Amun al-Haditha, 1989).

Ideology and Fostering Shared Aversions

Nasser used Arabism and left-wing discourse to wed officers ideologically to his regime. War Minister Mohammad Fawzi mentions in his memoirs that officers' training under Nasser was not merely technical. The military academy aimed to create the ideal Egyptian "revolutionary officer," i.e., one who shared the worldview of the Nasserite regime and was ready to be an "executive tool for achieving revolutionary goals." Nasser himself never tired of repeating to his officers that their role was not over after 1952, and that he believed in their capacity to lead Egypt because he has had throughout his life "faith in militarism." Each of them, Nasser hammered repeatedly, was to be "a revolutionary cell" among the mass of the people.[18]

The claims Nasser consistently conveyed to the officer corps and his countrymen at large centered around three fundamental arguments. First, Egypt was under permanent threat from within and without. Foreign powers and local forces were conspiring to keep the country underdeveloped and subjugated. Second, Egyptian parties had failed to tackle the challenge of national rebirth successfully. At best, they were incompetent, and at worst, complicit in conspiring against their own nation. Egyptians themselves were unprepared for the modernizing mission ahead for Egypt, and vulnerable to the manipulation of regressive forces. A pro-Nasser propaganda piece bluntly asserted in 1954 to be "unsatisfied with the level (*mustawa*) of the people," though it hoped the regime would raise its awareness and understanding.[19] Third, redistribution at home, combined with defiant radicalism abroad, represented Egypt's path to modernization and means of overcoming archaism. The military's role in achieving these goals was indispensable according to Nasser. To be sure, King Faruq never gave the armed forces an ideological mission to achieve prior to 1952, though clearly, he hoped to turn as many officers as possible against his rivals in the Wafd Party. But the Free Officers repeatedly framed the armed forces as the "vanguard and shield of the revolution" – and a protector in charge of the defense of the nation

---

[18] Fawzi asserted in this regard: "When I took over this job, I took upon myself developing what I termed as national and political awareness, stemming from the logic that the target of fighting by the armed forces is, after all, a political one, and whoever will be sacrificing himself to the nation has to understand the politics and be convinced by it." See 'Abdallah Imam, *Al-Fariq Mohammad Fawzi, al-Naksa, al-Istinzaf, al-Sijn* (Cairo: Dar al-Khayyal, 2001), 31 and 17. See also Ahmad Hashem, "Al-Jaysh wa-l-Dawla fi Masr: Tashabok al- 'Askari wa-l-Madani," Al Jazeera Center for Strategic Studies, June 1, 2015, http://studies.aljazeera.net/ar/reports/2015/05/201553111285692330.html (accessed July 7, 2015); and Sassoon, *Anatomy of Authoritarianism*, 78.

[19] Sharif Yuness, *Nida' al-Sha'b, Tarikh Naqdi li-l-Ideologia al-Nasiriyya* (Cairo: Dar al-Shuruq, 2012), 128.

"against internal exploitation and domination."[20] Nasser asserted tire-
lessly the task of the populist regime was pedagogical, not merely political
or economic, and the military would provide Egyptians with a model to
follow and a norm to which they could aspire. Though the "reactionaries"
(read: the king, the Wafd Party, the aristocratic landowners, the Muslim
Brotherhood, and the Communists) were able to hoodwink swathes of the
Egyptian people, they failed to fool the officers. And when the people
cried out for saviors, the officers heard the call and intervened to redeem
Egyptians from their enemies – and, ultimately, themselves. The military
was Egypt's critical "reform-minded organization."[21] Because the officers created the new order, they were entitled to lead it. And because their
patriotism and dedication shielded them from the corruption and decadence pervasive in Egyptian society, the latter would follow the former on
the path of national salvation and economic modernization, not the other
way around. In the words of Lacouture, civilians were to play "second
fiddle to the men in khaki."[22]

Liberating Egyptian soil from occupation was a major goal the new
regime set to accomplish in the wake of the coup. The British agreed in
October 1954 to complete the evacuation of the Suez Canal Zone, which
gave the officers a legitimacy boost. True consecration came, however, in
1956, with the nationalization of the Suez Canal. Nasser snatched political triumph from the jaws of military defeat after France, the UK, and
Israel invaded the Sinai, but were later forced into a humiliating retreat.
Fifty-five British- and French-owned firms were nationalized in the wake
of the Suez Crisis, an additional act of defiance that announced the
beginnings of the state's massive interference in the economic sector.[23]
Nasser's militancy had seemingly transformed Egypt almost overnight
into a regional power: one capable of standing up successfully to Western
hegemons, whose influence over the Middle East had shaped its destiny
and politics for so long. Redeeming Egyptian pride and establishing
Egyptian preeminence over the Arab world struck a deep emotional

---

[20] See Baker, *Egypt's Uncertain Revolution*, 48; and P. J. Vatikiotis, *The Egyptian Army in
Politics: Pattern for New Nations?* (Bloomington, IN: Indiana University Press, 1961), 239.
Quoting Nasser: "You, men of the armed forces, were on the march on 23 July . . . to save
the people from their woes and fulfill their hopes . . . you will force reactionaries to stop . . .
.the people has always suffered, and yelled and whispered, and were lost among different
ideologies and goals . . . they have often entrapped the people . . . but you have always
believed in principles and higher ideals . . . which is why you were never led astray the way
the people were." Yuness, *Nida' al-Sha'b*, 72.

[21] Jean Lacouture, *The Demigods: Charismatic Leadership in the Third World* (New York:
Alfred Knopf, 1970), 102.

[22] Ibid., 104.

[23] Anouar Abdel-Malek, *Egypt: Military Society: The Army Regime, the Left, and Social
Change under Nasser* (New York: Random House, 1968), xiv.

cord within the population at large and the officer corps in particular. Nasser knew that Faruq's tarnished nationalist credentials made him vulnerable to opposition. When Nasser and his colleagues conspired against him, they were able to credibly depict him as a sellout. The same would not hold true for disaffected officers after 1952. His militant stance and series of early foreign policy successes made Nasser unassailable from a nationalist perspective and, therefore, less vulnerable to domestic opposition – including the military type he feared the most.[24]

In addition to stoking enmity against foreign adversaries, Nasser also fostered resentment against "the enemy within," i.e., political parties. In one diatribe after another, the Nasserite discourse presented parties as divisive, corrupt, occupied strictly with narrow gains, and open channels for foreign interference in Egyptian affairs. The armed forces were to save Egypt from divisive partisanship (hizbiyya). Particularly guilty were the Communists and the Muslim Brotherhood. Nasser construed communism as the main enemy of Arab unionism, and no word was harsh enough in his invectives against the Communists – especially during the early years of his tenure – whom he considered stooges of Zionism and were headed in Egypt by a "Jewish woman"; they were morally loose, and worked diligently to spread chaos on behalf of Israel.[25] As for the Muslim Brothers, they were dangerous because their Islamic credentials placed them at a higher level than the Communists as Nasser's main competitors for Egyptians' loyalty and support. The Brothers were particularly worrying because they had long proved capable of infiltrating the officer corps, the military at large, and also the police. So well implanted were the Brothers in the armed forces, in fact, that they tipped off Nasser about an early conspiracy against him within NCO ranks in August 1952 – something his own services had failed to discover.[26] As the new regime and the powerful Islamist formation later became mortal enemies, Nasser argued that the Brothers transformed Islam into "a [drug] to numb the senses of this faithful people."[27] Nasserite propaganda relentlessly construed the Brothers as fanatics bent on using Islam instrumentally for political reasons; their true and only goal was seizing power. They, too, were a reactionary force, whose claim to have

---

[24] The Muslim Brotherhood did criticize Nasser for the moderation of his regime vis-à-vis Israel in his early years in power. The Brotherhood was also critical because Nasser conceded in the 1954 Anglo-Egyptian Treaty that Britain and Egypt would be allies should an outside power invade the region and that Britain would have the right to reoccupy the canal zone should war erupt. Nasser's realpolitik was decried as treason by the Brotherhood. The latter failed, however, to delegitimize Nasser outside its direct circles.

[25] Yuness, *Nida' al-Sha'b*, 119.   [26] Sirrs, *The Egyptian Intelligence Service*, 35.

[27] Yuness, *Nida' al-Sha'b*, 78.

a monopoly over religion was tantamount to "heresy and exploitation," and whose secretive military organizations were fundamentally antidemocratic. In sum, the Nasserite regime, supported by the armed forces, was to be Egypt's guarantee against succumbing to religious reaction, colonial powers, and atheist communism.

The memoirs of the officers who surrounded Nasser suggest they accepted the mission he entrusted the armed forces with, and believed in his incorruptibility, fundamental integrity, and dedication to Egypt. Sami Sharaf, a Free Officer who worked as Nasser's personal assistant, referred adoringly to his late boss in his memoirs as a "father and a teacher" whose very name "means freedom, and socialism, and unity."[28] The previously mentioned Abul-'Iz spoke of the Egyptian leader as a "giant" in his memoirs and highlighted his own emotional distress at seeing Nasser defeated in the wake of the military debacle in 1967.[29] 'Abdul-Latif al-Baghdadi, a founding member of the Free Officers who exited the political stage in 1964 over a disagreement with Nasser, wrote in his memoirs that the Ra'is (Nasser) "captured my soul" ("*malaka 'alayya nafsi*") and that he felt ready to die for him ("*kunto 'ala isti'dad li-l-tadhia binafsi fi sabilihi*"), when Nasser was facing the tripartite attack on Egypt in 1956 against overwhelming odds.[30] It is interesting to note that even officers whose careers suffered under Nasser referred to him respectfully in their memoirs. Ahmad Isma'el, who served as Egypt's war minister during the 1973 war, was twice dismissed from the military under Nasser. In 1967, Nasser sacked him in the wake of the Six-Day War. After returning him to service as chief of staff, Nasser discharged him yet again, following a successful Israeli raid in the Red Sea in September 1969. Isma'el had few reasons to love Nasser. Indeed, Sa'ad al-Din al-Shazli, who served as chief of staff under Isma'el in 1973, wrote that the latter "abhorred Nasser immensely" for firing him twice.[31] And yet in his memoirs, penned following Nasser's death and published decades later, Isma'el stressed Nasser's "patriotism and incorruptibility," and paid the Ra'is an emotional tribute:

I believed that no human being could do what this man did ... Nasser was a seasoned, skillful man, and we have no one like him, for he comes first, and whoever comes second after him is a far second. Thus, when I heard Nasser had died, I imagined at first that he had been assassinated. And then I learned he died of a heart attack, so I wept. I wept for the lost friend, and I wept for Egypt and

---

[28] Sami Sharaf, *Sanawat wa-Ayyam ma' 'Abdul Nasser, Shahadat Sami Sharaf, al-Kitab al-Awwal* (Cairo: al-Maktab al-Masri al-Hadith, 2014), 12 and 14.
[29] al-Gawadi, *Mudhakkarat*, 117.   [30] al-Baghadadi, *Mudhakkarat*, 354.
[31] al-Shazli, *Harb October, Mudhakkarat al-Fariq Sa'ad al-Din al-Shazli* (Cairo: Ru'ya li-l-Nashr wa-l-Tawzi', 2011), 227.

Egypt's misfortune. I wept because God did not give him time to take Egypt out of its quagmire, and he was the only who could.[32]

Other, similar examples abound. This is not to suggest that officers' memoirs were never critical of Nasser – they often were. The accounts, however, generally imply that officers did, indeed, believe that Nasser stood for something greater than himself. Eric Nordlinger pinpoints, in this regard, the "emotion-charged support" that Nasser elicited.[33] Simply put, Nasser's unquestionable personal integrity and his overall ideological justification of his rule worked. This was certainly true until 1967. It is also true, of course, that Nasser counted upon more than shared beliefs to keep the Egyptian armed forces on his side.

Promoting the Material Interests of the Military Elite

Under Nasser, the Egyptian officer corps began its decades-long transformation into a caste – one shielded by social clubs, cooperative stores, high-cost allowances, and military transportation, to name only a few privileges, from the travails that civilians in Egypt suffered in everyday life. Shortly after seizing power, the Free Officers increased military wages. Senior officers may have received as much as twice the salary of a minister, but mid-ranking and junior officers benefited from better pay, as well.[34] Scores were able to acquire sequestered properties that belonged, under the monarchy, to the Egyptian upper class or foreign nationals driven out of Egypt after 1952.[35] The military budget skyrocketed: defense expenditures multiplied sevenfold between 1960 and 1965, rising from 3.9 percent of the gross national product in 1950 to 12.3 percent in 1965.[36] The new regime also made sure to provide the armed forces with advanced weaponry delivered by the Soviets and their allies. Nasser said explicitly that he was channeling better equipment to the military so officers wouldn't "lose faith in the government."[37] In addition, the Institute of

---

[32] Magdi Gallad, ed., *Mushir al-Nasr, Mudhakkarat Ahmad Isma'el, Wazir al-Harbiyya fi Ma'rakat October 1973* (Cairo: Dar Nahdat Masr, 2013), 102–103. Salah Nasr, too, was sacked by Nasser from his position as director of the GID following the 1967 defeat. He was tried and sentenced to jail for twenty-five years. And yet Nasr opined in his memoirs that Nasser was incorruptible and "... the greatest Egyptian of all time" (*a'zam man anjabat Masr*). See 'Abdallah Imam, *Salah Nasr Yatadhakkar, al-Thawra, al-Mukhabarat, al-Naksa* (Cairo: Dar al-Khayyal, 1999), 122.

[33] Nordlinger, *Soldiers in Politics*, 115.

[34] Baker, *Egypt's Uncertain Revolution*, 57; and Fawzi, *Harb al-Sanawat al-Thalath*, 56.

[35] John Waterbury, *The Egypt of Nasser and Sadat: The Political Economy of Two Regimes* (Princeton, NJ: Princeton University Press, 1983), 337.

[36] Baker, *Egypt's Uncertain Revolution*, 56.

[37] Hashim, "The Egyptian Military, Part One," 5.

Higher Studies of National Defense was created to provide advanced courses in strategic studies. The creation of the rank of army general (*fariq awwal*) inflated the number of senior officers in the military.

Nasser also promoted the interests of the officers' caste in the government. The fact that two officers (Neguib and Nasser) had become the first presidents of the nascent republic, and that all vice presidents hailed from the armed forces, provided the most ostentatious symbols of military control of the state. Other signals of military supremacy in the Nasserite regime abound, however. As of June 1953, RCC members were occupying the most pivotal positions in the cabinet: the premiership (Neguib), the ministry of interior (Nasser), and the ministry of war (al-Baghdadi). The trend proved enduring: of all eighteen cabinets formed under Nasser between 1952 and 1970, only two were headed by civilians. Also, of all ministers appointed after 1954, 36.6 percent were officers, and Nasser himself occupied the premiership eight times.[38] Officers were appointed to ministries as diverse as foreign affairs, planning, culture, tourism, social affairs and labor, municipal and rural affairs, health, industry, culture and national guidance, and waqfs.[39] So pervasive was the presence of the military that in some cabinets, half the ministers hailed from the armed forces. The Sudqi Suleiman cabinet, installed in September 1966, and the Nasser cabinet, formed in June 1967, stand as cases in point, with 55.2 and 65.4 percent of ministers being ex-officers, respectively.[40] Tables 2.2, 2.3, and 2.4 show the extent to which first-rank positions in the Egyptian state were militarized in the wake of the 1952 coup.

Beyond cabinet positions, a progressive militarization of the bureaucracy began immediately after the 1952 coup, when RCC members stipulated that each of them would monitor the work of one or more ministries.[41] In order to make sure their directives were being implemented – but also to build a personal clientele inside the armed forces – the members of the RCC appointed hundreds of fellow officers as "advisors" and "representatives" in the bureaucracy. Diplomatic positions were particularly prized by the top brass. As of 1962, most Egyptian ambassadors to Europe hailed from the armed forces. Officers occupied 72 percent of Egyptian diplomatic positions overall.[42] The members of the Free Officers organization were especially privileged in their access to prized civilian jobs. Nasser promoted second- and third-ranking Free Officers to

---

[38] Imad Harb, "The Egyptian Military in Politics: Disengagement or Accommodation," *Middle East Journal* 57, no. 2 (Spring 2003): 269–290.
[39] Vatikiotis, *The Egyptian Army in Politics*, 54–55.   [40] Ibid., xxviii.
[41] Khaled Muhieddin, *Wa-l-Ana Atakallam* (Cairo: Markaz al-Ahram li-l-Tarjama wa-l-Nashr, 1992), 196.
[42] Fahmi, *I'tirafat Shams Badran*, 20.

Table 2.2 *The background of prime ministers under Nasser (1952–1970)*[43]

Prime minister	Professional background
'Ali Maher	Civilian
Mohammad Neguib	Military officer
Gamal 'Abdul Nasser	Military officer
Nur al-Din Tarraf	Civilian
Kamal al-Din Hussein	Military officer
'Ali Sabri	Military officer
Zakaria Muhieddin	Military officer
Mohammad Sudqi Suleiman	Military officer

Table 2.3 *The background of ministers of interior under Nasser (1952–1970)*

Minister of interior	Professional background
Gamal 'Abdul Nasser	Military officer
Zakaria Muhieddin	Military officer
'Abbas Radwan	Military officer
'Abdul-'Azim Fahmi	Police officer
Sha'rawi Gom'a	Military officer

high civilian positions, including positions in the nationalized enterprises.[44] When Shams Badran, Field Marshal 'Amer's chief secretary, became minister of defense in 1966, a memo was sent to all public administrations and companies forbidding them to fill vacant positions without prior authorization from the commander of the armed forces, 'Amer, who would only agree to appoint civilians if he himself had no military candidates in mind for job openings. Local government was especially militarized: in 1964, for instance, twenty-two of Egypt's twenty-six governors were officers (i.e., 84.61 percent).[45]

[43] I collected the data in Tables 2.2, 2.3, and 2.4 from various sources, especially memoirs of Egyptian officers I read. Particularly instructive were the memoirs of al-Baghdadi, Muhieddin, Hamrush, and Hammad, all of which I cite in this book.
[44] Be'eri, *Army Officers in Arab Politics and Society*, 247.
[45] Richard H. Dekmejian, "Egypt and Turkey: The Military in the Background," in *Soldiers, Peasants, and Bureaucrats: Civil-Military Relations in Communist and Modernizing Societies*, ed. Roman Kolkowicz and Andrzej Korbonski (London: George Allen & Unwin, 1982), 222. See also al-Baghdadi, *Mudhakkarat*, 172.

Table 2.4 *The background of ministers of war under Nasser (1952–1970)*

Minister of war	Professional background
Mohammad Neguib	Military officer
'Abdul-Latif al-Baghdadi	Military officer
Hussein al-Shaf'i	Military officer
'Abdul-Hakim 'Amer	Military officer
'Abdul-Wahab al-Beshri	Military officer/engineer
Shams Badran	Military officer
Amine Huweidi	Military officer
Mohammad Fawzi	Military officer

Nasser's intervention in Yemen (1962–1967) also proved useful as an occasion to keep the officers happy. Jesse Ferris notes that the Yemen war created a "privileged class of soldiers and civilians" who benefited so much from it, they developed an interest in its prolongation. The long list of material rewards bequeathed on servicemen fighting in Yemen included: travel bonuses, double-pay, preferential treatment in hospital care, access to vehicles, and country club membership. Veterans also benefitted from precedence in land grants from the state, including real estate confiscated during the campaign against "feudalism,"[46] as well as preferential treatment in public jobs. A governor reported in 1964 that 40 percent of open positions in state institutions within his governorates were reserved for Yemen war veterans and their families. In addition, returning soldiers could bring with them scarce consumer goods for their own use or for commercial purposes. Large-scale smuggling and black-market trade flourished.[47] Naturally, the biggest gains from the war went to Field Marshal 'Amer and his allies in the officer corps, for whom it was a financial windfall.[48] Nasser was aware that the officers were taking advantage of their military positions for personal gain. He didn't mind,

[46] The redistribution of confiscated property to military officers who constituted the Nasserite regime's main pillar of support gives credence to Zakaria Muhieddin, the prominent RCC member and longtime patron of Egyptian intelligence under Nasser. He argued that agricultural reform, expropriating private property from "reactionary" Egyptians, and the overall drive toward socialist transformation aimed, above all, at the "consolidation of political power by controlling the economy." See Ashraf al-Sharif, "Kamal al-Din Hussein wa-Wujuh Dawlat Yulyu al-Muhafiza," *Mada Masr*, October 1, 2015, www.madamasr.com/ar/opinion/politics (accessed October 4, 2015).
[47] See Jesse Ferris, *Nasser's Gamble: How Intervention in Yemen Caused the Six-Day War and the Decline of Egyptian Power* (Princeton, NJ: Princeton University Press, 2013), 199–205. See also Imam, *Al-Fariq*, 35.
[48] See also Hashim, "The Egyptian Military, Part One," 6.

as long as they were loyal. If anything, Nasser reckoned that the more corrupt an officer, the less likely he would pose a threat should he decide to sack him.[49]

Counterbalancing

Nasser counterbalanced the military with security and civilian organizations headed by loyalist barons such as ʿAli Sabri in the ruling Arab Socialist Union (ASU), Zakaria Muhieddin and Sami Sharaf in the intelligence apparatus, and Shaʿrawi Gomʿa in the ministry of interior. These barons enjoyed some degree of organizational support in their respective power bases. They competed with one another, but mainly with ʿAmer, for power. With that said, of all four pillars of the regime – the military, the ASU, the ministry of interior, and the intelligence services – the armed forces were the most powerful player in the game. Until his downfall in 1967, ʿAmer was the main contender capable of mounting a serious challenge to the presidency.

Nasser's first counterbalancing moves began early in his tenure. In June 1953, the Republican Guard was founded and placed under the direction of a loyalist officer, ʿAbdul-Mohsen Abul-Nur. A National Guard was also established, and provided military training for Egyptians eager to fight British occupation. In effect, the National Guard gave the new regime supervision over a partisan militia trained by military officers.[50] The most fundamental innovation was in restructuring intelligence agencies, however. Immediately after 1952, Nasser asked the Soviet Union for help in reorganizing the intelligence apparatus. The Soviets, at the time, suspected Nasser of right-wing militaristic tendencies, and they turned him down. Nasser had more luck with several German spies who had participated in the Second World War. They were invited to Cairo, where they taught their Egyptian counterparts the basics of intelligence-gathering and organization. In 1953, the CIA agreed to help, as well.[51]

Lieutenant Colonel Zakaria Muhieddin, RCC member and a close associate of Nasser, was appointed head of MI after the coup. Muhieddin quickly emerged as a capable spy chief and candidly told his subordinates that the main mission of the MI was to secure the new regime.[52] Under his leadership, MI officers monitored political

---

[49] Nutting, *Nasser*, 304.
[50] Abul-Nur ʿAbdul-Muhsen, *Al-Haqiqa ʿan Thawrat 23 Yulyu, Mudhakkarat ʿAbdul-Muhsen Abul-Nur* (Cairo: al-Hayʾa al-Masriyya li-l-Kitab, 2001), 35.
[51] Abul-Fadl ʿAbdul-Fattah, *Kunto Naʾiban li-Raʾis al-Mukhabarat* (Cairo: Dar al-Shuruq, 2001), 176–179.
[52] Ibid., 87.

opponents of the nascent order as well as one another. A whole section of the MI directorate was occupied by Hasan al-Tuhami, a shadowy figure of the Egyptian intelligence apparatus charged with sensitive missions under Nasser, and later Sadat. As it turned out, Nasser had asked al-Tuhami to keep the telephone conversations of his companions in the RCC under surveillance, which he did.[53]

The General Intelligence Service (GIS), a civilian spy agency, was created in 1954 and staffed with military officers loyal to the new regime. In its formative years, the GIS was headed by Muhieddin, Sabri, and Salah Nasr – all staunchly loyalist officers. Sabri was Nasser's aide-de-camp when he was appointed director of the GIS, and Nasr was ʿAmer's. The appointment of these specific men to lead the GIS reflected not only its rise to power, but also the importance placed by the new regime on building a reliable Mukhabarat apparatus.[54] Yet another, new intelligence agency was the Office of the Commander in Chief for Political Guidance (OCC), also staffed with pro-regime officers whose task was to create a network of officers/informants to monitor political opinions within the military, report on suspicious officers, and make sure that loyalist officers were rewarded.[55] Finally, the Special Section was renamed the General Investigations Directorate (GID) and expanded. These agencies spied upon military and civilian opponents of the regime as well as one another, thus performing the typical function of counter-balancing apparatuses in authoritarian regimes. Unsurprisingly, there was little love lost between the military and the organizations counter-balancing it, especially the GID.[56] Still, by 1955, the Nasserite regime could boast an "effective counter-intelligence service" skilled at infiltrating the ranks of both military and civilian enemies of the new order, according to a US report.[57]

Another innovation was the creation in March 1955 of the Presidential Information Bureau (PIB) (Secretaria al-Maʿlumat), a powerful intelligence apparatus under Nasser's direct control. This was headed by his trusted aide Sharaf, a former MI officer. Nasser gave him broad leeway to collect information from and on any state institution or source, domestic or foreign. Sharaf recruited experts from various bureaucracies to work in the bureau.[58] Originally a modest subdivision of the presidency

---

[53] Ibid., 174.   [54] Imam, *Salah Nasr*, 53.   [55] Ibid., 22.
[56] Kandil, *Soldiers, Spies, and Statesmen*, 75.
[57] Sirrs, *The Egyptian Intelligence Service*, 38.
[58] Sharaf's recruits included Nasser's daughter and GID operative Huda ʿAbdul Nasser, as well as Nasser's son-in-law, Ashraf Marwan, the husband of Mona ʿAbdul Nasser. Marwan eventually became a spy for Mossad, Israel's intelligence service. On Ashraf Marwan, see Uri Bar-Joseph, *The Angel: The Egyptian Spy Who Saved Israel* (New York: HarperCollins, 2016).

employing only three people, the bureau expanded into a vast network of analysts, diplomats, informants, and translators working around the clock to keep the flow of information streaming.

That the bureau had been created chiefly to keep an eye on the armed forces was not lost on 'Amer, who ordered Sharaf to steer away from the military top brass and from the MI. Sharaf did not comply, and quietly cultivated a network of loyalist officers who became Nasser's eyes and ears in the military institution. 'Amer also instructed the MI not to provide Sharaf with information unless previously authorized to do so by himself or his close associate Badran. The relationship between the PIB and the military commandership under 'Amer remained icy, at best. The same was true of the interaction between the bureau and the GIS when Nasr, an ally of 'Amer, was appointed to lead it in 1957.[59] Nasser was aware of interinstitutional rivalries pitting the armed forces, the intelligence organizations, and the civilian bureaucracies against one another. He fanned the competition between the different agencies of his regime as an additional guarantee for political survival.[60]

In 1962, the above-mentioned Arab Socialist Union (ASU) was established. Sharaf admits in his book on Nasser's ruling methods that the Egyptian president had become alarmed by the military's political influence and created the ASU as a civilian "counterweight to the armed forces."[61] Because the ASU was not, strictly speaking, a political party, but instead a mass popular organization open to all sectors of society, military personnel were allowed to join. Ostensibly, the ASU would devote itself to the revolution's great ideological missions, i.e., socialism, anti-imperialism, and Arab unity. In effect, however, the ASU had different purposes. First, as of 1964, running for parliament, professional orders, and even local community councils had become a function of ASU membership. This signaled to ambitious Egyptians that the regime was seeking to build a power base outside the military, and that a civilian route toward joining the ruling circles had opened. In other words, no longer was access to the power elite restricted to officers. This, in itself, pitted the ASU against the military, as both were competing for regime patronage. Second, the ASU quickly devolved into a massive surveillance organization, adding yet another layer to Nasser's sprawling security empire. In fact, the ASU even spied on the GIS, which caused the leader of the latter agency to complain to Nasser.[62] The ASU's leadership did

---

[59] On the formation of the Presidential Information Bureau, see Sharaf, *Sanawat*, 29–46.
[60] Imam, *Salah Nasr*, 171.
[61] Sami Sharaf, *'Abdul Nasser: Kayfa Hakama Masr* (Cairo: Madbuli al-Saghir, 1996), 228–229.
[62] Kandil, *Soldiers, Spies, and Statesmen*, 58.

not take its coup-proofing mission lightly. In 1964, the organization's youth branch chose the following topic to ponder during its summer camp: "How should ASU youth resist a possible coup?"[63] Only a year later, ASU informants discovered a Muslim Brotherhood plot to overthrow the regime.

In July 1963, the Arab Vanguard (al-Tali'a al-'Arabiyya) was created and modeled after the League of Communists in the former Yugoslavia. The Vanguard was a secret organization into which only the most committed members of the ASU were admitted. Nasser asked his close associates to form small cells of individuals committed to his regime so they could comprise the nucleus of the Vanguard. These operatives, in turn, were instructed to create additional cells until the numbers multiplied. Under the supervision of intelligence organizations capable of monitoring and vetoing adherence to the secret organization, the latter expanded to cover all Egyptian provinces as well as ministries, the parliament, universities, and youth organizations. Marxist intellectuals were allowed to join after communist organizations agreed to dissolve themselves. The founding documents of the Vanguard indicated that members were to receive military training in preparation for revolutionary struggle.[64] Some members became full-timers, and received salaries in exchange for their services to the Vanguard – and, by extension, the Nasserite regime. The main task of the Vanguard was to write reports denouncing "deviations" and "counter-revolutionary" tendencies in Egyptian institutions at large, but especially in the armed forces. In 1970, when the Ba'ath Party succeeded in recruiting officers in the armed forces and General Intelligence, Nasser blamed the Vanguard for negligence – a clear indicator of its coup-proofing and counter-espionage mission. In fact, the Vanguard's internal regulations were explicit about the report-writing duties of its operatives, and competition among them was fierce in this regard. Adherents could show zealotry if they uncovered conspiracies that others failed to expose.[65] Nasser instructed the leadership of the Vanguard, as well as its members at large, to write reports not just on the regime's opponents, but also on its leading figures. The Ra'is had little trust in his own men, and they, in return, distrusted and spied upon one another.[66] 'Amer was suspicious of Nasser's intentions, and

---

[63] Risa Brooks, *The Civil–Military Politics of Strategic Assessment* (Princeton, NJ: Princeton University Press, 2008), 76.

[64] 'Abdul-Ghaffar Shukr, *Al-Tali'a al-'Arabiyya, al-Tanzim al-Qawmi al-Sirri li-Gamal 'Abdul Nasser, 1965–1986* (Beirut: Markaz Dirasat al-Wihda al-'Arabiyya, 2015), 41.

[65] Nazih al-Ayubi, *Al-Dawla al-Markaziyya fi Masr* (Beirut: Markaz Dirasat al-Wihda al-'Arabiyya, 1989), 122.

[66] Kamal Khaled, *Rijal 'Abdul Nasser wa-l-Sadat* (Cairo: Dar al-'Adala, 1986), 295–296.

tried to infiltrate the new organization by planting his loyalists in sensitive Vanguard positions. 'Amer also maneuvered to keep the ASU away from his fiefdom in the armed forces, and tried to create his own "revolutionary organization" called al-Do'at (i.e., the Proselytizers). The clash between the Proselytizers and the Vanguard was immediate, and the former had to dissolve itself in 1966.[67]

The tug-of-war between the civilian and military wings of the Nasserite regime heightened following 1967, and the ASU argued that the defeat reflected a lack of revolutionary zeal in military ranks. For the ASU, the antidote to bureaucratization was the creation of an ideological military genuinely committed to the regime's revolutionary pan-Arab cause, and thus ready to die for it. In essence, the ASU was promoting a reinforced indoctrination of the armed forces via an Egyptian commissar system modeled along communist lines. The commissars would naturally hail from the Vanguard and the ASU at large, and the correlation of forces between officers and civilians would tilt decisively in favor of the latter. Though the defeat weakened the armed forces, this scenario was a nonstarter as far as the generals were concerned.

The counterbalancing mission of the ASU/Vanguard had never been lost on the top brass. As the ASU became publicly critical of the armed forces' performance in the Six-Day War, the animosity between it and the military intensified. Eventually, the ASU had to tone down its raw criticism, lest outraged officers turn on its patron – Nasser himself. Still, the ASU's attacks on the military and the pervasive popular resentment following the defeat restructured civil–military relations in a manner favorable to Nasser until his death in 1970.[68]

Coups under the Ba'ath Regime (1963–1970)[69]

The March 1963 coup that brought Ba'athist officers to power was a watershed in the history of Syria. The same was true of Hafez al-Asad's takeover in November 1970. Between these two putsches, Syrian officers hatched seven other plots, raising the number of coup attempts throughout the period to nine. Successful military interventionism during that time

---

[67] al-Ayubi, *Al-Dawla al-Markaziyya*, 121.   [68] Dekmejian, "Egypt and Turkey," 34.
[69] Note that some Syrian authors prefer to use the expression "neo-Ba'ath," in reference to the post-1963 party, to make a distinction between the original organization, co-founded by Michel Aflaq and Salahaldin al-Bitar, and the later party, dominated by officers from minority backgrounds. To the best of my knowledge, Muta' al-Safadi was the first to coin "neo-Ba'ath," but the expression became common later in the literature on Syria. See Muta' al-Safadi, *Hizb al-Ba'ath, Ma'sat al-Mawled, Ma'sat al-Nihaya* (Beirut: Dar al-Adab, 1964), 193. For the sake of simplicity, however, I will avoid the label "neo-Ba'ath" in what follows.

bore the signature of the Baʿathist Military Committee, established in early 1960 in Cairo. Three Alawi officers (Lieutenant Colonel Mohammad ʿOmran, Major Salah Jdid, and Captain Hafez al-Asad) and two Ismaʿilis (Major Ahmad al-Mir and Captain ʿAbdul-Karim al-Jundi) were the Committee's original members. Ten more officers were added progressively, until the number was capped at fifteen in the summer of 1963. To a certain extent, the military politics of Syria in the 1960s – and perhaps politics tout court – revolved around the struggles pitting the members of the Committee against their enemies – and one another.

To seize power in 1963, Baʿathist officers were forced to strike an alliance with their Nasserite peers and independents. Scores of Baʿathists had been purged from the armed forces between 1961 and 1963. Consequently, the Committee that masterminded the coup was in no position to challenge the status quo alone, and needed to coalesce with allies. At the same time, it never intended to share power – certainly not with Nasserites, whose plans to reestablish the UAR were anathema to Baʿathist officers. Lest we forget, the April 1962 Nasserite-Baʿathist coup foundered because the Nasserites called for instant union with Egypt, and the Baʿathists immediately withdrew their support because they did not subscribe to such a goal. The two sides collaborated better in March 1963, but the contradictions inherent to their alliance quickly escalated into renewed military activism. Only weeks after the March power grab, the Committee mounted a velvet coup, sacked scores of Nasserite officers from the armed forces, and drove the Nasserite defense minister and deputy chief of staff out of power.[70] Having thus overcome opposition, the Committee turned on itself in a deadly contest for power. In 1966, Field Marshal Amin al-Hafez decided to purge thirty officers of minority background from the military, but a coup ousted him from the chairmanship of the presidential council. Al-Hafez was not an original member of the Committee, but his seniority and background made him useful to its members, who needed a Sunni straw man in 1963. To a certain extent, al-Hafez was to the Committee what Neguib was to the

---

[70] There is a general agreement in the literature that Baʿathist officers positioned themselves to take control of fighting brigades and field positions in the armed forces after March 1963, whereas Nasserites were content to hold prestigious (but less operational) sinecures. Such divergence explains in part why the Baʿathists drove the Nasserites out of the armed forces, and not the other way around, although the latter may have technically outnumbered the former. Nabil al-Shueiri claims, in this regard, that the Baʿath Party threatened Baʿathist officers with expulsion, should they have accepted administrative instead of field positions. See Saqr Abu Fakhr, *Suria wa-Hutam al-Marakeb al-Mubaʾthara, Hiwar maʿ Nabil al-Shueiri, ʿAflaq wa-l-Baʿath wa-l- Muʾamarat wa-l-ʿAskar* (Beirut: al-Muʾassasa al-ʿArabiyya li-l-Dirasat wa-l-Nashr, 2005), 297. See also Mustafa Tlass, *Merʾat Hayati, al-ʿAqd al-Thani, 1958–1968* (Damascus: Dar Tlass li-l-Dirasat wa-l-Nashr wa-l-Tawziʾ, 2006), 373.

Egyptian Free Officers in 1952. By 1966, however, al-Hafez had outlived his usefulness, and was overthrown.[71] His downfall, combined with that of General Mohammad 'Omran,[72] a founding member of the Committee who defected to its Ba'athist civilian rivals, left only two players jockeying for the top job: Salah Jdid and Hafez al-Asad, both original members of the Committee. In 1970, the latter won the contest for supremacy – yet again via a military coup.

Five botched coup attempts under the Ba'ath Party are equally important to mention. Probably the most serious endeavor to overthrow the Committee and reestablish union with Egypt in the wake of the March 1963 coup was Colonel Jassem 'Alwan's failed putsch in July 1963. After the coup fizzled, military courts swiftly ordered the execution of twenty-seven mutinous officers while 'Alwan was exiled to Egypt in 1964.[73] Shortly after the fall of al-Hafez in February 1966, his supporters convinced senior Druze officer Hamad 'Ubayd to trigger a coup against the Committee. Originally a member, 'Ubayd had become disaffected with it, and tried unsuccessfully to oust his former associates from power in March 1966. Against the backdrop of a growing Alawi–Druze polarization as well as heightened confrontation between Ba'athist officers and the party's civilian wing, two other putsches were prepared in 1966. The first plot was led by Druze Major General Fahd al-Sha'ir, who built a military organization open to officers from different sects but excluding Alawis. And the second coup was mounted by Druze Major Salim Hatum, who recruited almost exclusively from his community and allegedly tried to assassinate Hafez al-Asad, Jdid, and other members of the Committee in 1965.[74] Both attempts failed. Major General Ahmad Suwaydani, the former chief of staff who was sacked in February 1968, tried to seize power in August of that year, but he, too, was unsuccessful. Suwaydani fled to Iraq, but was returned to Syria, where he was arrested. Tables 2.5 and 2.6 provide additional data on these coups and the officers of the Committee.

---

[71] On the coup d'état mounted against Amin al-Hafez, see Itamar Rabinovich, *Syria under the Ba'ath, 1963–1966: The Army–Party Symbiosis* (Jerusalem: Israel University Press, 1972), 195–202. See also a series of Al Jazeera interviews with Amin al-Hafez, aired in July 2001; especially, interviews 14 and 15, www.youtube.com/watch?v=vWKFeZ8TA aE and www.youtube.com/watch?v=Enjyc6uSooA (accessed April 7, 2017).

[72] 'Omran was assassinated in Tripoli, Lebanon, in 1972. It is widely believed that Hafez al-Asad ordered his intelligence to liquidate his former associate.

[73] Patrick Seale, *Asad: The Struggle for the Middle East* (Berkley, CA: University of California Press, 1988), 81–83. For more on the confrontation between Nasser and the Ba'ath Party, see Suleiman al-Firzli, *Hurub al-Nasiriyya wa-l-Ba'ath* (Beirut: Naufal, 2016).

[74] Tlass, *Mer'at Hayati, al-'Aqd al-Thani*, 563–565.

Table 2.5 *Coups under the Ba'ath Party (1963–1970)*[75]

Coup leader	Date	Outcome	Center of conspiracy
Ziad al-Hariri/Mohammad 'Omran/Salah Jdid	March 1963	Success	Damascus
Mohammad 'Omran/Salah Jdid/Hafez al-Asad	April 1963	Success	Damascus
Jassem 'Alwan	July 1963	Failure	Damascus
Salah Jdid/Hafez al-Asad /Salim Hatum	February 1966	Success	Damascus
Hamad 'Ubayd	March 1966	Failure	Aleppo
Fahd al-Sha'ir	August 1966	Failure	Damascus
Salim Hatum	September 1966	Failure	Damascus
Ahmad Suwaydani	August 1968	Failure	Damascus
Hafez al-Asad	November 1970	Success	Damascus

Table 2.6 *Officers in the Ba'athist Military Committee*[76]

Officer	Sect	Birthplace	Membership date
Mohammad 'Omran	'Alawi	Al-Makhram, Hama	Original member (1960)
Salah Jdid	'Alawi	Doueir Ba'abda, Lataqia	Original member (1960)
Hafez al-Asad	'Alawi	Al-Qerdaha, Lataqia	Original member (1960)
'Abdul-Karim al-Jundi	Ismai'li	Al-Salamiyya, Hama	Original member (1960)
Ahmad al-Mir	Ismai'li	Masiaf, Lataqia	Original member (1960)
Salim Hatum	Druze	Al-Suweida	Joined between 1961 and March 1963
Hamad 'Ubayd	Druze	Al-Suweida	Joined between 1961 and March 1963
Muhammad Rabah al-Tawil	Sunni	Lataqia	Joined between 1961 and March 1963

[75] I collected the data in this table from Nikolaos Van Dam, *The Struggle for Power in Syria: Politics and Society under Asad and the Ba'th Party* (New York: I.B. Tauris, 1996); and Seal, *Asad*.

[76] I collected the officers' sects and birthplaces from Zein al-'Abidin, *Al-Jaysh wa-l-Siasa*, 368. I obtained the membership dates from Seal, *Asad*, 61 and 500. For more on the Committee, see Tlass, *Mir'at Hayati, al-'Aqd al-Thani*, 154–155. Note that the five founders of the Committee, who remained its true leaders until the end, all hailed from minority backgrounds. Also note that most Sunnis who joined the Committee belonged to the rural lower classes. To a certain extent, the Committee represented a nexus between minority officers and poor rural Sunnis. Not a single officer from Damascus was ever recruited into the Committee.

Table 2.6 *(cont.)*

Officer	Sect	Birthplace	Membership date
Ahmad Suwaydani	Sunni	Huran	Joined between 1961 and March 1963
Musa al-Zu'bi	Sunni	Huran	Joined between 1961 and March 1963
Suleiman Haddad	'Alawi	Beit Yachout, Lataqia	Joined after the March 1963 coup (summer 1963)
'Othman Kana'an	'Alawi	Iskandarun	Joined after the March 1963 coup (summer 1963)
Mustafa Haj-'Ali	Sunni	Huran	Joined after the March 1963 coup (summer 1963)
Hussein Melhem	Sunni	Aleppo	Joined after the March 1963 coup (summer 1963)
Amin al-Hafez	Sunni	Aleppo	Joined after the March 1963 coup (summer 1963)

Why did coups remain pervasive under the Ba'ath Party, just as they had been in the previous era? Beyond the inevitable lust for power on the part of the officers, several variables converged to keep putsches ubiquitous in the Syria of the 1960s. Ideology was certainly one such factor – specifically the attitude toward the UAR. On one end of the spectrum, the separatist officers had smashed the union between Egypt and Syria, and were committed to the newly restored independence of their country. On the other, the Nasserite officers aimed to reinstate the UAR.

The Ba'athists played a complex game. Ideologically, they were unionists, and could not ally themselves with the separatist regime that stigmatized them. Instead, they pursued a rapprochement with the Nasserites and disaffected independents. All shared common enmity toward the traditional politicians back in power under the separatist regime. The UAR had proven a harrowing experience for the Ba'ath Party, after Nasser forced the party's Syrian branch to dissolve itself and rewarded its leaders with insignificant political sinecures. In essence, Nasser pushed the Ba'ath Party from the center to the margins in Syria. Consequently, trust between the two major forces in pan-Arab politics was irreversibly shattered. In sum, the Damascene separatist officers espoused a vision of

Syria ruled once more by the old order; the Ba'athists favored a radical hotbed; and Nasserite officers wanted Syria to be subsumed yet again under the UAR. These three projects were fundamentally incompatible, and the forces behind them were stuck in a zero-sum game. In the context of the time, coups were the natural consequence of a polarized political process lacking minimal ideological overlap between its components.[77]

Interestingly, the Ba'ath Party takeover did not heal Syria's ideological quarrels and power struggles. Internal Ba'athist fractures pitted a military wing – whose officers became the real masters of Syria after their successful coup in March 1963 – against civilians who argued that the party should control the gun, not the other way around.[78] The latter faction counted in its ranks the co-founders of the Ba'ath Party, Michel Aflaq and Salahaldin al-Bitar, as well as some supporters in the officer corps. The historical legitimacy of Aflaq and al-Bitar did give them weight as they jockeyed for power with officers, but the 1963 coup was strictly a military affair. Ba'athist civilians were barely informed that the military wing was mounting a takeover, and did not participate in the planning of the

---

[77] On the politics of the era and momentary alliance followed by intense confrontation between Nasserite and Ba'athist officers, see the work by a historical founding figure of the Ba'ath Party, Jalal al-Sayyed, *Hezb al-Ba'ath al-'Arabi* (Beirut: Dar al-Nahar, 1973), 172–184.

[78] Munif al-Razzaz, the secretary general of the Ba'ath Party who was ousted in 1966, gives a fascinating account in his memoirs on the internal power play that pitted the civilian leadership of the party against Ba'athist officers in the 1960s. According to al-Razzaz, the military wing of the party had always been poorly institutionalized, and consisted of officers who harbored Ba'athist sympathies but could still act independently of party leadership. On a strictly ideological level, the Ba'ath Party believed that the popular masses, not officers, were the driving force of progressive transformation. From a practical perspective, however, militaries were bursting irrepressibly into Arab politics, and the Akram al-Hurani faction in the Ba'ath Party was eager to seize power in collaboration with officers. The putschist roots of Nasser's regime had legitimized the idea of a coup in Syria, or so radical Ba'athists argued in the 1950s. Al-Razzaz maintains that the Ba'ath Party was reluctant to accept military interventionism, yet tempted by the possibilities it created for a party struggling to reach power democratically. The Ba'ath Party reckoned it could establish a middle ground by acknowledging that the party had military sympathizers, and by allowing Akram al-Hurani to cultivate them without officially creating a military organization under party control. Consequently, according to al-Razzaz, the Ba'athists were active as individuals in the armed forces, but the Ba'ath as a party was not. Arguing along similar lines, Ba'athist leader Mansur al-Atrash noted that the historical co-founders of the party, Michel Aflaq and Salahaldin al-Bitar, did not actually know the names of Ba'athist officers in the armed forces – only al-Hurani did. This means that Ba'athist civilian control over the military wing had been feeble from the start. It became weaker still following al-Hurani's break with the party after 1961. Al-Atrash states that Ba'athist civilians like himself initially believed that the officers would remain faithful to the party's mission and legitimate leaders out of sheer ideological commitment – an assumption he deemed "naïve," in retrospect. See Munif al-Razzaz, *Al-Tajriba al-Murra* (Beirut: Dar Ghandur li-l-Tiba'a wa-l-Nashr, 1966), 33–36. See also Mansur al-Atrash, *Al-Jil al-Mudan, Sira Dhatiyya* (Beirut: Riad al-Rayes, 2008), 235–236 and 345–346.

putsch, let alone its execution. This did little to strengthen them in the intra-party struggles of the 1960s.[79]

Friction between the two wings of the Ba'ath Party translated into intra-military tension, and escalated progressively until the February 1966 coup consolidated the officers' hegemony over the party and state. In the wake of the catastrophic 1967 defeat, the ruling Syrian elite became divided into two camps yet again. On the one hand, militant leftists led by Syria's strongman, Jdid, still advocated combative "anti-imperialism" abroad and revolutionary socialism at home, even at the price of alienating conservative Arab regimes and the local bourgeoisie. Another faction, headed by then minister of defense Hafez al-Asad, maintained that Syria needed to prioritize the strategic necessities of war with Israel over left-wing doctrinaire purity. The al-Asad camp was ready to collaborate with Arab regimes and social classes deemed "reactionary" by the radicals, should that prove helpful to Syria in shifting the correlation of forces with Israel in its favor. As the two rival groups traded insults and became embroiled in a bitter contest for supremacy, the stage was set for the November 1970 putsch that delivered Syria durably to Hafez al-Asad.[80]

It may be that collision between ambitious officers all competing for supremacy was inevitable, irrespective of the ideational divergences mentioned above. Indeed, it could be argued that the vehement sloganeering characteristic of the time served as a mere veneer for self-centered considerations, and that the true substance of the fervent ideological quarrels was political rivalry. It is difficult to weigh the exact influence of both factors – i.e., high-minded convictions and lust for power – though undoubtedly, they do not have to be mutually exclusive.

It is also certain that sectarian dynamics and identity politics did not lurk too far below the ideological surface. Think again of the relationship between Nasserite and Ba'athist officers as a case in point. While both Nasser and the Ba'ath Party preached Arab socialism, the former essentially appealed to Arab Sunnis in Syria, whereas the latter fared better with minorities.[81] Syrian Alawis were not generally enthusiastic about the UAR, which reduced them to demographic insignificance and trapped them once again in an overwhelmingly Sunni entity, only decades after their

---

[79] al-Atrash, *Al-Jil al-Mudan*, 342. It should be added that the fear of a Nasserite counter-coup also strengthened the military wing in the Ba'ath Party after 1963, as Ba'athist civilians were dependent upon the party's officers remaining in power.

[80] On the differences between Salah Jdid and Hafez al-Asad, see Hashem 'Othman, *Tarikh Suria al-Hadith, 'Ahd Hafez al-Asad, 1971–2000* (Beirut: Riad El-Rayyes Books, 2014), 37–41.

[81] Rabinovich, *Syria under the Ba'ath*, 14.

emancipation from the Ottoman Empire. In the words of Alain Chouet, Alawis felt swindled under the UAR and marginalized as a minority.[82] Perhaps understandably, Ba'athist officers in the Committee who hailed from predominantly minority backgrounds were in no hurry to hoist Nasser's flag once again in Damascus after the breakdown of the UAR.[83] In addition, minority officers had played a role in their country's affairs via the Ba'ath Party and the rightist Syrian Social Nationalist Party (SSNP) prior to union with Egypt, and had seen their activism curtailed after Nasser gutted Syrian politics and banned parties in the UAR. Consequently, Alawi officers had their own reasons for opposing unionism, especially against the backdrop of pervasive hostility toward unionism among their co-religionists.[84] While Ba'athist officers were not exclusively Alawi and some Nasserite officers were not Sunnis, the cleavage between the two political camps corresponded largely with – and, in turn, reinforced – the dividing line between Alawis and Sunnis in Syria.[85]

While foreign intervention did not play a major role in the coups of the 1960s, it is certain that the separatist coup had the sympathy, and possibly the backing, of conservative regimes in Saudi Arabia and Jordan.[86] Whether Riyadh and Amman knew in advance that the Damascene officers were plotting to overthrow the UAR, and actually provided them with intelligence or financial support, isn't clear. The other coups appeared to be purely internal to Syria; indeed, to the Ba'ath Party. Martin Seymour noted, for instance, that nothing suggests that the

---

[82] Alain Chouet, "Impact of Wielding Power on 'Alawi Cohesiveness,'" *Maghreb-Machrek*, no. 147 (January–March, 1995): 5.

[83] Matti Moosa goes so far as to assert that Alawi officers in the Committee were motivated by "full consciousness of communal solidarity and sectarianism." If Moosa is right to argue that such officers used the Ba'ath Party and its ideology instrumentally, then it is no wonder they proved to be anti-unionists from their first days in power. Matti Moosa, *Extremist Shiites: The Ghulat Sects* (New York: Syracuse University Press, 1988), 297.

[84] Al-Razzaz argues that antagonism toward Nasser was stronger among Ba'athist officers than in the party's civilian ranks, because the former lost more influence under the UAR and felt particularly persecuted by the Nasserite regime. Al-Razzaz, *Al-Tajriba al-Murra*, 87.

[85] Peter Gubser, "Minorities in Power: The Alawites of Syria," in *The Political Role of Minority Groups in the Middle East*, ed. R. D. McLaurin (New York: Praeger, 1979), 37–41. See also Hazem Saghieh, *Al-Ba'ath al-Suri, Tarikh Mujaz* (Beirut: Dar al-Saqi, 2012), 35; Rabinovich, *Syria under the Ba'ath*, 61; and Itamar Rabinovich, "The Compact Minorities and the Syrian State, 1918–45," *Journal of Contemporary History* 14, no. 4 (October 1979): 699. Note that Mustafa Tlass mentions in his memoirs that Christians in Aleppo were deeply distressed when news of the pro-Nasser coup spread in the city in April 1962. Misgivings vis-à-vis the UAR were not confined to Alawis among Syrian minorities. Tlass, *Mer'at Hayati, Al-'Aqd al-Thani*, 220–221. Note also that Syrian minorities are no exception, in this regard. Iraqi Kurds never applauded Arab unionist projects, nor did Lebanese Christians.

[86] Seale, *Asad*, 67. See also Rabinovitch, *Syria under the Ba'ath*, 149–150.

Russians were behind the 1966 coup.[87] This, in fact, is true of the 1968 and 1970 putsches, as well. Domestic politics were the main driving force behind putsches, the struggle for power, and political change.

Coup-Proofing under the Ba'ath Party (1963–1970)

The main coup-proofing tactics under the Ba'ath Party were counterbalancing and ethnic stacking. Favoritism along identity lines was not itself new in Syria. Hosni al-Za'im, Syria's first military dictator, cultivated Circassians and Kurds, while Adib al-Shishakli, the strongman in Damascus from December 1949 until 1954, favored Sunnis from Hama. Sunnis hailing from large urban centers – especially Damascus – were also favored under the AUR regime between 1958 and 1961. Still, the sheer scale of manipulation of ethnic loyalties that began with the 1963 Ba'athist rise to power was unprecedented as I show below.

Counterbalancing

In June 1963, the Ba'ath Party created the National Guard (al-Haras al-Qawmi), a para-military organization whose mission was to terrorize opponents in the streets and keep an eye on potential opposition in the military – especially from Nasserite quarters.[88] Mustafa Tlass states in his memoirs that the National Guard played a direct role in countering the failed military putsch mounted by Nasserite officers in July 1963.[89] In the late 1960s, after Hafez al-Asad, then minister of defense, secured his grip over the armed forces, his rival Jdid beefed up the Ba'athist commando organization al-Sa'iqa as well as the national security and General Intelligence services as a counterweight to the military. At this stage, counterbalancing was still in its infancy in Syria. It would later take different proportions under Hafez and Bashar al-Asad.

Ideology and Fostering Shared Aversions

Shortly after seizing power in 1963, Syria's new rulers began an extensive purge of the military. It is estimated that up to 700 officers were dismissed

---

[87] Martin Seymour, "The Dynamics of Power in Syria since the Break with Egypt," *Middle Eastern Studies* 16, no. 1 (January 1970): 42.

[88] See Gad Soffer, "The Role of the Officer Class in Syrian Politics and Society" (PhD diss., American University, 1968), 135. Note that the name of the organization was later changed to the Popular Army (al-Jaysh al-Sha'bi).

[89] Tlass, *Mer'at Hayati, al-'Aqd al-Thani*, 431–432.

from the armed forces in the wake of the Ba'athist coup.[90] Sunnis were over-represented among cashiered officers, while Alawis formed at least 50 percent of their replacements; it has been argued, in fact, that this figure was closer to 90 percent, including poorly trained reserve officers and Ba'athist school teachers.[91] Purges were particularly systematic in the armored brigades, the air force, and navy, where professional officers were almost completely replaced by new Ba'athist recruits.[92] The king-making forces crucial to coups, notably the Seventieth and Fifth Brigades, became particularly stacked with Alawis. By 1965, Sunni officers controlled only 25 to 30 percent of military units; but the ratio would further diminish later on.[93] The Committee also opted to create under its supervision a secretive Ba'athist Military Organization, in charge of penetrating important sectors of the armed forces. Trustworthy Ba'athist officers were coopted into the Organization, which gave the Committee control over hundreds of supporters spread in all regiments. This was especially concentrated around Damascus.[94] Two other purges followed the successful putsch mounted in 1966 against Amin al-Hafez and the failure of Major Salim Hatum's attempt to seize power that same year. Another massive dismissal of Sunni officers from Huran followed former chief of staff Suwaydani's botched coup attempt in 1968.[95] The number of al-Hafez, Hatum, and Suwaydani supporters sacked from the officer corps, the overwhelming majority of whom were Sunnis and Druze, is estimated at 400. They, too, were essentially replaced by Ba'athist Alawis.[96] Anti-

---

[90] Syrian intelligence officer Khalil Mustafa maintains in his memoirs that up to 85 percent of Syrian officers were dismissed, imprisoned, or executed in the immediate years that followed the March 1963 coup. The ratio may be exaggerated, though there is consensus in the literature that Ba'athist purges of the armed forces were, indeed, massive. See Khalil Mustafa, *Suqut al-Julan* (Cairo: Dar al-I'tisam, 1980), 22.

[91] Van Dam, *The Struggle for Power*, 32. See also Mustafa, *Suqut al-Julan*, 30.

[92] al-Safadi, *Hizb al-Ba'ath*, 339.

[93] Alasdair Drysdale, "Ethnicity in the Syrian Officer Corps: A Conceptualization," *Civilisations* 29, no. 3/4 (1979): 368.

[94] Provided they remained loyal, Ba'athist officers in the Military Organization could aspire to be rewarded with generous financial perks, promotions, and appointments in much-desired political or diplomatic sinecures. Sami al-Jundi mentions in his book that Hafez al-Assad and Salah Jdid appointed loyalist officers as military attachés in foreign countries whose language they ignored; several military attachés assigned to Paris were actually not conversant in French. Officers in perfect health were also sent on medical leaves to Paris, and reaped generous salaries for the duration of their stay abroad. Sami al-Jundi, *Al-Ba'ath* (Beirut: Dar al-Nahar, 1969), 156.

[95] Suwaydani himself was a Sunni from Huran and had a power base among his co-religionists from the region.

[96] Overall, in the decade preceding the 1967 war with Israel, more than 2,200 professional officers were sacked from the Syrian armed forces. Half were dismissed during the UAR, and half after the Ba'ath Party's 1963 putsch. This number amounted to about two thirds of the Syrian officer corps, which counted around 3,000 men in its ranks in 1963. Zein al-

Sunni discrimination in the officer corps also included practices such as stationing Sunni officers away from the capital and discriminating against Sunni applicants to the Military Academy in Homs. As sectarian engineering of military companies trickled down to the level of NCOs and soldiers, some units became all-Alawi from top to bottom.[97] All these practices were to endure, and would result in long-term effects upon Syria's politics and armed forces.

Until he was overthrown in 1966, President Amin al-Hafez tried to secure his grip on power by cultivating a Sunni base to counterbalance the rising minority officers. The latter's overt sectarian tactics did help al-Hafez cultivate his image as the Sunnis' champion and ultimate protector in the armed forces. At the same time, Sunni mobilization eased Jdid and Hafez al-Asad's drive to build a minority coalition that included most influential Alawi, Druze, and Isma'ili officers. To be sure, a handful of Druze officers, and even some Alawis, remained loyal to al-Hafez; and a few Sunnis threw in their lot with the Alawi-dominated faction. The officers' personal interests and vagaries of incessant power plays sometimes facilitated cross-sectarian alliances. And yet sectarian polarization and loyalty remained, nonetheless, the defining factor of Syrian military politics at the time. Minority officers were aware that they were increasingly overrepresented in the military, including its upper echelons. Had the Alawi camp lost to al-Hafez, the sectarian imbalance would have to be corrected – and possibly even flipped in favor of Sunnis. The risk of an al-Hafez triumph, for Alawi officers, was simply too big to be acceptable. In the words of Nikolaos Van Dam, and Munif al-Razzaz, respectively:

During the power struggle between al-Hafiz and Jadid, the manipulation with sectarian, regional, and tribal loyalties caused the tension within the Syrian armed forces to increase to such an extent that far-reaching polarization resulted between Sunnis and members of religious minorities. Sectarian contradistinction among the military consequently began to overshadow almost all other differences.[98]

When al-Hafiz and Jdid jockeyed for power, sectarian divisiveness became public in the ranks and sectarian antagonism grew increasingly violent, which left its marks on the armed forces, as all other contentious factors vanished, to be

'Abidin, *Al-Jaysh wa-l-Siasa*, 414. See also Be'eri, *Army Officers in Arab Politics and Society*, 335.
[97] See al-Razzaz, *Al-Tajriba al-Murra*, 158–159. See also al-Safadi, *Hizb al-Ba'ath*, 339–340 and 349; and Van Dam, *The Struggle for Power*, 32–36. Note that Alawi officers were also purged when their patrons (e.g., Mohammad 'Omran and Salah Jdid) lost the factional struggle for power. Many, however, were returned to service after pledging loyalty to Hafez al-Asad, who emerged triumphant in the intra-Alawi conflicts that pitted leading Alawi generals against one another in the second half of the 1960s.
[98] Van Dam, *The Struggle for Power*, 44.

replaced exclusively by the sectarian dimension (*yahull al-miqias al-ta'ifi mahall ay miqias akhar*).[99]

Should Ba'athist ideological claims and the party's purported efforts to create an "ideological military" (i.e., *jaysh 'aqa'idi*) count as coup-proofing, as well? I have argued in the theoretical section of this book that ideational beliefs can, indeed, wed officers to one another – and militaries to the ruling elite. The Ba'ath Party did stand for a unionist message that resonated with public opinion, in Syria and beyond in the Arab world. In the wake of the successful 1963 coup, the Committee devoted time and energy to building a network of party cells entrusted with the task of spreading Ba'athist ideology and messages in the armed forces. Minister of Defense Hafez al-Asad took an old Arab nationalist philosopher and ideologue, Zaki al-Arsuzi, out of retirement, and arranged for him to visit military barracks and lecture the men on Arab nationalism and the foundational beliefs of the Ba'ath Party. Relentlessly, Ba'athist officers claimed to be the standard-bearers of their proclaimed political faith, an avant-garde committed to building an ideological army as well as a unionist and anti-imperialist state. But whether officers took their own rhetoric seriously is questionable. Mohammad 'Omran, a co-founder of the Committee, argued candidly in his memoirs that the politics of Ba'athist officers following the 1963 turning point stood in direct contradiction to their ideology and professed beliefs.[100] 'Omran's observation is accurate on several important levels. For instance, Ba'athist ideology promotes Arab unionism, but the Ba'ath Party turned out to be more staunchly separatist than the regime it ousted. Once they captured power in Syria, the officers kept it – and that, in effect, meant that the UAR was not to be restored, and unionism was to remain a mere slogan. On the other hand, the party is ostensibly above sectarianism as well as against it. And yet Ba'athist officers used identity politics and manipulated sectarian loyalties as they struggled to keep their grip on power. For instance, Mohammad 'Omran recruited his faction almost exclusively from minority officers and stated explicitly that "Fatimid" officers must play their role in Syria and the armed forces (*"inn al-Fatimiyya yajib an ta'kudha dawraha"*).[101] Jdid, al-Hafez, and Hatum, all prominent Ba'athist officers, also competed for the loyalties of their

---

[99] al-Razzaz, *Al-Tajriba al-Murra*, 160.

[100] Mohammad 'Omran, *Tajribati fi al-Thawra* (Beirut: Dar al-Jil li-l-Tab' wa-l-Nashr wa-l-Tawzi', 1970), 23.

[101] By "Fatimid," 'Omran meant heterodox Muslim sects, i.e., Alawis, Druze, and Isma'ilis. See Van Dam, *The Struggle for Power*, 39.

sects (the Alawis, Sunnis, and Druze, respectively), and recruited military factions along confessional lines.

Mustafa Tlass relates in his memoirs how Sunni Ba'athist officers were inclined to support their fellow Sunni al-Hafez against the Alawi Jdid, out of sectarian solidarity.[102] In 1967, Sunni Ba'athists from the eastern Deir al-Zur asked Jdid to favor Sunni chief of staff Suwaydani over his Alawi rival, then minister of defense Hafez al-Asad, lest they accuse Jdid of sectarianism and spread rumors that a secretive supreme council of the Alawi sect controlled the agency of Alawi officers, who supposedly hid their true loyalties behind a veneer of Ba'athist loyalty.[103] Later on, as Jdid and Hafez al-Asad became locked in a bitter power struggle in the late 1960s, Ba'athist officer 'Izzat Jdid tried to mediate between the two, and urged them to tame their rivalry in the name of sectarian unity between fellow Alawi officers ("*maslahat al-ta'ifa taqtadi alla yatakhsam abna'uha*").[104] Tlass, a Hafez al-Asad loyalist, accused Jdid (but not Hafez al-Asad) of favoring Alawis.[105] I will show later on, however, that Hafez al-Asad filled the officer corps with Alawis and pushed sectarian stacking to an unprecedented level in the armed forces. Simply put, the Ba'ath Party's ostensive secularism did not prevent its officers from using identity politics as just another way of seizing power and keeping it. Consequently, the party became vulnerable to charges of ideological hypocrisy.[106] For instance, Muta' al-Safadi, a former Ba'athist, accused the party of framing as a class struggle what was, in essence, sectarian conflict targeting Sunnis:

> The party of unity became the bastion of minorities (*husn al-aqalliyat*), stimulating their separatist tendencies and isolationism and putting them on the offensive against the majority of the masses.[107]

Such indictments gained increasing traction after the Ba'ath Party broke with Nasser in the early 1960s, which did not help it acquire legitimacy or give credence to the officers' alleged pan-Arab unionist commitment. The depth of Sunni resentment was palpable in a series of sectarian incidents and violent mobilizations in the mid-1960s, which pitted regime opponents against Alawi civilians, or pro-regime forces, in Banias (Lataqia), Hama, and Homs. Also, Ba'athist Syria's underperformance in the conflicts with Israel did not strengthen Ba'athist officers' claims to

---

[102] See Tlass, *Mer'at Hayati, al-'Aqd al-Thani*, 513–514.   [103] Ibid., 865.

[104] See Tlass, *Mer'at Hayati, al-'Aqd al-Thaleth*, 347.   [105] Ibid.

[106] For an interesting analysis of the interplay between egoistic, sectarian, and ideological motivations in structuring the agency of Ba'athist officers, see Seymour, "The Dynamics of Power," 40–41.

[107] See al-Safadi, *Hizb al-Ba'ath*, 54.

be the shield and armor of the Arab world – certainly not in the Six-Day War. Add to this that the appeal of Arab socialism had receded progressively with the demise of Nasserism. Consequently, the Ba'athist regime in Syria appeared to be the champion of an increasingly decrepit ideology that party leaders themselves did not act upon.[108] If coup-proofing proved effective nonetheless – so much so that the regime was able to survive the 1967 debacle unchallenged – it was for reasons other than the alleged pan-Arab ideological commitment and purity of the party.

Conclusion

The putschists who founded the Free Officers and Ba'athist regimes were determined not to lose power the same way they seized it, and their coup-proofing methods delivered and subsequently endured. In Chapter 3, I ponder the evolution of coup-proofing in Egypt and Syria, and show in chapter 4 that its institutional legacy structured the militaries' response to the 2011 uprisings in both countries.

[108] Fabrice Balanche, *La région alaouite et le pouvoir syrien* (Paris: Editions Kharthala, 2006), 284.

3   Coups, Coup-Proofing, and the Neoliberal Age in Egypt and Syria

In 1970, Anwar Sadat became president of Egypt following the death of Gamal ʿAbdul Nasser. Saʿad al-Din al-Shazli, the Egyptian Armed Forces' (EAF) chief of staff during the 1973 October War, shows in his memoirs that regime security trumped national security considerations throughout Sadat's years in power. For instance, when Sadat allocated shipments of Soviet tanks to different military units, he made sure to keep a balance of power among the different mechanized brigades so none could pose a threat to his regime, even though the scattering of Soviet tanks among several formations, instead of concentrating them in a few, was less efficient from a strictly military perspective. Simply put, maintaining what al-Shazli labeled the "internal security equilibrium" (*al-tawazon al-amni al-dakhili*) in the armed forces trumped battle-related military concerns. On the other hand, Sadat counterbalanced Military Intelligence (MI) with General Intelligence and the ministry of interior's state security (Mabaheth Amn al-Dawla) by encouraging competition between the three organizations in order to reduce the likelihood of coups.[1]

The primacy of coup-proofing endured under Mubarak as well. Significantly, the Mubarak regime refrained from fostering the kind of maverick field officers who make mobile warfare possible. To this day, Egypt's strategic doctrine remains centered upon defense combat and trench-style fighting, which has repeatedly proven inferior to Israel's war-

---

[1] Saʿad al-Din al-Shazli, *Harb October, Mudhakkarat al-Fariq Saʿad al-Din al-Shazli* (Cairo: Ruʾya li-l-Nashr wa-l-Tawziʿ, 2011), 180, 192–193. Add to this that Sadat appointed Ahmed Ismaʿil as minister of defense in the October War in 1972, though he knew that Ismaʿil was terminally ill with cancer. As the war raged on, he had to be hospitalized and was absent from his duties. More importantly, he was not on speaking terms with his own chief of staff, the above-mentioned al-Shazli, who considered resigning when Ismaʿil was appointed war minister. That the two highest officers in the Egyptian military had been enemies for a decade did not facilitate cooperation between them and reflected negatively upon the Egyptian war effort, especially in the crucial last days of combat. Sadat, however, prioritized divide-and-rule tactics for the purpose of political control over the necessities of battlefield effectiveness.

of-movement style. The truth is, Blitzkrieg-style warfare makes military heroes out of tactically astute officers, which is precisely what the insecure Mubarak never wanted. In contrast, trench warfare places the centralization of military command in the hands of a few politically trusted generals. So deleterious was coup-proofing under Mubarak that the EAF became operationally incapable of conducting yearly military maneuvers with their American allies.[2] In other words, nothing was more important for successive Egyptian regimes than successful coup-proofing – not even preparing the EAF to achieve their full military potential in a dangerous regional environment. Accordingly, coup-proofing tactics considered efficient became a fixture of civil–military relations for decades, hence their impact during the 2011 turning point.

As for Syria, the ruthlessness of Hafez al-Asad's coup-proofing reflects the vulnerability of his regime and his own insecurities as a ruler hailing from a minority background. There was no guarantee that al-Asad would survive in power after seizing it in 1970. Still, coup-proofing under his regime worked, and the late president maintained the tactics that gutted Syrian military politics throughout his long career. His son and heir, Bashar, replaced older generals with younger ones but kept the fundamental rules of the game unchanged: coup-proofing was central under him as it was under his father, and along similar lines. This means that the Syrian armed forces operating during the 2011 uprising were molded by political control mechanisms set in place since the early 1960s.

Coups under Sadat

Sadat consolidated his hold on power in May 1971, after outmaneuvering several coup-plotters, including his own war minister, Mohammad Fawzi. Sadat was assassinated in October 1981 during a coup attempt led by a former Military Intelligence officer, ʿAbbud al-Zumur. Between these plots marking Sadat's rise to power and his demise, six other military conspiracies punctuated his turbulent tenure. Coup-proofing the armed forces was no less a necessity under Sadat than it had been under Nasser.

Politicking in the Egyptian military commenced immediately following Nasser's death on September 28, 1970. Mohammad Sadeq was then the EAF's chief of staff. In his memoirs, Sadeq related that Fawzi lost no time

[2] Roger Owen, "Military Presidents in Arab States," *The International Journal of Middle East Studies* 43, no. 3 (August 2011): 395. See also Henry M. Clement and Robert Springborg, "A Tunisian Solution For Egypt's Military: Why Egypt's Military Will Not Be Able to Govern," *Foreign Affairs*, February 21, 2011, www.foreignaffairs.com/articles/tunisi a/2011–02-21/tunisian-solution-egypt-s-military (accessed August 7, 2014).

assigning three of his aides to command armored brigades stationed in Cairo (the Central Military District, in the EAF's jargon) only hours after Nasser died in a move intended to secure control over the center of political power. Sadeq rejected the new appointments, and Fawzi rescinded his orders. The tug-of-war between the two men had begun, however, and the opening salvos in the post-Nasser power play were shot even before the Ra'is was buried.[3]

Sadat had been Nasser's vice president at the time of his death, and was deemed a political lightweight who could serve as a transitional president until key military, security, and political players in the system reordered power. When it became clear that Sadat did not intend to serve as front man, his opponents prepared to stage a military takeover in April 1971 – and failed. Sadeq was still chief of staff, and spearheaded the pro-Sadat camp in the EAF. His loyalty to the president paid off: as the anti-Sadat intrigue fizzled, Fawzi was jailed, and Sadeq replaced him as war minister and commander of the armed forces.[4] Sadat had survived the first coup attempt under his tenure.

Only eighteen months later, a second military conspiracy was discovered, and a ring of high-ranking coup-plotters was dismantled. By that time, Sadeq had fallen from grace with Sadat, and the latter dismissed him. His supporters in the armed forces, however, formed a secretive "Save Egypt" movement and prepared to seize power. As it turned out, MI was heavily involved in the new plot, along with senior officers occupying sensitive positions in the Central Military District, al-Sa'iqa Special Forces, and armored brigades. Sadeq himself was not implicated in the coup, but Sadat placed him under house arrest nonetheless, and sacked the MI's director, Major General Muhrez Mustafa.[5]

The third plot unfolded in April 1974 as a conspiracy from below and collusion between Islamists inside the military and radical militants outside it, under the leadership of Palestinian activist Saleh Sarieh. The conspirators planned to seize the Technical Military Academy (al-Kulliyya al-Faniyya al-'Askariyya), use the arsenal of heavy weaponry stacked within to occupy the parliament and ASU headquarters, and declare the Islamic Republic of Egypt after assassinating Sadat. One conspirator had a change of heart at the last minute, and leaked the plan to the interior ministry's State Security Investigations Service (SSIS), also called Mabaheth Amn al-Dawla. The coup attempt foundered, but the nexus between military and civilian Islamist activists heralded the same

---

[3] See Sadeq's memoirs in al-Gawadi, *Fi A'qab al-Naksa*, 300.   [4] Ibid., 304–314.
[5] On this coup attempt led by Major General 'Ali 'Abdul-Khabir, see the memoirs of al-Shazli, *Harb October*, 240–245.

combination of militants that would try to seize power in 1981 and kill Sadat in the process.[6] It was rumored at the time that former RCC member Hussein al-Shaf'i, Sadat's vice president, was involved in the Technical Military Academy coup attempt. Sadat did not dismiss the possibility, and allegedly opined that al-Shaf'i was not incapable of trying to overthrow him ("*ye'melha Hussein*").[7] Still, no tangible evidence ever corroborated these suspicions: al-Shaf'i himself accused the Mabaheth of trying to implicate him in the affair, along with former war minister Sadeq and former chief of staff al-Shazli.[8] As in 1965, military officers and the ministry of interior were trading accusations, but this time, the roles were reversed. In 1974, the Mabaheth charged officers with plotting against the regime, while in 1965, the MI had blamed the Mabaheth for failing to uncover an alleged Islamist plot.

Little information is available about the fourth and fifth plots in June 1975 and June 1977. We do know, however, that forty-three officers were arrested following the first conspiracy, and that the second centered upon naval officers in Alexandria. In June 1978, the exiled al-Shazli called upon the military to remove Sadat and, subsequently, fourteen paratroopers were jailed for supporting him.[9] Following the signature of the Camp David Accords in September 1978, a new Free Officers organization circulated pamphlets within the armed forces accusing the American experts training Egyptian officers of spying on them and promoting ideological transformations incompatible with the military's identity and history. Alarmed by intelligence reports, Sadat turned to al-Gamasy, who downplayed news of saber-rattling in the armed forces.[10] But al-Gamasy's assurances were proven wrong: in March 1981, the MI dismantled an Islamist ring founded by a Jordanian student at Alexandria University, Wisam al-Rahhal. This effort was headed in the armed forces by armored brigades Major 'Isam al-Qamari, who had converted several mid-ranking officers to his cause. Al-Qamari eschewed arrest for a while

---

[6] Sirrs, *A History of the Mukhabarat*, 42.

[7] See also the account of Ahmad al-Raggal, who participated in the planning of the 1974 Technical Military Academy operation but defected to presidential security, in Mustafa Kamil, "Infirad 'al-Rijal' Yahki Qissat Awwal Inqilab 'Askari Islami 'ala al-Sadat," *Mobtada*, April 3, 2015, www.mobtada.com/news_details.php?ID=313387 (accessed April 15, 2015).

[8] 'Abdallah Imam, *Haqiqat al-Sadat* (Cairo: Mu'assasat Rose al-Youssef li-l-Sahafa wa-l-Tiba'a wa-l-Nashr, 1986), 224.

[9] Richard H. Dekmejian, "Egypt and Turkey: The Military in the Background," in *Soldiers, Peasants and Bureaucrats: Civil–Military Relations in Communist and Modernizing Societies*, ed. Roman Kolkowicz and Andrzej Korbonski (London: George Allen & Unwin, 1982), 38–39.

[10] Ghali Shukri, *Al-Thawra al-Mudada fi Masr* (Cairo: Kitab al-Ahali, 1987), 451.

and went underground, moving from one hideout to another until he was finally arrested in October 1981.[11]

That very same month, yet another Islamist plot to seize power was unfolding. Ayman al-Zawahiri, the future leader of al-Qaeda, was then a young Egyptian doctor and Islamist activist convinced that only a military coup could "pluck the regime from the roots."[12] He wasn't alone in thinking along these lines. After a distinguished record in service, Abbud al-Zumur retired from the armed forces as a lieutenant colonel in the MI reconnaissance branch and a 1973 war hero. Along with al-Zawahiri, 'Abdul-Salam Farag, and other leaders of the al-Jihad militant Islamist group, al-Zumur recruited mid-ranking and junior officers in the military, such as air force lieutenant colonel 'Isam al-Tuhami, air force captain Ahmad Moussa, and the commander of airport guards, Colonel Ahmad al-Maqrabani.[13] A sergeant in Unit 55, stationed around the defense ministry, was to provide the conspirators with weaponry stolen from its arsenal. Al-Zumur devised a scheme to control the defense and interior ministries, the telephone and telegraph buildings, and state radio and television. The process leading to regime overthrow was to begin with an attempt on Sadat's life during the annual victory parade celebrating the crossing of the Suez Canal on the first day of the October War. The task was entrusted to artillery first lieutenant Khaled al-Islambuli and a small cell of militants, including a former air defense officer and a reserve first lieutenant. On October 6, 1981, al-Islambuli and his associates struck successfully: Sadat was assassinated, along with nine others. The rest of the plan failed, however, and the plotters were apprehended.[14]

Whether some sectors in the armed forces facilitated the attack on Sadat against a backdrop of heightened polarization in civil–military relations, or the breach in security measures surrounding the president was due to incompetence, remains a hotly debated question. It was rumored that al-Shazli had masterminded the plot and created a secretive movement in the armed forces that had recruited Sadat's killers. Al-Shazli himself confessed to *Newsweek* that he was "overjoyed" by Sadat's execution, which he considered a "step in the right direction." He also hinted that he was, indeed, the driving force behind the young officers who killed Sadat, and that the operation had been part of a greater

[11] Fu'ad 'Allam, *Al-Ikhwan wa-Ana, Min al-Manshiyya ila al-Minassah* (Cairo: Akhbar al-Yawm, 1996), 413–415.

[12] Lawrence Wright, *The Terror Years: From Al-Qaeda to the Islamic State* (New York: Vintage, 2017), 31.

[13] 'Adel Hammuda, *Ightial Ra'is, bi-l-Watha'iq, Asrar Ightial Anwar al-Sadat* (Cairo: Dar Iqra', 1985), 59.

[14] See Mahmud Fawzi, *Al-Nabawi Isma'il wa-Juzur Hadithat al-Minassah* (Cairo: Dar al-Nashr Haitieh, 1991), 161–166. See also Sirrs, *A History of the Mukhabarat*, 143–145.

Table 3.1 *Coup plots under Sadat (1970–1981)*

	Date	Leading officers involved	Outcome
(1)	April/May 1971	Mohammad Fawzi (general/war minister and commander of the EAF)	Failure
(2)	November 1972	'Ali 'Abdul-Khabir (major general/ commander of the Central Military Region)	Failure
(3)	April 1974	-	Failure
(4)	June 1975	-	Failure
(5)	June 1977	-	Failure
(6)	August 1978	Sa'ad al-Din al-Shazli (lieutenant general/former chief of staff)	Failure
(7)	March 1981	'Isam al-Qamari (major/armored brigades)	Failure
(8)	October 1981	'Abbud al-Zumur (retired lieutenant colonel/Military Intelligence)	Sadat's assassination

scheme to overthrow the Egyptian regime. But al-Shazli's boasting was never corroborated. He had been sacked from the armed forces in 1973, a year before al-Islambuli was admitted into the military academy. While al-Shazli remained popular within the ranks and in Egyptian society at large for his role in the October War, he had no connection with al-Islambuli and his associates, and no role in Sadat's violent end.[15] Table 3.1 presents a recapitulation of the above-mentioned conspiracies.

Coup-Proofing under Sadat

Sadat's coup-proofing strategy combined a mixture of ideational and material elements in addition to counterbalancing and divide and rule. Two tactics that he employed later proved to be of particular long-term significance for Egypt: empowering the interior ministry even further, and tolerating unprecedented levels of corruption among the military elite.

Ideology and Fostering Shared Aversions

In his study on Nasser, Richard Dekmejian wrote that the pervasive mood in Egypt following its setback in the 1948 war was inward-looking, nationalistic, and extremely hostile to Pan-Arabism.[16] The 1967 Naksa

---

[15] Hammuda, *Ightial Ra'is*, 50–52.
[16] Richard H. Dekmejian, *Egypt under Nasir: A Study in Political Dynamics* (London: Hodder & Stoughton, 1972), 93.

("Setback," or Six-Day War) was far more devastating to Egypt than 1948, and it was, perhaps, inevitable that isolationist tendencies would resurface again after the war. The breakup of the UAR in 1961 had already been an embarrassment from an ideological perspective. Many argued that if Nasser in Egypt and the Ba'ath Party in Syria, both paragons of Arab nationalism, could not make unionism work, then maybe the conceptual underpinnings of the whole experiment were questionable. As it turned out, *Qutrism* – local patriotism in opposition to pan-Arab unionism – was anything but a spent force in Egypt and Syria. The very name "United Arab Republic" drew the ire of some officers in Cairo, who argued that Egypt was the oldest name in the history of humankind, and the UAR would make the appellation disappear.[17] Syrians, for their part, complained that Egyptian officers were gradually controlling the Syrian military, and that embassies were leaving Damascus to Cairo. It was also rumored that Egyptian peasants were flocking to Syria to occupy the most fertile lands in the countryside.[18] The breakdown of the UAR was acrimonious and heightened intra-Arab tensions. Nasser and the Ba'ath Party had once partnered under a common ideological platform, but by 1963, they had become enemies. The Nasser/Ba'ath Party split deteriorated into full confrontation after the Ba'athists triggered a successful coup in March 1963 and took power in Damascus – but subsequently refused to bring Syria back into the fold of the UAR.

And then the 1967 turning point came. The crisis opened as a series of deadly border clashes between Israel and Syria in 1966. Egypt eventually moved troops to Sinai, hoping that a show of force would prevent Israel from escalating tensions. Nasser was hoping to avoid war, but still signaled that Cairo would not be a bystander, should Israel attack Syria. When Israel called his bluff and hostilities began, the Syrian military did little to take the heat off Egyptian troops in Sinai, who alone bore the full brunt of the Israeli attack in the first days of the war. The view from Cairo was this: a conflict that began for the sake of defending Syria ended with a crushing defeat for Egyptian arms, while the Syrians watched the Israeli juggernaut slaughter thousands of Egyptian soldiers in Sinai without budging. Egypt felt betrayed. In the September 1970 Arab League summit in Cairo, a bitter Nasser complained about having been sucked into war by the Yemenis in 1962 and again by the Syrians in 1967 (*"warratuna"*). Arab governments, according to Nasser, issued communiqués, but the Egyptians fought the actual wars – Arabs were abusing Egypt (*"istikrad"*). If Nasser himself was rancorous about Egypt's Arab

---

[17] al-Baghdadi, *Mudhakkarat*, 135.   [18] Seale, *Asad*, 58–59.

brethren, then it should not be surprising that resentment ran deep among Egyptians less committed than Nasser to pan-Arab ideology.[19]

These transformations paved the way for Sadat's subsequent ideational about-face. He behaved as the ultimate *Qutrist* – one ready to switch sides in the Cold War, display open religious zeal to the extent of calling himself the "Believer President" (*al-Ra'is al-Mu'men*), feed incorrect war plans to his Syrian partners in 1973, and then turn his back completely on the Arab world to pursue a separate peace deal with Israel. Inevitably, Sadat alienated the Nasserite and leftist intelligentsia as well as sections of the articulate public, who remained committed to the ideals of pan-Arab solidarity. Yet the military top brass were generally sensitive to Sadat's Egypt-first orientation, and ready to be convinced that throughout the Arab–Israeli conflict, "it was Egyptians who died while other Arab states postured and orated,"[20] or that "Egypt [was] heavily indebted while the rich Arabs [were] depositing billions of dollars in foreign banks."[21] Sadat's underlying argument was that the military had paid a heavy price to fulfill Egypt's Arab commitments. It fought in 1948 to defend the Palestinians; from 1962 to 1967 to help the Yemenis; and in June 1967 to take the pressure off the Syrians. After their honorable performance in 1973, it was time for the armed forces to be shielded from further confrontation with Israel, and for Egypt to prioritize its own interests. Sadat's retreat from the flamboyant pan-Arab engagement of Nasser, symbolized by the country's name change from the United Arab Republic to the Arab Republic of Egypt, was in tune with the mainstream political sympathies of the officer corps, which had become, by the time he took office, "impervious" to radical pan-Arab ideological appeals.[22] Billboards in major cities proclaiming "Egypt First" or "Egypt First, Second, and Last" captured the pervasive mood in the military and society at large.[23] Not even the Palestinian cause escaped Egyptian resentment at the time. In an informative account of his experiences as an Egyptian-Armenian conscript in the military following 1967, Nubar Aroyan recounts:

---

[19] The Syrians were particularly loathed in Egyptian military circles because they had allegedly "bitten the hand that fed them" in 1967. After the guns fell silent and the scale of the disaster became known, Nasserism entered into a twilight zone against the backdrop of a major ideological crisis that had damaged the appeal of militant Pan-Arabism. See Mussa Sabri, *Watha'iq Harb October* (Cairo: al-Maktab al-Masri al-Hadith, 1975), 142–143 and 199.

[20] Thomas W. Lipman, *Egypt after Nasser: Sadat, Peace, and the Mirage of Prosperity* (St. Paul, MN: Paragon House, 1989), 183.

[21] Jason Brownlee, "Peace before Freedom: Diplomacy and Repression in Sadat's Egypt," *Political Science Quarterly* 126, no. 4 (Winter 2011): 641–668.

[22] Hinnebusch, *Egyptian Politics*, 127.   [23] Baker, *Egypt's Uncertain Revolution*, 142.

And generally, Palestine was blamed as the root of all problems. The name Palestine (*Falasteen* in Arabic) was bisected into *Falas/Teen* (bankruptcy/mud), the most common expression of bitterness being *Awwelha falas, akherha teen* (starts with bankruptcy, ends with mud).[24]

Reflecting the same disenchantment with the Palestinian cause, an anonymous senior officer serving under Sadat maintained:

When I heard the news about the Israel visit [Sadat's trip to Jerusalem] ... I was pleased. The other officers said they liked it, but no one was sure the other was telling the truth. Later, more relaxed in the evening, we realized that everyone truly felt the same .... What Sadat has done should have been done years ago. ... We would fight and die defending our national interests, but we have died enough for the Palestinians. I accept that this, in effect, means war – war of some sort with the Palestinians. It will be a very rough ride for Egypt. I am an Egyptian first and an Arab second .... The army is ready to die for Egypt, but not for the Palestinians. No military coup could succeed in persuading the officers at large to send their men to die for a fight which is not theirs. We die for Egypt.[25]

That Nasser had led them to three military defeats in less than two decades under the banner of Pan-Arabism (i.e., the Suez War of 1956, the 1962 intervention in Yemen, and the June War in 1967 with Israel) had not been lost on the armed forces. The 1967 debacle was particularly humiliating. Officers were taunted by civilians in the streets of Cairo, and a song mocking their performance became the emblematic tune of the postwar sixties.[26] In 1973, the Egyptian military performed better and inflicted heavy casualties upon Israeli troops stationed in Sinai, especially during the first days of the war. Though other battles ended under less-favorable circumstances, Egyptian prowess was undeniable and plain for the world to see. By then, however, Egyptian officers were weary of the never-ending war with Israel, and understood that they would be trounced yet again should they fight. Sadat's realignment and ideational message was appealing for three reasons. First, Sadat absolved the armed forces from the responsibility of the 1967 Naksa. He wrote in his memoirs that the armed forces were "the victim[s], not the cause, of the June 1967 defeat," and his regime actively propagated this view, which implied that ʿAmer's poor leadership and dysfunctional relationship with Nasser had

---

[24] Nubar Aroyan, *Diary of a Soldier in the Egyptian Military: A Peek Inside the Egyptian Army* (Bloomington, IN: WestBrow Press, 2012), 6.

[25] See the "Views from Abroad" section published by the *Journal of Palestine Studies* 7, no. 2 (1978): 159–161.

[26] Written by popular poet Ahmad Fouad Najm and performed by Sheikh Imam, the song entitled "How Sweet Is the Homecoming of Our Officers from the Frontline" (*Ya Mahla Rag ʾit Zubbatna min Khat al-Nar*) captured Egypt's bitterness at the officers' corruption and dismal performance in the war. Available at: www.youtube.com/watch?v=4IWaH N2YDXg (accessed January 15, 2015).

caused the debacle, not the incompetence of Egypt's soldiers.[27] This, of course, was precisely what the military wanted to hear – and what senior figures such as war ministers Amine Howeidi, Kamal Hasan ʿAli, or field marshal al-Gamasy explicitly said in their memoirs.[28] And second, Sadat restored military morale in the wake of 1973. Military spokesmen had always argued that the armed forces were not given the opportunity to fight in 1967, and their initial battlefield successes in 1973 gave credibility to their claim.[29] Sadat actually congratulated his troops repeatedly on becoming the sixth military force in the world. And finally, his inward orientation shielded the armed forces from further unwinnable confrontations with Israel and spared them additional involvement in the cauldron of Arab politics. The ideational link that wedded the military to the Sadat regime rested upon his postwar image as the redeemer of Egypt's military honor, which, according to him, Nasser had tarnished.

On the other hand, Sadat also played on Egyptian pride and sense of victimhood as he referred to his Arab critics as "dwarfs," "bedouins," "treacherous," and "dogs" who expected Egypt to keep fighting their wars gratuitously, yet dared to diminish and criticize his country.[30] Over and over again from 1975 onward, in speeches to the military, he systematically lashed out at radical Arabs supposedly conspiring against Egypt:

We lose no occasion to defend the Palestinian cause, whereas the Palestinians themselves are busy hiring themselves as mercenaries and terrorists in brothels and cabarets. Let them know that Egypt will remain Egypt . . . and Mother Egypt will stamp dwarfs (*Masr sa tadus al-aqzam*). Egypt will stamp these dwarfs, whatever the cost may be . . ..[31]

I was prepared to speak on behalf of the Golan. But no. Let these dirty Alawis speak for it. These are people who have lost all life's meaning. Let them face their people in Syria and let them solve it. We shall see what they will achieve. I could have brought them the Golan but I am not responsible for it while the Alawis are in power. . . . [King] Faysal [of Saudi Arabia] told me that Hafiz al-Asad is Alawi and

---

[27] Anwar al-Sadat, *Al-Bahth ʿan al-Dhat, Qissat Hayati* (Cairo: al-Maktab al-Masri al-Hadith, 1979), 200.

[28] Huweidi, *Al-Foras al-Daʾiʿa*, 74, 77, 83; Kamal Hasan ʿAli, *Mashawir al-ʿOmr fi al-Harb wa-l-Mukhabarat wa-l-Siasa, Asrar wa-Khafaya 70 Aman min ʿOmr Masr* (Cairo: Dar al-Shuruq, 1994), 212–218; and al-Gamasy, *Mudhakkarat*, 68.

[29] Baker, *Egypt's Uncertain Revolution*, 159.

[30] Heikal, *Kharif al-Ghadab*, 314. See also Sadat's scathing attack on the Emir of Kuwait and other Arab opponents. Available at: www.youtube.com/watch?v=Kwmd4VrOsZM (accessed January 5, 2016).

[31] These Sadat speeches are available online at: http://sadat.bibalex.org/Historic_Docume nts/Historic_Docs_All.aspx?TabName=Speech&page=29#Gallery (accessed January 9, 2016).

Ba'thist, and the one is more evil than the other . . . . Faysal also told me: How can you hold hands with the Syrian Ba'thists?[32]

Other examples in the same vein abound. In sum, Sadat maintained that it would be naïve for Egypt's armed forces to keep sacrificing themselves for the sake of the Arab cause, only to be met with ungratefulness and backstabbing. His message resonated with the officer corps. To be sure, the military's former mission as defender of the Arab nation and engine of social change was abandoned when Sadat's regime made peace with Israel and opened Egypt to the forces of the market. But what the officers lost in prestige as shields of the Arab nation and revolutionary redistributors of wealth under Nasser, they gained as liberators of Sinai and successful defenders of Egypt under Sadat.

Promoting the Material Interests of the Military Elite

In the wake of the 1973 war, Sadat abruptly took Egypt out of state socialism and into unfettered laissez-faire capitalism. Law 43, enacted in 1974, heralded the beginning of a new economic era in Egypt. The state monopoly on banks was lifted, and the private sector promoted. The mechanisms set in place by the new policies fostered foreign investment as well as the emergence of a nascent class of economic winners comprised of private entrepreneurs and state bureaucrats who sold public assets in exchange for generous kickbacks. Real-estate speculators and agents of foreign capital thrived, while import activities nurtured the rise of a new bourgeoisie of middlemen and compradors. Under Sadat's *infitah* (open-door policy), corruption reached unprecedented heights as "fat cats" turned into "fat cows," according to Mamdouh Salem, Sadat's own prime minister.[33]

Mohammad Hasanein Heikal's hatred of Sadat is well-known, and his book on the Sadat era should be read with this in mind. Still, when Heikal used the epithet *al-Nahb al-Munazzam* (Organized Larceny) to describe the unencumbered cronyism unleashed by Sadat's neoliberal turn, he was hardly exaggerating. The saga of Rashad 'Othman is quite representative in this regard. A migrant worker from Upper Egypt, 'Othman drifted in 1970 to Alexandria, where he made subsistence wages working as a porter. A few years later, 'Othman was a rich man. By 1981, he was a multimillionaire, a National Democratic Party (NDP) leader in Alexandria, and an MP. Eventually, 'Othman was prosecuted, and

[32] Van Dam, *The Struggle for Power in Syria*, 93.
[33] See Bilal Fadl, "Al-Sadat wa-Ma Adraka Ma al-Sadat," part 4, *al-Arabi al-Jadid*, December 30, 2015, www.alaraby.co.uk/opinion/2015/12/30/ما-أدراك-وما-السادات 4-السادات (accessed January 27, 2016).

spent most of the 1980s in jail, his fall triggered by his failure to keep his patrons happy. The very essence of *infitah* meant that Egypt's nouveaux riches could accumulate wealth unhindered, and only a handful of the new caste of businessmen was ever bothered by monitoring agencies.[34] Sadat went as far as terminating the Bureau of Administrative Oversight (Jihaz al-Raqaba al-Idariyya), the very mission of which was to investigate fraudulent practices and misuse of public resources. In effect, Sadat gave a "green light for corruption" in Egypt.[35]

This macroeconomic background structured the financial dimension of civil–military relations under Sadat. It is true, of course, that the Egyptian president "demilitarized" his government. Under Sadat, 17 percent of ministers had a military background between 1971 and 1974, and around 8 percent did between 1974 and 1981. Overall, the ratio of ministers who came from the military throughout Sadat's years in office was close to 12.8 percent.[36] In addition, fewer generals became ambassadors or governors under Sadat than under Nasser. The trend was toward civilianization, especially in the wake of the 1973 war. Yet it would be a mistake to assume that Sadat failed to promote the material interests of the top brass. Indeed, it should be remembered that the seeds of the military's economic empire, which later flourished under Mubarak's long tenure, were planted during Sadat's mandate.

The military's economic involvement gave the Egyptian generals a new public role to play in a time of peace, just when the postwar period was reducing the need for their presence as the nation's bulwark against Israel. The strategic rationale behind the military's economic mission was threefold: (1) Rebranding the armed forces as a major contributor to Egypt's prosperity, and thus deserving the same reverence and special treatment it had enjoyed in wartimes; (2) avoiding the layoff of thousands of officers no longer needed in the military after the signature of the Camp David Accords; and (3) finding new venues for the top brass to pursue their private interests. ʿAbdul-Halim Abu Ghazalah, the last commander of the armed forces appointed under Sadat, masterminded the military's turn toward the economy,[37] but he could not have done so absent the encouragement of Sadat himself.

---

[34] On the Rashad ʿOthman affair and similar incidents under Sadat, see Heikal, *Kharif al-Ghadab*, 328–352.

[35] Imam, *Haqiqat al-Sadat*, 196.

[36] Mark N. Cooper, "The Demilitarization of the Egyptian Cabinet," *International Journal of Middle East Studies* 14, no. 2 (May 1982): 208. See also Sassoon, *Anatomy of Authoritarianism*, 82.

[37] Mohammad al-Baz, *Al-Mushir wa-l-Fariq, al-Malaffat al-Siasiyya li-Tantawi wa-ʿAnnan, Maʿarik al-Ashbah bayna al-Ikhwan wa-l-Jaysh* (Cairo: Kunuz li-l-Tawziʿ wa-l-Nashr, 2014), 25.

In 1975, Egypt established the Arab Organization for Industrialization (AOI). Initially, the aim was to lay the foundation of the Arab military industry, and the AOI quickly invested in rocket, missile, and military vehicle production. Progressively, however, the AOI's activities came to include the manufacture of nonmilitary products, such as railway and metro accessories and plastic and fiberglass elements. In addition, the AOI became involved in a wide range of infrastructure projects, including river water purification and seawater desalination.

In 1979, the state-owned National Services Project Organization (NSPO, or Jihaz al-Khidma al-Wataniyya) was founded. It comprised several commercial enterprises – all producing nonmilitary products, yet all run by retired generals. Supervision over the AOI and NSPO dividends was nominal under the pretext that military finance was a "national security" issue. Unsurprisingly, in an environment kept deliberately loose, crass material games became rife among senior officers, scores of whom reinvented themselves as consultants to foreign capital-seeking opportunities in Egypt or middlemen between the private and public sectors. Sadat had no interest in stemming the tide of profiteering and corruption, because his regime's generosity kept the generals loyal. In addition, the military elite, sullied with illegal activities, became less capable of turning against Sadat, who could take legal action against them if they ceased their devotion to his regime.[38]

Still, not everyone in the armed forces was happy. While the generals were making their way into the rarefied circles of economic power, their subordinates in the officer corps were struggling with spiraling inflation, given their meager and fixed incomes. This, of course, was true of employees in the entire Egyptian public sector.[39] Officers' salaries were not raised consistently with the increased cost of living. A *Financial Times* report noted that a novice secretary working for a foreign company in Egypt made more money than a military colonel.[40] Simply put, the new-found money at the top did not trickle down – nor could it have. In the second half of the 1970s, an increasing number of young officers resigned from their jobs in the military to seek employment in the private sector. Between 1974 and 1978, fifty officers and scores of soldiers left the armed forces to sell their services abroad as armed mercenaries in international security companies. The number of yearly applicants to the

---

[38] Waterbury, *The Egypt of Nasser and Sadat*, 349.
[39] Curtis R. Ryan, "Political Strategies and Regime Survival in Egypt," *Journal of Third World Studies* 18, no. 2 (Fall 2011): 25–46.
[40] Charles Richards, "Defense Forces Seek a Role," *Financial Times*, June 7, 1982, quoted in Ahmed 'Abdalla, ed., *Al-Jaysh wa-l-Dimoqratiyya fi Masr* (Cairo: Sina li-l-Nashr, 1990), 67.

military academy dropped by 16.5 percent; and soldiers were illegally selling state-owned arms to the highest bidder.[41] The generational divide line in the officer corps was stark under the monarchy and somewhat less pronounced under Nasser. During Sadat's last years, the friction between the top brass and the younger officers was again a hallmark of military affairs in Egypt.

Counterbalancing

As previously mentioned, Nasser counted increasingly upon the ASU – especially the Vanguard – to countervail the military in the sixties. Under Sadat, the Vanguard was dissolved and the ASU restructured to allow for multipartism.[42] The transitional Party of Egypt (Hizb Masr) was founded to defend Sadat's politics, but it was soon replaced by the National Democratic Party (NDP, or al-Hizb al-Watani al-Dimoqrati) in 1977. The Vanguard's 150,000 operatives simply shifted their loyalties to the new ruling party. Their experience in intelligence-gathering was needed, because the NDP's main tasks under Sadat (collecting information, writing reports, and counterweighting the armed forces) did not differ from Nasser's ASU.[43] To be sure, the NDP aspired to become a genuine mass party. Sadat himself hoped that the NDP would reach different sectors of Egyptian society, including the lower strata, and provide his regime with organized popular support. Thousands did flock to the ruling party to benefit from the regime's clientelistic practices. Beyond self-centered considerations, however, the political commitment of the party's adherents was always questionable. The NDP's lackluster performance during the 2011 popular mobilizations only confirmed suspicions first expressed decades earlier.[44]

Significantly, it was during Sadat's tenure that a police officer, Mamduh Salem, was appointed prime minister for the first time in Egypt. A Sadat loyalist, Salem served as minister of interior in 1971 and deputy prime minister in 1972, and then headed the government five times between 1975 and 1978. Salem also presided over the pro-Sadat party, Hizb Masr, before his eclipse at the end of the 1970s. Equally noteworthy is the fact that all three of the ministers Sadat appointed to

---

[41] Shukri, *Al-Thawra al-Mudada*, 450.
[42] By the end of the 1970s, the ASU was defunct.
[43] Kandil, *Soldiers, Spies, and Statesmen*, 158–168. See also Raymond A. Hinnebusch, "Egypt under Sadat: Elite, Power Structure, and Political Change in a Post-populist State," *Social Problems* 28, no. 4 (April 1981): 459–460.
[44] Ehud Ya'ari, "Sadat's Pyramid of Power," *The Jerusalem Quarterly* 14 (Winter 1980): 121.

head the ministry of interior –Salem, Assayed Fahmi, and al-Nabawi Isma'il – hailed from the police. This practice, which stands in stark contrast to Nasser's habit of appointing military officers to the same position, has endured since then.[45]

Isma'il was a particularly forceful figure. One specific incident reveals the influence he enjoyed under Sadat, and, by extension, the newfound prominence of the interior ministry. Sadat had decided to create the NDP to replace Hizb Masr without actually dissolving the latter; however, when its MPs gathered in the parliament to deliberate on whether or not to shift their loyalties to the new party, Isma'il stormed into their meeting and ordered them to join the NDP immediately. And when some MPs opined that they preferred to wait at least until they had read the NDP's program, Isma'il retorted that Sadat's party did not need a program, since the president was already putting his ideas into practice. Finally, when Salem resigned from Hizb Masr and his supporters planned a demonstration to ask him to remain party leader, Isma'il simply prevented them from doing so.[46]

Under Sadat, the staunchly loyalist ministry of interior became a center of power like never before. It is significant that when some Third Army contingents protested against Sadat's conciliatory policy and ceasefire agreement in 1974, the ministry of interior sent police forces to contain them, and fighting erupted between soldiers and policemen.[47] It is also important to note that Sadat's own aide-de-camp, Major General Fawzi 'Abdul-Hafez, hailed from the police, not the armed forces. To be sure, the police apparatus was already a partner in the ruling elite under Nasser, but the spectacular empowerment of the ministry of interior, which later culminated under Mubarak, goes back unquestionably to the Sadat presidency. Table 3.2 lists police officers appointed governor under Nasser and Sadat.

The financial resources made available for exponential growth of the ministry of interior stood as yet another sign of presidential favor. In the mid-1970s, an anti-terrorist brigade was added to the SSIS.[48] And later on, the police founded its own special forces, modeled along the military's al-Sa'iqa.[49] The Central Security Forces were equipped with armored vehicles, which they had originally lacked, and embarked upon a massive recruitment program. By 1977, they had ballooned to 300,000, three times their size in the early 1970s. 1977 was, in fact, a crucible year for the Sadat regime. Massive bread riots triggered by the termination of state

---

[45] The appointment of police Major General 'Abdel-'Azim Fahmi as interior minister under Nasser was the exception that confirmed the rule.
[46] Fawzi, *Al-Nabawi Isma'il*, 23–35.   [47] Dekmejian, "Egypt and Turkey," 37.
[48] 'Allam, *Al-Ikhwan wa-Ana*, 285.   [49] Fawzi, *Al-Nabawi Isma'il*, 136.

Table 3.2 *Police officers appointed governors under Nasser and Sadat*[50]

Name of police officers appointed governor under Nasser (1952–1970)	Year of appointment/governorate	Name of police officers appointed governor under Sadat (1970–1981)	Year of appointment/governorate
(1) Sadiq 'Abdul-Latif	1960 (Alexandria)	(1) Mustafa 'Alwani Karim	1971 (Manufiyya)
(2) Mahmud Tal'at	1960 (Suez)	(2) Hussein Kamel Mustafa	1971 (Manufiyya)
(3) 'Abdul-Ra'uf 'Asem	1960 (Qina)	(3) Hussein Rihani	1971 (Kafr al-Sheikh)
(4) 'Abdul-'Aziz 'Ali	1960 (Sharqia)	(4) Mohammad Ahmad al-Minyawi	1972 (Dumiat)
(5) 'Abdul-Hafiz Abu Ghanima	1960 (Qaliubiyya)	(5) Shafiq 'Ismat	1973 (Bani Sweif)
(6) Mohammad Hasan Khurshid	1960 (Suhaj)	(6) 'Abdul-Halim Hatata	1974 (Buheira)
(7) 'Abdul-Hamid Khayrat	1961 (Suhaj)	(7) Mahmud Younes al-Ansari	1974 (Aswan)
(8) 'Abdullah Ghabara	1961 (Qina)	(8) 'Abdul-Hafiz Bajuri	1976 (Qina)
(9) 'Abdul-Salam Khafaji	1962 (Sharqiyya)	(9) Kamal Kheirallah	1976 (Suhaj)
(10) Yussef Hafez	1964 (Manufiyya)	(10) Husni Taha Najib	1977 (Suhaj)
(11) Mohammad Sayf al-Yazal	1964 (Suez)	(11) Sa'd al-Sharbini	1978 (Buheira)
(12) Ahmad Mohammad 'Ali	1964 (Gharbiyya)	(12) Mohammad Fathalla Saleme	1978 (Kafr al-Sheikh)
(13) Hasan Kamel Mohammad	1965 (Manufiyya)	(13) Mohammad Amine Mitiks	1979 (Sharqiyya)
(14) Mamduh Salem	1967 (Asyut)	(14) Kamal al-Hadidi	1980 (Minia)
(15) Hasan Rushdi Ibrahim	1967 (Port Said)	(15) Tharwat 'Atallah	1980 (Suhaj)
(16) Mahmud al-Siba'i	1968 (Qaliubiyya)	(16) Mohammad Salahiddin Ibrahim	1981 (Minia)
(17) Salah Mujahed	1968 (Dumiat)		

[50] Mohammad al-Gawadi, *Qadat al-Shurta al-Masriyya, 1952–2002: Dirasa Tahliliyya wa-Mawsu'at Shakhsiyyat* (Cairo: Madbuli, 2003), 681–697.

subsidies on basic foodstuffs engulfed Egypt on January 18 and 19 of that year. The ministry of interior was overwhelmed by the size of the protests, and Sadat reluctantly asked the armed forces to reestablish public order. The military leadership agreed to help, but only after the government had rescinded its policy. A barrage of announcements that Sadat had reinstituted state subsidies was aired while the armed forces were deploying. The top brass were not certain their subordinates in the military hierarchy would comply if ordered to open fire on civilians, because they, too, were suffering from Egypt's economic circumstances. Thus, the generals hoped to diffuse the situation and avoid, to the greatest extent possible, pitting their troops against unarmed demonstrators.[51] Eventually, the tide of protests subsided, but the regime had suffered a major blow. Sadat had worried that the military could stage a coup after its units deployed in the streets of Cairo, and instructed the police to monitor the troops.[52] After his generals saved the day, it became clear to the president that strengthening the police was obligatory – not just to counterbalance the armed forces, but also to reduce the regime's dependency on them.[53] Sadat pledged to crush similar uprisings with brutal force in the future. His were no idle threats: the president asked the US to provide the Egyptian police with the training and weaponry for riot control, and his request was received positively.[54]

Divide-and-Rule Tactics

A constant turnover in the commandership of the armed forces was a hallmark of the Sadat presidency, as shown in Table 3.3.

The first war ministers under Sadat, Fawzi and Sadeq, were sacked over profound strategic divergences with the president. Fawzi favored restarting the war of attrition that Nasser had waged on Israel between 1967 and 1970, but Sadat opposed the idea emphatically, and argued that Egyptian defenses were incapable of stopping Israeli retaliatory raids on the interior, namely, Upper Egypt.[55] As the relationship between Sadat and his war minister deteriorated, Fawzi accused Sadat of selling out to

---

[51] Heikal, *Kharif al-Ghadab*, 189.   [52] Kandil, *Soldiers, Spies, and Statesmen*, 169.

[53] Al-Nabawi Isma'il argued, in this regard, that while it was business as usual for the police to face civilians, calling on the armed forces to intervene in internal security affairs signaled weakness – hence the plan to reinforce the police, with which he was engaged. See Fawzi, *al-Nabawi Isma'il*, 137–138.

[54] Hasan Abu Basha, *Fi al-Amn wa-l-Siasa, Mudhakkarat Hasan Abu Basha* (Cairo: Dar al-Hilal, 1990), 22; and Kandil, *Soldiers, Spies, and Statesmen*, 170.

[55] 'Amr Yossef, "Sadat as Supreme Commander," *The Journal of Strategic Studies* 37, no. 4 (2014): 532–555.

Table 3.3 *Reshuffling of military commandership under Sadat*

	War minister	Tenure
(1)	Mohammad Fawzi	1970–1971
(2)	Mohammad Sadeq	1971–1972
(3)	Ahmed Isma'il[56]	1972–1974
(4)	'Abdul-Ghani al-Gamasy	1974–1978
(5)	Kamal Hassan 'Ali	1978–1980
(6)	Ahmad Badawi[57]	1980–1981
(7)	'Abdul-Halim Abu Ghazala	1981

the Americans and betraying Nasser's legacy.[58] Shortly after Fawzi's downfall, Sadeq's relations with Sadat soured, because he, too, opposed the president's military strategy for the next round with Israel. Sadat advocated a limited war despite (or, perhaps, because of) Israel's military superiority, whereas his new war minister, Sadeq, rejected engaging the Israelis in a restricted conflict. This, he warned, might lead to the destruction of the armed forces. Sadeq favored postponing the war with Israel until the Egyptian military became ready to wage total combat intended to liberate Egypt's occupied territories.[59] Sadat opposed immobilism, however, because he was aware of its domestic political consequences; and also because he was banking on a negotiated settlement under American patronage after the war. The quarrel between the two men became bitter, and Sadat blamed Sadeq for failing to prepare the armed forces for battle.[60] In addition to divergence over strategy, Sadeq's popularity in military ranks did not endear him to Sadat; nor did reports fed to him by the General Intelligence Service (GIS) boss Ahmed Isma'il, claiming that despite Sadeq's public criticism of the Soviets, the Russians were in fact grooming the war minister to become president.[61]

While these frictions hastened the disgrace of Sadeq and Fawzi before him, later events suggest in retrospect that compliance would not have saved them, anyway. Think of general 'Abdul-Ghani al-Gamasy, whom Sadat appointed war minister in 1974, as a case in point. To be

---

[56] Ahmed Isma'il died of cancer in December 1974.
[57] Ahmad Badawi died in a helicopter crash along with thirteen senior officers in March 1981. It has been argued that Badawi was preparing a coup, and that Sadat and Mubarak were behind the tragic accident that cost Badawi and the other generals their lives.
[58] al-Gawadi, *Mudhakkarat*, 307. See also Heikal, *Kharif al-Ghadab*, 104.
[59] Huweidi, *Al-Foras al-Da'i'a*, 321–324.
[60] al-Sadat, *Al-Bahth 'an al-Dhat*, 247–249. See also Heikal, *Kharif al-Ghadab*, 114.
[61] Sirrs, *The Egyptian Intelligence Service*, 126.

sure, al-Gamasy, too, harbored deep misgivings about Sadat's strategic decision-making. In his memoirs, al-Gamasy notes bitterly that the 1973 correspondence between Sadat and Henry Kissinger revealed Egyptian military secrets to the United States, and, by extension, Israel, while the Egyptian armed forces were still battling the Israelis in Sinai. Moreover, he wrote that Sadat's interference in military operational planning had detrimental effects on the Egyptian armed forces' performance during the 1973 war. Finally, he was horrified by Sadat's concessions pertaining to Egyptian deployment and military presence in Sinai, to which the latter had agreed in order to secure a peace deal with Israel following the war.[62] However, for all his reservations, al-Gamasy never challenged Sadat, and dutifully executed whatever orders the president issued. He wrote explicitly that while the top brass have a right to express their opinions candidly on military and strategic affairs, it is their duty to obey the orders of the president, even when he decides to ignore their advice.[63] In this regard, al-Gamasy represented the prototype of the military professional who understands and accepts the principle of civilian supremacy and control of the armed forces. Yet he was sacked, along with his chief of staff, Muhammad ʿAli Fahmi, in 1978.

The next war minister, Kamal Hassan ʿAli, was far more a Sadat loyalist than al-Gamasy. Still, ʿAli was reassigned to the state department only two years after Sadat appointed him. Significantly, he notes in his memoirs that Sadat gave him no reason for his transfer to the state department, other than stating that two years as war minister were enough ("kifaya kida ʿaleik wizarit al-difa").[64] This means that while divergence with the president hastened turnover, obedient loyalty did not prevent it. The only war minister under Sadat who was spared the president's reshuffling practices was Ahmed Ismaʿil, and there was good reason for this. As mentioned previously, Ismaʿil was terminally ill with cancer, and Sadat admitted publicly in 1977 that he was privy to Ismaʿil's health condition when he appointed him war minister in 1972.[65] Sadat, then, didn't need to worry about the dying general, who passed away in 1974. In sum, Sadat wanted full control over the armed forces, and the quick turnover meant that no war minister spent enough time at the apex of the military hierarchy to cultivate a large power base, as ʿAmer had done under Nasser. As an additional perk, rapid reshuffling meant that the commandership of the armed forces was frequently up for grabs, and the permanent race to the top pitted ambitious generals against one another to play into Sadat's divide-and-rule tactics.

---

[62] al-Gamasy, *Mudhakkarat*, 350 and 391; see also 500–501.   [63] Ibid., 421.
[64] ʿAli, *Mashawir al-ʿOmr*, 441.   [65] al-Shazli, *Harb October*, 229.

Coups under Mubarak

Hosni Mubarak was sitting beside Sadat when the latter was assassinated, and he was hurried away from the scene, wondering whether a coup was unfolding. This meant that the early hours of Mubarak's ascent to power as president were already marked by worries about military loyalty. The regime quickly imposed a state of emergency, and blocked Suez roads to inhibit potential coup-plotters from entering Cairo. The SSIS and the Republican Guard were very active in securing major cities. Foreign observers noted the absence of military detachments in the streets of the Egyptian capital, which signaled a lack of trust in the armed forces.[66] Notwithstanding the talk about the EAF's alleged eclipse after the 1973 war, they still maintained the capacity to topple the government, had they harbored the will to do so. Consequently, the military was Mubarak's "key worry" as he tried to consolidate power and hundreds were dismissed from service to purge the ranks of suspected radical elements.[67] To be sure, coup attempts turned out to be less frequent – and civil–military relations comparatively less tumultuous – under Mubarak than under his predecessors. However, not unlike Egyptian presidents before him, Mubarak faced military-based conspiracies. 'Ali al-Raggal argues correctly in this regard that the EAF remained "a source of permanent threat" throughout Mubarak's tenure. Thus, effective coup-proofing conditioned the political survival of Mubarak, just as it had structured Nasser's and Sadat's.[68]

In 1986, mid-ranking and junior officers plotted to topple Mubarak's regime. They, too, had links with Islamists, and the affair showed again the capacity and willingness of religious extremists to infiltrate the armed forces in the lower echelons of the officer corps. MI uncovered the

[66] Sirrs, *The Egyptian Intelligence Service*, 150–151.
[67] Ahmed S. Hashim, "The Egyptian Military, Part Two: From Mubarak Onward," *Middle East Policy Council* 18, no. 4 (Winter 2011): 106, www.mepc.org/egyptian-military-part-two-mubarak-onward (accessed March 3, 2015). See also Joseph Kechichian and Jeanne Nazimek, "Challenges to the Military in Egypt," *Middle East Policy Council* 5, no. 3 (September 1997), www.mepc.org/challenges-military-egypt (accessed July 12, 2017).
[68] 'Ali al-Raggal, "Al-Tawari' ka-Qanun wa-Ideologia li-l-Hokm fi 'Asr Mubarak," *Al-Safir*, June 2, 2016, http://arabi.assafir.com/Article/25/4984 (accessed June 2, 2016). Note, on the other hand, Mubarak also faced several assassination attempts, the most dangerous of which happened in Addis Ababa in June 1995. The alertness of his security team from the Republican Guard (RG) saved Mubarak's life, which probably contributed to the rise in prominence of the RG under his rule. See the interview with Mubarak's personal bodyguard, Major General Ra'fat al-Hujeiri, published by the Egyptian daily *al-Wafd*, August 7, 2014, 'Al-Liwa Ra'fat al-Hujeiri: Mubarak Naja min 6 Muhwalat Ightial ... Wa Wafat Hafidihi Qadat 'Alayh', https://alwafd.news/720314/حوارات-وملفات (اللواء-رأفت-الحجيري-مبارك-نجا-من-6-محاولات-اغتيال-ووفاة-حفيده-قضت-علي ه-) (accessed August 9, 2015).

attempt and foiled it, but the intrigue showed that unrest was still brewing among young officers.[69] Mubarak's rivalry with his war minister, Field Marshal ʿAbdul-Halim Abu Ghazalah, heightened the threat of military interventionism throughout the 1980s. Sadat appointed Abu Ghazalah as his war minister in March 1981, and Mubarak kept him. The two men had, until then, been personal friends and allies. Mubarak soon became apprehensive of Abu Ghazalah's clout in the armed forces, however, and offered him the vice presidency in exchange for his resignation from the military – a bargain the field marshal turned down.[70] In February 1986, when rumors of military service extension triggered violent riots among Central Security Forces (CSF) conscripts in Cairo, Mubarak was originally reluctant to ask the armed forces to quell the mutiny, lest a coup follow military deployment in the streets of the capital. Eventually the armed forces crushed the CSF revolt but Mubarak's fears were not unfounded. The memoirs of Kamal al-Genzuri, Egypt's former prime minister, reveal that senior officers surrounding Abu Ghazalah did, indeed, incite him to overthrow Mubarak ("*khallasna menno*").[71] Abu Ghazalah chose to keep Mubarak in power, but the latter removed him from office in 1989.[72]

The appointment of Yussef Sabri Abu Taleb as war minister for a brief interlude, followed by Hussein Tantawi in 1991, eased the relationship between the president and the commandership of the armed forces. Both Abu Taleb and Tantawi were uncharismatic officers and staunch Mubarak loyalists. Quiescence at the top, however, did not necessarily mean that the threat of military interventionism vanished. First, Abu Ghazalah maintained a faithful military following, especially among generals who owed him their promotions. These officers, in turn, had allies and friends in the armed forces, and the threat of a pro-Abu Ghazalah movement in the EAF lingered for years after the field marshal had been removed from office.[73] Second, in 1993, another young officers' coup was thwarted. Major

---

[69] Hashim, "The Egyptian Military, Part Two," 107.

[70] Robert Springborg, *Mubarak's Egypt: Fragmentation of the Political Order* (Boulder, CO: Westview, 1989), 100–102. For more on Abu Ghazalah, see Zeinab Abul-Magd, "Zaman al-Thamaninat al-Jamil: Ayyam Abu Ghazalah," *Al-Manassa*, December 30, 2015, https://almanassa.com/ar/story/664 (accessed January 9, 2016); Amira Fikri, *Al-Mushir Mohammad ʿAbdul-Halim Abu Ghazalah, Masirat Hayat* (Cairo: Dar al-Jumhuriyya, 2010); and Mohammad al-Baz, *Al Mushir, Qissat Suʿud wa-Inhiar Abu Ghazalah* (Cairo: Kunuz li-l-Tawziʿ wa-l-Nashr, 2007).

[71] Interview with Kamal al-Ganzuri, *Al-Mugaz*, December 15, 2013, http://almogaz.com /news/politics/2013/12/15/1234680 (accessed December 15, 2013).

[72] Abu Ghazalah had, by then, lost Washington's favor over his involvement in an unsuccessful scheme to smuggle complex missile parts from America to Egypt.

[73] Cassandra, "The Impending Crisis in Egypt," *Middle East Journal* 49, no. 1 (Winter 1995): 23.

Hisham Ahmed Selim had studied closely the 1952 Free Officers takeover, and headed a small group of military and civilian Islamists bent on overthrowing the regime and killing Mubarak. This time, it was the SSIS that infiltrated the conspirators and botched their scheme.[74] In a trial of Islamists that same year, five military personnel recruited by the jihadi "Vanguards of Islam" stood accused.[75] The attempts by Islamists to infiltrate the armed forces were systematic and deliberate. A central tenet of Ayman al-Zawahiri's al-Jihad doctrine was to trigger regime change and create a new Islamist order in Egypt via a military-led putsch.[76]

Unlike Nasser and Sadat, Mubarak had no great mission to entrust to the military. Redistributive radicalism at home and militant anti-imperialism abroad had been abandoned, and Sinai was liberated under his predecessor. Egypt's ostracism in the Arab world eventually ended, and the Arab League moved back to its headquarters in Cairo. However, the latter jettisoned the leadership ambitions of old. In the words of an observer of Egyptian politics:

While Mubarak disposes of the state power he inherited from Gamal Abdul Nasser and Anwar al-Sadat, he can neither claim the legacy of either man, nor claim to be the progenitor of a new "ism."[77]

To be sure, Egyptian nationalism had long structured the discourse of the military. The Mubarak regime was unable to reverse Egypt's unambiguous regional decline, however, and was thus hardly a symbol of Egyptian pride. Mubarak joined the American-led coalition against Iraq in 1991, supported the American invasion of that country in 2003, and was on Israel's side in its 2006 war with Hezbollah. None of this endeared Mubarak to Egyptian public opinion. In addition, his regime was mired by persistent corruption rumors, which were particularly detrimental. Widespread stories of lucrative commissions diverted to the country's first family damaged Mubarak's early image of personal integrity, and prevented him from standing credibly as a patriotic leader dedicated to the welfare of his impoverished people. Thus, the regime's nationalist credentials were deeply tarnished.

Nor was there an alternative set of beliefs shaping the worldview of Egyptian soldiers. Turkish officers operated for a long time as defenders

---

[74] See "Asrar Awwal Inqilab 'Askari 'ala Mubarak," *Donya al-Watan,* September 1, 2012, www.alwatanvoice.com/arabic/news/2012/09/01/313210.html (accessed May 16, 2017).
[75] Hashim, "The Egyptian Military, Part Two," 111.
[76] Sirrs, *The Egyptian Intelligence Service,* 163.
[77] Cassandra, "The Impending Crisis," 10. See also Samer Soliman, "The Political Economy of Mubarak's Fall," in *Arab Spring in Egypt: Revolution and Beyond,* ed. Bahgat Korany and Rabab El-Mahdi (Cairo: The American University in Cairo Press, 2014), 59.

of secularism. In Iran, the Islamic Revolutionary Guard Corps (IRGC) is committed to a mixture of fundamentalist Islam and nationalist power projection. Despite specific cases of radical infiltration, the Egyptian officers are not Islamists. Women wearing the full veil, or niqab, were denied entry into military clubs, and loathing of the Muslim Brotherhood runs very deep in the officer corps – especially within its higher echelons. According to an Egyptian journalist close to the Supreme Council of the Armed Forces (SCAF), military officers "[do] not consider the Brothers to be Egyptians at all (*"mush masriyyin"*).[78]*Majallat al-Nasr*, the armed forces magazine, ran several articles in the 1990s pertaining to religious extremism and how to fight it. For instance, *al-Nasr* published in January 1993 the minutes of a meeting between Lieutenant General Salih Halbi and military personnel, whom he urged not to be fooled by Islamist propaganda. Halbi maintained that "terrorist," not "fundamentalist," was the accurate word to designate Islamist activists whose attacks on innocents falsified the meaning of Islam.[79] In 2004, even as the military elite gave public support to the Mubarak regime's economic orientations, they warned that the social repercussions of neoliberalism and the woes of ordinary Egyptians could provide a political opening from which the Muslim Brotherhood would benefit.[80] In this regard, at least, the generals were in full harmony with their president. Mubarak was almost as personally hostile to the Muslim Brotherhood as Nasser was in his day, and he endorsed officers known for their anti-Islamist zeal. Sami ʿAnan, whom Mubarak promoted to EAF chief of staff in 2005, reportedly came to the attention of the former president because of his diligence in fighting religious radicals.[81]

And still, the officers aren't secularists, either. Abu Ghazalah stressed repeatedly in the 1980s the Quranic roots of Egypt's military strategy. Ahmed ʿAbdullah noted, in this regard, that the military elite under Abu Ghazalah dedicated considerable time and effort to bolster their Islamic credentials.[82] This orientation endured beyond the latter's tenure as commander of the armed forces. For instance, Tantawi urged his soldiers in 2007 to emulate the Prophet Muhammad and take him as a role model for their lives.[83] *Al-Nasr* relayed a similar message, and occasionally featured articles expressing pride in the Prophet's victorious battles and military prowess. Verses from the Quran adorn the first pages of officers' theses and instructors' reports at the Nasser Military Academy

---

[78] Hicham Bou Nassif, "Coups and Nascent Democracies: The Military and Egypt's Failed Consolidation," *Democratization* 24, no. 1 (January 2017): 8.

[79] Sassoon, *Anatomy of Authoritarianism*, 99.   [80] Cook, *Ruling but Not Governing*, 81.

[81] al-Baz, *Al-Mushir*, 50.   [82] ʿAbdalla, ed., *Al-Jaysh wa-l-Dimoqratiyya*, 27.

[83] See Egyptian newspapers on December 7, 2007.

in Cairo.[84] Today, an increasing number of officers' wives wear the Islamic veil, including Egypt's current first lady. Egyptian officers are thus committed neither to Islamism nor to secularism; and nor are they dedicated to socialism or neoliberalism. Ideationally, they are "neutral,"[85] and, indeed, "emasculated."[86] And while the officers still look uneasily upon Israel's military might and train to fight the Hebrew state – the Badr-96 exercises in 1996 named Israel specifically as a target – the Camp David Accords ushered in an era of unbroken peace, and war with Israel has not lurked on the horizon for decades. Not even the Israeli invasion of Lebanon in 1982, the outbreak of several Palestinian intifadas as of 1987, or the rise to power of Israel's arch-hawk Ariel Sharon in 2001 threatened the cooperation between the two countries. Simply put, Mubarak did not develop any link binding the military as a whole to his rule via shared ideological commitments.[87]

Nor, for that matter, did Mubarak resort to Sadat-style divide-and-rule tactics or permanent reshuffling of senior officers. Mubarak's presidential tenure was three times as long as Sadat's, and yet both appointed seven generals as chief of staff. Officers promoted to chief of staff spent, on average, less than two years in their position under Sadat, and twice as long under Mubarak.[88] The latter's war ministers also held long tenures. Abu Ghazalah remained commander of the armed forces for eight years, between 1981 and 1989. And while his successor, Abu Taleb, kept his position for only two years, Mubarak's third war minister, appointed in 1991, was his last: Tantawi's tenure as commander of the military stretched for more than two decades.

Coup-Proofing under Mubarak

To coup-proof his regime, Mubarak counted essentially upon promoting the interests of the military elite and counterbalancing.

[84] Personal observation by the author during a visit to Nasser Higher Military Academy in Cairo, July 2012.

[85] Zeinab Abul-Magd, "The Egyptian Republic of Retired Generals," *Foreign Policy*, May 8, 2012, http://foreignpolicy.com/2012/05/08/the-egyptian-republic-of-retired-generals (accessed May 12, 2017). See also Yezid Sayigh, "Above the State: The Officers' Republic in Egypt," Carnegie Middle East Center, August 1, 2012, http://carnegie-mec.org/2012/08/01/above-state-officers-republic-in-egypt-pub-48972 (accessed November 22, 2017).

[86] Hashim, "The Egyptian Military, Part Two," 121.

[87] Sayigh, "Above the State." See also Hashim, "The Egyptian Military, Part Two," 121; and Springborg, *Mubarak's Egypt*, 40.

[88] See Kirk S. Campbell, "Civil–Military Relations and Political Liberalization: A Comparative Study of the Military's Corporateness and Political Values in Egypt, Syria, Turkey, and Pakistan" (PhD diss., George Washington University, 2009), 123.

Promoting the Material Interests of the Military Elite

Mubarak's years in power were extremely good for his generals, who benefitted from the expansion of military-controlled business enterprises. The major military bodies engaged in economic activities under Mubarak were the ministry of military production, the Arab Organization for Industrialization (AOI), and the National Service Projects Organization (NSPO). Together, they form what Robert Springborg labeled "Military, Inc."[89] Some scholars have argued that the military controlled 25 to 40 percent of the Egyptian economy under Mubarak, which is an exaggeration.[90] A former minister of trade, Rashid Mohammad Rashid, gauged the size of the military economy at "less than 10 percent."[91] In an interview in Cairo, prominent Egyptian economist Ahmad Sayyid al-Naggar maintained that the military controls less than 5 percent of the economy. Later, al-Naggar suggested that the military's share of the GDP did not exceed 1.8 percent.[92] Because the generals jealously shroud their economic affairs in secrecy, speculations pertaining to the exact size of their business remain inconclusive. And yet even if the lowest estimations were accurate, that would still mean that hundreds of millions of dollars circulate within the military economy, unmonitored by the parliament or public civilian agencies. The official alibis for the military's business involvement range from securing financial self-sufficiency as defense budgets decline, to channeling surplus goods to local markets. They also include cultivating a modern industrial base that fosters development in Egypt and putting the alleged dexterity of officers as economic managers to use. An obvious aim, however, remains unstated: securing personal enrichment for senior officers, and, by extension, their political loyalty to the powers that be.

---

[89] See Nadine Marroushi, "US Expert: Leadership of 'Military Inc.' Is Running Egypt," *Egypt Independent*, October 26, 2011, www.egyptindependent.com/us-expert-leadership -military-inc-running-egypt (accessed July 22, 2017).

[90] Nimrod Raphaeli, "Egyptian Army's Pervasive Role in National Economy," The Middle East Media Research Institute, Inquiry and Analysis Series no. 1001, July 29, 2013, www .memri.org/reports/egyptian-armys-pervasive-role-national-economy (accessed April 5, 2015).

[91] See David D. Kirkpatrick, "Egyptians Say Military Discourages an Open Economy," *The New York Times*, February 17, 2011, www.nytimes.com/2011/02/18/world/middleeast/ 18military.html (accessed January 8, 2016).

[92] Interview with Ahmad Sayyid al-Naggar (June 18, 2012), Cairo. See also Ahmad Sayyid al-Naggar, "Iqtisad al-Jaysh bayna al-Tahwil wa-Mantiq Tafkik al-Dawla," *Al-Ahram*, April 12, 2012, www.ahram.org.eg/Archive/866/2012/4/11/4/142891.aspx (accessed June 10, 2015); and Ahmad Sayyid al-Naggar, "Madha Yurid al-Gharb min Iqtisad al-Jaysh al-Masri," *Dunia al-Watan*, October 10, 2013, https://pulpit.alwatanvoice.com/c ontent/print/308621.html (accessed November 27, 2015).

Mubarak's economic liberalization drive provided his top brass with an opportunity to develop their business ventures. Privatized state companies were for sale, and the military appropriated them. For instance, the AOI bought Egypt's only wagons manufacturing plant in 2004. A year later, the AOI signed an agreement with Japan's Mitsubishi to produce metro and tram wagons, and eventually invited Mitsubishi to develop metro lines in Greater Cairo. "Military, Inc." was also involved in the auto industry. The armed forces signaled their interest in acquiring the state-owned El-Nasr Automotive Manufacturing Company (NASCO) in 2010, and they did so three years later. Combined with the military-owned Arab American Vehicles (AAV), NASCO positioned the military to sign deals with international carmakers – including Chrysler, Hyundai, Wrangler, Cherokee, Toyota, and others – to assemble new car models in Egyptian plants and sell them locally. As of 2003, the military had expanded into maritime and river transport companies, and appropriated the Egyptian Company for Ship Repairs and Building, Alexandria Shipyard, as well as the Nile Company for River Transport. The latter evolved into a colossal owner of riverine lands and ports along the Nile. Among other facilities, the company owns the Aswan port, which is critical for trade between Egypt and Sudan. The military also operates in strategic sectors, such as steelmaking and cement. The Mubarak regime provided the resources needed to modernize the military-owned Abu Za'bal Company for Engineering Industry and several giant steel-makers, including the German SMS Siemag, which partnered with the Egyptian top brass to develop this venture. The Abu Za'bal Company generated huge profits for the military from Egypt's expanding construction market. The same was true of the 'Arish Cement Factory in North Sinai, established in 2010 in partnership with a Chinese company.[93] In addition, the military has built and operates toll highways, bridges, and ports. It owns and manages mines and quarries, chic hotels, wedding halls, social clubs, and sporting arenas. Other fields of military economic activity include real-estate ventures and housing projects, food, dairies, medical and electrical production, water management, and land reclamation projects. Through Queen Service, which is part of the NSPO, the military is also active in the thriving field of private security companies. In the words of Zeinab Abul-Magd, military business is "everywhere."[94]

The military's control of public land has been particularly profitable in terms of rent extraction. Egypt is a populous country, its inhabitants

---

[93] Zeinab Abul-Magd, *Militarizing the Nation: The Army, Business, and Revolution in Egypt* (New York: Columbia University Press, 2017), 127–133.
[94] Ibid., 151.

dwelling mainly in the overcrowded Nile Valley. The congested settlements need to expand east and west toward the desert, which makes public land a precious resource. Consequently, the allocation and management of land is a critical prerogative. The military benefits, in this regard, from dual leeway: (1) The ministry of defense determines which land will remain under exclusive military control due to security-related considerations, and (2) the ministry of defense has the right to open land previously controlled by the military to the private sector or civilian state agencies. In other words, the military can alter the labeling of Egypt's public land, which forms 94 percent of its national territory. Irrepressible urban expansion toward the desert is a boon for the military, and so are the multiple investment opportunities in the immense tracts of land around the Nile. The Armed Forces Land Projects Organization (AFLPO), which Mubarak established by presidential decree in 1982, handles the sale of military-owned land and manages the subsequent returns.[95]

The reasons for the rapid expansion of the military's economic sphere are twofold. First, Mubarak's support has been unwavering, and profitable government contracts have been easy to win. Add to this generous tax breaks and cheap labor provided by conscripts-turned-slave workers, and it becomes easy to understand why private entrepreneurs in Egypt bemoan unfair competition stemming from the state's preferential treatment of military business. Second, foreign investors and giant international corporations, in particular, favor partnerships with the EAF over other local economic players, because they understand that the military's political clout translates into business advantages. On the one hand, the military can deal efficiently with bureaucratic hurdles, if necessary, by ignoring them altogether. On the other, it has the physical capacity to protect its investment sites during times of political turbulence. Finally, workers operating in the military's economic sphere are not unionized, and are less likely to mobilize against draconian labor conditions. If they do, the Military Police (MP) intervene to disperse them. In addition, the ministry of military production managing the EAF's economic sphere is "awash with cash," and politically well-connected. All of these conditions make the military a perfect business partner for global corporations.[96] Particularly salient in the last years under Mubarak was the deepening

---

[95] 'Abdul-Fattah Barayez, "This Land Is Their Land: Egypt's Military and the Economy," *Jadaliyya*, January 25, 2016, www.jadaliyya.com/pages/index/23671/%E 2%80%9Cthis-land-is-their-land%E2%80%9D_egypt%E2%80%99s-military-and-t he (accessed January 28, 2017). See also Hillel Frisch, "Guns and Butter in the Egyptian Army," *Middle East Review of International Affairs* 5, no. 2 (Summer 2001): 8.

[96] Raphaeli, "Egyptian Army's Pervasive Role."

partnership between "Military, Inc." and Gulf capital. The oil boom in the 2000s provided Gulf conglomerates with a stream of cash flow readily transferable into Foreign Direct Investment (FDI). Egypt was an appealing destination for several reasons, including economic liberalization, geographical proximity, political stability, and an abundance of cheap labor. The Kuwaiti group Kharafi partnered with the military to launch the Arab Company for Computer Manufacturing, which produces 750,000 computers per year. Other joint ventures between the group and the military include the International Pipe Industry Company, which serves the regional hydrocarbons industry, and the Maxalto project, which channels German technology into the manufacture of smart cards. Capital from the UAE and Kuwait has also flowed to the Suez Canal Development Project, with the goal of expanding port capacity. The military is heavily involved.[97]

The generals enriched themselves as administrators of military business. In addition, they secured appointments in local government as governors, deputy governors, and heads of city councils (ro'asa' ahya'). Military retirees also secured plum civilian jobs in the state bureaucracy, especially the ministries of housing and public transportation. Egypt's officers are pensioned off young: typically in their forties, if they are discharged at the rank of colonel or brigadier general, or in their fifties, if they reach top-brass positions such as major general or lieutenant general.[98] Higher ranks upon retirement usually correlate with a greater likelihood of securing the most profitable sinecures. It should be noted here that the monthly salary of active major generals and brigadier generals under Mubarak hovered around $700 to $800. After retirement, the pension of a major general was $500 in addition to a lump sum that amounts to $6,670. These are modest remunerations. But managers of the military's economic sphere and other state-owned commercial companies reaped handsome earnings purportedly ranging from $16,670 to $166,670 per month.[99] Appointments in particularly lucrative companies, in combination with discrete business transactions, raised the annual income of the luckiest generals to $16.67 million.[100] These are significant sums by any standard, but in the context of poverty-stricken Egypt, they are colossal – even more so as Mubarak also lavished on the

---

[97] Shana Marshall and Joshua Stacher, "Egypt's Generals and Transnational Capital," *The Middle East Report and Information Project* 262 (Spring 2012), www.merip.org/mer/me r262/egypts-generals-transnational-capital (accessed June 25, 2015). See also L. S., "Continuing Business by Other Means: Egypt's Military Economy," *Mute*, May 30, 2014, www.metamute.org/editorial/articles/continuing-business-other-means-egypts-military-economy (accessed April 17, 2015).

[98] Abul-Magd, "The Egyptian Republic."   [99] Sayigh, "Above the State," 5.

[100] Ibid., 19.

top brass direct cash payments known in the armed forces as loyalty bonuses (*'alawat wala'*), or loyalty envelopes (*zuruf wala'*).[101] Understandably, the competition to rise in the hierarchy and secure these much-desired promotions was fierce. Absolute allegiance and deep entrenchment within loyalist networks preconditioned the reaping of plums. Conformism and apolitical subservience to the regime were prized and characteristically rewarded. The system was not conceived to promote, let alone create, mavericks, free-thinkers, or the outspoken.

Counterbalancing

Throughout Mubarak's long tenure, the interior ministry kept growing. Estimations of the number of personnel under the control of the ministry range between 1 and 1.7 million, including 850,000 policemen and staff, and 300,000 to 400,000 paid informers.[102] Tens of thousands of hired thugs (*baltagiyya*) working for the police should also be added to the picture. The budget of the interior ministry expanded, rising from $1.05 billion in 1990 to $3.6 billion in 2008 – a rate of increase three times that of the defense budget.[103] These numbers made the interior ministry the second-largest public employer after the education ministry.[104] And although the troops controlled by the interior ministry never became a match for the armed forces in terms of firepower, in strict military terms, they did represent two to three times the size of the EAF. Through sheer numbers, they would have had to be taken into consideration in any balance-of-power calculation, had the military – or a section of it – decided to move against Mubarak.

That Mubarak intended the interior ministry, and particularly its SSIS,[105] to play an important role in maintaining regime security became clear early on. The MI was tainted by Sadat's assassination within the

---

[101] According to 'Abdul-Khaleq Faruq, an economist who wrote extensively on the political economy of corruption in Egypt, the estimated number of officers who used to benefit from direct cash payments under Mubarak is 2,000, including most major generals, and some brigadier generals. Interview in Cairo (July 5, 2012). For more on this issue, see Hicham Bou Nassif, "Wedded to Mubarak: The Second Career and Financial Rewards of Egypt's Military Elite from 1981 till 2011," *The Middle East Journal* 67, no. 1 (Winter 2013): 141–144.

[102] Yezid Sayigh, "Missed Opportunity: The Politics of Police Reform in Egypt and Tunisia," Carnegie Middle East Center, March 7, 2015, http://carnegieendowment .org/files/missed_opportunity.pdf (accessed April 18, 2016).

[103] Sayigh, "Above the State," 6.

[104] 'Abdul-Khaleq Faruq, *Judhur al-Fasad al-Idari fi Masr, Bi'at al-'Amal wa-Siasat al-Ujur wa-l-Murattabat fi Masr, 1963–2002* (Cairo: Dar al-Shuruq, 2008), 277.

[105] The name of the SSIS was dissolved following the 2011 uprising, and replaced by the National Security Agency (NSA).

EAF's premises. At worst, it was implicated in the conspiracy against Sadat, and at best, it had failed to protect the president, and was ineffectual. It was the SSIS – principally Unit 75, which specialized in counterterrorism – that examined potential military involvement in the assassination.[106] In essence, this meant that the SSIS was given leeway to investigate armed forces personnel – never a welcome prospect from the military's perspective.

Three factors enhanced the SSIS's growing prominence. First, six of seven interior ministers appointed under Mubarak came from the SSIS, as Table 3.4 shows. This gave the SSIS prestige, influence, and access to the uppermost circles of power. Second, the resources made available to the SSIS allowed it to purchase cutting-edge control technologies, and also facilitated its recruitment drive. It boasted 100,000 policemen and informers, who made it a true pillar of the Mubarak regime and unquestionably the most powerful police organization in Egypt.[107] And third, it played a major role in penetrating the Muslim Brotherhood and keeping radical jihadi organizations in check. SSIS officers developed a sense of being the true and ultimate bulwark against a Muslim Brotherhood takeover of Egypt, and felt entitled to conduct extensive surveillance activities that pervaded Egyptian society and politics. The vigilance of the agency included military officers who knew they were under the watchful eye of the interior ministry, and deeply resented it. In this regard, the SSIS was trespassing on MI territory, and officers were cognizant that a negative report by SSIS informers could have a deleterious effect on their careers, in the armed forces and beyond.[108]

The friction between the interior ministry and the armed forces sometimes escalated into open confrontation. For instance, in March 2009, Military Academy cadets attacked and burned a police station in Cairo, where one of their colleagues had been mistreated. Repeated similar incidents, both before and after Mubarak's fall, reveal the depth of

---

[106] Sirrs, *The Egyptian Intelligence Service*, 151.

[107] See ʿOmar ʿAshur in Khaled ʿAbdul-ʿAl, "Siraʿ al-Jaysh wa-l-Dakhiliyya fi Masr ... al-Maʿraka ʿala al-Nufudh," *Al-ʿArabi al-Jadid*, April 15, 2015, www.alaraby.co.uk/investigations/2015/4/15/صراع-الجيش-والداخلية-في-مصر-المعركة-على-النفوذ (accessed March 16, 2016).

[108] It is rumored that the military retrieved records of tapped telephone conversations pertaining to the top brass from SSIS stations when the latter were attacked by angry demonstrators and security collapsed in Cairo during the events of the Arab Spring. See Mohammad Husni, "Durus Mustafada min al-Tasribat ... Mujaz Hal al-Dawla al-Masriyya," *Noon Post*, December 6, 2014, www.noonpost.org/content/4595 (accessed December 10, 2014).

Table 3.4 *Ministers of interior under Mubarak*[109]

	Name	Professional background
(1)	Al-Nabawi Isma'il	SSIS
(2)	Hasan Abu Basha	SSIS
(3)	Ahmad Rushdi	SSIS
(4)	Zaki Badr	SSIS
(5)	Mohammad 'Abdul-Halim Mussa	SSIS
(6)	Hasan al-Olfi	State Treasury Investigations Service
(7)	Habib al-'Adli	SSIS

animosity between soldiers and policemen in Egypt.[110] President 'Abdul-Fattah al-Sisi, a former MI director under Mubarak, allegedly called the Egyptian police a "million-man mafia."[111]

In order to wed the interior ministry to his regime, Mubarak turned a blind eye to its corruption. The notorious special funds in the interior ministry channeled millions of dollars to loyalist police officers in princely salaries and cash payments. Multiple sources kept the funds awash with money, including revenue from speeding tickets and assets seized from drug traffickers. By law, such sums belonged to the state's public treasury, but regime security prevailed over legal considerations.[112] Some senior officers in the interior ministry earned monthly salaries as high as $83,000, according to Mostafa al-Kashef, a retired police major general.[113] Reports show that former interior minister Habib al-'Adli distributed millions of dollars to his subordinates in the form of rewards and monetary incentives (*hawafez*). For instance, a former SSIS senior officer, Major General Mohsen Suleiman al-Fahham, received more than $2 million in direct installments under al-'Adli. A former first assistant to

---

[109] See Dina al-Husseini's report on Egyptian interior ministers, "Wuzara' Dakhiliyyat Masr min al-Sadat li-l-Sissi," *al-Bawaba News*, September 3, 2015, www.albawabhnews.com/1160398 (accessed September 15, 2015).

[110] 'Ali al-Raggal, "Alat al-Qatl fi al-Dawla wa-l-Mawja al-Thawriyya al-Qadima," *Al-Safir*, December 31, 2015, http://assafir.com/Article/1/464433/RssFeed (accessed December 31, 2015).

[111] See Peter Hessler, "Egypt's Failed Revolution," *The New Yorker*, January 2, 2017, www.newyorker.com/magazine/2017/01/02/egypts-failed-revolution (accessed January 2, 2017).

[112] See Ahmad Mansur's interview with 'Abdul-Khaleq Faruq on Al Jazeera (March 26, 2012).

[113] Hanem al-Finchi, "Al-Kashef: Mukalamat Telephone Tahmi Tujjar Mukhaddarat," *Al-Wafd*, April 1, 2011, www.ahram.org.eg/News/857/38/216600.aspx (accessed March 27, 2015).

al-'Adli, Major General Isma'il Mohammad al-Sha'er, cashed out with $575,195. In 2016, an Egyptian court forced these two officials, along with seventy-eight others in the interior ministry, to restore $17 million back to the public treasury.[114] In a different case, al-Fahham was again ordered to return more than $1.9 million.[115] In addition, police generals were involved in shady real-estate deals. Two former SSIS directors, Major General Hasan 'Abdul-Rahman and Major General Salah Saleme, stand as cases in point. In 2013, they were prosecuted for acquiring underpriced agricultural land and profiteering in resale operations.[116]

Positions in the economic sphere run by the interior ministry provided an additional source of income for the generals. Al-Fateh was the first interior ministry company to engage in commercial activities. Established in 2000, it manages the ministry's construction and restoration projects. It has also signed deals with other public and private entities. Al-Mustaqbal is another pillar of "Interior, Inc." Also established in 2000, the company is active in several sectors, including energy, real estate, and agriculture. Yet another, the Civil Information Technology Company (CITC), manages the Egyptian National ID project. CITC also develops and sells software programs. In addition, the ministry's industrial zone boasts eight plants manufacturing clothing, shoes, and furniture.[117] Police generals are pervasive in these enterprises, and earn substantial salaries for running them. Al-'Adli's first assistant, police Major General Fu'ad Yussef, was a special example in this regard. His monthly revenue stemming from the ministry's economic sphere exceeded a million dollars.[118]

Beyond the interior ministry's economic sphere, police retirees were allotted plum civilian jobs in local government. For instance, 34 of all 156 governors (i.e., 22 percent) appointed under Mubarak hailed from the

[114] Ahmad Chalabi and Yosri al-Badri, "Al-Dawla Tastarid 178 Maliun Jineih fi Fasad al-Dakhiliyya," *Egypt Independent*, January 28, 2016, www.almasryalyoum.com/news/det ails/882701 (accessed January 28, 2016).

[115] See the report "Bel-Arqam ... Fasad al-Dakhliyya fi 'Ahd al-'Adli," *Barlamani*, January 29, 2016, www.parlmany.com/News/7/33804 (accessed February 1, 2016).

[116] Mamduh al-Wali and 'Abdul-Nasser Salemeh, "Tawarrut Ru'assa Amn al-Dawla al-Sabiqayn fi al-Istila' 'ala Aradi," *Al-Ahram*, June 21, 2013, www.ahram.org.eg/News/857/38/216600.aspx (accessed June 21, 2013).

[117] Khaled 'Abdul-'Al, "Imbiatoriat al-Shurta al-Masriyya al-Iqtisadiyya," *Al-'Arabi al-Jadid*, December 30, 2016, www.alaraby.co.uk/investigations/2016/12/29/إمبراطورية-الشرطة-المصرية-الـ1 (accessed December 30, 2016).

[118] 'Abdul-Rahman Kamal, "130 Alf Jineih Towaza' 'ala al-Dubbat wa-l-Umana' al-Muqarrabin Yawmiyyan ... wa-Musa'ed al-Wazir li-l-Shu'un al-Maliyya Yataqada 7 Malayin Shahriyyan," *Al-Sha'ab*, November 26, 2013, https://travel-alone.xyz/?ts_id=1 (accessed April 3, 2020).

interior ministry.[119] Some governorates, such as al-Minya in Upper Egypt, became a reserved domain for police generals. All of al-Minya's eight governors appointed under Mubarak hailed from the interior ministry. In turn, the governors hired scores of their peers and colleagues as special assistants and consultants. The corruption of police retirees appointed in local government mirrored that of the military.[120]

Police generals were also appointed in private security firms that had proliferated since the 1980s. Falcon was a case in point. Established in 2006 by the Commercial International Bank (CIB), it quickly became prominent in the field. Originally manned by 400 employees, Falcon boasted 6,000 by the time Mubarak fell, and eventually 12,000 in 2014. Scores of Falcon administrators and trainers hailed from the police, the intelligence services, and the military. Care Services is another important player in the field, which has also provided sinecures to police and military retirees. It is interesting to note that while plums in security firms were already good under Mubarak, they became even more readily available after his downfall. Political instability naturally allowed the firms to expand, and the need for former officers to run them became greater.[121]

A different level of police corruption revolves around its agency in everyday life. The Egyptian police are notorious for their brutality, and people dwelling in underprivileged neighborhoods are particularly vulnerable to their heavy-handedness. Egyptians bribe police officers to curry favor with them and to avoid physical or moral abuse. Crimes perpetrated by policemen in exchange for kickbacks include abetting drug traffickers by leaking sensitive information about raids and anti-narcotic campaigns; helping organized crime involved in car robberies; engaging in contraband activities; extorting money from prisoners to allow them access to medical treatment; and facilitating prisoners' escape from jail.[122] By the end of Mubarak's tenure, a deep rift had begun to separate the police from Egyptian citizens, who mocked its claim to be

---

[119] Bou Nassif, "Wedded to Mubarak," 517.

[120] Ashraf Kamal, "Al-Fasad Yadrub Diwan 'Aam al-Minia," Al-Wafd, February 3, 2016, https://alwafd.news/المحافظات/1037107-الفساد-يضرب-ديوان-عام-المنيا (accessed February 3, 2016). See also 'Ali Khaled and Ahmad Hussein, "Siraj-Din al-Rubi Muhami Dubbat al-Shurta al-Muttahamin bi-l-Fasad ... Thamen Liwa' Shurta 'Aala Maq'ad Mohafiz al-Minia 'Ala al-Tawali," Al-Badil, August 5, 2011, www.masress.com/elbadil/53424 (accessed April 3, 2020).

[121] 'Ali al-Raggal, "Tashaddhi al-Dawla al-Masriyya," Al-Safir, October 12, 2015, http://assafir.com/Article/69/461062 (accessed October 12, 2015). See also Mahmud 'Abdallah, "Hares Amn ... Wazifa bi-la Mu'ahhalat," Al-Badil, January 12, 2017.

[122] Leila Khaled, "Fasad al-Shorta fi Masr ... Khams Turuq li-Isitighlal al-Muwatinin," Al-'Arabi al-Jadid, 30 May 30, 2016, www.alaraby.co.uk/investigations/2016/5/30/فساد الشرطة-في-مصر-5-طرق-لاستغلال-المواطنين (accessed June 1, 2016).

serving a higher purpose and maintaining order. Still, politically connected police officers were, in effect, above the law.[123]

The Republican Guard (RG) was another privileged body throughout Mubarak's years in power. The RG could only boast 600 soldiers in the 1950s. This number doubled under Sadat, and later ballooned to more than 7,000 men under Mubarak. An elite force, the RG is provided with sophisticated weaponry, including air-defense missiles and state-of-the-art M1A1 Abrams tanks.[124] It is barracked strategically in Dahshur, 35 kilometers south of Cairo, and is thus favorably positioned to defend the capital, should mutinous troops stage a putsch. To be sure, the RG cannot, by itself, stop the EAF as a whole from triggering a coup. But had a few brigades moved against Mubarak, a loyalist RG would have been a serious obstacle to potential coup-plotters. Mubarak cultivated the allegiance of RG commanders via prestigious appointments in the armed forces and post-retirement plum jobs. Consider the highest post in the military hierarchy, for instance. Traditionally, commanders of the armed forces hailed from the second or the third field army, but Tantawi was commander of the RG when he was appointed minister of defense in 1991. The pattern continued with Magdi Hatata and Hamdi Wahiba, respectively the fifth and sixth RG commanders under Mubarak, both of whom were elevated to chief of staff of the armed forces. The generals were also hired as chairmen of the Arab Industrial Organization (AIO) upon their retirement. Interestingly, three former RG commanders were twice appointed governors of South Sinai under Mubarak, i.e., Mamduh Zuhayri (1993, 1996); Mustafa ʿAfifi Ismaʿil (1997, 1999); and Muhammad Hani Mitwalli (2006, 2008). The reason for this is straightforward. Mubarak used to vacation frequently in Sharm al-Sheikh, which is located in South Sinai. He needed to entrust the province to governors he knew well, and RG commanders were a natural choice in this regard.[125]

Lastly, the Central Security Forces (CSF) grew exponentially under Mubarak, eventually boasting 450,000 men. Observers agree that the rapid expansion of the CSF reflected Mubarak's need for a parallel military institution as yet another counterweight to the armed forces.[126] The main mission of the CSF was to handle unrest, and, consequently, to

---

[123] On everyday interaction between the police and Egyptian citizens, see Salwa Ismail, "The Egyptian Revolution against the Police," *Social Research* 79, no. 2 (Summer 2012): 435–462.

[124] Nabil Sayf, "Al-Haras al-Jumhuri … Men al-Malik Faruq ila Mursi," *Al-Wafd*, 12 September, 2012, https://alwafd.news/ملفات-محلية/263841-الحرس-الجمهوري-من-الملك-فاروق-إلي-«مرسي» (accessed 14 July, 2014).

[125] Interview with retired army Major General Talʿat Musallim, Cairo (June 27, 2012).

[126] See, for instance, Frisch, "Guns and Butter," 6.

reduce the regime's dependency on the military to squelch internal dissent. And that the CSF did. It was the CSF that quelled urban riots, such as the 1992 Edku uprising in the northern Buheira governorate. In 2006 in al-Mafruza (Alexandria), and in 2008 in Toson (also in Alexandria), the CSF forcibly expelled residents allegedly squatting on private properties marked for real-estate development. In these and other similar instances, the CSF functioned as the regime's deadly heavy hand.[127] Yet the CSF fell short of functioning as effectively as the regime had hoped it would: as mentioned previously, in 1986, they rioted. And in 2011, they collapsed when faced with massive demonstrations. The CSF was also more vulnerable than other military formations to Islamist infiltration, as their conscripts hailed from the lower-middle classes of the Egyptian population, a segment traditionally susceptible to radical ideologies.[128]

Coups under the al-Asad Dynasty

Coup attempts receded in Syria after Hafez al-Asad rose to power in 1970, then stopped altogether. Writing on the rise and fall of Syrian generals who followed one another in quick succession for fifteen years after independence, Gad Soffer noted, "Each one of these had been the strong man in Syria, a strong man for a day."[129] From a comparative perspective, al-Asad's long tenure represents a paradigmatic shift – not for the lack of challengers to his rule, but because they were all unsuccessful. The information available on military conspiracies under al-Asad is murky, and to this day, there are more allegations and speculations about coup attempts during his tenure than incontrovertible data. Seemingly, supporters of Salah Jdid in the armed forces plotted a coup in 1972, and again in 1976, in order to restore him to power according to a 1978 CIA report.[130] At the time, the "Jdidists" were particularly worrying for al-Asad, because they were solidly implanted in his regime's three

---

[127] 'Ali al-Raggal, "Masr: Jihaz al-Dakhiliyya wa-l-Neoliberaliyya," *Al-Safir*, November 10, 2016, http://arabi.assafir.com/Article/5521 (accessed November 10, 2016).

[128] See also Kechichian and Nazimek, "Challenges."

[129] Soffer, "The Role of the Officer Class," 49.

[130] See CIA document N'RDP80T00634A00010052-5, "Syria without Assad: Succession Politics," 13, approved for release May 25, 2006, www.cia.gov/library/readingroom/do cs/CIA-RDP80T00634A000400010052-5.pdf (accessed May 26, 2018). The same document maintains that resentment against al-Asad lingered within some quarters of the officer corps among Alawi supporters of General Mohammad 'Omran, who was assassinated in 1972. Pro-'Omran officers never plotted a coup, however, and refrained from collaborating with supporters of Jdid. This played into the hands of the al-Asad regime. See also Van Dam, *The Struggle for Power in Syria*, 69.

pillars of power: the ruling party, the Alawi community, and the military–security complex.

Also in 1972, a group of Sunni officers alienated by Alawi hegemony over the armed forces reportedly conspired to overthrow the regime with Iraqi help, and failed.[131] A 1976 CIA report maintains that the Syrian regime discovered and foiled another plot led by pro-Iraqi elements in the ruling party and officer corps in 1975.[132] Mustafa Tlass mentions in his memoirs that Naji Jamil, a Sunni officer who was the first commander of the air force under al-Asad, connived to create a Sunni power base in the military as a stepping-stone toward seizing power. Allegedly, Jamil tried to recruit Sunni minister of interior and former director of General Intelligence 'Adnan Dabagh into his plot, and had planned to capture Rif'at al-Asad as the first step in a process designed to overthrow the regime.[133] Whether such assertions are true is debatable. We do know, however, that Jamil was permanently ousted from the circles of power in 1978 amidst heightened sectarian polarization in the armed forces. In fact, intra-military antagonism erupted violently in June 1979, when a fundamentalist Sunni captain and several accomplices killed eighty-three Alawi cadets at the Aleppo Artillery School. The Aleppo incident showed that the military was not immune to radical infiltration, and thus compounded the regime's security fears. In response, the authorities cashiered 400 military officers to prevent further Islamist penetration of the armed forces, thus reducing even further the Sunni presence within the officer corps. At the time, Sunnis still formed the majority in Syria's air force, and several Sunni pilots were forbidden to fly their jets, according to French expert on Syria Michel Seurat.[134] On the other hand, forty officers accused of being affiliated with the opposition were arrested in the last months of 1979 – and then nine more before the year ended.[135] In May 1980, rumors circulated that 900 Sunni officers and NCOs had

---

[131] See a report published by *Zaman al-Wasl*, January 2, 2018, www.zamanalwsl.net/news/article/84305/ (accessed July 12, 2018). Another report on the same website, published on January 15, 2018, gives additional details on the coup attempt. Available at: www.zamanalwsl.net/news/article/84619/ (accessed July 15, 2018).

[132] See CIA document RDP85T00353R000100270005-25X1, "Asad's Domestic Position," 7, approved for release September 29, 2003, www.cia.gov/library/readingroom/docs/CIA-RDP85T00353R000100270005-2.pdf (accessed June 25, 2018).

[133] Tlass, *Mer'āt Hayati, al-'Aqd al-Thalith*, 476–477. Interestingly, Jamil had not completed pilot courses and, therefore, was not yet a pilot when he was appointed to lead the Syrian armed forces. He was an al-Asad loyalist at the time, and that secured his rise to power in the military hierarchy.

[134] Michel Seurat (writing as Paul Maler), "La Société Syrienne Contre Son Etat," *Le Monde Diplomatique* (April 1980): 5. See also Middle East Watch, *Syria Unmasked: The Suppression of Human Rights by the Asad Regime* (New Haven, CT: Yale University Press, 1991), 10.

[135] Seurat, Ibid.

been purged from the military and security agencies. In April 1981, more Sunni officers were struck from the lists, some of whom were later sentenced to death for treason.[136] A former Syrian deputy prime minister, whom I have met and who wishes to remain anonymous, maintained that Sunni officers in the air force plotted a coup in 1981, yet again with Iraqi support. Several of them were executed when their plans were discovered.[137] In the wake of the tense period stretching from the Aleppo incident in 1979 to the Hama massacre in 1982, the regime accentuated the Alawitization of its coercive apparatus as its dependency on its sectarian base increased. The next challenge came from within Alawi ranks. In 1984, Rif'at al-Asad deployed troops in the Syrian capital, after his brother Hafez fell seriously ill in November 1983. For a while, Rif'at appeared poised to seize power, but Hafez's recovery thwarted his plans.[138] Yahya Sadowski maintains that two additional coups against Hafez al-Asad brewed in 1982 and again in 1987 – both staged by "idealistic Alawi officers," according to him.[139]

To the best of my knowledge, no other military conspiracy was hatched or reported in the remaining years of Hafez al-Asad's rule. A 1986 CIA assessment speculated that Syria's "strong tradition of coup-plotting" could reassert itself, should the Syrian president appoint his brother Rif'at as successor, mishandle brinkmanship with Israel, or suffer a serious reverse in Lebanon.[140] None of these hypotheses materialized, however, and military interventionism remained dormant. Overall, the literature agrees that coup-proofing effectively ended threats to Hafez al-Asad's grip on Syria in the second half of his long tenure.[141] When Bashar al-Asad rose to power, some observers questioned whether he would be able to impose his authority over Syria's generals. For instance, Uri

---

[136] Zein al-'Abidin, Al-Jaysh wa-l-Siasa, 440.
[137] Interview in Beirut (December 22, 2016).   [138] Seale, Asad, 430–437.
[139] Yahya M. Sadowski, "Patronage and the Ba'ath: Corruption and Control in Contemporary Syria," Arab Studies Quarterly 19, no. 4 (Fall 1987): 445 and 459. Reportedly, at least fifty officers were involved in the abortive 1982 coup. See Jack Anderson, "Syrian Factions Challenge Assad for Dominance," The Washington Post, July 15, 1983, CIA approved for release April 13, 2012, www.cia.gov/library/read ingroom/docs/CIA-RDP90-00965R000100140058-6.pdf (accessed May 25, 2018).
[140] See CIA document N'CIA-RDP86t01017r000100770001-5, "Syria: Scenarios of Dramatic Political Change," approved for release February 15, 2011, www.cia.gov/lib rary/readingroom/document/cia-rdp86t01017r000100770001-5 (accessed June 12, 2018).
[141] See Ridwan Ziade, Al-Sulta wa-l-Istikhbarat fi Suria (Beirut: Riad El-Rayyes Books, 2013), 70. See also Michael Eisenstadt, "Syria's Defense Companies: Profile of a Praetorian Unit," unpublished paper, 1984, 1; and Nicholas Van Dam, "Sectarian and Regional Factionalism in the Syrian Elite," Middle East Journal 32, no. 2 (Spring 1978): 210.

Lubrani, an Israeli diplomat and longtime coordinator of Israeli activities in Lebanon, opined in June 2000:

They (the Syrians) have crowned a 34-year-old fellow. They made him the military commander overnight. It is not too hard to guess what the generals in the Syrian Army are thinking. I would say that he has barely a 50 percent chance of survival.[142]

Such speculations proved unwarranted, and the smoothness of the power transfer reflected the regime's entrenchment and cohesiveness. No putsch or coup attempt was reported under the tenure of Bashar al-Asad, either before or after the outbreak of the Syrian Civil War. In sum, until the regime stabilized in the 1980s, the al-Asads were threatened by Sunnis unreconciled to Alawi rule as well as by rival Alawi challengers. Since then, the military has been effectively transformed into an obedient watchdog. Next, I ponder the coup-proofing techniques of the al-Asad dynasty and study their effect on the armed forces' response to the 2011 uprising.

Coup-Proofing under the al-Asad Dynasty

Several rival power centers in Syria had become spent forces prior to Hafez al-Asad's successful putsch in 1970, for reasons having little or nothing or to do with his agency. The right-wing Syrian Socialist Nationalist Party (SSNP) once mustered a strong following in the officer corps; however, the SSNP had been marginalized in the 1950s and 1960s, and its sympathizers purged from the armed forces. Meanwhile, the intra-Sunni struggle for power had weakened the community's political leadership as well as Sunni officers' clout in the military. Additionally, Druze officers with autonomous power bases were neutralized in the wake of 1963. After al-Asad emerged triumphant from the power play that opposed him to Jdid, he became the undisputed master of Syria.

And yet he felt insecure at the top. He had good reason to feel this way, considering Syria's recent history and the series of internal challenges he faced early in his reign. Stopping coups was a priority for the Syrian leader from his first days in power.[143] To secure his grip over the coercive apparatus, al-Asad devised a complex coup-proofing strategy and wedded his officers to the status quo via ideational and non-ideational bonds. Ethnic stacking and all-in-the-family tactics were central to his coup-

---

[142] See Eyal Zisser, "The Syrian Army on the Domestic and External Fronts," in *Armed Forces in the Middle East: Politics and Strategy*, ed. Barry Rubin and Thomas Keaney (London: Frank Cass, 2002), 115.
[143] See Seale, *Asad*, 181.

proofing system, and his ultimate guarantee for regime survival. But al-Asad wielded other techniques as well, including counterbalancing and promoting the financial interests of his generals. In essence, Bashar al-Asad's coup-proofing was a continuation of his father's.

Ideology and Fostering Shared Aversions

Fabrice Balanche noted in his book on Syria that the Ba'athist regime worked deliberately to buttress the country's sectarian identities, irre-spectively of its ostensibly anti-communitarian rhetoric.[144] Nowhere was such a policy more pronounced than in the coercive apparatus, in which ethnic stacking wedded the intelligence sector and military forces to the al-Asad dynasty. To be sure, the Alawitization of the Syrian military began immediately in the wake of the 1963 coup; but the process only accelerated under Hafez al-Asad from 1970 onward. Three dimensions are particularly important to pinpoint in this regard. First, recruitment into the armed forces, and particularly the military academy, favored the president's community at the expense of all others. According to retired Brigadier General Mohammad Shahime, whom I interviewed in Turkey:

When Hafez al-Asad came to power in 1970, Sunni numbers in the officer corps were still significant. He changed that. I graduated from the military academy in 1973. Our cohort numbered 1,100 officers that year, and Sunnis were in the hundreds. I don't have the exact figures, but I would not be surprised to know that Sunnis formed up to half of cohorts in the early 1970s. My son-in-law graduated from the military academy in 2001. There were 300 officers who graduated that year, 250 of whom were Alawis, while 50 hailed from all other communities combined.[145]

The findings of scholars working on Syria corroborate such claims. Zisser contends that at the time of al-Asad's death in 2000, 90 percent of officers carrying the rank of general were Alawis.[146] For his part, Batatu notes that Alawi generals commanded only two of the five regular army divisions in 1973. By 1992, Syria had nine regular divisions, seven of which were led by Alawi senior officers.[147] Balanche concedes that there are no statistical data pertaining to the sectarian distribution of the rank and file in the

[144] Balanche, *La région alaouite*, 41.
[145] Interview with retired Brigadier General Mohammad Shahime (Army), Antakya, Turkey (May 7, 2014).
[146] Eyal Zisser, "Appearance and Reality: Syria's Decision-Making Structure," *Middle East Review of International Affairs* (May 1998), www.rubincenter.org/1998/05/zisser-1998-05-05/ (accessed March 7, 2016).
[147] Hanna Batatu, *Syria's Peasantry, the Descendants of Its Lesser Rural Notables, and Their Politics* (Princeton, NJ: Princeton University Press, 1999).

Syrian military, but speculates that Alawis form a majority in the lower echelons of the armed forces, as well, and not just in the officer corps. He also maintains that military camps around Damascus, Homs, and Hama are almost exclusively inhabited by Alawi families.[148] In order for such a clear overrepresentation of a minority group to be possible, ethnic stacking must have been systematic and unrelenting throughout al-Asad's tenure.

Second, the regime built praetorian units as quasi all-Alawi forces on the level of officers, NCOs, and rank and file. Until 1984, the Defense Companies (Saraya al-Difa') were the linchpin of this paramilitary system, with 90 percent of their personnel reportedly Alawi.[149] Later, the RG and the Fourth Armored Brigades replaced the Companies as the regime's premier paramilitary units, but maintained their all-Alawi composition, especially in the officer corps. Third, the different intelligence organizations were packed with Alawis on all levels of personnel, and Alawi dominance is particularly glaring in the security sector. Three Alawi figures are especially important to mention in this regard: namely, Mohammad al-Khawli, 'Ali Duba, and Mohammad Nassif Kheir-Beik. General al-Khawli headed Air Force Intelligence from 1963 until 1988, and was al-Asad's most trusted advisor in security matters. He is believed to have encouraged his boss's proclivity to ethnically stack the officer corps with Alawis. In 1988, al-Asad relieved al-Khawli from his office under American and British pressure in the wake of a botched Syrian attempt to bomb an EL AL Israeli Airlines plane at Heathrow Airport, but al-Khawli remained nonetheless an influential member in the regime's inner circle and reemerged in 1994 as commander of the air force.[150]

General Duba was the MI boss from 1974 to 1999 and, like Hafez al-Asad's rival Jdid, belonged to the Matawira Alawi tribal confederation. Yet Duba chose al-Asad over Jdid, which helped the former secure the loyalty of a substantial number of Matawira tribesmen. As for General Kheir-Beik, he remained chief of the internal security branch (Sector 251) of General Intelligence from 1975 to 1999 and was in charge of the sensitive Iran/Hezbollah dossier. His prominence paved the way for other members from his clan to occupy sensitive positions in the military–

---

[148] Balanche, *La région alaouite*, 150.   [149] Eisenstadt, "Syria's Defense Companies," 3.
[150] On the removal of al-Khawli from the Air Force Intelligence Directorate, see William Beecher, "Syrians Are Said to Suspend Terror Role," *Boston Globe*, February 1, 1987, CIA approved for release December 21, 2011, www.cia.gov/library/readingroom/docs/CIA-RDP90-00965R000100420001-7.pdf (accessed May 28, 2018). See also David B. Ottaway, "Syrian Connection to Terrorism Probed: 'New and Very Disturbing' Evidence," *The Washington Post*, June 1, 1986, CIA approved for release May 4, 2012, www.cia.gov/library/readingroom/docs/CIA-RDP90-00965R000604900038-5.pdf (accessed May 28, 2018).

security archipelago, including his brother 'Isam (director of cabinet for defense minister Tlass) in addition to several cousins and nephews such as Mu'in Nassif (former commander of the defense brigades), Fu'ad Nassif (chief of Section 225 in internal security), and 'Ali Nassif (deputy director of external security).[151] The long tenures of the three generals suggest that al-Asad, unlike Sadat in Egypt, did not feel compelled to rotate his senior associates, and appreciated continuity.[152]

It is difficult to understate the power of such men and the other "Alawi barons," the upper crust of the senior Alawi officers leading the regime's security agencies as well as its military and paramilitary forces. The events of 1983–1984 that led to the downfall of Rif'at al-Asad are telling in terms of who wielded actual power in Syria after Hafez al-Asad himself. When the president was momentarily incapacitated due to deteriorating health conditions, the Alawi barons rallied around Rif'at al-Asad, who prepared to replace his dying brother as head of state. When the president recovered, the generals pledged continued loyalty to him, and Rifa't was eliminated as a contender for power. Such dynamics structuring the political fortunes and fate of Syria unfolded within an informal network of strong Alawi generals. The formal institutions of state and party mattered little when the Alawi top brass jockeyed for power.[153]

That some Sunnis did occupy leadership positions in the officer corps does not undermine the thesis of Alawi hegemony. Mustafa Tlass, Hekmat al-Shehabi, and Naji Jamil were the most prominent Sunni officers serving under Hafez al-Asad, as minister of defense, chief of staff, and commander of the air force, respectively. In addition, al-Asad appointed mostly Sunni generals to lead the General Intelligence. One Alawi or another would always keep an eye on the Sunni top brass, however. I have mentioned previously that Alawi officer 'Isam Nassif Kheir-Beik "abetted" Tlass in performing his duties as director of cabinet. Another Alawi general, Shafiq Fayyad, did the same as deputy minister of defense. 'Ali Aslan, an Alawi, was al-Shehabi's deputy chief of staff. Another Alawi general, Mohammad al-Khawli, was director of Air Force Intelligence when Jamil led the air force. This is not to suggest that Sunni generals were mere figureheads, but it is clear that the authority of their Alawi seconds checked theirs. For instance, even when Jamil was head of the air force, al-Khawli had to have prior knowledge of combat or training missions before an aircraft could take off from any Syrian airfield. And the Sunni generals who led the General Intelligence were never the most powerful figures within it. The

---

[151] Chouet, "Impact of Wielding Power," 10.

[152] See Ziade, *Al-Sulta wa-l-Istikhbarat*, 103 and 111.

[153] Eyal Zisser, "Decision Making in Asad's Syria," The Washington Institute Policy Focus, research memorandum no. 35 (February 1998), 16.

unmovable Alawi security baron, General Mohammad Nassif Kheir-Beik, definitely was.[154]

A word is due here on the Murshidis. These are the followers of the Alawi religious figure and political leader Suleiman al-Murshid, who coalesced after years of persecution by central authorities in Damascus into a militant and cohesive subsect of Syrian Alawis. The first post-independence Syrian government executed al-Murshid in 1946, and the successive regimes were very harsh on his followers. In contrast, Hafez al-Asad released Saji al-Murshid, Suleiman's son and successor, from house arrest, and recognized his authority over his followers. Saji's brother, al-Nur al-Mudi', became a real-estate entrepreneur and business partner of Rif at al-Asad. He was awarded public contracts that secured his family's fortune as well as his own. Under al-Asad, Murshidi MPs were elected to the parliament in 1977 for the first time in Syrian history. It later became customary that three seats be allocated to the sect. Jawbat Burghal, a Murshidi fiefdom in the Alawi countryside, was transformed into an administrative regional center that created dozens of public ser- vice jobs for its inhabitants – yet another sign of presidential favor.[155] In exchange, Murshidi leaders enlisted their community members in the loyalist camp, thousands of whom (young men) were recruited into the regime's paramilitary forces – especially the defense brigades, and, even- tually, the Fourth Armored Division. Reportedly, the Murshidis showed particular zeal during the 1982 Hama massacre. And their loyalty to Hafez al-Asad was an important reason behind the failure of Rif at al-Asad's bid to seize power in 1983–1984.[156]

All-in-the-family tactics functioned as another aspect of identity poli- tics in the military, and a permanent fixture of the regime's coup-proofing strategy. In addition to the al-Asad clan, two other families are particu- larly important to pinpoint, in this regard: the Makhlufs, al-Asad's in- laws, and the Kheir-Beiks, who hail from the Kalbiyah Alawi tribal confederation, like the al-Asads themselves. Hafez al-Asad began appointing relatives to senior military positions as defense minister, and continued to do so after he seized power in 1970. Al-Asad's brother, Rif at, became commander of the powerful paramilitary Defense Companies (Saraya al-Difa') deployed in Damascus. 'Adnan al-Asad, a cousin of the president, led the Struggle Companies (Saraya al-Sira'),

[154] Batatu, *Syria's Peasantry*, 226.   [155] Balanche, *La région alaouite*, 158.
[156] See CIA document no. CIA-RDP85T00314R000200140002-4, "Syria: The Succession Struggle and Rif at's Prospects," 5, approved for release January 31, 2011, www.cia.gov/library/readingroom/docs/CIA-RDP85T00314R000200140002-4.pdf (accessed June 12, 2018). On the relationship between Hafez al-Asad and the Murshidis, see also Zein al-'Abidin, *Al-Jaysh wa-l-Siasa*, 500 and 506–507.

yet another paramilitary unit deployed in Damascus. 'Adnan Makhluf, Asad's brother-in-law, was in charge of the regime's Republican Guard. In the early 1990s, al-Asad's eldest son, Basel, who was being groomed to succeed his father, became a staff member of the Presidential Guard and a commander of an elite armored brigade, though he was only a major in the armed forces. For their part, the Kheir-Beiks were especially prominent in the sprawling security sector, as shown previously. Table 3.5

Table 3.5 *Prominent officers under Hafez al-Asad, by sectarian and family affiliation*[157]

Name	Position	Family tie with the al-Asads	Sectarian affiliation
Basel al-Asad	Officer in the Presidential Guard	Hafez al-Asad's son	Alawi
Bashar al-Asad	Officer in the Presidential Guard	Hafez al-Asad's son	Alawi
Maher al-Asad	Officer in the Fourth Armored Division	Hafez al-Asad's son	Alawi
Rif'at al-Asad	Commander of the Defense Companies	Hafez al-Asad's brother	Alawi
'Adnan al-Asad	Commander of the Struggle Companies	Hafez al-Asad's nephew	Alawi
Shafiq Fayyad	Deputy minister of defense	Hafez al-Asad's brother-in-law. His son ('Ala') married Rif'at al-Asad's daughter (Lamia)	Alawi
'Adnan Makhluf	Commander of the Republican Guard	Cousin of Hafez al-Asad's wife (Anisa Makhluf)	Alawi
'Ali Haydar	Commander of the Special Forces	Hafez al-Asad's brother-in-Law	Alawi
'Ali Aslan	Deputy chief of staff	-	Alawi
Ghazi Kan'an	Military Intelligence chief in Lebanon	His son married a daughter of Hafez al-Asad's brother, Jamil	Alawi
Naji Jamil	Air force commander	-	Sunni
Ibrahim Huwayja	Director of Air Force Intelligence	-	Alawi
Mustafa Tlass	Minister of defense	-	Sunni

[157] See Kjetil Selvik, "Roots of Fragmentation: The Army and Regime Survival in Syria," *CMI Insight*, no. 2 (April 2014): 1, www.cmi.no/publications/file/5127-roots-of-fragmentation.pdf (accessed June 5, 2016).

Table 3.5 *(cont.)*

Name	Position	Family tie with the al-Asads	Sectarian affiliation
Hekmat al-Shehabi	Chief of staff	-	Sunni
Mohammad Nassif Kheir-Beik	Officer in General Intelligence – Sector 251	-	Alawi
'Isam Nassif Kheir-Beik	Director of cabinet for defense minister Mustafa Tlass	-	Alawi
Mu'in Nassif Kheir-Beik	Commander of the Fortieth Brigade – the Defense Companies	Rif'at al-Asad's son-in-law	Alawi
Ibrahim Safi	Commander of Syrian troops in Lebanon	-	Alawi
Hasan Turkmani	Deputy chief of staff	-	Sunni
'Ali Malahefji	Air force commander	-	Alawi
'Ali Habib Mahmoud	Commander of the Special Forces	-	Alawi
'Ali al-Saleh	Air defense commander	-	Alawi
Bahjat Suleiman	Senior officer in General Intelligence – Sector 251	-	Alawi
'Ali Zaza	Commander of military security	-	Sunni

shows the extent of Alawi overrepresentation among the regime's top brass generically, as well as the family affiliations of prominent officers under Hafez al-Asad. Tables 3.6, 3.7, and 3.8 trace the sectarian affiliation of commanders of specific sectors particularly important to regime security.

The ethnic stacking of the Syrian armed forces continued under Bashar al-Asad. Until he defected from the Republican Guard in 2012, Brigadier General Manaf Tlass was a regime insider and personal friend of Bashar. According to Tlass, out of Syria's 40,000 officers, 30,000 are Alawi, 8,000 Sunni, and 2,000 from all religious communities combined, including Christian, Druze, and Ismai'li.[158] The percentage of Alawis among Syria's career soldiers remains unclear, though some argue that on

---

[158] See Kjetil Selvik, "Roots of Fragmentation: The Army and Regime Survival in Syria," *CMI Insight*, no. 2 (April 2014): 1, www.cmi.no/publications/file/5127-roots-of-fragmentation.pdf (accessed June 5, 2016).

Table 3.6 *Directors of Air Force Intelligence under Hafez al-Asad, by sectarian affiliation*

Name	Tenure	Family tie with the al-Asads	Sectarian affiliation
Mohammad al-Khawli	1971–1988	-	Alawi
Ibrahim Huwayjah	1988–2002	-	Alawi

Table 3.7 *Directors of Military Intelligence under Hafez al-Asad, by sectarian affiliation*

Name	Tenure	Family tie with the al-Asads	Sectarian affiliation
Hikmat al-Shihabi	1970–1974	-	Sunni
ʻAli Duba	1974–1999	-	Alawi
Hasan Khalil	1999–2005	-	Alawi

Table 3.8 *Directors of General Intelligence under Hafez al-Asad, by sectarian affiliation*

Name	Tenure	Family Tie with the al-Asads	Sectarian affiliation
ʻAdnan Dabbagh	1971–1976	-	Sunni
ʻAli al-Madani	1976–1979	-	Sunni
Nazih Zreir	1979–1984	-	Sunni
Fuʼad ʻAbsi	1984–1987	-	Sunni
Majed Saʻid	1987–1994	-	Sunni
Bashir al-Najjar	1994–1998	-	Sunni
ʻAli Huri	1998–2005	-	Alawi

the eve of the 2011 uprising, 70 percent hailed from the president's co-ethnics.[159] Specific organizational measures guarantee not only that Alawi cadets are overwhelmingly represented in the military academy, but also that the Syrian top brass will, in essence, hail from the president's co-ethnics. Sunni officers remain a minority, and Sunni generals are still

[159] In contrast, most of Syria's 300,000 conscripts are Sunnis, reflecting the community's demographic weight in the country. See Rheva Bhalla, "Making Sense of the Syrian Uprising," May 5, 2011, *Stratfor*, https://worldview.stratfor.com/article/making-sense-syrian-crisis-0 (accessed June 20, 2018).

systematically flanked with Alawi subordinates, as they were under Hafez al-Asad, so that any order they give could be neutralized in the lower echelons if need be.[160]

In fact, there is an overall agreement among Sunni officers who defected from the Syrian armed forces after 2011 that the Alawitization of the officer corps has increased in the last decade, and that Sunni officers have suffered from more discrimination in the military under Bashar than under his father. According to Tlass:

> For 30 years, Hafiz al-Asad was commander-in-chief of the army, surrounded by two Sunni deputies, Mustafa Tlass from Rastan and Hikmat Shihabi from al-Bab, in the Aleppo countryside. The two were rivals, competing with each other. He also maintained the Sunni Naji Jamil from the outskirts of Deir-el Zour in a prominent position. In 2009, Bashar al-Asad was the army's supreme commander. His minister of defense, ʿAli Habib, was an ʿAlawi, and so was his deputy, ʿAli Ayyub. The chief of staff of the armed forces, Dawud Rajiha, was a Christian, while his deputies, Asif Shwakat and Munir Adnuf, were both ʿAlawis. The first Sunni to appear in this hierarchy was Fahed Jasim al-Freij, as the seventh or eighth most influential person.[161]

Tlass's thesis is debatable. To be sure, his father, minister of defense Mustafa Tlass, and chief of staff Hikmat al-Shihabi were nominally number two and three in the military hierarchy, respectively. And yet their authority never rivaled that of the Alawi barons who functioned as the actual masters of the armed forces under Hafez al-Asad's watchful eyes. Tlass also forgets that the Sunni commander of the air force to whom he refers, Jamil, was ousted in 1978. Finally, it is interesting to note that Sunni officers directed two of Syria's three most powerful intelligence agencies at the beginning of Hafez al-Asad's tenure, but none at the end it. As Tables 3.8, 3.9, and 3.10 show, Air Force Intelligence, Military Intelligence, and General Intelligence were all under Alawi control when Hafez al-Asad died in 2000. This suggests that the drive to reinforce Alawi hegemony even further was already palpable in the last years that preceded Bashar al-Asad's rise to power. Yet, Tlass's statement is important, because it reflects a widespread perception among Sunni officers that Bashar actually reduced whatever meager role they were allowed to play in the armed forces while continuing his father's tradition of appointing family members in sensitive positions in the military

---

[160] See Zénobie, "Syrie: un Officier Supérieur Parle," *Le Monde Diplomatique*, September 7, 2011, www.monde-diplomatique.fr/carnet/2011-09-07-Syrie-un-officier-superieur-parle (accessed September 7, 2011).
[161] Selvik, "Roots of Fragmentation," 2–3.

Table 3.9 *Prominent Alawi officers who are relatives of Bashar al-Asad*[162]

Name	Position	Family tie with Bashar al-Asad
Maher al-Asad	The regime's enforcer and longtime de facto commander of the Fourth Armored Division (he was officially appointed to lead it in April 2018)	Brother
Asef Shawkat	Deputy defense minister and chief of Military Intelligence (he was described as "the key figure overseeing Syria's security apparatus"[163] before being killed in July 2012)	Brother-in-law
Hafez Makhluf	Officer in the General Intelligence Directorate (GID)	First cousin (and brother of tycoon Rami Makhluf)
Iyad Makhluf	Officer in the Republican Guard	First cousin (and brother of tycoon Rami Makhluf)
Talal Makhluf	Commander of the Republican Guard	Cousin
Muhsin Makhluf	Commander of the Eleventh Armored Division	Cousin
Dhu al-Himma Shalish	Officer in charge of presidential security	First cousin
Riad Shalish	The long-serving director of the governmental Military Housing Establishment	First cousin (and brother of Dhu al-Himma Shalish)
Sakhr Shalish	Military officer	Cousin (and nephew of Dhu al-Himma Shalish)
'Ayham al-Asad	Officer in the Republican Guard	Cousin (his father, Kamal, was a half-brother of Hafez al-Asad. His wife, Kinda Makhluf, is the sister of tycoon Rami Makhluf, and a first cousin of Bashar al-Asad)
Ha'el al-Asad	Commander of the Military Police in the Fourth Armored Division	Cousin (brother of Hilal al-Asad)

---

[162] I gleaned the data in this table from various interviews I conducted while working on Syria. I also used several reports, including one published in *Al-Sharq al-Awsat*, March 25, 2015, https://aawsat.com/home/article/320071/رجال-الأسد (accessed March 29, 2016).

[163] See Sean Boyne, "Assad Purges Security Chiefs to Smooth the Way for Succession," *Jane's Intelligence Review* 11, no. 6 (June 1999): 4.

Table 3.9 *(cont.)*

Name	Position	Family tie with Bashar al-Asad
Hilal al-Asad	Commander of the Military Police in the Fourth Armored Division/Commander of the Latkia branch in the paramilitary National Defense Force (he died in battle in March 2014)	Cousin (brother of Ha'el al-Asad)
Zuheir al-Asad	Commander of the First Armored Division (he played a central role during the Syrian uprising in repressing demonstrations throughout the "Triangle of Death." i.e., the Rif Dimashq, Quneitra, and Dar'a governorates)	Cousin (his father, Tawfiq, was a half-brother of Hafez al-Asad)
'Atef Najib	Officer in the Political Security Directorate (he headed political security in the southern city of Dar'a when the Syrian revolution began in 2011)	First cousin

security. Table 3.9 shows that all-in-the-family tactics indeed remained a feature of the Syrian military under Bashar.

In addition, Alawi presence remained overwhelming in commandership positions in the armed forces throughout Bashar al-Asad's tenure. Of twelve divisions forming the regular army in 2011, only two – Divisions 7 and 10 – had Sunni commanders. The rest were all led by Alawi generals.[164] Ethnic stacking is particularly palpable in the security and paramilitary sectors, as shown in Tables 3.10, 3.11, and 3.12.

Promoting the Material Interests of the Military Elite

In addition to ethnic stacking, Hafez al-Asad wedded the military top brass to his rule by promoting their material interests. Whether al-Asad himself was corrupt or not, we cannot know, because the veil of the Syrian regime is impenetrable at this level. Overall, scholars seem convinced that the late president was more interested in power than

---

[164] Hicham Bou Nassif, "Second-Class: The Grievances of Sunni Officers in the Syrian Armed Forces," *Journal of Strategic Studies* 38, no. 5 (August 2015): 22.

Table 3.10 *Directors of Syrian intelligence agencies in charge of controlling the armed forces under Bashar al-Asad, by sectarian affiliation*[165]

Director of Air Force Intelligence (2000–2011)	Sectarian affiliation	Director of Military Intelligence (2000–2011)	Sectarian affiliation
Major General Ibrahim Huwayjah	Alawi	Major General Hasan Khalil	Alawi
Major General 'Izz al-Din Isma'il	Alawi	Major General Asef Shawkat	Alawi
Major General 'Abdul-Fattah Qudsieh	Alawi	Major General 'Abdul-Fattah Qudsieh	Alawi
Major General Jamil Hasan	Alawi	Major General Rafiq Shehade	Alawi

Table 3.11 *Commanders of the Republican Guard and the Fourth Armored Division under Bashar al-Asad, by sectarian affiliation*[166]

Commander of the Republican Guard (2000–2011)	Sectarian affiliation	Commander of the Fourth Armored Division (2000–2011)	Sectarian affiliation
Major General 'Ali Hassan	Alawi	Major General Mahmud 'Ammar	Alawi
Major General Nureddin Naqqar	Alawi	Major General 'Ali 'Ammar	Alawi
Major General Shu'eib Suleiman	Alawi	Major General Mohammad 'Ali Dargham	Alawi
Major General Badi' 'Ali	Alawi		

Table 3.12 *Commanders of the Special Forces and the Airborne Special Forces under Bashar al-Asad, by sectarian affiliation*[167]

Commander of the Special Forces (2000–2011)	Sectarian affiliation	Commander of the Airborne Special Forces (2000–2011)	Sectarian affiliation
Major General 'Ali Habib	Alawi	Major General 'Ali Suleiman	Alawi
Major General Subhi al-Tayyib	Sunni	Major General Mohammad Hussein al-Hussein	Alawi
Major General Ra'if Dallul	Alawi		
Major General Jum'a al-Ahmad	Alawi		
Major General Fu'ad Hammud	Alawi		

[165] Ibid., 21–24.   [166] Ibid.   [167] Ibid.

in the concomitant luxuries.[168] With that said, al-Asad wielded significant financial means which he used to purchase loyalty, despite the poverty of the Syrian state. Three resources mattered in particular: (1) Military expenditures, which accounted in the early 1970s for 35 percent of Syria's budget and peaked at 40 percent in 1987, before dropping afterwards. Defense spending was a reserved domain for the president as supreme commander of the armed forces, and consequently remained above the supervision of public monitoring agencies.[169] (2) Syria's petroleum sector. According to a 1988 CIA study, Syria's oil output was at 170,000 barrels per day (bpd) in the early 1980s. By mid-1988, it had risen to 250,000 bpd, and continued increasing until it reached 300,000 bpd at the end of the year.[170] Eliyahu Kanovsky estimates the output at 160,000 bpd in 1985, 405,000 bpd in 1990, and 610,000 bpd in 1995.[171] While the numbers are somewhat disputed, there is general agreement in the literature that Syria's oil export revenues provided the regime with much-needed hard currency that fluctuated between $2 billion and $3 billion yearly, according to a range of estimates. These sums were also under the discretion of the president. It was al-Asad, not the successive Syrian cabinets, who decided how to spend the oil rent.[172] (3) The drug trade, which blossomed under Syrian control during the civil war in neighboring Lebanon. According to US reports, the trade was worth around $4 billion yearly.[173] Even Israeli sources admit that al-Asad himself was not involved in narcotics trafficking. And yet in several pillars of his regime, the activity had his tacit acknowledgment – indeed, his "blessing."[174] The US Drug Enforcement Agency (DEA) estimated

---

[168] See, for instance, Batatu, *Syria's Peasantry*, 243.

[169] See Volker Perthes, *The Political Economy of Syria under Asad* (New York: I.B. Tauris, 1995), 31; and the study of Bashir Zein al-'Abidin on corruption in Syria: "Malaf al-Fasad fi Suria, al-Halaqa al-Rabi'a: Romuz al-Fasad, al-Asad," *Majallat al-Sunna*, no. 100, October 2000, http://sunah.org/main/393-3-ةقلحلا-يروري-يفـداسفـلا-فلم-تافلم اسد-لآ-داسفـلا-زومر-ةعبارلا.html (accessed April 25, 2018).

[170] See CIA report: "Syria: Facing the Economic Constraints of the 1990s," document no. CIA-RDP90T00100R000500760001-5, approved for release March 13, 2014, www.cia.gov/library/readingroom/docs/CIA-RDP90T00100R000500760001-5.pdf (accessed May 28, 2018).

[171] Eliyahu Kanovsky, "Syria's Troubled Economic Future," *Middle East Quarterly* 4, no. 2 (1997), www.meforum.org/articles/other/syria-s-troubled-economic-future (accessed May 29, 2018).

[172] Zein al-'Abidin, "Malaf al-Fasad fi Suria."

[173] James Bruce, "Changes in the Syrian High Command," *Jane's Intelligence Review* 7, no. 3 (1995): 127.

[174] See Yonah Alexander, "The Politics of Terror," *The Washington Times*, March 11, 1987, www.reaganlibrary.gov/sites/default/files/digitallibrary/smof/publicliaison/green/Box-0 27/40-219-6927378-027-017-2017.pdf (accessed June 25, 2018).

that the Syrian regime reaped around a billion dollars per year in the 1980s from the drug trade.[175] It may be irrelevant to note that the actual monthly salary of a senior officer in Syria averaged $150 during the 1990s, a modest sum even by Syrian standards.[176] Resources stemming from the defense budget, oil, and drug money combined gave the al-Asad regime leeway to maintain large patronage networks, the main beneficiaries of which led princely lives as long as they remained loyal.

In addition to lavishing direct handouts on his top generals, al-Asad turned a blind eye to their lucrative illegal activities. The involvement of Rifʿat al-Asad in narcotics trafficking stands as a notorious case in point. From 1976 to 2005, Syria controlled much of Lebanon's territory, including the fertile Beqaa valley in the east. Opium production in Lebanon was meager prior to Syrian deployment, and poppies were only cultivated in a few dozen hectares in the Beqaa. By 1986, a decade later, opium was grown on 1,500 hectares, with an average yield of 25 kilos per hectare; narcotics production kept expanding throughout the 1980s, progressively transforming Lebanon into a major producer of opium and a central shipping hub for the global cocaine trade.[177]

The drug trade generated a fortune for the powerful Syrian generals involved. In order to avoid turf wars, the Syrian top brass controlling the Beqaa during the Lebanese Civil War (1975–1990) agreed to carve the territory between them, and recognized each other's exclusive economic spheres of influence. For instance, after a quarrel between intelligence generals Mohammad Ghanem and Ghazi Kanʿan, they reached a settlement according to which the former exacted a tribute from drug smugglers at the Lebanese border post of al-Masnaʿ. The latter did the same in the Lebanese city of Shtaura. Similar "treaties" kept the peace among top-ranking Syrian officials and allowed the drug business to flourish.[178] Secret processing laboratories converting opium into heroin were originally set in the Beqaa, but from 1987 onward, they were

---

[175] See Claude Moniquet and Vanja Luksic's fascinating account on Rifʿat al-Asad's control of the Lebanese drug trade, "Armes, drogue, voitures: le traffic Syrien," *L'Express*, May 8, 1987, 34–41.

[176] See Zisser, "The Syrian Army," 120.

[177] See James A. Paul, *Human Rights in Syria: A Middle East Watch Report* (New York: Human Rights Watch, 1990), 148, https://books.google.com/books?id=NxjxWYWnl wC&printsec=frontcover&source=gbs_ge_summary_r&cad=0#v=onepage&q&f=false (accessed August 15, 2017).

[178] See Jack Anderson, "Syrians Aiding Heroin Traffic in Bekaa Valley," *The Washington Post*, February 1, 1984, CIA approved for release December 21, 2011, www.cia.gov/li brary/readingroom/docs/CIA-RDP90-00965R000100130129-8.pdf (accessed May 26, 2018).

reportedly operating in Aleppo, Damascus, Homs, and Lataqia in order to meet the rising demand. The yield passed through Syrian and rival Lebanese militias' checkpoints, as the French magazine *L'Express* reported in a detailed investigation published in 1987. Al-Asad's generals used their military vehicles and helicopters to expedite the drug crop to the Syrian-controlled port city of Tripoli, in northern Lebanon, and would export it from there.[179]

Rif'at al-Asad quickly established himself as a powerful drug czar in the Syrian–Lebanese cartel, recruiting Syrian officers and diplomats to expand his activities. In August 1977, a Lebanese hashish cargo was seized at Leonardo da Vinci International Airport in Italy. According to a CIA document, the Italian ambassador in Beirut revealed that the cargo had been shipped from Damascus under the supervision of Rif'at.[180] In May 1985, Spain expelled the Syrian consul general from Madrid and the chief of security from the Syrian embassy after seizing heroin cargos shipped to two high-ranking diplomats. As it turned out, both were close to Rif'at, and operated as supervisors of Syrian-sponsored drug laboratories in the Costa Brava of Spain. In 1986, three Syrian diplomats were expelled from Italy when a gang of drug smugglers was caught in the northern Italian port city of Trieste, exposing the implication of the diplomats in the trafficking.[181] In 1990, a French court convicted Syrian Military Intelligence operatives for endeavoring to smuggle into France eight tons of Lebanese hash-ish loaded in Tripoli.[182] In 1992, the director of the Military Intelligence Service (MIS) Branch 293, Brigadier General Ahmad 'Abbud, was sacked from the armed forces along with forty-six other officers after the Interpol identified them as members of Syria's drug cartel. This embarrassed the regime publicly.[183] As these and other similar incidents were publicized, Syrian diplomatic pouches became notorious for the extensive transport of drugs and weapons into Europe.

[179] Moniquet and Luksic, "Armes, drogue, voitures," 35.
[180] CIA document, "International Narcotics Development," 15, no. N'CIA-RDP7900912A001800010017-2, approved for release May 12, 2009, www.cia.gov/libr ary/readingroom/docs/CIA-RDP79T00912A001800010017-2.pdf (accessed May 26, 2018).
[181] See Middle East Insider, "Syria: Narcotics Center of the Middle East," *Middle East Insider Report* 16, no. 38 (1989): 32, www.larouchepub.com/eiw/public/1989/eirv16n38 -19890921/eirv16n38-19890921_032-syria_narcotics_center_of_the_mi.pdf (accessed May 7, 2017).
[182] Jonathan V. Marshall, *The Lebanese Connection: Corruption, Civil War, and the International Drug Traffic* (Stanford, CA: Stanford University Press, 2012), 120.
[183] See a report published by *Elaph*, August 8, 2008, http://elaph.com/Web/NewsPapers/ 2008/8/355067.htm (accessed June 25, 2018).

The relationship between Rif'at and businessman Mondher al-Kassar is important to pinpoint in this regard. Al-Kassar gained notoriety for being a Syrian drug lord engaged in narcotics trafficking in Italy, Spain, and France, as well as for his involvement in the Contras scandal with Oliver North. Significantly, he was known as "The Drug Prince of Marbella," because he maintained lavish residences in Spain from which he operated. Among other shadowy deals, he partnered with Canadian cocaine dealers to establish drug trade networks between Brazil and Europe, and with the East German government-owned shipping line DSR to organize weapon shipments from Cyprus. Al-Kassar ran his activities via the Bovega Company, ostensibly a commercial enterprise engaged in legitimate activities. In 1987, a joint investigation in Italy and Spain revealed that he was only operating as a front man on behalf of Rif'at and his son Firas.[184]

Rif'at also made money plundering Lebanon. Jokes circulated in Lebanon and Syria that the powerful general was not only the brother of the Syrian president, but also the "King of Oriental Carpets" because he instructed his troops to confiscate valuable goods from wealthy Lebanese mansions. Other booty included furniture and automobiles. Notoriously, Rif'at established a market in the Syrian capital from which his soldiers publicly sold goods looted from Lebanon, or simply confiscated from public agencies. The aforementioned businessman al-Kassar was valuable in this regard, as well. His connections in the drug underworld proved useful in establishing networks active in the export of stolen cars from Europe to Lebanon, where they would be repaired in garages operating under Syrian supervision before being sold on Middle Eastern markets. Yet another source of income for the enterprising Rif'at was racketeering: imposing a fee on large businesses in Syria for the licenses required to start and run commercial companies. They also provided "protection."[185] Arrangements like these were in particularly high demand prior to the liberalization of the economy, which began timidly in the early 1990s and accelerated later on. The absence of banking laws and traditions left businesses vulnerable to bureaucratic depredation and capriciousness. Partnerships with officialdom, and especially with influential military and security actors in the regime, were needed in order for businessmen to feel safe about their investments in Syria.[186]

---

[184] See Middle East Insider, "Syria: Narcotics Center of the Middle East," 34.

[185] Ibid. See also Paul, *Human Rights in Syria*, 48.

[186] This nexus between private capital and well-positioned protectors inside the regime has been referred to in the literature on Syria as the "military–mercantile" complex, or, more colorfully, the alliance between "sharks and dinosaurs." See Gary C. Gambill, "The

While Rif'at's illegal activities were particularly notorious, he was not the only Syrian general who used his power to enrich himself. A recent study on security sector reform in Syria noted that Hafez al-Asad allowed the commanders of his coercive apparatus to accumulate "obscene wealth" while simultaneously preparing corruption files to be used against them, should they grow excessively ambitious.[187] Another study showed that unlike the Chinese and Cuban models, military involvement in economic activities in Syria operated on individual rather than institutional levels. In other words, the military economic sphere under al-Asad meant that several hundred officers with close connections to the regime's center of power gained access to lucrative businesses – not the armed forces, as such.[188] The contentions of both studies are particularly accurate for the era stretching from 1973 onward. In the wake of the Arab–Israeli War that year, and against the backdrop of soaring oil prices, a windfall of international loans and Arab financial help spawn an economic boom in Syria. Al-Asad allowed the Syrian top brass to benefit from the capital inflow by entering into partnerships with prominent businessmen, a trend that has since proved enduring. Progressively, the economy became compartmentalized, as some sectors became fiefdoms from which top-brass generals could extract resources. For example, Rif'at al-Asad controlled the Military Housing Establishment (Mu'assasat al-Iskan al-'Askari) in charge of building officers' residences; General Shafiq Fayyad (Third Armored Brigade) handled the importation of construction materials; and General 'Ali Haydar (Special Forces) was active in the food-packing industry. These and other senior officers also developed business interests in economic sectors pertaining to public works, construction, and the manufacture of batteries and bottled mineral water. Whether the bourgeoisie traditionally active in these and other fields actually wanted to partner with the generals didn't really matter. The only alternative to doing so was selling the businesses to them at undervalued prices.[189]

As for General 'Ali Duba (Military Intelligence), he partnered with Rif'at in the running of the Lebanese narcotics trade, and

---

Political Obstacles to Economic Reform in Syria," *Middle East Intelligence Bulletin* 3, no. 7 (July 2011), www.shrc.org/en/?p=19864 (accessed May 26, 2017).

[187] See Maen Tallaa, "The Syrian Security Sector and the Need for Structural and Functional Change," *Omran for Strategic Studies* (November 2016): 8, http://khamakarpress.com/201 6/11/18/the-syrian-security-services-and-the-need-for-structural-and-functional-change/ (accessed March 8, 2017).

[188] Frank O. Mora and Quintan Wiktorowicz, "Economic Reform and the Military: China, Cuba, and Syria in Comparative Perspective," *International Journal of Comparative Sociology* 44, no. 2 (April 2003): 109.

[189] Chouet, "Impact of Wielding Power," 7.

made money trading favor with the above-mentioned al-Kassar, who married his wife's sister in 1981.[190] General Mohammad Nassif Kheir-Beik (Internal Security) was a silent partner of prominent businessman Saʾib al-Nahhas, a Shia Damascene known for his intimate relationships with the Iranian regime.[191] For his part, long-serving chief of staff Hikmat al-Shihabi was reportedly invested in one of Lebanon's major mobile phone companies, Libancell, in which the sons of a former Lebanese defense minister fronted for his offspring and those of Syrian vice president ʿAbdul-Halim Khaddam.[192] Another compartmentalization under Hafez al-Asad was geographical in nature: senior officers deployed to specific regions in Syria transformed them into economic fiefdoms. For instance, General Ibrahim Safi led the First Armored Division deployed in southern Damascus, whereas General Shafiq Fayyad's Third Armored Division was stationed in the northern part of the capital. This gave both senior officers leeway to do business within their respective sectors. Safi and Fayyad were said to engage in extensive smuggling activities as well as real estate in collaboration with General ʿAli Haydar (Special Forces), and General Ghazi Kanʿan (Military Intelligence), both of whom were said to have created "islands of wealth and power" as commanders of military and intelligence units in Lebanon.[193]

Defense minister Mustafa Tlass, too, was involved in smuggling from Lebanon. According to a report entitled "Syrian Involvement in Drug-Related Activities in Lebanon," released by the Israeli police in the early 1990s, Tlass – in addition to generals Duba and Kanaʿan – issued travel passes allowing drug traffickers to move in Lebanon and Syria unhindered by Syrian checkpoints in exchange for a "hefty payment."[194] In November 1992, the democratic staff of the US House Judiciary's Subcommittee on Crime and Criminal Justice issued a study providing additional details on this specific matter. Tlass reportedly sold 1,000 laissez-passers in 1989 alone for $10,000 each.[195] In addition, the US

[190] See Marshall, *The Lebanese Connection*, 128; and Bruce, "Changes in the Syrian High Command," 127.
[191] Batatu, *Syria's Peasantry*, 243.
[192] Reinoud Leenders, *Spoils of Truth: Corruption and State-building in Postwar Lebanon* (Ithaca, NY: Cornell University Press, 2012), 155.
[193] Bassam Haddad, "The Economic Price of Regime Security: Mistrust, State-Business Networks, and Economic Stagnation in Syria, 1986–2000" (PhD diss., Georgetown University, 2002), 225. See also Zein al-ʿAbidin, *Al-Jaysh wa-l-Siasa*, 460.
[194] Marshall, *The Lebanese Connection*, 115.
[195] See, "Syria, President Bush, and Drugs – The Administration Next Iraq Gate," 12, report prepared by the Subcommittee on Crime and Criminal Justice of the Committee of the Judiciary, November 23, 1992, https://babel.hathitrust.org/cgi/pt?id=purl .32754075290498;view=1up;seq=16 (accessed July 26, 2018).

Federal Bureau of Investigation (FBI) maintained in a 1991 report that Tlass had received bribes in order to facilitate the shipping out of Lebanon of more than three tons of Lebanese hashish. The cargo was eventually seized in Boston.[196] Reportedly, Tlass regularly exaggerated the quantities of steel, wood, and cement required for his ministry. The government would purchase or import the amounts required by Tlass, who would then sell the large excesses on the black market via civilian middlemen.[197]

Counterfeiting was another important source of income. In the late 1980s, Syrian officers deployed in the Beqaa began running high-quality forgeries producing US and European currencies. By 1993, Syrian counterfeiting of US hundred-dollar bills in Lebanon "sky-rocketed," according to US intelligence sources. Eventually, the activity came to an end after the US government exerted intense pressure on the Syrian regime, but its barons had, by then, pocketed perhaps as much as $1 billion from their venture.[198] The military members of the ruling coalition also benefitted from currency manipulation, skimming off taxes by way of corrupt custom regulations. Favorable loans were made possible by governmental monopoly on the banking sector. In addition, Hafez al-Asad allowed his generals to transform compulsory military service into yet another source of income. Conscripts would be summoned for service and then released in exchange for bribes. Officers of the Military Intelligence were particularly engaged in such schemes. In 1982, conscription officers could buy their way out of the military for 20,000 Syrian pounds (the equivalent of $5,128 at that year's rate of exchange). The sum was 18,000 pounds ($4,615) and 15,000 pounds ($3,846) for NCOs and soldiers, respectively.[199] Military commanders would also confiscate food intended for con-scripts and then sell it back to them via privately owned cafeterias they operated and owned.

Other inventive scenarios include arrangements between conscripts who worked in liberal professions and their commanders, according to which the former were allowed to resume work as doctors, lawyers, or engineers while ostensibly doing their military service, in exchange for sharing their income with senior officers in charge of the units to which

---

[196] Ibid., 120.
[197] Mahmud Sadeq, *Hiwar hawla Suria* (London: Dar ʿOkaz, 1993), 236–237. See also Zein al-ʿAbidin, *Al-Jaysh wa-l-Siasa*, 461.
[198] Gary C. Gambill, "Syria after Lebanon: Hooked on Lebanon," *The Middle East Quarterly* 12, no. 4 (Fall 2005), www.meforum.org/articles/2005/syria-after-lebanon-hooked-on-lebanon (accessed June 22, 2018).
[199] Sadeq, *Hiwar hawla Suria*, 231.

they were assigned. In this way, any commander leading even a relatively small unit of conscripts was guaranteed an extra source of income. This could be especially significant if upper-class Syrians served under him. As for poor conscripts, they would be put to work as virtual slave laborers on farms owned by the military elite, or serve their generals as chauffeurs, carpenters, and electricians active in whatever moneymaking activities their commanders happen to be engaged in during their military service.[200] Officers working in Syria's intelligence organizations were in a privileged position to extort resources, because citizens' everyday transactions with the state's bureaucracy required a background check. This was used to obtain import licenses, study-abroad scholarships, and so forth. The Kurdish minority in Syria and the anguished families of abducted Lebanese languishing in Syrian jails were a constant source of revenue – the former to acquire passports and the latter to be allowed prison visits. Thus, the opportunities for Mukhabarat officers to racketeer were virtually limitless.[201]

In this regard, coup-proofing under Bashar al-Asad proved a fundamental continuation of his father's system, though under a different economic zeitgeist. The hesitant opening of the economy that began with the enactment of Law 10 in 1991 – which aimed to encourage private investment – morphed into a neoliberal turn a decade later. In the words of Raymond Hinnebusch, Bashar's economic planners strived to transform Syria into "a version of Lebanon" by transferring the responsibility for growth to the private sector and emphasizing banking, tourism, commerce, and especially cross-regional trade.[202] Some of the old guard felt threatened by change, and reflexively clung to the non-competitive economic environment that had proven conducive to wealth accumulation through corruption and patronage. The malaise of the old guard was compounded by Syria's retreat from Lebanon in 2005, which reduced the ability of Syrian generals to loot that country – an unwelcome turning point that unfolded against a backdrop of dwindling revenues from the oil and drug sectors. However, it soon became clear that neoliberalism under Bashar was quickly converting into crony-capitalism. In 2006, Syria ranked 93rd in the Transparency International Corruption Perception Index, which included 163 countries that year. By 2008, Syria's ranking on the same index had fallen to 147th on a list of 180

---

[200] 'Abdallah al-Dahamesha, *Suria, Mazra'at al-Asad* (Beirut: Dar al-Nawa'ir, 2011), 4–43.

[201] Balanche, *La région alaouite*, 149–150. See also Middle East Watch, *Syria Unmasked*, 41.

[202] Raymond A. Hinnebusch, "Syria: From 'Authoritarian Upgrading' to Revolution," *International Affairs* 88, no. 1 (January 2012): 101.

countries, and again to 178th out of 180 in 2017.[203] Throughout the 2000s, the "military–mercantile" complex turned its attention to promising sectors such as real estate, tourism, communication, and transportation. The generals understood that although the economic environment had changed, they themselves were still in highly privileged positions: their political influence was tantamount to opportunity. The Military Housing Establishment, for example, competed successfully to win a major contract from an American-based hotel chain. Access to cheap building materials and labor, in addition to political protection and support, gave Milhouse a competitive advantage over its rivals in the private sector. On the other hand, the new regulations stipulated that as of 2001, 25 percent of all shares of foreign banks henceforth allowed to operate in Syria must be Syrian. Cronyism meant that regime allies, namely, senior officers, were set to benefit from such accommodations.[204] Writing on networks that benefitted from the gradual development of Syria's private sector from the 1990s onward, Bassam Haddad noted that the commanders of the coercive apparatus were, with the top political leadership, the main beneficiaries of economic transformations that moved Syria from state socialism to laissez-faire. In the words of Haddad:

Directly below the top leadership category is that of the army and security services. This category includes not only top generals and heads of the nine major security apparatuses, but also their deputies, loyal underlings, and former heads of security. Numbering several hundred, with a few dozen exceptional strongmen at the helm, these individuals have been able to convert their coercive power, and in some cases their institutional positionality, into significant wealth. However, due to the military nature of their work, their involvement in private business is usually through partners. In that capacity, they act as "protectors" of businessmen, who usually compensate them handsomely. Not surprisingly, most of the offspring of powerful figures in the army and security services opted for private careers as they came of age in the mid-to late 1990s. Together, fathers, sons, and daughters form a significant power and financial bloc among the state bourgeoisie as a whole, and it is difficult in this "familial" context to separate the public from the private.[205]

---

[203] For 2006 and beyond, see the Transparency International Yearly Corruption Perceptions Index. Available at: www.transparency.org/country/SYR (accessed June 1, 2018).

[204] See Mora and Wiktorowicz, "Economic Reform and the Military," 114. See also Bassam Haddad, "Change and Stasis in Syria: One Step Forward," *Middle East Report*, no. 213, Millennial Middle East: Changing Orders, Shifting Borders (Winter 1999): 23–27.

[205] Bassam Haddad, *Business Networks in Syria: The Political Economy of Authoritarian Resilience* (Stanford, CA: Stanford University Press, 2012), 68. Writing along similar lines, Anna Borshchevskaya noted: "Once a business becomes profitable, the Assad government either demands a share of profit or simply does not allow it to operate." See Anna Borshchevskaya, "Sponsored Corruption and Neglected Reform in Syria," *Middle*

Rami Makhluf and Firas Tlass are clear illustrations of the nexus between the military–security complex and the rising business class. As mentioned previously, the Makhlufs are the al-Asads' in-laws, who occupy sensitive positions in the regime's coercive apparatus. Rami is Bashar al-Asad's first cousin. Unlike his two brothers – Hafez Makhluf, a brigadier general in the General Intelligence Directorate (GID), and Iyad Makhluf, also a GID officer – Rami eschewed a military career and took over the economic empire created by his father Mohammad, the brother of Hafez al-Asad's wife, Anisa Makhluf. Quickly, Rami became an influential tycoon, especially after he started Syria's largest cellular network company, Syriatel, in the early 2000s. On the eve of the uprising in 2011, he was reportedly worth $5 billion, and dominated 60 percent of the Syrian economy. Famously dubbed a "poster boy for corruption" in US diplomatic cables, Rami held stakes in several oil and gas companies, duty-free shops, luxury car import companies, the banking sector, and Sham Holding, probably Syria's biggest private company.[206]

As for Firas Tlass, he is the son of former defense minister Mustafa Tlass and the brother of Brigadier General Manaf Tlass, who served as battalion commander in Syria's elite Republican Guard until his defection in 2012. Firas was a prominent businessman until his family's break with the regime following the Syrian uprising. A magnate who developed assets in real estate, banking, and food distribution, he holds a fortune said to be second only to Rami's. The money reaped by these two men, and businessmen who shared their background, was not only theirs, but also that of their clans. Documents released via Swiss leaks – i.e., the 2015 journalistic investigation of a giant tax-evasion scheme in which the British multinational bank HSBC was involved – show that Rami's brothers, officers Hafez and Iyad, actually co-own the family's business empire.[207] Rami also partnered with his cousin Maher, Bashar's brother and commander of the Fourth Armored Division, in various business

---

East Quarterly 17, no. 3 (Summer 2010), www.meforum.org/articles/2010/sponsored-corruption-and-neglected-reform-in-syria (accessed June 1, 2018).

[206] See Juliette Garside and David Pegg, "Mossack Fonseca Serviced Assad Cousin's Firms Despite Syria Corruption Fears," *The Guardian*, April 5, 2016, www.theguardian.com/news/2016/apr/05/mossack-fonseca-panama-papers-rami-makhlouf-syria-assad-hsbc (accessed May 29, 2016).

[207] A fourth brother, Ihab, is also a co-owner. See a report on the Makhluf business empire published by *The New Arab*, August 17, 2015, www.alaraby.co.uk/english/features/2015/8/17/exclusive-assads-sanctions-busting-ties-to-israeli-business-tycoon (accessed May 30, 2018).

ventures in Lebanon.[208] And when Alawi intelligence general Suheil al-Hasan created the loyalist special division Tiger Forces (Quwaat al-Nimr) in 2013, he counted upon Rami to fund his elite unit. Similarly, prominent Alawi businessman Ayman Jaber funded the paramilitary force Desert Hawks (Suqur al-Sahra'), headed by his brother, officer Muhrez Jaber.[209] On the other hand, when Brigadier General Manaf Tlass defected and tried to reinvent himself as a military commander of the opposition, his brother Firas bankrolled the Faruq Brigades, an anti-regime militia that operated in the Tlass family's native al-Rastan, in Homs. Civilian riches in Syria's elite families were at the officers' disposal, as well, when circumstances required the latter to use them.[210]

Under Bashar, just as it had been under his father, the most influential military security figures of the regime became financial magnates in their own right. The president's brother, Major General Maher al-Asad, is a case in point. Reports suggest that he secured a billion dollars from shady deals with the Saddam Hussein regime centered upon the oil-for-food program enacted by the UN in the 1990s and early 2000s. Maher is invariably mentioned as the main culprit behind a money-laundering scheme that led to the collapse of the Lebanese bank al-Madina in 2003. An al-Madina banker at the heart of the scandal provided detailed information on the implication of Syrian and Lebanese officials in the affair. She estimated that Maher had extracted $50 million from the bank as "gifts" to himself and his civilian associates.[211] According to *Fortune* magazine, roughly a billion dollars in illegal kickbacks syphoned by Iraqi officials were laundered by the bank, with 25 percent going to their Lebanese and Syrian counterparts, including Maher. In addition, the brother of the Syrian president reportedly controls the Sheraton hotel network as well as several media outlets comprising the online site Sham

---

[208] See Shmuel Bar, "Bashar's Syria: The Regime and Its Strategic Worldview," *Comparative Strategy*, no. 25 (2006): 395, www.offiziere.ch/wp-content/uploads/Shmuel_Bar_2.pdf (accessed May 30, 2018).

[209] See Muhannad al-Haj ʿAli, "Limadha Yulahiq al-Asad Rijal Aʿmalih," *Al-Modon*, June 1, 2016, www.almodon.com/opinion/2018/6/1/لماذا-يلاحق-الأسد-رجال-أعماله (accessed June 1, 2018).

[210] See Kheder Khaddour, "Strength in Weakness: The Syrian Army's Accidental Resilience," Carnegie Middle East Center: Regional Insight, March 14, 2016, http://carnegie-mec.org/2016/03/14/strength-in-weakness-syrian-army-s-accidental-resilience-pub-62968 (accessed May 29, 2018). See also Kiril Semenov, "Who Controls Syria? The Al-Assad Family, the Inner Circle, and the Tycoons," Russian International Affairs Council, February 14, 2018, http://russiancouncil.ru/en/analytics-and-comments/analytics/who-controls-syria-the-al-assad-family-the-inner-circle-and-the-tycoons/ (accessed May 29, 2018). Note that Mustafa Tlass is not the only general and magnate whose offspring turned to business. The sons of Chief of Staff Hikmat al-Shihabi, General ʿAli Duba, and General Bahjat Suleiman did the same – among others.

[211] Hasan Sabra, *Laʿnta Lubnan* (Beirut: Difaf Publishing, 2016), 74–76.

Press. Maher handles his ventures via the media mogul Mohammad Hamsho as well as businessmen Khaled Qaddur and Ra'if al-Quwatli, all of whom act as his front men and silent partners.[212]

General Dhu al-Himma Shalish is another example of an officer-turned -businessman under Bashar al-Asad. Shalish, who is Bashar's first cousin and head of presidential security, owns the SES International Corp, sanctioned by the US government for facilitating the trans-shipment of defense-related material to the Saddam Hussein regime in violation of UN sanctions imposed upon Iraq in the 1990s. In essence, SES would ship weapons and military equipment to Syria, then quietly transport them to Iraq in exchange for kickbacks.[213] Reportedly, SES go-between transactions from 2000 until the breakdown of the Iraqi regime in 2003 amounted to $86.4 million. As for Dhu al-Himma's brother, General Riad Shalish, he was active in construction and contracting deals in the private sector in addition to managing Syria's Military Housing Establishment. Riad amassed a fortune and was sanctioned by the European Union, along with other businessmen, for funding the violence of the Syrian regime in the wake of the 2011 uprising.[214]

Officers hailing from the al-Asad, Makhluf, and Shalish families belong to the upper crust of Syria's elite. Theirs is the realm of big business and high-scale corruption. Their fancy mansions, built on the best plots of land, have become landmarks in the Alawi hinterland, and attest to the opulence of these families. This newfound social position and prosperity explain, at least in part, why the generals have an interest in upholding the very favorable status quo. With that said, Bashar al-Asad did not promote the interests of only this restricted category of officers. The top brass from outside the circle of the ruling families also benefitted from the regime's generosity – and tolerance of corrupt practices. Until 2005, Syrian generals deployed in Lebanon invariably found ways to benefit financially

---

[212] See Mitchell Prothero, "Beirut Bombshell," *Fortune* on *CNN Money*, May 4, 2006, http://money.cnn.com/2006/05/01/news/international/lebanon_fortune_051506/ (accessed May 30, 2018). See also Benjamin Barthe, "Ces Oligarques Syriens qui Tiennent à bout de Bras le Regime Assad," *Le Monde*, May 30, 2014, www.lemonde.fr/international/article/2014/05/30/ces-oligarques-syriens-qui-tiennent-a-bout-de-bras-le-regime-assad_4429096_3210.html (accessed May 30, 2018).

[213] See the US Department of Treasury press release, June 9, 2005, www.treasury.gov /press-center/press-releases/Pages/js2487.aspx (accessed May 30, 2018). See also Bar, "Bashar's Syria," 395; and "Iraq Survey Group Final Report," Global Security, 2004, www.globalsecurity.org/wmd/library/report/2004/isg-final-report/isg -final-report_vol1_rfp-04-02.htm (accessed March 15, 2017).

[214] See the *Official Journal of the European Union* 54, Decision 2011/273/CFSP (June 24, 2011), http://eur-lex.europa.eu/LexUriServ/LexUriServ.do?uri=OJ:L:2011:164:FUL L:EN:PDF (accessed May 30, 2018). See also a report on the Shalishs published by the news website *Enabbaladi*, December 6, 2017, www.enabbaladi.net/archives/189266 (accessed May 30, 2018).

from Syria's presence there – especially via smuggling activities.[215] Two generals are particularly important to mention in this regard: Ghazi Kanʿan, longtime head of Syria's security apparatus in Lebanon, and his successor in 2003, Rustum Ghazale. The two men were Lebanon's de facto rulers until 2005, and made vast fortunes from various schemes, including extorting money from Lebanese politicians eager to win their favor. Ghazale, in particular, reaped $120 million from the above-mentioned al-Madina affair.[216] In 2007, a joint plan was enacted under the auspices of the defense ministry and loyalist businessmen that allowed retired officers to buy luxury cars at discounted and tax-free rates via payments deducted from pension payouts. Officers could then choose to sell the cars and make profit from tax savings, or keep them and enjoy the enhanced social status that such cars projected onto their owners in Syria.

Despite this excess, the bulk of Syrian officers eked out a meager living – especially in the lower echelons. Officers' salaries remained modest under Bashar al-Asad, and fluctuated between $400 and $800 monthly.[217] To compensate, the regime turned a blind eye when mid-ranking and junior officers took bribes in exchange for granting soldiers rights to leave, or engaged in different kinds of petty extortion. In the words of Selvik:

Clearly, the banality of corruption in the army was not a secret to anyone. But the regime could not afford to alienate the corporate interests of a pivotal political pillar. All the more so because the purchasing power of Syrian officer salaries had fallen over the years. Discontent within the officer corps was latent, and allowing some rent-seeking was a way for the regime to compensate. Several of the interviewees expressed that they had felt encouraged to engage in small-scale corruption. A former colonel in the Republican Guard saw this as a strategy to assure that he would stay quiet in the face of large-scale corruption. Everyone was to become an accomplice, along with the men at the pyramid's apex.[218]

In addition to tolerating pervasive corruption and predatory practices, Bashar al-Asad appointed several retired senior officers to gubernatorial and diplomatic positions. An officer I interviewed estimated that dozens of the top brass were awarded plum civilian jobs after retirement under Bashar.[219]

---

[215] Najib Ghadabian, "The New Asad: Dynamics of Continuity and Change in Syria," *Middle East Journal* 55, no. 4 (Autumn 2001): 629. See also Hasan Sabra, *Suria, Suqut al-ʿAʾila, ʾAwdat al-Watan* (Beirut: Arab Scientific Publishers, 2013), 234–240.
[216] Sabra, *Laʾnta Lubnan*, 71.   [217] Khaddour, "Strength in Weakness."
[218] Selvik, "Roots of Fragmentation," 4.
[219] Examples include, but are not restricted to, Major General Mohamad al-Hannous (Governor of Daraʿa); Major General ʿAbdul Qader al-Sheikh (Governor of Lataqia); Major General Ghassan ʿAbdul-ʿAl (Governor of Homs); Major General Wajih Ismaʿel (Ambassador to Jordan); and Major General Bahjat Suleiman (Ambassador to Jordan). Interview with retired Brigadier General Mohammad Shahime.

In comparison with so much generosity lavished on the top of the military hierarchy, the material benefits available for mid-ranking and junior officers were meager. A word is due here on military housing projects. The so-called "Suburb of al-Asad" (Dahiet al-Asad, or Dahia in colloquial Syrian) is a large residential complex in northeast Damascus that gives Syrian officers the opportunity to own property in the Syrian capital. The first apartments became available for officers under Hafez al-Asad in the early 1990s, but Dahia kept expanding until it covered 250 hectares and housed more than 100,000 residents by 2011. It is not luxurious, and suffers from typical problems that plague everyday life in under-privileged neighborhoods in Damascus, such as unrepaired streets, water and electrical outages, and mediocre garbage dump-servicing. In essence, the complex hosts mid-ranking officers. Very few major generals live in Dahia, and not a single higher-ranking officer does. It earned the unflattering sobriquet of the "army of sandal-wearers" (*jaysh abu shehhata*) because its inhabitants were dismissed by wealthier Syrians as poorly educated members of the lower classes. Still, for officers hailing from the countryside or disadvantaged urban neighborhoods, owning property in Damascus was a sign of much-desired social ascent. Add to this the fact that living in Dahia offered practical advantages for officers and their dependents – most notably, proximity to the best educational and health centers in the country. Perhaps it is understandable, therefore, that a slogan on Dahia's entrance declared it to be "the gift of President Hafez al-Asad to the officers in the Syrian Arab Army and their families." Because Dahia's apartments were coveted, the regime wanted to remind its officers to whom they owed the privilege each time they returned home.[220] Such liberalities did mitigate the effects of Syria's financial crisis in the lower echelons of the officer corps, but only in a relative sense. By and large, the bulk of Syria's mid-ranking and junior officers were struggling to make ends meet, and felt the brunt of the country's economic morass just like other sectors of the country's lower-middle classes.[221]

[220] See Kheder Khaddour, "Assad's Officer Ghetto: Why the Syrian Army Remains Loyal," Carnegie Middle East Center: Regional Insight, November 4, 2015, http://carnegie-mec.org/2015/11/04/assad-s-officer-ghetto-why-syrian-army-remains-loyal-pub-61449 (accessed May 31, 2018). Other military housing complexes have also been built in Aleppo, Deir al-Zur, and Tartus.

[221] Several Sunni officers I interviewed maintained that Dahia was essentially Alawi, and was part of an overall plan to surround Sunni cities with loyalist suburbs. According to Lieutenant Colonel Yasser Jaber: "Alawis [have] expanded everywhere in Syrian cities in the last decades, namely, in Damascus and Homs. Damascus is now surrounded with Alawi neighborhoods in the north and the west, such as al-Sumariyya, Mazze 86, and

Counterbalancing

Hafez al-Asad's counterbalancing system was intricate, and probably the most complex in the Arab world. In essence, the late Syrian president used five paramilitary units as well as four intelligence organizations to keep the armed forces in check and secure his grip over Syria. Combined, this posed a formidable defense ring protecting the regime's center of power in Damascus. The failure of al-Asad's challengers to unseat him, and the subsequent longevity of his tenure, are in no small part a function of successful counterbalancing tactics.

From their establishment in 1971 until their disbanding in the mid-1980s, the Defense Companies were the Syrian regime's first paramilitary unit. The companies were not answerable to the ministry of defense and were thus free from the military's chain of command – unlike, say, the Syrian Special Forces. Because their affiliation with the armed forces was more theoretical than real, they were strictly liable to Hafez al-Asad. As the president's praetorians, the companies were allowed to add irregular auxiliaries to their ranks such as Baʿath Party militias (10,000 strong), the Alawi Society of the Imam ʿAli al-Murtada (4,000 strong), and the Alawi militia of the Lebanese Arab Democratic Party (2,000 strong). Overall, the companies consisted of approximately 35,000 to 50,000 men, according to varying estimates, and mustered armored units, commando regiments, and their own intelligence branch. They were almost exclusively staffed by Alawis and led by generals who hailed overwhelmingly from the president's hometown or were his relatives and associates. Their commander was none other than Rifʿat al-Asad, the president's brother. Because their main task was checking the armed forces and preventing coups, the companies were deployed in Damascus around sensitive sites, such as the defense ministry and the TV station. This kept them physically close to the centers of power, and eased daily contact between their leaders and the al-Asads.[222]

The Republican Guard was another important praetorian unit established under Hafez al-Asad and tasked with counterbalancing

---

ʿIsh al-Warwar. There is also the al-Asad Dahia, which offers cheap housing for the popular classes, and which is overwhelmingly Alawi. In Homs, the neighborhoods of al-Zahra, ʿAkrama al-Jadida, al-Nuzha, and al-ʿAbbasiyya are all almost exclusively Alawi. The armed forces played a direct role in this systematic ethnic restructuring of Syrian cities because most of these neighborhoods initially emerged as military housing; then hospitals were added, and schools followed. The military localities were eventually transformed into full-blown Alawi-controlled districts. We used to discuss these new dynamics in the intimacy of our families, and fret about them a lot. But we felt powerless, until the revolution came." Interview, Antakya, Turkey (May 13, 2014).

[222] The best study on the Defense Companies remains Eisenstadt's "Syria's Defense Companies," especially pp. 1–7.

the armed forces as well as the Defense Companies. The Republican Guard protected the presidential palace in Damascus, and was in charge of Hafez al-Asad's personal security and that of visiting dignitaries. When al-Asad became president, he transferred from his fiefdom in the air force about 1,000 Alawi loyalists to form the nucleus of the Guard. The force became particularly prominent after its role in the 1984 crisis that pitted the two al-Asad brothers against each other. In the wake of Rif'at's downfall, Hafez promoted the commander of the Republican Guard, 'Adnan Makhluf, to brigadier general, and commissioned him to transform his unit into an alternative to the disgraced Defense Companies. The Guard quickly ballooned to 9,000 men operating autonomously from the armed forces and was strictly responsive to Hafez. According to a CIA document, the Guard was the first Syrian unit to receive the state-of-the-art Russian tank T72-M1981/3, which had never before been deployed outside of the ex-Soviet Union. And when Syria halted or cancelled the purchase of defense materials due to its financial troubles in the mid-1980s, the Guard was exempt from austerity measures.[223] Three of Hafez's four sons served at different points in the Guard: Basel, Bashar, and Maher al-Asad. So did Manaf Tlass, the son of defense minister Mustafa Tlass. It is believed that Republican Guard officers received significant handouts extracted from the oil rent in order to wed them further to the regime.[224]

Equally important to Hafez al-Asad's counterbalancing system were his intelligence agencies: the Air Force Intelligence Directorate (AFID), the Military Intelligence Service (MIS), the General Intelligence Directorate (GID), and the Political Security Directorate (PSD). To these agencies must be added the intelligence unit of the Defense Companies, which was highly active until the companies were dissolved.[225] In the early 1990s, conservative estimates put the number of people working for different intelligence organizations in Syria at 50,000; other conjectures maintained that the number was three times higher. Even if the lower

---

[223] CIA document N'CIA-RDP88T00096R000500590001-3, "Syria's Elite Military Unit: Key to Stability and Succession," 9, approved for release January 9, 2012, www.cia.gov /library/readingroom/docs/CIA-RDP88T00096R000500590001-3.pdf   (accessed June 18, 2018).

[224] See Al Jazeera's report on the Syrian Republican Guard, January 14, 2015, www.aljazeera.net/news/reportsandinterviews/2015/1/14/الحرس-الجمهوري-السوري (accessed June 16, 2018).

[225] The other paramilitary units also had their own intelligence branches, which should be added to the security archipelago – though their sizes were modest in comparison with the intelligence branch of the Defense Companies, let alone the four main intelligence agencies.

assessments were accurate, they would still make the Syrian security apparatus one of the most extensive in the world, in proportion with the size of the population. The frequent arrests of military officers, security personnel, and government employees revealed the extent to which the security apparatus was inward-looking and the regime fearful of threats from within. Al-Asad opponents have long argued, in this regard, that the AFID and the MIS – both notorious for torturing officers suspected of disloyalty to the regime – were more focused on quashing dissent in the armed forces than collecting data relevant to national security.[226]

The AFID was established early under Hafez al-Asad's tenure, and was considered to be the most loyal and efficient of all security organizations. While all of Syria's intelligence agencies were stacked with Alawis, it is widely believed that the percentage of non-Alawi officers was particularly low in the AFID.[227] Sunnis were well-represented among Syrian pilots, and the core mission of the AFID was to make sure they did not threaten the regime.[228] With that said, and despite its name, the AFID's task was never restricted to the air force alone, and it was feared within the Syrian armed forces and society at large. The authority of the ministry of defense over the AFID was only theoretical, as the intelligence complex answered to Hafez al-Asad directly. As for the MIS, it was the largest intelligence agency in terms of manpower, and was allegedly responsible for more torture and death in Syria than any other security organization.[229] The MIS assigned a security officer (*zabit amn*) and several informers to every military company in order to report on its personnel. The MIS also controlled Syria's Military Police, and was known for playing a crucial role in Lebanon, whereas the AFID specialized in covert operations abroad, the GID in monitoring the activities of the ruling Ba'ath Party, and the PSD in keeping a close watch on left-wing dissidents.[230]

Though boundaries between the different organizations were clear in theory, they were blurred in practice, which allowed for a great deal of overlap and rivalry. In order to reduce the excesses of the security complex decentralization, Hafez al-Asad created in the mid-1980s a Presidential Intelligence Committee in charge of coordinating the work of the intelligence agencies. The latter's autonomy was never seriously curtailed, however, and their competition endured. Such intra-regime friction served the interests of Hafez, as each agency checked the

---

[226] See Middle East Watch, *Syria Unmasked*, 40–41. See also Batatu, *Syria's Peasantry*, 240; and Sassoon, *Anatomy of Authoritarianism*, 95.
[227] See Tallaa, "The Syrian Security Services."
[228] See Bhalla, "Making Sense of the Syrian Crisis."
[229] Bruce, "Changes in the Syrian High Command," 127.
[230] Rathmell, "Syria's Intelligence Services."

power of the other and prevented it from accumulating too much clout. This left him in a position of complete control, and assured him access to different sources of information via trusted security lieutenants, who were all unswervingly answerable to him.[231]

Counterbalancing remained a central coup-proofing tactic in Syria under Bashar al-Asad. The Republican Guard consists of approximately 10,000 fighters, and its importance as a praetorian unit is undiminished. The Guard is still positioned in the Qasiun military complex overseeing Damascus's northern suburbs, which puts it in a "good position to counteract a coup."[232] After old-guard generals retired, Bashar filled several important positions with officers from the Guard, which operated as his personal fiefdom in the military–security complex.[233] As previously made clear, all generals appointed by Bashar to lead the Guard are Alawi, and the unit itself is almost completely stacked with the president's co-ethnics. The powerful Kheir-Beik Alawi clan is particularly pervasive in the Guard, and occupies major leading positions in its Security Company 101. The Guard's core task is still securing Damascus where it is deployed. With that said, the regime used the Guard to quell several disturbances outside the capital, such as the 2001 confrontations between local Druze and tribal Sunnis in southwestern Huran, the 2004 Kurdish uprising in northeastern Qamishli, and the 2005 clashes between Alawis and Isma'ilis in northwestern Masyaf.[234]

Another important all-Alawi praetorian unit is the Fourth Armored Division, which absorbed thousands of the Defense Companies' personnel after they were disbanded under Hafez al-Asad. The Division is positioned at the Mazzeh military complex above the capital's southern suburbs. Reports on the Division's manpower range from 15,000 to 50,000 normally stationed at the gateways of Damascus, but not in the city itself. The Division's personnel receive special training and are equipped with the best weaponry in Syria, including advanced Russian T72 tanks. The Division comprises a paratrooper regiment, engineering, and chemistry and Military Police battalions, in addition to several armored and infantry brigades. The Division's Branch 293, pertaining to officers' affairs, prepares special lists of candidates hailing from loyalist backgrounds to be admitted into the military and air force academies. As

---

[231] Seale, *Asad*, 428; and Middle East Watch, *Syria Unmasked*, 42. See also C. A. Wege, "Assad's Legions: The Syrian Intelligence Services," *The International Journal of Intelligence and Counterintelligence* 4, no. 1 (Spring 1990): 97.

[232] See Joseph Holliday, "The Assad Regime: From Counterinsurgency to Civil War," *Middle East Security* 8, Institute for the Study of War (March 2013): 44.

[233] 'Azmi Beshara, *Suria: Darb al-Alam, Muhawala fi al-Tarikh al-Rahin* (Doha: al-Markaz al-'Arabi li-l-Abhath wa-Dirasat al-Siasat, 2013), 302–303.

[234] See Tallaa, "The Syrian Security Services," 21.

for the Division's security office, it operates as a small, autonomous organization, but coordinates its activities with the country's main intelligence agencies. Finally, the anti-tank Struggle Companies provide an additional outer ring of defense for the capital in conjunction with the Third Armored Division and the eight to ten commando regiments of the Special Forces.[235]

The four main intelligence agencies that were active under Hafez al-Asad are still operational under Bashar. Estimations about the number of people employed in their different branches range from 100,000 to 200,000 operatives, which means that Syrians remained heavily spied upon after Hafez's demise.[236] The Air Force Intelligence Directorate (AFID) is still known for possessing the most sophisticated intelligence technology and skillful manpower, as well as for being particularly stacked with Alawis. The Military Intelligence Service (MIS) remains focused upon monitoring the armed forces – with the exception of the air force and air defense, both of which are under the supervision of the AFID. The MIS's Branch 294 keeps an eye on all troop movements, which it must approve beforehand. Its delegates in different units are answerable to the branch, not to their commanding officers, and report directly to it on the loyalty and political opinions of the troops. Branch 293 provides an additional layer of surveillance, and focuses exclusively upon the monitoring of military officers. The latter are promoted, transferred, or imprisoned as a function of reports submitted by Branch 293, the chief of which has the privilege of being able to contact Bashar al-Asad directly. According to a Sunni senior officer who defected in 2011, the armed forces cannot move a tank without the prior permission of the MIS, because the troops are "the executive power (*al-sulta al-tanfiziyya*) of the MIS, not of the military's commandership."[237] Another Sunni officer complained that if three Sunnis in the armed forces sit together for tea, the MIS could summon them to interrogate them over why they met.[238] As for the PSD and the GID, they have been in a state of permanent friction under Bashar due to the relative overlap of their mission. The latter has

[235] Ibid. See also Michael Eisenstadt, "Who Rules Syria? Bashar al-Asad and the Alawi Barons," Policy Watch, report no. 472, Washington Institute for Near East Policy, June 21, 2000, www.washingtoninstitute.org/policy-analysis/view/who-rules-syria-bashar-al-asad-and-the-alawi-barons (accessed June 22, 2018); and Zénobie, "Syrie."

[236] See a report on Syria's intelligence agencies published by *al-'Arabi al-Jadid*, April 13, 2015, www.alaraby.co.uk/politics/2015/4/13/استخبارات-النظام-السوري-مافيات-بصفة- أجهزة-أمنية (accessed June 22, 2018); and Zein al-'Abidin, *Al-Jaysh wa-l-Siasa*, 485.

[237] Zenobie, "Syrie"; and Tallaa, "The Syrian Security Services," 14–15.

[238] Interview with Major Mahmud 'Abbud (The Military Engineering Academy), Al-Rihanle, Turkey (May 15, 2014).

been especially active in keeping a watchful eye on police and interior security forces.[239]

Conclusion

The interior ministry became a central pillar of the coercive apparatus immediately after the breakdown of the Egyptian monarchy in 1952. And Nasser promoted the interests of the military elite as shown previously. Sadat pushed both dynamics further than Nasser ever did – and Mubarak outclassed his predecessors on both accounts. In Syria, too, the al-Asads counterbalanced the armed forces; and they wielded identity politics with deadly efficiency. And just like Nasser, Sadat, and Mubarak, the al-Asads tolerated top-brass corruption. In both Egypt and Syria, senior military commanders benefitted economically from allegiance to the regime; this was done in a quasi-institutionalized form through loyalty bonuses and post-retirement careers in Cairo, and on a more individual basis through enrichment opportunities in drug trafficking and rent extraction in Damascus. In both cases this led to a growing gap between the military elite (those who were effectively regime cronies) and their subordinates. In 2011, we were thus looking at two militaries whose leaders were loyalists, in which grievances related to counterbalancing had created tensions in regular troops, and in which top-brass profiteering had generated a gap between generals and younger officers, because money never trickled down. And yet coup-proofing bridged intra-military gaps in one case but not the other, as I show in Chapter 4. The consequences were tremendous.

---

[239] Zein al-ʿAbidin, *Al-Jaysh wa-l-Siasa*, 488.

4 How Coup-Proofing Structured Military Response to Protest in Egypt and Syria

The Egyptian uprising of 2011 began on January 25, eleven days after the ouster of Tunisia's autocrat Zein al-'Abidin Ben 'Ali. Given the historically different relationships between the regimes and their armed forces in Cairo and Tunis, it was not certain that the Egyptian military would refrain from using violence against protesters like the Tunisian soldiers did. And yet, the Egyptian armed forces did not rally behind Mubarak and mete out brutality as many feared they would. There is a puzzling question here: Why did two armies with radically different roles in regime formation and subsequent trajectories both desist from forcefully upholding the status quo? More precisely: Why did the armed forces in Egypt seemingly turn their back on a regime that was traditionally theirs? On the other hand: What explains the enduring loyalty of the bulk of the armed forces during the Syrian endgame, or the quick disintegration of the Libyan troops? In the following chapters, I answer these questions through the theoretical prism I developed earlier in this book.

The 2011 Uprising and the Fall of Mubarak: Explaining Military Behavior

The argument I make in this book is straightforward: the Egyptian military elite did not mete out violence in 2011 because they were unable to do so. The literature on regime change has long established that influential generals are unlikely to favor autocratic breakdowns especially in the absence of pacts enshrining prerogatives and guaranteeing impunity.[1] This insight is important to understand the agency of the Supreme Council of the Armed Forces (SCAF) during the endgame scenario of 2011. I contend that the SCAF remained an anti-revolutionary force committed to preserving the status quo until the very last days of

---

[1] See O'Donnell and Schmitter, *Transitions from Authoritarian Rule*. See also Kevin Koehler, "Political Militaries in Popular Uprisings: A Comparative Perspective on the Arab Spring," *International Political Science Review* 38, no. 3 (2017): 367.

Mubarak's tenure. The generals were opposed to humiliating Mubarak and did not want for him to go down ignominiously – this was particularly true of the defense minister and commander of the armed forces, Field Marshal Tantawi. Their subordinates in the officer corps, however, were not ready to open fire on their countrymen in order to keep Mubarak in power. And so the generals accepted regime breakdown to safeguard the cohesion of the armed forces and because they were bereft of options. To put it differently, the military elite couldn't save Mubarak, so they chose not to go down with him.

Counterbalancing and Discontent

The Egyptian military officers look at the interior ministry as a hated rival. My interviewees in Cairo expressed a loathing of the police that was unadulterated and pervasive:

It wasn't a secret that vast sums of money were allocated to the police under Mubarak. This fostered resentment among officers, especially in the lower echelons who were particularly hit by the economic crisis.[2]

Mubarak spoiled the police to coup-proof his regime against the military. Habib al-'Adly was interior minister for twelve years and he spent billions on beefing up the police. We used to scoff that he who covers himself with the police is naked (al-mitghatti bi-l-shurta 'aryan). 2011 proved us right.[3]

The attention Mubarak gave to the police alienated the officers who were struggling financially under his tenure. We didn't stop the police from mistreating civilians but we despised it.[4]

I heard similar comments invariably each time I interviewed military officers in Cairo. I argued in Chapter 1 that counterbalancing is effective from a coup-proofing perspective but can also foster estrangement in the armed forces vis-à-vis the powers that be. Egypt is an illustration of such dynamics. Just like Nasser and Sadat before him, Mubarak counterbalanced the armed forces with an increasingly assertive interior ministry. That Egypt was at peace following the 1978 Camp David Accords was conducive in this regard. The post-radical age in Egyptian foreign policy indeed implied that adventures requiring massive military deployments abroad – such as the Nasser-era war in Yemen – were passé. This meant that the EAF (Egyptian Armed Forces) could no longer claim absolute priority over other public institutions the way they did following the 1967 defeat. In contrast, the interior ministry's public profile kept rising. On

---

[2] Interview with retired Major General Tal'at Musallim (army), Cairo (July 27, 2012).
[3] Interview with retired Brigadier General A. Gaber (army), Cairo (June 12, 2012).
[4] Interview with a retired rear admiral (navy) who did not wish to be named, Cairo (August 2, 2012).

the one hand, the police was very much involved in squelching internal dissent and the fight against radical jihadi groups throughout the 1990s. Emergency law strengthened the clout of the interior ministry – policemen could kill or take bribes while remaining in effect unaccountable.[5] On the other, interior minister Habib al-ʿAdly became a trusted ally of the Mubarak dynasty in the 2000s. Al-ʿAdly was a critical supporter of *tawrith*, or passing power from the president to his ambitious son, Gamal. This also gave the police prominence, as the rise of the younger Mubarak appeared inexorable in the last years of his father's presidency. And so the interior ministry increasingly took on the allure of a state within a state in the 2000s – one that was pervasive and ruthless.[6] Al-ʿAdly's men grew so confident that police officers were sometimes disrespectful of their junior peers in the armed forces.[7] The latter were understandably reluctant in 2011 to kill ordinary Egyptians in order to save a regime they increasingly associated with their rivals.

That said, the military top brass were still within the presidential ruling coalition in 2011. Consequently, the generals remained committed to the regime, despite the increasing prominence of the police. I have shown previously the extent to which the Mubarak regime went to promote the interests of the top brass. I add here that at every comparative level, the military generals received more from the regime than their peers in the police. The budget represents a case in point. In a real police state, the interior ministry systematically outshines the military in the squabble for greater shares of the budget. This never happened in Egypt. And despite the spectacular rise in assets allocated to the interior ministry in Egypt, they always remained inferior to those of the ministry of defense. One consequence was the divergent compensation allocated to conscripts serving in the military, and their interior ministry counterparts: both were severely underpaid and exploited, but the former still made four times as much as the latter.[8] In fact, the police never overtook the military in the competition for state resources under the Mubarak regime, even if the $1.3 billion in annual aid from the US is excluded from the defense budget.[9]

In addition, "Military, Inc." dwarfed "Interior, Inc." The latter only began developing in the 2000s, and never reached the scale of the former.

---

[5] Interview with Maye Kassem, an Egyptian academic, Cairo (February 7, 2014).
[6] This was particularly true of the interior ministry's SSIS.
[7] Interview with Ahmad Sayyid al-Naggar, Cairo (June 18, 2012).
[8] Christopher S. Read, "Allegiance: Egypt Security Forces" (master's thesis, Naval Postgraduate School, Monterey, California, 2013), 20, https://apps.dtic.mil/dtic/tr/full text/u2/a620384.pdf (accessed February 2, 2014).
[9] Sayigh, "Above the State," 7.

Companies established by the interior ministry mainly handle the work of the same ministry: for instance, fabricating national ID cards or manufacturing road signs. We still lack detailed studies about interior ministry business, but everything we know suggests that it lags behind the military's economic realm by far. Finally, while both military and police generals were appointed to coveted civilian jobs, the former systematically received more than the latter. Local government stands as an excellent example. Police influence under Mubarak reached its height in the 2000s – of all fifty-nine governors appointed during that decade, twelve hailed from the police (22 percent), but twenty-six were military generals (44 percent). Overall, thirty-four governors appointed throughout Mubarak's tenure were police generals (22 percent) and sixty-three came from the armed forces (40 percent).[10] In the words of a police general and former assistant to the interior minister:

We have our own slice of the cake, but the armed forces have the cake itself.[11]

It could not have been otherwise. Mubarak was vice president when the military saved the regime from certain collapse in 1977, and he was president when the military quelled the Central Security Forces (CSF) in 1986. In both instances, it was the EAF that acted as the final line of defense for the officers' republic, not the police. And while the fight against radical Islamists fell within the realm of the interior ministry, the armed forces intervened when necessary: the EAF's action against Islamist radicals at Luxor in Upper Egypt in 1997 is but one example. In 1988, Ahmed 'Abdalla argued that the Egyptian military was "the ultimate barrier against an Islamic takeover of power by extra-parliamentary means."[12] This remained true throughout Mubarak's tenure, and gave the military political weight. Significantly, while Mubarak never appointed a vice president until the very end, the candidates for the job were always senior military officers, from Field Marshal Abu Ghazalah in the 1980s to 'Omar Suleiman and Field Marshal Tantawi later on. That a police general should be appointed vice president was unthinkable. On the other hand, while a police coup was unimaginable in Egypt, a military coup was, of course, anything but. While this meant that the regime needed to strengthen the interior ministry as a counterweight to the EAF, it also forced Mubarak to cultivate the loyalty of the top brass to keep them quiescent. And that Mubarak did diligently, as I demonstrated earlier. To quote Yasser El-Shimy at length:

[10] Bou Nassif, "Wedded to Mubarak," 517.
[11] See Yasser El-Shimy, "Unveiling the Gun: Why Praetorian Armies Decide to Rule, the Case of Egypt (2011–2013)" (PhD diss., Boston University, 2016), 95.
[12] 'Abdalla, "The Armed Forces," 1465.

The Egyptian army is not a mere prop in the coercive apparatus of an authoritarian regime, to be sure, but rather is the central pillar upon which all else rests. If it withholds support, the structure comes crumbling down. This is why Mubarak's resignation and the dissolution of the NDP did not spell an end to non-democratic rule in Egypt. It was the end of that system's external façade. The praetorian system remained, even as its civilian veneer was replaced by something else. Put differently, contemplate a counter-factual: what if the police, widely considered to be the strongest coercive pillar of Mubarak's regime, had attempted to force the three-decade-long tyrant into retirement, and take over the political reins itself? Would they have been able to do so, and design a "transition"? This is simply unimaginable, given the diminished legitimacy, political power, and coercive capabilities enjoyed by the police force compared to the EAF. The truth is, political regimes in Egypt had staked their claim to rule Egypt since the 1952 military coup, upon their association with . . . the EAF. This decades-long political system shuffles the cards occasionally, but never in a way that has undermined the abiding prominence of generals.[13]

El-Shimy is not alone in pinpointing the continued importance of the EAF under Mubarak. The truth is many scholars are skeptical per the "military decline" thesis. Yezid Sayigh, for instance, argues that the EAF remained a "key player" in the various institutions surrounding Mubarak, because it played "an indispensable role in regime maintenance."[14] Roger Owen maintains that the "increasingly elderly commanders" of the EAF were "significant members of the president's crony elite."[15] Philippe Droz-Vincent argues that the Mubarak regime "relied on the military as [a] backbone."[16] For his part, Anthony H. Cordesman notes that senior officers around Mubarak occupied key posts in the system, and had a vested interest in preventing change and keeping the status quo. "None are symbols of progress and change," wrote Cordesman about the Egyptian top brass.[17] I concur. Counterbalancing under Mubarak embittered the military at large, especially the young officers and soldiers, but it never implied that the interior ministry marginalized the SCAF and its negative repercussions on the generals were largely mitigated by Mubarak's extreme generosity toward them. Consequently, the military elite were not happy to see Mubarak humiliated. I show below that the generals lacked the capacity, not the will, to break the popular mobilizations in 2011.

---

[13] El-Shimy, "Unveiling the Gun," 32.   [14] Sayigh, "Above the State," 6–7.
[15] Owen, "Military Presidents," 395.
[16] Philippe Droz-Vincent, "Prospects for 'Democratic Control of the Armed Forces'? Comparative Insights and Lessons for the Arab World in Transition," *Armed Forces & Society* 40, no. 4 (2014): 711.
[17] Anthony H. Cordesman, "If Mubarak Leaves: The Role of the Egyptian Military," Center for Strategic and International Studies, February 10, 2011, www.csis.org/analysis/if-mubarak-leaves-role-egyptian-military (accessed May 15, 2014).

A Tale of Two Officer Corps

As previously discussed in Chapter 1, senior officers have the authority to issue orders, but their actual implementation is predicated upon the willingness of their subordinates to execute them. At the time of the 2011 uprising in Egypt, had the commander of the EAF, Field Marshal Tantawi, and his chief of staff, Lieutenant General Sami ʿAnan, ordered their troops to quell the popular uprising, they themselves would not have been the ones opening fire on civilians demonstrating in Tahrir Square. The same holds true for other SCAF generals, as well as the military elite at large. In contrast, mid-ranking and junior officers, in addition to the rank and file, would have been directly in charge of what would have inevitably become a protracted slaughter throughout Egypt possibly leading to the deaths of thousands. Would these officers and their soldiers have obeyed orders to shoot civilians?

This chapter has established that Mubarak wedded the top brass to his rule through a system of material incentives built upon pecuniary rewards and the promise of a highly remunerated post-retirement career. In contrast, the mid-ranking and junior officers did considerably less well during Mubarak's tenure because the rewards were exclusively distributed among the senior commanders. A retired general talking anonymously to Reuters reckoned that the beneficiaries of patronage in the armed forces were "concentrated in about 15 percent" of officers representing the military top brass. In this system, the perks did not trickle down to subordinates in the officer corps, let alone NCOs and soldiers at large. Pointedly, the range of young officers' monthly wages under Mubarak was between $333 and $414, which is the rough equivalent of a cab driver's income in Cairo in a good month.[18] These salaries are quite ludicrous in comparison with other Arab countries – say, for instance, the United Arab Emirates (UAE), where colonels make $36,000 per month.[19] Egyptian officers' wives have to work to make ends meet, and to be able to afford private schooling for their children.[20] Under these conditions, it is unsurprising that retired generals bemoan the fact that the military profession is "no longer an attractive option for ambitious young people."[21] Nor is it startling that military recruiters fail to entice the well-educated members of the urban elite, for whom the prospects of a career

---

[18] See Marwa Awad, "Special Report: In Egypt's Military, a March for Change," Reuters, April 10, 2012, www.reuters.com/article/us-egypt-army-idUSBRE8390IV20120410 (accessed March 12, 2014).

[19] Gaub, *Guardians of the Arab State*, 35.   [20] Cassandra, "The Impending Crisis," 21.

[21] See Elisabeth Bumiller, "Egypt Stability Hinges on a Divided Military," *The New York Times*, February 5, 2011, www.nytimes.com/2011/02/06/world/middleeast/06military.html (accessed February 12, 2015).

in the EAF are unappealing.[22] To be sure, the armed forces do offer mid-ranking and junior officers some advantages in terms of housing and healthcare. Overall, young officers do better than their peers in civilian administration. However, it is certain that these officers were deeply unhappy with their economic situation, like most Egyptians under Mubarak:

A freshly graduated second lieutenant from the military academy earns 2,000 pounds a month, maximum ($280). He may pay parts of his salary as a monthly installment for an apartment. But he also may have to wait for years, sometimes three to five, to get that apartment. He also benefits from a loan to buy a car, and from a good healthcare system in military hospitals. He doesn't get any help paying for the education of his children. Under these conditions, junior and mid-ranking officers were struggling financially. There was a widespread feeling among Egyptians that the regime was stealing the country – that there was a group of thieves around Gamal Mubarak pillaging Egypt. The officers were certainly aware of what the people were saying, and they were affected by the prevalent atmosphere. This was particularly true among junior officers, who were not able to get married because of a lack of financial means. They were very critical of Mubarak.[23]

The biggest drain on our salaries is education. The public educational system is crumbling; officers typically send their children to private schools and universities, and struggle to pay the tuition. We receive no help from the state in that regard. Nor could the state provide better salaries. When we used to complain, we used to be told that officers are public servants, and that the state could not raise the salaries of military public servants alone and leave the rest lagging too far behind. To raise the salaries of officers, the state needed to raise the salaries of other public servants, as well, and that was a measure it could not afford to take.[24]

Egyptian officers, in general, have better living conditions than most Egyptians. We benefit from the following advantages: First, our salaries are relatively better than civilian civil servants with the same level of education. Second, we can get loans to buy apartments with an easy mortgage stretching over thirty years. Third, we can get loans to buy goods (*sila' mu'ammira*) such as cars, TVs, refrigerators, and so forth. That being said, we were aware that Gamal and his cronies were making millions, whereas we were living barely at ease. The Mubarak regime, and Gamal in particular, became unpopular within our ranks.[25]

---

[22] Hazem Kandil, "Back on Horse? The Military between Two Revolutions," in *Arab Spring in Egypt*, 186.

[23] Interview with retired Major General Mohammad Qadri Sa'id (army), Cairo (July 1, 2012).

[24] Interview with a retired brigadier general (army) who did not wish to be named, Cairo (August 15, 2012).

[25] Interview with a retired rear admiral (navy) who did not wish to be named, Cairo (August 2, 2012).

Mid-level officers are usually career professionals who are not part of the political side of the military. They have won considerable public respect and support over the years, but they also have lost status, as a new class of businessmen and profiteers has acquired great wealth and the disparities in income have grown. Most can now buy less by the way of housing, education for the children, and the key elements of middle-class living than in the past.[26]

This means that young officers were struggling financially under Mubarak, in sharp contrast with the thriving military elite. Ahmed Hashim pinpoints accurately in this regard the "vast gulf" separating the "pampered senior command" from their subordinates, who were resentful of slow promotions and low pay.[27] The dichotomy between the senior officers and their subordinates did not go unnoticed prior to the uprising. Cables from the WikiLeaks website reveal that foreign diplomats described mid-level officers as "generally disgruntled" in 2008, reporting that "the mid-level officers do not necessarily share their superiors' fealty to the regime," and that Field Marshal Tantawi was unwaveringly loyal to the president but unpopular among young officers who dismissed him as "Mubarak's poodle."[28] A 2011 account penned by an anonymous young reserve officer in the EAF confirmed such reports. The officer maintained that his commanders deliberately distributed bad regulation food served on dirty plates and with dirty spoons. Soldiers were forced to buy their own rations from military cafeterias run by the generals. The latter's discourse about their achievements in the 1973 Yom Kippur War ran increasingly hollow and no longer convinced their subordinates, according to the whistleblowing officer: "Back then, they [i.e., the generals] had a cause to fight for – now it's all just bullshit and corruption."[29]

The friction between the upper and lower levels of the officer corps set the background for the military elite's behavior in 2011. The agency of Egypt's top brass throughout the uprising reflected both their preferences

---

[26] Cordesman, "If Mubarak Leaves."

[27] Hashim, "The Egyptian Military, Part Two," 121.

[28] See Cable ID: 08CAIRO0291, "Academics See the Military as in Decline, But Retaining Strong Influence," September 23, 2008, https://wikileaks.org/plusd/cables/08CAIR O2091_a.html (accessed May 8, 2015). Along similar lines, the Egyptian journalist 'Abdul-'Azim Hammad argues that young Egyptian officers blamed Tantawi for all the problems from which Egypt was suffering. According to Hammad, Tantawi's lack of a support base among mid-ranking and junior officers precluded any political ambitions the aging general might have harbored after the fall of Mubarak, lest a presidential bid trigger a coup. See 'Abdul-'Azim Hammad, *Al-Thawra al-Ta'iha, Sira' al-Khudha, wa-l-Lihia, wa-l-Midan, Ru'yat Shahed 'Ayan* (Cairo: al-Mahrousa, 2013), 30.

[29] Jack Shenker, "Egyptian Arms Officer's Diary of Military Life in a Revolution," *The Guardian*, December 28, 2011, www.theguardian.com/world/2011/dec/28/egyptian-military-officers-diary (accessed November 27, 2014).

(leaning toward the regime) and their inability to uphold the status quo without jeopardizing the cohesiveness of the military – and by extension their control over it. Recall that the regime unleashed its full force against the protestors during four days of fierce street battles at the beginning of the uprising. From January 25 to 28, 2011, clashes between the demonstrators, on one hand, and the police and CSF, on the other, were so violent that Cairo was described as a "war zone."[30] At least 840 people died in the confrontations of the Egyptian uprising, and 6,467 were wounded, mostly civilians from underprivileged backgrounds according to Amnesty International.[31] Had the SCAF opposed the bloodshed, it could have stopped it; the police and the CSF combined were no match for the military's superior firepower. The armed forces, however, remained in their barracks as long as the police and the CSF were confronting the demonstrators. They only intervened when Mubarak ordered them to do so when the embattled pro-regime forces collapsed on January 28. On that day, Mubarak decreed in his capacity as commander-in-chief a nighttime curfew in Cairo, Alexandria, and Suez, and ordered the military to implement the decision in cooperation with the defeated police. The SCAF immediately deployed troops in the streets of restive cities, advised civilians to avoid assembling in groups, and warned them that anyone who breaks the curfew "will be in danger."[32] On January 30, Mubarak conferred with defense minister Tantawi, chief of staff 'Anan, and other senior military commanders in a meeting that was highly covered by state media. Meanwhile, the SCAF sent jets to fly menacingly at low altitudes over the crowds in Tahrir Square. In the fluid atmosphere of the time, the demonstrators were uncertain about the intention of the military, and the sight of jets buzzing Tahrir sent an intimidating signal that some protesters likened to "terrorism."[33]

On January 31, a military spokesperson declared on state TV that the armed forces recognized the legitimacy of the protesters' demands and pledged that the military "will not resort to use of force against

---

[30] "Protests in Egypt and Unrest in Middle East – As It Happened," *The Guardian*, January 25, 2011, www.theguardian.com/global/blog/2011/jan/25/middleeast-tunisia (accessed March 12, 2014). See also "Egyptian Revolution Cost At Least 846 Lives," CBS News, April 19, 2011, www.cbsnews.com/news/egyptian-revolution-cost-at-least-846-lives (accessed June 15, 2013).

[31] "Egypt Rises: Killings, Detentions, and Torture in the '25 January Revolution,'" Amnesty International, May 19, 2011, 8, www.amnesty.org/download/Documents/320 00/mde120272011en.pdf (accessed March 5, 2014).

[32] BBC News, "Egypt Protests: Curfew Defied in Cairo and Other Cities," January 29, 2011, www.bbc.com/news/world-middle-east-12314799 (accessed May 12, 2013).

[33] *Associated Press*, January 30, 2011.

our great people."[34] This statement signaled to the opposition that the SCAF had turned against Mubarak. But two days later, on February 2, when regime loyalists launched the infamous Battle of the Camel and repeatedly attacked protesters in Tahrir Square, the SCAF ordered the troops to remain on the sidelines. The loyalists used knives and firebombers in their assault on the demonstrators but the army did little to prevent them from entering the square; eye-witness accounts actually suggest that some Military Intelligence (MI) units had cooperated with Mubarak's hired thugs. It is significant to note that when Mubarak supporters climbed onto roofs to rain Molotov cocktails down on the protesters, the soldiers were ordered not to intervene.[35] And when demonstrators begged a senior military officer present in Tahrir to protect them from the thugs, he retorted: "But aren't they Egyptian? ... You want me to fire at Egyptians?"[36] Furthermore, a lieutenant colonel berated the demonstrators who were, according to him, "going to rip the country apart," and inquired about the "money" coming in to organize the protests, thus repeating Mubarak's accusations that the uprising was the work of hostile foreigners seeking to destabilize Egypt.[37] Meanwhile, the MI was abducting activists opposed to Mubarak, some of whom were tortured to death.[38] The MI was also doing all it could to prevent foreign journalists from covering the escalating situation, including detaining them.[39] The Military Police (MP) too were engaged in arbitrary arrests of journalists, human rights activists, and protesters – some of whom were tortured and electroshocked in the military prison at the Heikstep base (east of Cairo). In fact, reports suggest that the MP was responsible for most cases of torture during the Egyptian

---

[34] See Ian Black, Jack Shenker, and Chris McGreal, "Egypt Set for Mass Protest as Army Rules Out Force," *The Guardian*, January 31, 2011, www.theguardian.com/world/2011/jan/31/egyptian-army-pledges-no-force (accessed June 15, 2013).

[35] Neil Ketchley, "The Army and the People Are One Hand! Fraternization and the 25th January Egyptian Revolution," *Comparative Studies in Society and History* 56, no. 1 (January 2014): 174–175.

[36] See David D. Kirkpatrick and Kareem Fahim, "Mubarak's Allies and Foes Clash in Egypt," *The New York Times*, February 2, 2011, www.nytimes.com/2011/02/03/world/middleeast/03egypt.html (accessed January 18, 2014).

[37] See Wendell Steavenson, "On the Square: Were the Egyptian Protesters Right to Trust the Military?" *The New Yorker*, February 21, 2011, www.newyorker.com/magazine/2011/02/28/on-the-square-wendell-steavenson (accessed April 4, 2020).

[38] See Evan Hill and Muhammad Mansour, "Egypt's Army Took Part in Torture and Killings during Revolution, Report Shows," *The Guardian*, April 10, 2013, www.theguardian.com/world/2013/apr/10/egypt-army-torture-killings-revolution (accessed January 18, 2014).

[39] Steven A. Cook, *The Struggle for Egypt: From Nasser to Tahrir Square* (New York: Oxford University Press, 2012), 288.

uprising, not the interior ministry.[40] A Western diplomat noted correctly that though Field Marshal Tantawi was not ordering his troops to open fire on civilians, he was "perfectly happy to arrest people."[41] It was never guaranteed that the protesters would push back against assailants and eventually win the day on February 2, but they did and saved the uprising from defeat; however, they owe little to the SCAF in this regard. Lest we forget, the two military bodies that rivaled with the interior ministry in meting out violence to protesters, the MI and the MP, were led by two sitting members of the SCAF, 'Abdul-Fattah al-Sisi, and Hamdi Badin, respectively.

The facts surrounding these happenings are complex and the SCAF's role seemingly ambivalent. Two things are certain, however: (1) The generals instructed their subordinates to stand idle when hired regime supporters exerted extreme violence on behalf of their masters, and the fate of the uprising hanged in the balance. Indeed, the military moved tanks to clear the way for the thugs' road to Tahrir.[42] (2) The SCAF's action in this specific context corresponds, in effect, to supporting the regime as Joshua Stacher has correctly noted.[43] Robert Springborg has argued in this regard that the SCAF was "orchestrating events" and "making possible the various forms of assault on the protesters."[44] William C. Taylor maintained that the SCAF's actions during the crisis "debunk the narrative that the military was ambitiously waiting for a period of domestic upheaval in order to reassert its authority over Mubarak and his acolytes in MoI."[45] Along similar lines, Holger Albrecht and Dina Bishara noted that the SCAF met without Mubarak only on February 10, though soldiers had been deployed as early as January 28, and concluded persuasively that the SCAF was, in fact, "reluctant to drive Mubarak out" until it ran out of options.[46] And if we add to this that the SCAF gave Mubarak time to make several interventions on national TV, offering a mixture of concessions and promises provided the protesters disperse, it becomes unambiguous that the SCAF did whatever it could to help the embattled president, short of ordering

---

[40] See Human Rights Watch report, "Egypt: Investigate Arrests of Activists, Journalists," February 9, 2011, www.hrw.org/news/2011/02/09/egypt-investigate-arrests-activists-journalists (accessed January 12, 2014); and "Egypt Rises," 70–80.

[41] Steavenson, "On the Square."   [42] "Egypt Rises," 36.

[43] Joshua Stacher, *Adaptable Autocrats: Regime Power in Egypt and Syria* (Stanford, CA: Stanford University Press, 2012), 11.

[44] Quoted in Bumiller, "Egypt Stability."

[45] William C. Taylor, *Military Responses to the Arab Uprising and the Future of Civil–Military Relations in the Middle East: Analysis from Egypt, Tunisia, Libya, and Syria* (New York: Palgrave Macmillan, 2014), 127. Note that "MoI" here refers to the ministry of interior.

[46] Holger Albrecht and Dina Bishara, "Back on Horseback: The Military and Political Transformation in Egypt," *Middle East Law and Governance* 3, no. 1–2 (2011): 16.

a full-scale massacre of protesters. Lest we forget, Mubarak pledged on February 1 that he would not run again in the September 2011 elections. He promised reforms and struck an emotional chord with the public when he said he wished to die in his homeland. By that time, the turmoil of the last week had exhausted many Egyptians who ached for normalcy and were ready to tolerate Mubarak for eight additional months if that would stop the violence.[47] Had it not been for the Battle of the Camel that unfolded a day later, Mubarak's strategy could have worked – and the SCAF did nothing to undercut it. Senior officers, including members of the SCAF, were asked several times to explain the reason for their inaction during the first days of the revolution. Their answers reveal indeed that the military elite were far from eager to force Mubarak to step down:

At the beginning, we gave the presidential institution full opportunity to manage events. If it were able to succeed, nothing would have happened. We would have pulled our people back to the barracks. But they were incapable of responding to the events.[48]

We gave Mubarak a chance to fix the deteriorating situation, but he could not. So we had to intervene.[49]

The Egyptian military will not do what the Tunisian counterparts did with Ben Ali.[50]

The army in Tunisia put pressure on Ben Ali to leave. We are not going to do that here. The army here is loyal to this country and to the regime.[51]

I asked the generals I met in Cairo if they believe that their colleagues were sincere when they made such statements and my interviewees overwhelmingly said they did – and that they were thinking along similar lines themselves when the events were unfolding. In other words, I found no

---

[47] See International Crisis Group, "Popular Protest in North Africa and throughout the Middle East: Egypt Victorious?" Middle East and North Africa report no. 101, February 24, 2011, 9, www.crisisgroup.org/file/1549/download?token=fY0Ba424 (accessed March 7, 2015).

[48] See Lally Weymouth, "Egyptian Generals Speak about the Revolution, Elections," *The Washington Post*, May 18, 2011, www.washingtonpost.com/world/middle-east/egyptian-generals-speak-about-revolution-elections/2011/05/16/AF7AiU6G_story.html?utm_term=.e8a659988cfb (accessed April 25, 2014).

[49] See interview with a SCAF general (December 13, 2011) in international Crisis Group, "Lost in Transition: The World according to Egypt's SCAF," Middle East and North Africa report no. 121, April 24, 2012, www.crisisgroup.org/middle-east-north-africa/north-africa/egypt/lost-transition-world-according-egypt-s-scaf (accessed February 5, 2014).

[50] Egyptian Chief of Staff/Lieutenant General Sami ʿAnan, speaking in Washington during the first day of the mobilization in Egypt. See Atef Said, "The Paradox of Transition to 'Democracy' under Military Rule," *Social Research* 79, no. 2 (Summer 2012): 401.

[51] Retired Egyptian General Hosam Sowilan, quoted in David D. Kirkpatrick, "Mubarak Orders Crackdown, with Revolt Sweeping Egypt," *The New York Times*, January 28, 2011, www.nytimes.com/2011/01/29/world/middleeast/29unrest.html (accessed March 27, 2014).

discrepancy between what some of the top brass said publicly and what others repeated to me privately. This review of events suggests that the SCAF was not neutral in 2011, let alone favorable to the uprising. The generals initially hoped that Mubarak's repeated TV appearances would diffuse the situation or that his thugs would cow demonstrators. When it became clear that these hopes were misplaced, the military elite balked at issuing orders for the troops to shoot protesters, because they were "unable to guarantee anything else."[52] The fact is the signals sent from the streets of Cairo were unmistakable: soldiers and protesters were hugging and fraternizing on TV. From the beginning, the demonstrators followed what has been labeled the "hug a soldier" method and treated army soldiers "almost with adulation."[53] They sang the national anthem, spoke with the military personnel, and begged for their support; the mid-level officers and their soldiers responded positively to such tactics.[54] For instance, when worried demonstrators asked a lead tank commander in Tahrir Square whether he would open fire on them, he answered, "No, I will never do that, not even if I am given that order."[55] Other tank commanders in Tahrir were tearing off headsets over which they received orders from their superiors; some called their families for advice and were told not to kill civilians even if that entailed insubordination.[56] One colonel pledged to cut his own hands "before firing one bullet" on the protesters.[57] Captain Majed Bulus vowed publicly to commit suicide if the military meted out violence to civilians. Bulus made headlines when he instructed his troops to defend the protesters during the Battle of the Camel thus ignoring the SCAF's explicit orders to remain neutral. The young officer was seen sobbing in sorrow for the death of protesters that day.[58] Throughout the uprising, journalists covering the events reported on fraternization between the lower echelons of the military and the protesters – and the latter scrawling political slogans on tanks in

---

[52] Read, "Allegiance," 49.

[53] David D. Kirkpatrick and Mona El-Naggar, "Protest's Old Guard Falls In behind the Young," *The New York Times*, January 30, 2011, www.nytimes.com/2011/01/31/world/middleeast/31opposition.html (accessed January 15, 2013). See also Marwa Awad, "Egypt Army Seeks to Free Tahrir Square for Traffic," Reuters, February 5, 2011, www.reuters.com/article/us-egypt-protests/egypt-army-seeks-to-free-tahrir-square-for-traffic-idUSTRE7141S820110205 (accessed January 5, 2014).

[54] Read, "Allegiance," 32.

[55] Wendell Steavenson, *Circling the Square: Stories from the Egyptian Revolution* (New York: HarperCollins, 2015), 18.

[56] See Robert Fisk, "As Mubarak Clings On ... What Now for Egypt," *The Independent*, February 11, 2011, www.independent.co.uk/voices/commentators/fisk/robert-fisk-as-mubarak-clings-on-what-now-for-egypt-2211287.html (accessed June 5, 2013).

[57] Kandil, *Soldiers, Spies, and Statesmen*, 226.

[58] See Egyptian daily *Al-Ahram*'s report on Captain Majed Bulus, March 5, 2011, http://gate.ahram.org.eg/News/45415.aspx (accessed March 14, 2019).

Tahrir Square.[59] Hazem Kandil observed, in this regard, that the army was "visibly supportive of the revolt without waiting for instruction from above."[60] It is unlikely that this took the SCAF by surprise. The job of the Military Intelligence in any armed force is to keep a close watch on the officer corps and report to the commandership about the political opinions of its members. Tantawi must have known long before 2011 that his men loathed Mubarak and his ambitious son, Gamal. Furthermore, the interaction between the troops and the protesters made it completely clear for the SCAF that the officers in the field could at best be instructed to remain on the sidelines, but would not slaughter thousands to keep Mubarak in power. In fact, even neutrality proved too much to bear for some mid-ranking and junior officers who defected outright to the protesters: Major Ahmad Shuman, Major ʿAmr Metwalli, and Major Tamer Badr publicly went over to the uprising on February 10, and called for Mubarak's ouster while wearing their military uniform. Fifteen other mid-ranking and junior officers quickly joined them, and pledged to support the uprising.[61] Their defection greatly alarmed the SCAF, who feared that a cascade of desertions would follow; Field Marshal Tantawi found the prospect of officers in uniform speaking on Al Jazeera particularly worrying.[62] On the same day, the commander of the Cairo military district and SCAF member Major General Hasan al-Roweini told his colleagues that the troops were not ready to open fire on the crowd "for any extended period of time" and warned repeatedly of an "Iranian scenario" should the situation escalate.[63] It is important to give

[59] See, for instance, David D. Kirkpatrick, "Mubarak's Grip On Power Is Shaken," *The New York Times*, January 31, 2011, www.nytimes.com/2011/02/01/world/middleeast/01egypt.html (accessed March 5, 2014). Even the lower echelons of the police were not always ready to fire on civilians. The testimony of a protester to the International Crisis Group (ICG) is interesting, in this regard: "I faced off with a riot policeman, both of us screaming and pleading with each other, him yelling, 'Don't approach,' and me yelling, 'Don't shoot!' He clearly didn't want to. I saw another officer holding a tear gas gun who said to the guy next to him, 'I can't do this, this is wrong,' and then ran behind a security vehicle and gave the gun to someone else." See International Crisis Group, "Egypt Victorious," 4.

[60] Kandil, *Soldiers, Spies, and Statesmen*, 226.

[61] See Marwa Awad, "Egypt Army Officer Says 15 Others Join Protesters," Reuters, February 11, 2011, www.reuters.com/article/us-egypt-protest-officers/egypt-army-officer-says-15-others-join-protesters-idUSTRE71A12V20110211 (accessed June 4, 2013).

[62] Interview with retired Major General Mohammad Qadri Saʿid, Cairo (June 10, 2012). See Omar Ashour, "Ballots versus Bullets: The Crisis of Civil–Military Relations in Egypt," Brookings, September 3, 2013, www.brookings.edu/articles/ballots-versus-bullets-the-crisis-of-civil-military-relations-in-egypt (accessed March 20, 2019).

[63] See Sidney Blumenthal, "Intel Report and Options: What Really Happened and What Should Happen Now," WikiLeaks, February 21, 2011, https://wikileaks.org/clinton-emails/emailid/13117 (accessed April 5, 2016).

al-Roweini's words the attention they deserve. The careful Mubarak was known for hand-picking particularly pliable generals for the position of Cairo military district commander;[64] al-Roweini was a loyalist. And yet, the general was forced to caution that the Egyptian high command faced the real possibility of losing control over the lower military echelons who might defect to the uprising should the situation escalate. Reportedly, Tantawi himself told Mubarak as much in the last conversation between the two men prior to the latter's downfall:

Mr. President, your presence in power is no longer sustainable. I consider myself to be a son of yours, and I urge you to leave office because the alternative to that is war in the streets (harb shaware'), and the military is disinclined to fight the people in the streets; all our officers and soldiers have brothers or relatives demonstrating in Egypt's squares.[65]

Tantawi had always believed that the first mission of the EAF was to protect Egypt's legitimate order (al-shar'iyya), of which Mubarak was the symbol.[66] The general and his fellow SCAF counterparts had originally hoped Mubarak could stay in office until the end of his term in September 2011, and manage a smooth and dignified transition of power.[67] Mubarak was still president when, on February 5, SCAF's General al-Roweini visited the protesters in Tahrir and asked them to disperse in order to preserve "what's left of Egypt." When the demonstrators responded with shouts clamoring again for Mubarak's resignation, al-Roweini stepped down from a podium he was standing on saying: "I will not speak amid such chants."[68] Later on the same day, al-Roweini claimed that demonstrators had forcefully prevented ordinary Egyptians from leaving the streets. He dismissed the popular movement as "silly business" and "fuss" (zeita); he also asserted that "no one can apply pressure on the government" (ma haddish yi'dar yidghat 'ala al-hukuma).[69] Having failed to convince the crowds to empty Tahrir, the SCAF ordered its troops on

[64] Taylor, Military Responses, 132.
[65] Mohammad al-Baz, Al-Mushir wa-l-Fariq, 221. Note that Tantawi told Mubarak during a hospital visit in October 2014 that the SCAF was acting to preserve the cohesiveness of the EAF (tamasok al-jaysh) throughout the events that led to the former president's downfall three years earlier. See Egyptian daily Al-Yawm al-Sabi'"s report on Tantawi's visit on October 19, 2014.
[66] Hammad, Al-Thawra al-Ta'iha, 52.
[67] Dina Shehata, "The Fall of the Pharaoh: How Hosni Mubarak's Reign Came to an End," Foreign Affairs 90, no. 3 (May/June 2011): 31.
[68] See Marwa Awad and Dina Zayed, "Army Tries to Limit Cairo Protest Camp Space," Reuters, February 6, 2011, https://uk.reuters.com/article/uk-egypt-protests-army/army-tries-to-limit-cairo-protest-camp-space-idUKTRE71527J20110206 (accessed January 16, 2014). See also al-Baz, Al-Mushir wa-l-Fariq, 240.
[69] Al-Ruweini's video is available at: www.youtube.com/watch?v=DkNS4RghLLQ&list=PLB4098476254686E8 (accessed June 5, 2015). See also Steavenson, "On the Square."

February 6, and again on February 9, to move armored vehicles into the Square and fire shots of live ammunition into the air to clear the protesters – or corral them into a small circle – and get traffic moving again.[70] In essence, the SCAF was trying to reestablish normalcy in Tahrir while Mubarak was clinging to power. But the SCAF's tactics failed and the protests continued with an influx of labor unions.[71] On February 10, Mubarak gave his last speech and pledged to remain in office until the end of his term – the ensuing popular outrage and escalation of protest signaled to the SCAF that the uprising will not fizzle as long as Mubarak remained president. It took the threat of a general insurrection throughout Egypt for the military elite to exert pressure upon Mubarak to relinquish the presidency on February 11, thirteen days after they had become the supreme arbiter of the situation unfolding in Cairo, on January 29 – in contradistinction, the Tunisian autocrat Zein al-ʿAbidin Ben ʿAli was ousted only three days after the military secured control over Tunis on January 11, 2011. Specifically, the Egyptian top brass removed Mubarak from office after two things became clear: first, that dislodging protesters from Tahrir Square would require a bloodbath. And second, that ordering troops to fire would trigger a mutiny in the lower ranks, and thus jeopardize the generals' survival.[72] And yet even then, the top brass still hoped that Mubarak's exit would be "graceful" and that their patron would "go with dignity."[73] I dwelled briefly in the introduction of this book on the quagmire of the military leadership during the 1985 popular uprising in Sudan: the loyalist and change-resistant Tantawi was in 2011 a latter-day Siwar al-Dahab.

Interestingly, the generals' fealty to their benefactor outlived his downfall. For instance, both Tantawi and ʿAnan denied repeatedly that Mubarak had ever ordered them to open fire on the protesters. By doing so, the two men paved the way for Egyptian courts to be lenient toward the former president. Tantawi later made sure to visit Mubarak in hospital in 2014. ʿAnan allegedly kept a portrait of Mubarak hanging in his house and argued recurrently after 2011 that Mubarak did not deserve

---

[70] See Reuters blog, "Unrest in Egypt," http://live.reuters.com/Event/Unrest_in_Egypt?P age=0 (accessed June 7, 2015), especially pp. 24–25.

[71] Reportedly, the commander of the second field army, General Mohammad Farid Hegazy, and General ʿAbdul-Fattah al-Sisi, both of whom were SCAF members in 2011, were critical of Tantawi's "patience" and favored a muscular approach vis-à-vis demonstrators. See Taylor, *Military Responses*, 128. Interestingly, al-Sisi, who seized power in 2013, appointed Hegazy as chief of staff of the armed forces in 2017.

[72] Bumiller, "Egypt Stability."

[73] Ibid. See also Steven A. Cook, "Five Things You Need to Know about the Egyptian Armed Forces," Council on Foreign Relations, January 31, 2011, www.cfr.org/blog/five-things-you-need-know-about-egyptian-armed-forces (accessed February 5, 2019).

being overthrown and jailed. Reportedly, he wept because Mubarak was humiliated in his old age.[74] Other senior officers have expressed similar sentiments. For instance, the former commander of the Republican Guard, Major General Najib ʿAbdul-Salam, denied that Mubarak had ever ordered the Guard to open fire on the protesters, and contended that the former president "loved the people." ʿAbdul-Salam confessed that he cried when Mubarak was forced to leave the presidential palace in 2011.[75] Several retired generals maintained in different interviews that Mubarak was "very patriotic," and that he protected Egypt's territorial integrity and refused to give up on Tiran and Sanafir – two islands that ʿAbdul-Fattah al-Sisi, the strongman currently ruling Egypt, ceded to Saudi Arabia.[76] My interviewees in Cairo were retired senior officers, and they overwhelmingly defended Mubarak's regime; those with criticisms directed them at some of Mubarak's aides, his sons, or corrupt NDP figures, but never at the former president himself. I found nothing during my fieldwork to imply that the relationship between Mubarak and the military elite had reached a breaking point because of *tawrith*, or for any other reason, prior to the 2011 uprising. And thus, the reasons for their behavior in 2011, I argue, must be searched for elsewhere.

Note that there is a quasi-consensus in the literature that cracking down on protesters was not an option the Egyptian top brass could seriously have considered. Hillel Frisch pinpoints the "obvious unwillingness" of the generals to set low-ranking officers and the rank and file against civilians.[77] Zoltan Barany and Steven Cook both maintain that the officers and enlisted men would probably have refused to obey orders, had the generals instructed them to open fire on civilians.[78] Ahmed S. Hashim and Philippe Droz-Vincent argue that shooting at the protesters would have threatened the unity of the Egyptian military.[79] Droz-Vincent actually contends that guarding the cohesion of the EAF was "at the core" of

[74] al-Baz, *Al-Mushir wa-l-Fariq*, 9 and 106.
[75] See Sadiq al-ʿIssawi's interview with Major General Najib ʿAbdul-Salam, *Al-Tahrir*, February 11, 2015, www.tahrirnews.com/Story/241098/-الأسبق-الجمهوري-الحرس-قائد بكيت-وأنا-أرى-طائرة-مبارك-تغادر-القصر/مصر (accessed February 12, 2015).
[76] See Hazem al-ʿObeidi's interview with Major General Rifʿat al-Hujeiri (Republican Guard), *Al-Wafd*, August 7, 2014. See also *Al-Masry al-Youm*'s interview with former commander of the Republican Guard, Major General Mohammad Hani Metwalli, April 10, 2016, www.almasryalyoum.com/news/details/926329 (accessed May 1, 2016).
[77] Hillel Frisch, "The Egyptian Army and Egypt's 'Spring,'" *Journal of Strategic Studies* 36, no. 2 (April 2013): 193.
[78] Zoltan Barany, "Comparing the Arab Revolts: The Role of the Military," *Journal of Democracy* 22, no. 4 (October 2011): 29. Cook, *The Struggle For Egypt*, 287.
[79] See Ahmed S. Hashim, "The Man on Horseback: The Role of the Military in the Arab Revolutions and in Their Aftermaths, 2011–2015," *Middle East Perspectives* 7 (October 2015): 10. See also Droz-Vincent, "From Fighting Formal Wars," 394.

the SCAF's decision to force Mubarak out of power after giving him "every opportunity" to save his regime prior to his eventual downfall.[80] Kandil maintains, for his part, that although the Egyptian military elite remained loyal to Mubarak, they were under pressure from the officer corps to refrain from opening fire upon civilians. Consequently, the generals had to accept the downfall of their "old political master" in order to avoid fracturing the armed forces.[81] My interviews in Cairo overwhelmingly corroborate these assessments:

The Egyptian mid-ranking and junior officers would not have obeyed orders to shoot on civilians; they were not psychologically prepared to do so.[82]

Had Tantawi issued orders to shoot on the people, the officer corps would have splintered between a minority ready to carry out orders, and a majority that would have refused to obey. The armed forces would have disintegrated; a scenario of civil war would have followed.[83]

Tantawi was personally loyal to Mubarak. He tried to save him ... But had the SCAF ordered the mid-ranking and junior officers to shoot on civilians, they would have turned their weapons against the SCAF. The officer corps would have splintered along generational lines. Tantawi refrained from opening fire on the protesters not to protect the revolution, but to safeguard the unity of the armed forces.[84]

The SCAF originally deployed the armed forces in the streets to protect the Mubarak regime, but was quickly forced to accept the fact that the regime could not be saved. It felt that if it gave orders to shoot, they wouldn't be executed – in other words, that the mid-ranking and young officers would rebel against such orders. I think the generals were right in this regard. I had many encounters with young officers when the events were unfolding. They were tense, and did not want to shoot on civilians. One lieutenant told me that the smallest weapon in his possession, the AK47, was still a deadly armament. Had he been ordered to use it, the AK47 alone could have caused a slaughter which he was unwilling to perpetrate.[85]

These quotes are straightforward. In three rounds of fieldwork in Cairo in 2011, 2012, and 2014, I kept hearing the same arguments from my interviewees. Despite their continued loyalty to Mubarak, the Egyptian

[80] Droz-Vincent, "Prospects," 702–703. Derek Lutterbeck makes a similar argument in "Arab Uprisings, Armed Forces, and Civil–Military Relations," *Armed Forces & Society* 39, no. 1 (2013): 37.

[81] Hazem Kandil, *The Power Triangle: Military, Security, and Politics in Regime Change* (New York: Oxford University Press, 2016), 325.

[82] Interview with retired Major General Mohammad Qadri Sa'id, Cairo (July 1, 2012).

[83] Interview with retired Major General Tal'at Musallim, Cairo (July 27, 2012).

[84] Interview with 'Abdullah al-Sinnawi, Egyptian daily *Al-Shuruq* columnist and commentator on affairs of the Egyptian armed forces, Cairo (July 2, 2012).

[85] Interview with Hisham Qassem, publisher and co-founder of the Egyptian daily *Al-Masry al-Youm*, Cairo (July 5, 2012).

military elite lacked the capacity to quell the uprising. Mubarak's coup-proofing techniques only delivered the loyalty of the upper echelon of the officer corps. The president and the generals developed solid bonds of mutual interest, but no such links existed between Mubarak and the younger officers. Nor were they wedded to him ideationally, through a conception of common threat or shared aversions. The homogenous nature of Egyptian society precluded Mubarak from "othering" the pro-testers along sectarian lines, the way Bashar al-Asad had done in Syria. Nor could the Mubarak regime credibly argue that the masses of Egyptians who took to the streets were supporters of the Muslim Brotherhood or religious fanatics.

This means that Mubarak's coercive system was built upon an inher-ent contradiction. While mid-ranking and junior officers would be in charge of cracking down on civilians should the armed forces be required to uphold the status quo, they were not the ones who actually benefited from the regime, and they felt no special loyalty toward it. Junior officers under Mubarak were spending their youthful decades in relative poverty until they reached retirement age and became eligible for plum jobs – but only if they had proven themselves absolutely loyal and had been promoted to higher ranks. The latter, in fact, did not guarantee automatically hitting the jackpot despite the regime's lar-gesse, because the number of retired senior officers exceeded the coveted slots Mubarak had to offer, though it is true that the former president did whatever he could to keep the greatest number of top brass satisfied.[86] Mid-ranking and junior officers knew that after years of service spent living on inadequate salaries, they may well become young military retirees subsisting on meager pensions. These officers were also aware that the loyalist civilian and military elite were enriching themselves while they struggled to make ends meet. Unsurprisingly, those without a special interest in the status quo were not prepared to kill their unarmed countrymen in order to uphold it.

Tellingly, the divergence in disposition between the top brass and younger officers continued after the fall of Mubarak. For instance, on April 8, 2011, twenty-two officers took to Tahrir Square and joined demonstrators calling for the SCAF to hand power to civilians and protesting the slow pace of Mubarak's trial. These "soldiers of con-science" who ignored strict EAF regulations forbidding military person-nel to participate in political activities were all junior officers, mostly lieutenants and captains. They were sentenced to ten years' incarceration though the term was eventually reduced to three years in prison. An EAF

[86] Hashim, "The Egyptian Military, Part Two," 107.

spokesman accused these men of trying "to cause a chasm between Egyptians and their Army," and activists feared that dozens of deserting officers have been arrested while their families were terrorized into silence.[87] Also, in October 2011, around 500 mid-ranking and junior officers stationed in Alexandria assembled at the headquarters of the Air Defense Academy to protest harsh treatment and low wages in an open rebellion that lasted several days. Young officers present at the gathering accused their senior colleagues of hoarding millions while they themselves struggled to make ends meet. Military sources speaking anonymously about the Alexandria protest told a Reuters correspondent that they were tired of "a very few top officers becoming rich" and hoped the revolution would be their chance to secure "better treatment, salaries, and improved conditions and training." A major complained that his peers were struggling financially like most Egyptians because money was not trickling down to them. "You have to reach a specific rank before wealth is unlocked," he said.[88] Soon afterwards, another junior officer told a foreign correspondent that his colleagues were outraged because the SCAF was involving the troops in police-like operations and warned that "there are certain things they [the SCAF] know they cannot make us do." An alarmed SCAF reacted to the agitation by accelerating the promotion of scores of young officers to appease them and lavishing regular payments of up to $11,600 on colonels and generals. In addition, when protests were staged in Tahrir Square, the SCAF distributed extra pay to secure the obedience of the mid-level and junior officers. Robert Springborg argued at the time that Field Marshal Tantawi was "frightened to death" lest his subordinates trigger a coup and was deliberately provoking a confrontation with the US to bolster his credentials in the military[89] Still, the malaise in the lower echelons persisted, and the SCAF was aware that the young officers were restive, indeed "relatively pro-revolution" in the words of a reserve officer who spoke namelessly to *The Guardian*.[90]

---

[87] See Patrick Galey, "Soldiers of Conscience," *Foreign Policy*, January 24, 2011, https://foreignpolicy.com/2012/01/24/soldiers-of-conscience/ (accessed March 15, 2019). See also ʿAli al-Raggal, "Riwayat Ma Jara fi Masr fi al-Ayyam al-Hasima," *Al-Safir*, April 21, 2016, http://assafir.com/Article/1/489170/RssFeed (accessed April 21, 2016). All but one of the April 8 officers were later pardoned by minister of defense ʿAbdul-Fattah al-Sisi.

[88] See Awad, "Special Report."

[89] See Galey, "Why the Egyptian Military Fears a Captains' Revolt."

[90] See Shenker, "Egyptian Army Officer's Diary." Interestingly, a foreign diplomat in Cairo opined at the time: "[The SCAF] is not giving out orders that could be disobeyed, not even potentially. It knows it cannot ask its soldiers to do something they don't want to do. If it asks soldiers to, say, fire on protesters, the SCAF knows it could end up with

Alternative Explanations of Military Behavior in 2011 Egypt

Tawrith

A pervasive argument in the literature maintains that the SCAF refrained from defending Mubarak in 2011 because the generals opposed *tawrith* (i.e., as stated earlier, the grooming of the younger Mubarak as a potential successor to his father). According to this narrative, Gamal Mubarak alienated the generals because he allied himself with the interior ministry as well as wealthy businessmen who competed with "Military, Inc." for profit. Consequently, the SCAF looked favorably upon the 2011 uprising as a godsend conducive to checking Gamal's presidential ambitions. Some elements in this argument are beyond dispute and I concur that Egyptian officers overall did not look favorably upon *tawrith*. But even had the SCAF supported Gamal, it could not have ordered the troops to open fire on the protesters in 2011 as I showed above. For this and other reasons I discuss below, I maintain that *tawrith* may not have been central to the SCAF's calculations during the 2011 uprising. Also, I contend that the alleged threat that Gamal posed to the SCAF and the latter's supposed alienation from the Mubarak regime should not be exaggerated – in the words of Egyptian scholar Omar Ashour, the SCAF never ceased to believe "that the principle elements of the status quo should be maintained" despite the political rise of Gamal Mubarak.[91] Nor should we forget that the generals loathed the Muslim Brotherhood as well as the liberal and leftist activists far more than they ever hated the younger Mubarak. In sum, we should remember that the SCAF acted as a quintessentially anti-revolutionary military clique in 2011, and beyond. The friction with the Mubarak clan over *tawrith* did not mean that the SCAF ever embraced democratic transition, or harbored sympathy toward its supporters even for tactical reasons.

A majority of my military interviewees in Cairo were critical of the younger Mubarak and his allies as the *tawrith* argument would expect them to be indeed. One retired general claimed in fact that the military was ready to trigger a coup in order to prevent *tawrith*. Most, however,

something like the Russian Revolution." See Galey, "Why the Egyptian Military Fears a Captains' Revolt."

[91] Ashour, "Ballots versus Bullets." See also, Omar Ashour, "Bullets Beat Ballots: The Arab Uprisings and Civil–Military Relations in Egypt," in *Revisiting the Arab Uprisings: The Politics of a Revolutionary Moment*, ed. Stephane Lacroix and Jean-Pierre Filiu (New York: Oxford University Press, 2018).

denied the existence of such plans.[92] And several interviewees actually contended that Gamal or any other loyalist civilian figure would have been acceptable as president, provided they upheld the status quo. According to a retired rear admiral I interviewed:

The SCAF is the locus of corruption in the armed forces. This is why the military elite prefer one of their own to be president, because high-ranking officers know how the financial rewards system operates, and would not spoil the generals' affairs. But in fact, even a civilian would do [this] if he understood the game and did not intervene in military business. What is certain is that SCAF cannot afford to have an unfriendly president at the helm, irrespective of his background. The money is too big, and corruption too entrenched. Most SCAF members would go to prison if an unfriendly president decided to investigate their affairs. Also, the money would have to be paid back to the state.[93]

Would Gamal Mubarak have been an "unfriendly president" toward the military top brass? Answers to hypothetical questions are by necessity speculative. Still, little suggests that Gamal would have threatened military business or prevented the generals from enriching themselves. First, Gamal was not an anti-corruption crusader in any way. It is hard to imagine him acting in the name of any kind of higher national interest to prevent the generals from pilfering the state. Second, Gamal was a regime insider – arguably, the ultimate insider under his father – and thus privy to its inner workings. The importance of keeping the generals quiescent could not have escaped him. It should be remembered, in this regard, that Hosni Mubarak became even more generous toward the generals during his last years in power.[94] For his part, Gamal actively courted the military top brass, and his efforts were at least partially successful. For instance, General Magdi Sha'rawi, the commander of the Egyptian Air Force from 2002 until 2008, converted a wing in the headquarters of the air force in New Egypt into private quarters for Gamal. Hamdi Wahiba, the general who preceded Sami 'Anan as chief of staff (2001–2005), was also known for his warm bonds with both Gamal and his older brother, 'Ala'. Gamal wove a friendly relationship

---

[92] Several senior officers also publicly denied that the armed forces were planning a coup against Mubarak. See, for instance, the interview of Major General Najib 'Abdul-Salam with the Egyptian daily *Al-Masry al-Youm*, August 8, 2014, www.almasryalyoum.com/news/details/497057 (accessed August 8, 2014).

[93] Interview with a retired rear admiral (navy) who did not wish to be named, Cairo (August 2, 2012).

[94] The top-brass share of gubernatorial appointments illustrates this dynamic. The ratio of officers-turned-governors rose from 30 percent in the 1980s to 44 percent in the last decade of his tenure. See Bou Nassif, "Wedded to Mubarak," 517. The military's economic sphere also expanded in the 2000s, with Mubarak's blessing and encouragement.

with chief of staff Sami ʿAnan, as well: both Gamal and ʿAla' were invited to the wedding of ʿAnan's daughter, which highlighted the cordial relations between the three men. As for General Najib ʿAbdul-Salam, a former head of the Republican Guard, he kept a picture of the Mubarak brothers, Gamal and ʿAla', in his office. It is doubtful that Gamal would have enjoyed such warm relationships with some of Egypt's most influential generals had they suspected him of planning to challenge the power or abolish the privileges of the military elite.[95] Finally, as shown previously, neoliberalism brought prosperity to the generals who started thriving partnerships with state-bred tycoons such as the Zayat brothers, or the Osman and Sawiris families. The idea that the SCAF was a pillar of protectionism increasingly alienated by Gamal Mubarak's unbridled neoliberalism is a myth that does not stand to the careful analysis of facts.[96]

Had the younger Mubarak become president, it is unlikely he would have allowed loyalist magnates to put his regime on a dangerous collision course with his powerful generals. Pro-Gamal businessmen and the top brass had all prospered in the 2000s, and little suggests they would not have done the same under a Gamal presidency. The fact is Gamal and the military elite were far from being each other's ideological nemesis. This was true in the geopolitical realm as well, not just in economic affairs. Lest we forget, the Egyptian top brass wanted peace with Israel maintained. In addition, the generals had long identified Iran and its extensions in Lebanon (i.e., Hezbollah), and Gaza (i.e., Hamas) as their main enemy. That Hamas in particular worried the Egyptian military has been amply documented.[97] A nexus between a revisionist Muslim Brotherhood regime in Cairo, Iran, and a Hamas-dominated Gaza strip would have been a nightmare scenario from the generals' perspective. The Brotherhood had long criticized Egypt's "special relations" with the United States and pushed for a tougher Egyptian stance against Israel. In 1991, when the Egyptian military sent troops to fight alongside the

---

[95] al-Baz, *Al-Mushir wa-l-Fariq*, especially pp. 28, 51, 54, and 99.

[96] John Sfakianakis, "The Whales of the Nile: Networks, Businessmen, and Bureaucrats during the Era of Privatization in Egypt," in *Networks of Privileges in the Middle East*, ed. Steven Heydemann (New York: Palgrave Macmillan, 2004), 87–91. To quote the Egyptian academic Samer Suleiman, in this regard: "The SCAF was not directly threatened by Gamal Mubarak. The latter had neither the ability nor the interest in taking on the military's economic empire. The truth is the SCAF would have been able to strike a deal with Gamal, but the latter was hated in the officer corps, let alone society at large. That put pressure on the SCAF's generals who understood that a pro-Gamal stance would threaten the unity of the armed forces." Interview with Samer Suleiman, Cairo (July 5, 2012).

[97] See US embassy cable published by *The Guardian*, February 3, 2011, www.theguardian.com /world/us-embassy-cables-documents/146040 (accessed October 7, 2014).

American-led international coalition against Iraqi troops in Kuwait, the Brotherhood hailed Iraqi President Saddam Hussein as "a symbol of resistance" against Western imperialism. That same year, the Brotherhood declared itself opposed to the Madrid peace conference, which it described as yet another plot to "preempt any attempt for a possible renaissance of the [Islamic] nation to recover its vitality and unity." The Mubarak regime, of course, supported the conference. This meant that the Brotherhood was accusing Mubarak, and, by extension, the generals supporting him, of selling out to the US. Should the Brotherhood or any other populist party have ever come to power, the generals worried that Egypt could be taken into uncharted regional waters.[98] In sharp contrast, Gamal would have represented a continuation of his father's politics in this regard.

In addition, nothing guaranteed that a Muslim Brotherhood presidency would not open the SCAF's corruption file under Hosni Mubarak, whereas it was certain that Gamal would not do so for obvious reasons. On the other hand, the Brotherhood enjoyed strong popular support, and availed itself of a highly motivated and disciplined party machine. As such, it would need the generals far less to shore up its rule than the younger Mubarak. But precisely because it depended on its electoral base, the Brotherhood – or any other democratically elected politician for that matter – might have been tempted to satisfy popular expectations for social justice by rethinking the neoliberal policies that had served the interest of the top brass so well. In contrast, a reconfigured authoritarian rule under Gamal would be less sensitive to societal pressure. In brief, the top brass wanted to continue flourishing, and to eschew regional adventurism. The SCAF felt no urge to be in the political limelight or to establish direct military rule – in the words of Tarek Masoud, the Egyptian military elite have "little stomach for the business of day-to-day governance."[99] But nor did the generals intend to become marginal either or to let elected officials run Egypt's foreign and defense policies. A Gamal presidency could have delivered all of these goals in the context of a SCAF-friendly balancing act. This may explain why American diplomats in Cairo reported prior to 2011 that the SCAF did not actually oppose *tawrith*.[100] In fact, Egyptian MP and regime insider Mustafa al-

---

[98] Tarek Masoud, "The Upheavals in Egypt and Tunisia: The Road to (and from) Liberation Square, *Journal of Democracy* 22, no. 3 (July 2011): 26. See also Cook, *Ruling But Not Governing*, 86–87.

[99] Masoud, "The Upheavals in Egypt and Tunisia," 26.

[100] See US embassy cable published by *The Telegraph*, February 15, 2011, www.telegraph.co.uk/news/wikileaks-files/egypt-wikileaks-cables/8327232/XXXXX XXXXXXX-MILITARY-WILL-ENSURE-TRANSFER-OF-POWER.html

Fiqi maintained explicitly and repeatedly in 2009 and 2010 that Gamal would be the NDP's only candidate, should his father decide not to run in the 2011 presidential elections – and that the military institution supported Gamal's candidacy. Al-Fiqi's assertions circulated widely in Egypt at the time. The SCAF never rebutted his statements, either directly or indirectly, via its famous "authorized military source" (*masdar 'askari mas'ul*). Quoting a 2010 al-Fiqi interview:

He [Gamal] is the NDP's candidate should the presidential seat become empty …. I believe that the military institution will support that … [Gamal] will be a civilian president but the son of a military president, and his appointment will reflect the continued loyalty to his father; choosing him as president is the safest way to stability, since there is no vice president, and considering the plurality of candidates.[101]

On the other hand, competition to succeed Mubarak would have pitted presidential hopefuls, including military generals, against one another, whereas a Gamal presidency would have kept the cohesion of the top brass intact. Lest we forget, the ailing Tantawi was an unlikely successor to Mubarak for various reasons, including age, health, and weak support within the EAF. But until the end of Mubarak's years in power, no other general had ever mustered enough support to unify the military around him. Writing in 2001 about former chief of staff Magdi Hatata, Mohammad Abdul-'Aziz and Yussef Hussein noted that though Hatata was popular among the top brass, he had failed to accrue the "formidable patronage support system" needed to emerge as the military's candidate for the top job.[102] This assessment was also valid with regard to Hatata's successors, generals Hamdi Waheeba and Sami 'Anan. The latter harbored unmistakable presidential ambitions, but Tantawi was enthusiastic about his prospects.[103] And the intelligence background of 'Omar Suleiman made his candidacy a red herring for the generals, who vetoed candidates hailing from the security services.[104] A struggle for power typically accompanied by purges and counter-purges within the higher echelons would have been disastrous for the military elite. It would also have been made completely unnecessary by the Gamal option. Jason

---

(accessed January 4, 2014). See also Masoud, "The Upheavals in Egypt and Tunisia," 26.

[101] See Mahmud Muslim's interview with Mustafa al-Fiqi, *Al-Masry al-Youm*, January 12, 2010, http://today.almasryalyoum.com/article2.aspx?ArticleID=239948 (accessed February 23, 2014).

[102] Muhammad 'Abdul-Aziz and Youssef Hussein, "The President, the Son, and the Military: The Question of Succession in Egypt," *The Arab Studies Journal* 9/10, no. 2/1 (Fall 2001/Spring 2002): 76.

[103] On the interaction between Tantawi and 'Anan, see al-Baz, *Al-Mushir wa-l-Fariq*, 11.

[104] 'Abdul-'Aziz and Hussein, "The President," 75.

Brownlee argued in 2007 that the Egyptian top brass "might not only accept, but even endorse a hereditary transition" that would deliver the presidency to Gamal.[105] This assessment goes against conventional wisdom on the topic, but I hope I have shown why I find it plausible.

Even if we accept the premise that opposition to Gamal structured military agency in 2011, several variables would still need to be examined. First, the collapse of the police on January 28, 2011, followed by the EAF's deployment in the streets of Cairo, shifted the correlation of forces decisively within the Mubarak regime in favor of the military top brass. Three events unfolding on January 29 are important to pinpoint: (1) Ahmed ʿEzz, the steel magnate widely perceived to be Gamal's enforcer and engineer of his rise to power resigned from the ruling National Democratic Party (NDP). (2) Hosni Mubarak appointed a senior military officer, air force General Ahmad Shafiq, prime minister. Shafiq's cabinet was almost free of Gamal's cronies, who had previously been pervasive. (3) Hosni Mubarak swore in ʿOmar Suleiman, the chief of the General Intelligence Service (GIS) as vice president.[106] With Tantawi still leading the armed forces as minister of defense, the appointments of Shafiq and Suleiman effectively put generals hailing from the military establishment in control of the regime's key positions. These developments unmistakably ended Gamal's presidential ambitions. In fact, Suleiman lost no time in declaring to Egyptian state TV on February 3 that Gamal would not run in the upcoming presidential elections. Two days later, on February 5, Hosni Mubarak announced Gamal's resignation from the NDP.[107]

To argue that even after January 29, opposition to Gamal was the main factor (let alone the sole influence) weighing upon the generals is to forget that his presidency was no longer in the cards thirteen days before the end of the uprising, and that they themselves had become the masters of the country. In the meantime, the Muslim Brotherhood was playing an increasingly assertive role in the popular mobilization. The Brotherhood's prominence in the streets became particularly clear during the Battle of the Camel, when its youth played a crucial role in pushing Mubarak's supporters out of Tahrir Square on February 2. It is doubtful that the Egyptian generals would have supported any street protest since

---

[105] Jason Brownlee, "The Heir Apparency of Gamal Mubarak," *Arab Studies Journal* 15/16, no. 2/1 (Fall 2007/Spring 2008): 51.

[106] Mubarak also dangled the vice presidency in front of Field Marshal Tantawi. See Ahmad Shafiq's interview with *Al-Hayat*, May 9, 2013, www.alhayat.com/Details/511 865 (accessed September 5, 2014).

[107] See *Haaretz*, February 3, 2011, www.haaretz.com/world-news/report-gamal-mubarak-will-not-seek-egyptian-presidency-1.341070 (accessed February 15, 2015).

their distrust of "disorderly" popular movements is unshakable, as Eva Bellin has correctly noted.[108] But it is even less likely that the generals would have applauded a popular uprising bent on bringing down a regime historically their own while simultaneously opening the doors of power to their old Islamist nemeses. This was particularly true in the wake of Gamal's demise. Lest we forget, the Brotherhood had long proved its electoral prowess in the context of Egyptian professional orders and campuses – and even in parliamentary elections, when they were not completely rigged.[109] It was clear that democratic transition would inevitably bring the Brotherhood to center stage in Egyptian politics. This would have been the equivalent of a political earthquake in Egypt, and yet the generals were notoriously characterized by a profound "reluctance to change."[110] Contra much of the literature, prominent Egyptian historian Khaled Fahmy maintained that the Egyptian military elite perceived the 2011 uprising as a "grave error" (khata' fadeh) and that tawrith was for them only a "small detail" (joz'an saghiran) in the grand scheme of threatening events unfolding that year.[111] I concur on both accounts.

In order to wrestle back power after millions of Egyptians took to the streets in January 2011, the SCAF needed to use overwhelming violence and shape a reconfigured autocracy with Gamal and his cronies out of the way. This, of course, was precisely what the generals did later on. In the Maspero massacre of October 2011, the military slaughtered thirty Coptic Christians who were protesting peacefully the burning of a church in Upper Egypt. Omar Ashour noted in this regard that the SCAF needed at the time to create "demons" in order to strengthen the internal cohesion of the armed forces and Copts represented "an easy target against which to rally soldiers and officers."[112] In August 2013, the SCAF sanctioned an even bloodier massacre, in Cairo's Rabi'a al-'Adawiyya Square, where the army and security forces slaughtered

---

[108] Eva Bellin, "The Puzzle of Democratic Divergence in the Arab World: Theory Confronts Experience in Egypt and Tunisia," Political Science Quarterly 133, no. 3 (Fall 2018): 449.

[109] For instance, in 2005, the Brothers won 86 seats in Egypt's 454-seat parliament; more seats would have gone to the Brotherhood that year had the regime loosened its grip on electoral procedures.

[110] Droz-Vincent, "Prospects," 703.

[111] See Basma al-Mahid's interview with Khaled Fahmy, published by al-Minassa, December 1, 2018, https://almanassa.com/ar/story/11220 (accessed December 1, 2018).

[112] Ashour, "Ballots versus Bullets." Though Copts represent nearly 10 percent of Egyptians, their numbers in the officer corps are negligible and there are few if any senior EAF commanders hailing from a Christian background. In the words of a reserve officer, the military sees the Copts as "less important" because they are a minority. See Shenker, "Egyptian Army Officer's Diary."

approximately 1,000 unarmed supporters of the Muslim Brotherhood. I maintain that the only reason the military elite didn't follow the same blood-drenched path in January 2011 was that they couldn't do so at that point in time. The massive anti-Mubarak uprising was clearly nonsectarian and nonpartisan, though Brotherhood supporters were, evidently, part of the picture. The inclusiveness of the January protests prevented the SCAF from framing them credibly as a Coptic or a Brotherhood plot. Consequently, the SCAF was unable to transform the military's antipathy vis-à-vis the Copts and loathing of the Brotherhood into violence.

In sum, I accept the argument that Mubarak and his military officers did not see eye to eye on *tawrith*. And yet I maintain that the friction between the president and the SCAF unfolded between allies who never ceased to be so until Mubarak's breakdown. Field Marshal Tantawi, in particular, remained loyal to the former president, and the SCAF overall was too involved in Mubarak-era corruption to be enthusiastic about his downfall. When Mubarak's rule crumbled, the top brass sacrificed him to safeguard the regime in which they prospered. At that point in time, it was expedient for the generals to frame themselves as critics of the former president. But that was mere political convenience; the SCAF in 2011 was anti-revolutionary from day one – certainly since the end of the younger Mubarak's presidential dreams.

US Influence

Yet another hypothesis surrounding military behavior in 2011 suggests that American pressure may have forced Egyptian generals to refrain from cracking down on the popular protests.[113] *The New York Times* reported on February 5, 2011, that Robert Gates and Admiral Mike Mullen, the American defense secretary and chairman of the joint chiefs of staff, respectively, called their Egyptian counterparts when protests were unfolding in Egypt and expressed hope that the military would "keep enough peace on the streets so that talks with opposition leaders could begin."[114] The SCAF later earned compliments from President Obama immediately after Mubarak's resignation, for serving Egypt "patriotically" throughout the uprising.[115] It may, indeed, be factual that the Obama administration did lobby the SCAF not to use violence against

---

[113] See Stephan Roll, "Managing Change: How Egypt's Military Leadership Shaped the Transformation," *Mediterranean Politics* 21, no. 1 (October 2015): 25.

[114] Bumiller, "Egypt Stability."

[115] See "Obama's Remarks on the Resignation of Mubarak," *The New York Times*, February 11, 2011, www.nytimes.com/2011/02/12/world/middleeast/12diplo-text.html (accessed March 19, 2014).

civilians, though we can't ascertain this for a fact until diplomatic archives become available for researchers. Irrespective of what really happened on this front during the heated days leading to Mubarak's downfall, one question remains important to ponder: Could Washington have stirred the generals on a course they loathed, had they possessed the capacity to crush the uprising?

It is certain that Egypt's alliance with America matters to Egyptian generals. As mentioned previously, the yearly sum provided by the American aid program to Egypt amounts to $1.3 billion. The EAF uses these sums to acquire advanced military technology from American companies, and takes pride in their possession of state-of-the-art weaponry. In addition, Egyptian officers are regularly sent to train in American military academies, and the two countries collaborate on security affairs and anti-terrorism activities. America's clout as a global power directly involved in Middle East politics heightens for Egypt the importance of maintaining cordial relations with Washington.

And still it is analytically wrong to imagine that the Egyptian military elite react to American designs for Egypt like an apple falling by the force of gravity. Lest we forget, the aging high command under Mubarak was mostly Soviet-trained. Officers educated in American military schools did not form a privileged caste or receive any special treatment. They were not promoted to commandership positions faster than less well-trained officers. This betrays a deliberate attempt to keep American influence to a minimum in the officer corps, and nothing suggests the US was ever able to force the Egyptian military command to change course.[116] That America matters does not make it omnipotent everywhere, all the time; there are limits to the clout of even a superpower. For instance, in 1979, Cairo rebuffed repeated American demands to permit the establishment of a US military base on the Red Sea. Nor would the Sadat regime, at the time, allow the US to use two air bases in Sinai that Israel had evacuated. From 1982 to 1984, the Reagan administration renewed US demands to establish military presence on the Red Sea, but Mubarak did not prove any more malleable than his predecessor, and America's entreaties were again rejected.[117] Similarly, Field Marshal Tantawi snubbed repeated American demands in the 1990s for the military to play a greater role alongside the interior ministry in fighting terrorism. Tantawi would only agree to intervene against radical groups as a last resort, and in conditions

---

[116] Cassandra, "The Impending Crisis," 26.
[117] Abul-Magd, *Militarizing the Nation*, 85. South Vietnamese officers who developed close ties with the Americans faced similar suspicions, and struggled to be promoted because the authorities feared that they would use their political capital with the US to seize power. See Talmadge, *The Dictator's Army*, 249.

of extreme urgency.[118] In a 2007 meeting with the US ambassador in Cairo, Francis J. Ricciardone Jr., Tantawi warned him that Egypt's history with colonialism makes it particularly sensitive to foreign intervention, and that Americans who believe they can pressure the military in matters pertaining to its domestic role "should know this will not work."[119] Tantawi's were not empty words. In a 2008 memo released by WikiLeaks, American diplomats again lamented their inability to convince the defense minister to include threats stemming from piracy, border security, and counter-terrorism in the mission of the EAF. The diplomats lambasted Tantawi for being fixated with achieving strategic parity with Israel, thirty-one years after the Camp David Accords. They conceded, however, that the "the aging leadership" of the EAF had resisted their efforts and remained determined to train the troops in conventional warfare; the diplomats singled out Tantawi as the "chief impediment" to US efforts to foster close military ties with Cairo.[120] The US's limited leeway over its ally was made clear one more time in the wake of Mubarak's fall in 2011, when the Obama administration failed to change Tantawi's decisions pertaining to the sequencing of the legislative and presidential elections, and drafting the new constitution.[121]

This is not to suggest, of course, that Sadat, Mubarak, or Tantawi were symbols of Arab "steadfastness" vis-à-vis America; they themselves never pretended as much, since Sadat had realigned Egyptian foreign policy away from Nasser-era radicalism. Still, the Egyptian elite were never American stooges devoid of autonomous agency in the internal realm. Steven Cook asserts convincingly that "Washington has far less ability to shape events in Egypt than commonly believed."[122] Similarly, Marc Lynch highlights the limits of American power in the Middle East and writes that US influence on events during the Arab uprisings in particular was "far less than most Americans or Arabs believe."[123] Both contentions may go against entrenched conventional wisdoms but remain nonetheless fundamentally right.

---

[118] al-Baz, *Al-Mushir wa-l-Fariq*, 228.

[119] See WikiLeaks cable "Defense Minister Tantawi on Mil-to-Mil Relations," https://wikileaks.org/plusd/cables/07CAIRO2801_a.html (accessed March 6, 2019).

[120] See *Al-Watan Daily*, "US Frustrated with Egyptian Military, Show Wikileaks," January 1, 2011, https://wikileaks.org/gifiles/attach/134/134658_03.pdf (accessed March 3, 2019).

[121] David Schenker, "Washington's Limited Influence in Egypt," Washington Institute for Near East Policy, September 15, 2011, www.washingtoninstitute.org/policy-analysis/view/washingtons-limited-influence-in-egypt (accessed January 15, 2019).

[122] Cook, *The Struggle for Egypt*, 302.

[123] Marc Lynch, *The New Arab Wars: Uprisings and Anarchy in the Middle East* (New York: PublicAffairs, 2016), xiii.

In his June 2009 speech in Cairo, Barack Obama promised to support the struggle for democracy and the rule of law "everywhere." Later on, the Obama administration did criticize – mildly – the Mubarak regime for extending the emergency law, but Cairo again ignored Washington. American aid to Egypt was unaffected, and secretary of defense Robert Gates maintained that military support to the EAF would continue to be provided "without conditions."[124] In April 2013, US ambassador to Egypt Anne Peterson sent encrypted messages to Washington warning that a coup was brewing in Cairo. The Obama administration dispatched then secretary of defense Chuck Hagel to Egypt to warn the SCAF that Washington would punish a coup, and to remind the commander of the armed forces General 'Abdul-Fattah al-Sisi that American law dictated an immediate cutoff of military aid to armed forces overthrowing elected officials. General al-Sisi told Hagel that the Muslim Brotherhood was evil, and that he, Hagel, "[could] not understand it like we understand it here." Hagel conceded that he didn't live in Cairo, whereas al-Sisi did, and that it was for the general to decide what was best for Egypt. Therefore, when Obama warned Morsi in their last conversation on July 1 that the Egyptian military was not "taking direction" from the US, he was speaking the truth. Two days later, al-Sisi deposed Morsi and seized power.

This and other similar episodes debunk the image of an overbearing America dealing with allegedly meek and obedient Egyptian military clients.[125] Note that following the July 2013 coup, Washington lobbied Cairo doggedly to bring the ousted Muslim Brotherhood back into the political process. Former deputy secretary of state William J. Burns publicly condemned the al-Sisi regime's "politically motivated arrests," and called for a dialogue including "all sides and political parties" in a barely disguised hint to the Muslim Brotherhood. The generals, however, ignored Washington's calls to restart the democratic process following the military takeover.[126] And yet Egypt's relations with America did not collapse; Washington accepted the fait accompli, and soon, business on the Cairo/Washington nexus was back to normal. The fact is Washington's interests still trump rhetorical commitments to democracy

---

[124] Adam Shatz, "Mubarak's Last Breath," *London Review of Books* 32, no. 10 (May 2010), www.lrb.co.uk/v32/n10/adam-shatz/mubaraks-last-breath (accessed March 2, 2013).

[125] See David D. Kirkpatrick, "The White House and the Strongman," *The New York Times*, July 27, 2018, www.nytimes.com/2018/07/27/sunday-review/obama-egypt-coup-trump.html (accessed August 16, 2018).

[126] See *The Washington Post*, July 17, 2013, "Egypt Ignores Washington after U.S. Policy Missteps," www.washingtonpost.com/opinions/egypt-ignores-washington-after-us-policy-missteps/2013/07/17/7c26fdb2-ef0b-11e2-9008-61e94a7ea20d_story.html?utm_term=.20d6c2ecb728 (accessed June 1, 2014).

and human rights.[127] And while America's influence in Cairo is real, it should not be exaggerated.

Nor should the importance of US military aid to Egypt be overstated. First, while the EAF still receives $1.3 billion dollars per annum from the US, the value of this sum in real terms has decreased by 50 percent.[128] Second, the military budget has expanded over the years, which means that American aid accounts for less in absolute terms. According to Zeinab Abul-Magd:

> Under Abu Ghazala in 1984, the Egyptian military budget was 1.8 billion dollars, in a total state budget of 15 billion dollars. This meant that U.S. aid amounted to more than 70 percent of the military's budget, and about nine percent of the state budget. Under General Abd al-Fattah al-Sisi today, the military budget is about four billion dollars, with a total state budget of about 95 billion dollars. This means that U.S. military aid has decreased to around 30 percent of the official military budget, and only 1.3 percent of the state budget. More importantly, the Egyptian military annually earns hundreds of millions of dollars from off-budgetary revenue through its vast business empire in the civilian sector. For example, it is known that the military was recently able to afford to lend the state as much as two billion dollars.[129]

Abul-Magd concludes correctly that the generals cannot always be expected to "follow Washington's lead." This inference stands true for 2011: had they perpetrated a massacre that year, America would have condemned the use of violence against civilians, and quickly dropped its moral objections to safeguard a stable association with an important ally in a turbulent region. This scenario, in fact, is no mere speculation; it's exactly what happened in the wake of the August 2013 Rabi'a al-'Adawiyya massacre that I mentioned previously. America remonstrated Cairo, but did not reduce its aid to the Egyptian military, let alone suspend it. Nothing suggests that Washington would have behaved any differently had the generals cracked down on the 2011 uprising. The alleged worries of the Egyptian military elite over America's reaction to

---

[127] See *The Washington Post*, July 9, 2013, "The Post's View: Egypt, Obama Double Down on Failed Policies," www.washingtonpost.com/opinions/the-posts-view-egypt-obama-double-down-on-failed-policies/2013/07/09/9ab085dc-e8c1-11e2-aa9f-c03a72e2d342_story.html?utm_term=.e1d883d24dba (accessed March 12, 2014).

[128] Frisch, "Guns and Butter," 1. Gulf money, by far, supersedes American aid. Between 2013 and 2015 alone, Gulf assistance to Egypt has been estimated at $20 billion. See Shana Marshall, "The Egyptian Armed Forces and the Remaking of an Economic Empire," Carnegie Middle East Center, April 15, 2015, 4, http://carnegie-mec.org/20 15/04/15/egyptian-armed-forces-and-remaking-of-economic-empire-pub-59726 (accessed April 30, 2015).

[129] See Zeinab Abul-Magd, "US Military Aid to Egypt Lost Value," *Jadaliyya*, July 25, 2013, www.jadaliyya.com/pages/index/13186/us-military-aid-to-egypt-lost-value#_ed n6 (accessed December 9, 2013).

whatever violence they inflicted on the Egyptian people should not be overestimated.[130]

Conclusion of the Egyptian Case Study

Promoting the interests of the military elite has always been central to the coup-proofing strategies of successive Egyptian regimes. This was already true under Nasser and Sadat; and Mubarak promoted the material interests of the military elite further. The top brass indeed did very well throughout Mubarak's tenure; the mid-ranking and junior officers did not. This was especially true during the last decade of his rule, when inflation compounded the economic struggle of public sector employees, including military personnel. When Nasser and the Free Officers seized power, the EAF numbered almost 65,000 men. Under Mubarak, this number hovered at half a million. In and of themselves, numbers do not make coups more or less frequent since military seizures of power have been triggered by small and large armed forces alike. It is true, however, that colonels, majors, and captains are more dangerous in smaller armies than in larger ones. Ahmed 'Abdulla has made the argument that the massive size of the Egyptian military reduced the likelihood of coups triggered by a small military clique. A successful putsch, should one occur in contemporary Egypt, would be more likely to be staged by the upper echelons of the military institution.[131] This may explain, at least in part, why Mubarak could afford to neglect the junior officers in the military. It must be added, of course, that Egypt is a poor country in which public servants are underpaid – officers included. In Mubarak's time, drastic increases in public wages were unaffordable, and civilian public servants could not be left lagging too far behind officers. Mubarak did not spoil the tens of thousands of mid-ranking and junior officers manning the lower echelons of the military hierarchy – because he couldn't. This, combined with the lack of ideational ties between the president and junior officers, confined Mubarak's loyalists to the upper echelons. Their allegiance alone was not enough to uphold the status quo in 2011.

The transformative events that followed the breakdown of the Mubarak regime are beyond the scope of this chapter – specifically the 2013 coup that allowed military dictator 'Abdul-Fattah al-Sisi to seize power and prevent democratic consolidation in Egypt. And yet a brief

---

[130] Along similar lines, Greitens found that American or international influence was not decisive in shaping state violence in East Asia. See Greitens, *Dictators and Their Secret Police*, 61–62.

[131] 'Abdalla, ed., *Al-Jaysh wa-l-Dimoqratiyya*, 25.

word is due here on the continued tension along intergenerational lines in the Egyptian military in the wake of Mubarak's breakdown. The fact is al-Sisi replicated several aspects of Mubarak's coup-proofing system, and was arguably even more generous to high-ranking generals than Mubarak ever was. In September 2019, Mohammad ʿAli, a self-exiled Egyptian actor and businessman who worked as a military contractor for fifteen years, released a series of videos on social media exposing the corruption of al-Sisi, his family, and the top brass. The videos appeared credible because ʿAli was a regime insider and a loyalist-turned-whistleblower. The intricate details of graft that ʿAli provided circulated widely in Egypt and galvanized renewed popular protests in Tahrir Square. In response, al-Sisi worried publicly lest ʿAli's charges trigger turmoil inside the Egyptian military by pitting low-level officers (al-dubbat al-sughayyarin) against their superiors. Al-Sisi's reply suggests that the strongman wasn't especially concerned about the reaction of the Egyptian top brass to the allegations, but clearly fretted about the effects of such videos on their subordinates.[132] ʿAli's videos, as well as al-Sisi's rejoinder, show that the intergenerational dynamics that I describe in this chapter are still very much at play in Egypt. Should al-Sisi face an endgame scenario, these dynamics may cripple yet again the ability of the top brass to save their president benefactor just as they did in 2011.

The 2011 Uprising and the Survival of al-Asad: Explaining Military Behavior

I have argued previously in this book that counterbalancing alienates the military if authoritarian regimes favor institutional rivals. In addition, I showed that privileging the material interests of senior officers creates friction with mid-ranking and junior subordinates, should the money fail to trickle down. Both dynamics are at play in Syria. The Bashar al-Asad regime clearly indulges its praetorian units over the armed forces and the top brass over young officers. The fact is counterbalancing and the promotion of the material interests of the military elite function as staples of coup-proofing in Syria as much they do in Egypt. Yet military behavior in 2011 differed radically in the two countries. I maintain that it was the ideational dimension – at work in Syria, but not in Egypt – that explains the divergence, and, by extension, the Syrian regime's capacity to use force against civilian demonstrators.

---

[132] The first video released by Mohammad ʿAli is available at: www.youtube.com/watch?v=UdAuRx3efHU (accessed September 7, 2019). Al-Sisi's reply is available at: www.youtube.com/watch?v=_jeWpw2Px2Q (accessed September 21, 2019).

Shared Aversions: The Tie That Binds

Fabrice Balanche observed in 2006:

Hafez al-Asad ... used religion instrumentally in his own community to unify
Alawi ranks around him. It was sufficient to evoke the past persecution of Alawis
and their economic exploitation by great Sunni landowners to strengthen Alawi
cohesion. But it is the fear of the promised bloodbath should Alawis lose power
that makes the sectarian chord vibrate the most. The massacre of Alawi cadets in
Aleppo's military academy in 1979 and the wave of assassinations (perpetrated by
the Muslim Brothers) which targeted Alawi figures between 1979 and 1982 have
reinforced intra-Alawi solidarity and fealty toward president Hafez al-Asad, along
the following logic: "*Anta ma'a al-Asad, anta ma'a nafsak*" (You are with Assad,
you are with yourself.)[133]

It is difficult to overemphasize the judiciousness of these observations.
Even prior to the 2011 turning point and its violent aftermath, intercommunal relationships in Syria were fraught with tension, especially along
the Sunni/Alawi dividing line. The sources of Sunni resentment were
multiple. Religious Sunnis still harbored age-old biases against Alawis
as a "heretical sect."[134] After a decade of fieldwork in Syria, Balanche
concluded that most Sunnis considered their Alawi countrymen to
be atheists and disbelievers (*kafirin*).[135] Whether this is so, indeed,
remains debatable, but there is no doubt that religiosity had been on the
rise in Syria – and that Islamization correlated traditionally with an
unfavorable perception of heterodox communities.[136] On the other
hand, old Sunni dynasties hadn't forgotten that they ran Syrian cities
for centuries until Alawi officers dislodged them from their privileged
positions. While some déclassé Sunnis accommodated themselves to
(and actually benefited from) the new ruling class, others still viewed
the post-1963 elite as usurpers. It is important to understand, in this

---

[133] Balanche, *La région*, 154. Along similar lines, Joshua Landis and Zoltan Barany noted in
the wake of the 2011 uprising that Alawis overall seem convinced that their physical
survival is at stake, and that they will be "driven to the sea" if the al-Asad regime
crumbles. See the interview with Joshua Landis, "A Great Sorting Out: The Future of
Minorities in the Middle East," *Al Noor* (Spring 2016), www.bcalnoor.org/single-post
/2016/09/03/A-Great-Sorting-Out-The-Future-of-Minorities-in-the-Middle-East
(accessed July 7, 2017). See also Zoltan Barany, "Why Most Syrian Officers Remain
Loyal to Assad," Arab Center for Research and Policy Studies, June 17, 2013,
www.dohainstitute.org/en/PoliticalStudies/Pages/Why_Most_Syrian_Officers_Remai
n_Loyal_to_Assad.aspx (accessed June 26, 2018).
[134] Theodore McLauchlin, "The Loyalty Trap: Regime Ethnic Exclusion, Commitment
Problems, and Civil War Duration in Syria and Beyond," *Security Studies* 27, no. 2
(2018): 342.
[135] Balanche, *La région*, 217.
[136] Yahya Sadowski pinpoints, in this regard, the Syrian Islamists' "virulent hatred of the
Alawi heresiarchs." See Sadowski, "Patronage and the Ba'ath," 451.

regard, the damage inflicted upon the Sunni psyche by the evident inferiority status in Syria and the humiliating situation of living as a majority supposedly ruled by a minority. Tellingly, a Sunni insurgent said to a foreign journalist that Alawis, after the conflict, would "return to their natural place" in Syrian society.[137] In addition, the fear instigated by the heavy-handed security services in the Syrian population at large had morphed into generalized distrust and loathing of Alawis as such because of their overrepresentation in the intelligence sector. Lest we forget, regime violence against Sunnis did not begin in 2011, and was never restricted to the Muslim Brotherhood alone. Even Patrick Seale, who wrote an otherwise sympathetic biography of Hafez al-Asad, admits that thousands of Sunni civilians were slaughtered during the notorious Hama massacre in 1982 by the all-Alawi Defense Companies *after* the city fell.[138] Human rights organizations have documented a series of other horrendous massacres of Sunnis that may not have reached Hama's level of violence, but were extremely bloody, nonetheless.[139] These horrors were never forgotten in Syria, though it was convenient to "act as if"[140] they had been in order to remain on the regime's safe side. Sunni resentment was particularly intense in Hama, which remains scarred by the 1982 tragedy, and in Homs and Latakia, where the demographic weight of the Alawi community is significant and communal dividing lines are firmly entrenched.[141] Perhaps inevitably, the hatred inspired by the regime mutated into animosity vis-à-vis its Alawi clientele. To be sure,

---

[137] See Nir Rosen, "Among the Alawites," *London Review of Books* 34, no. 18 (September 2012), www.lrb.co.uk/v34/n18/nir-rosen/among-the-alawites (accessed July 18, 2018).

[138] Seale, *Asad*, 333.

[139] For an informative read on human rights violations under the Hafez al-Asad regime, see the Syrian Human Rights Committee's "Report on the Human Rights Situation in Syria over a 20-Year Period, 1979–1999," London, 2001, https://wikileaks.org/gifiles/attach/150/150649_SYRIAN%20HUMAN%20RIGHTS%20COMMITTEE.pdf (accessed April 15, 2018).

[140] On the public falsification of preferences in Syria, see Lisa Wedeen, *Ambiguities of Domination: Politics, Rhetoric, and Symbols in Contemporary Syria* (Chicago, IL: The University of Chicago Press, 2015).

[141] Two signs of sectarian friction in Homs prior to the 2011 uprising are the scarcity of intercommunal marriages and the fact that different communities tended to cluster together in separate neighborhoods. An Alawi dentist living in Homs told a Syrian researcher that the city was "already geographically divided before March 2011 .... Not that we had any problems with Sunnis, but we couldn't live together. Our customs are different." Another Alawi interviewee opined that it had been important for his community to maintain secure and open roads between Homs and the surrounding (Alawi) villages for security reasons. Said the interviewee: "This way, if anything happens, (villagers) are ready to come help us, or we can flee from the city to the villages." See Khader Khaddour (writing under the pseudonym 'Aziz Nakkash): "The Alawite Dilemma in Homs: Survival, Solidarity, and the Making of a Community," Friedrich Ebert Stiftung Institute, March 2013, http://library.fes.de/pdf-files/iez/09825.pdf (accessed August 1, 2018).

Alawis, as such, do not govern Syria. The regime's leading elite and its core in the military–security complex, however, are overwhelmingly Alawi, and the sect is perceived as the regime's hardcore constituency.

A similar dynamic is true in terms of ordinary acts of violence committed by pro-regime armed thugs (*shabbiha*). They inspired so much fear that the Alawi accent itself became dreaded in Syria, and non-Alawis would sometimes imitate it in order to project an image of power. The truth is, not all *shabbiha* are Alawis, and some of their victims are. But the stereotype of its members is that of an impoverished violent Alawi thug fanatically devoted to the leaders of his community and biased against Sunnis. The rise of the *shabbiha* in the 1980s and the daily indignities they inflicted upon ordinary Sunnis only compounded the latter's dislike of Alawis.[142] In addition, class resentment and economic hardship heightened sectarian animosity. Syria's neoliberal turn failed to bring prosperity to the vast majority of its citizens, regardless of sect. A UNDP report found in 2009 that 33.6 percent of the population (6.7 million Syrians) were poor, and that 12.3 percent (2.4 million) were living in extreme poverty, making less than $2 per day. Syrians were already struggling when a severe drought hit the land between 2006 and 2010, leaving in its wake a devastated countryside. The northeastern and southern regions were particularly hard-hit – and both are overwhelmingly Sunni. Because the ruling elite are mainly Alawi, the sect came to be perceived as benefiting disproportionately and unfairly from power, while the rest of the population toiled to make ends meet. Thus, class and sectarian cleavages reinforced one another, as regime cronies prospered in a new economic scene seemingly unfavorable to everyone else.[143]

Ill feeling went both ways. Syrian Alawis are not a monolithic group – no more than Sunnis are. By and large, Alawis from the coast (the Sahel or the Latakia governorate) have more intimate connections with the ruling elite than Alawis from the interior (the Dakhel in the Homs-Hama region). And within the Sahel itself, some families are better represented in the upper echelons of the military–security complex, and are consequently more influential than others. In addition, not all Alawis are

---

[142] On the *shabbiha* phenomenon, see a study by Yassin al-Haj Salih, "The Syrian Shabiha and Their State: Statehood & Participation," Heinrich Böll Stiftung, April 16, 2012, https://lb.boell.org/en/2014/03/03/syrian-shabiha-and-their-state-statehood-participation (accessed June 18, 2018).

[143] See UNDP report, "Poverty and Inequality in Syria, 1997–2007," www.undp.org/content/dam/rbas/doc/poverty/BG_15_Poverty%20and%20Inequality%20in%20Syria_Fe B.pdf (accessed July 7, 2018). See also Raymond A. Hinnebusch, "Understanding Regime Divergence in the Post-uprising Arab State," *Journal of Historical Sociology* 31, no. 1 (2018): 42–43, https://onlinelibrary.wiley.com/doi/pdf/10.1111/johs.12190 (accessed July 3, 2018).

equally devoted to the al-Asad dynasty, and some have counted among its historical opponents. While all of these differentiations are real, they become functionally insignificant when communal survival appears to be at stake and existential fears structure political perceptions.[144] The fact remains that most Alawis adhere to a view of their community's history as an unbroken string of persecution under Sunni rule. Alawi separatism during the mandate reflected minority fears of renewed subjugation in a Sunni-dominated entity as much as French divide-and-rule tactics. And until the 1963 coup, Alawi apprehension about the young republic was not unfounded. The community was indeed on the political margin in addition to being impoverished. For a critical mass of Alawis, the al-Asad regime represents a historical reparation of past wrongs and a guarantee against future injustices. Sadowski observed in 1987 that countryside recruits in the armed forces have proven themselves ready to kill civilians and Islamist insurgents alike in order to defend the regime.[145] Writing in 1995, Chouet noted a disposition among Alawi officers to "raze the capital" should they be forced to leave it.[146] Both observations reflect entrenched Alawi animosity vis-à-vis Sunnis combined with a sense of atavistic insecurity and fears of Sunni revanchism should the al-Asad regime crumble. Also writing about Alawi politics in the 1980s, David Roberts and Hanna Batatu noted perspicaciously that the Alawis have "created so many blood-feuds" in the last two decades that they fear "a dreadful settlement of accounts" and "dire consequences" should the al-Asad regime crumble.[147]

Such contentions were true when they were written, and even more so in 2011, for the regime's heavy-handedness had never receded in the meantime. The sight of massive demonstrations leaving mosques after Friday prayers and clamoring in public squares for regime breakdown was frightening to loyalists. To survive the uprising, Bashar al-Asad played

---

[144] For an excellent study on the internal complexity of the Alawi community and the attitudes of Alawis in the Homs region vis-à-vis the Syrian conflict, see Khaddour, "The Alawite Dilemma." See also an informative report by Maxime Othman published by the news website *Daraj*, February 27, 2019, https://daraj.com/15063/ (accessed March 1, 2019).

[145] Sadowski, "Patronage and the Ba'ath," 453.

[146] Chouet, "Impact of Wielding Power," 11.

[147] David Roberts, *The Ba'ath and the Creation of Modern Syria* (London: Routledge, 1987), 145. Hanna Batatu, "Some Observations on the Social Roots of Syria's Ruling, Military Group and the Causes for Its Dominance," *Middle East Journal* 35, no. 3 (Summer 1981): 336. It is said, in this regard, that when Hafez al-Asad died in 2000, some Alawis prepared to leave Damascus and return to their villages because they feared that the hour of reckoning and Sunni retribution had finally come. See Salwa Ismail, *The Rule of Violence: Subjectivity, Memory and Government in Syria* (New York: Cambridge University Press, 2018), 88.

a game similar to his father's. Early in the uprising, the regime's propaganda machine persistently spread rumors that demonstrators were chanting "Alawis to the graves, Christians to Beirut" (el-'Alawiyye 'aal-tabut, wel Masihiyye 'aa Beirut), and framed the demonstrations as a fundamentalist revolt stirred by "Sunni Terrorist Jihadis."[148] More importantly, the al-Asad regime released dozens of Islamist prisoners, knowing in advance that they would join the uprising and contribute to its escalation toward violence and religious radicalization.[149] Many did exactly that, including the notorious Zahran 'Allush, a powerful warlord who lost no time after his release in founding the salafi Jaysh al-Islam and calling to "cleanse" Damascus from all Shia and Alawi presence. The same is true for Hasan 'Abbud of Ahrar al-Sham, another extremist faction.[150]

In essence, al-Asad used devastating violence against Sunnis, and then framed reactions from the Sunni side as an attack on Alawis, as such. These tactics paid off, and bereft Alawis from choice. Swathes of the community came to perceive the uprising as an existential threat, though a handful of Alawis actually threw in their lot with the secular opposition.[151] The historical narrative of victimhood colored Alawi perception of events, and the leaderless opposition movement proved unwilling or simply unable to assuage minority anxiety. Meanwhile, the regime's overpowering violence against Sunni civilians increased the latter's anti-Alawi bias, leaving even Alawis who did not support the regime in need of protection. Alawi officers and soldiers in the armed forces became largely convinced that the demonstrators were driven by sectarian hatred and that what awaited their community, should the

---

[148] See Alimar Lakzani and Roy Gutman, "In Tartous, Syria, Women Wear Black, Youth Are in Hiding, and Bitterness Grows," *The Nation*, May 15, 2017, www.thenation.com /article/in-tartous-syria-women-wear-black-youth-are-in-hiding-and-bitterness-grows/ (accessed July 5, 2018). Interestingly, Syrian officers received messages from their military leadership warning them of upcoming attacks by Islamists in late 2010 and early 2011, after events began unfolding in Tunisia and prior to the beginning of the Syrian chapter of the Arab Spring, let alone its later radicalization. See Khaddour, "The Alawite Dilemma."

[149] See Kathy Gilsinan, "How Syria's Uprising Spawned a Jihad," *The Atlantic*, March 16, 2016, www.theatlantic.com/international/archive/2016/03/syria-civil-war-five-years/47 4006/ (accessed July 11, 2018).

[150] On Zahran 'Allush, see Joshua Landis, "Zahran 'Alloush: His Ideology and Beliefs," *Syria Comment*, December 15, 2013, www.joshualandis.com/blog/zahran-alloush/ (accessed July 11, 2018). See also Christopher Philips, "The World Abetted Asad's Victory in Syria," *The Atlantic*, August 4, 2018, www.theatlantic.com/international/arc hive/2018/08/assad-victory-syria/566522/ (accessed August 14, 2018).

[151] See Synaps Network report, "Picking Up the Pieces: How Syrian Society Has Changed," August 6, 2018, www.synaps.network/picking-up-the-pieces (accessed August 6, 2018).

regime break down, was slaughter. As early as July 2011, an Alawi officer confessed to a French reporter that he was tired of killing demonstrators and was disappointed with the regime, but that he kept imagining the Muslim Brotherhood seizing power and butchering his community. Said the officer:

When I imagine such scenes, I cease distinguishing who is in front of me, and I attack (*je fonce*).[152]

Along similar lines, another Alawi officer told a Syrian researcher that the uprising threatened nothing less than his community's physical survival:

We are a minority here, and the Sunnis want to drive us out ... the question isn't about Bashar al-Asad as a person, but if he goes, Alawites will be in danger, especially those in and around Homs, and more so than those on the coast.[153]

Such fears of upcoming massacres and second-class citizenship or dhimmitude in post-al-Asad Syria structured the reaction of Alawis within the military–security complex. Minority apprehensions and an essentialist view of the Sunnis as extremists help to explain the willingness of regime loyalists to perpetrate massacres literally from the first days of the uprising, despite the largely peaceful nature of the demonstrations. I stated earlier that militaries are typically loath to repress the civilians they are supposed to protect, and that internal policing missions sometimes facilitate loyalty shifts in the coercive apparatus. The events in Syria, however, unfolded differently. True, thousands deserted the armed forces in the wake of 2011, but moral outrage triggered by repression broke along identity lines. Alawis in the military–security complex remained overwhelmingly loyal, with defection essentially confined to Sunni officers and soldiers. In fact, the revolt deepened a "sense of isolation" among Alawi officers who viewed the protests through the prism of the 1979 slaughter at the Aleppo artillery school, and other attacks on their sect.[154]

It should be noted here that the anti-Alawi tirades of Sheikh 'Adnan al-'Ar'our, a Syrian Sunni religious figure, heightened sectarian antagonism in Syria. Al-'Ar'our threatened on a Saudi television network in June 2011 to mince the Alawi supporters of al-Asad in grinders, and to "feed their flesh to the dogs."[155] Such inflammatory rhetoric accompanied the rise of the al-Qaeda-affiliated al-Nusra front and eventually ISIS,

---

[152] See Georges Malbrunot, "60,000 centurions Alaouites protègent le clan Assad," *Le Figaro*, July 31, 2011, www.lefigaro.fr/international/2011/07/31/01003-20110731ART FIG00201-60000-centurions-alaouites-protegent-le-clan-assad.php (accessed July 16, 2016).

[153] Khaddour, "The Alawite Dilemma."   [154] Khaddour, "Assad's Officer Ghetto."

[155] Al-'Ar'our's video is available at: www.youtube.com/watch?v=5fFIU2SQu6o (accessed July 11, 2018).

confirming the Alawi's worst fears and giving credence to the regime's propaganda. Alawis were soon convinced that the 2011 uprising threatened their physical presence in Syria – and that Alawi soldiers and officers serving in the military–security complex had additional reasons to fear for their lives should the regime fall.[156] Against this background, defection became tantamount to treason of one's own community and family. If anything, when Alawi officers did criticize the al-Asad regime, it was for allegedly failing to use enough violence to nip the uprising in the bud:

In the time of President Hafez al-Assad in the 1980s, these people were given a painful blow. It was almost lethal, particularly in Hama. I was a young first lieutenant. The decision, at that time, was a wise one. This time, we did not settle the matter from the beginning, which is why we have ended up where we are. But it was the decision of the leadership. As for me, my view was different. Take, for example, the students at the [Tiananmen] square in China, which changed China. If the Chinese state had not settled the student chaos, China would have been lost, and the West would have destroyed it.[157]

Syrians can only be controlled if you scare them . . . . If Hafez were still alive, this would never have happened.[158]

The views from the Sunni quarters in the armed forces were often different. Unlike their Alawi colleagues, Sunni officers had no reflexive reason to defend an Alawi-dominated regime. It could have been possible, of course, to wed them ideationally to the ruling Ba'ath Party, but the officers had long since become disillusioned with the regime's ideological pretenses. Several of my interviewees in Turkey stated that they had always been cynical about the official discourse, and candidly acknowledged that they had joined the military (and stayed in it) in order to make a living. My interviewees repeatedly asserted that corruption had seriously dented the military's fighting capacity, but was nonetheless accepted and quasi-institutionalized. The reason for this, they argued, was easy to understand. The regime was not interested in fighting Israel – only in coup-proofing and political survival. The rise of the Iran/Hezbollah axis compounded the officers' malaise. They suspected that

---

[156] See Rosen, "Among the Alawites." See also Hugh Macleod and Anna-Sofie Flamand, "Inside Syria's Shabiha Death Squads," *The Star*, June 15, 2012, www.thestar.com/news/world/2012/06/15/inside_syrias_shabiha_death_squads.html (accessed July 8, 2018).

[157] Interview with Lieutenant General Jamil al-Hasan, head of Syria's Air Force Intelligence Directorate, with a Russian news site on November 2016. See Aron Lund, "A Voice from the Shadows," *Diwan*, November 25, 2016, https://carnegie-mec.org/diwan/662 40 (accessed July 7, 2018).

[158] Interview with a junior Alawi officer and military judge. See Khaddour, "The Alawite Dilemma."

sectarianism was behind Syria's close identification with Teheran and its regional proxies. I asked all the Sunni Syrian officers I interviewed whether they believed prior to the 2011 turning point that the al-Asad regime was part of an alleged "Shia crescent" in the region, and all said they did. The Sunni officers' ideational affinity with the regime was simply nonexistent:

> The anti-Israeli and anti-imperialist bravado of the regime is not credible. They speak of Arab nationalism and practice systematic anti-Sunni discrimination. How do nationalism and sectarianism go hand in hand? My family is Ba'athist. Until I entered the military academy, I used to believe in the slogans of the Ba'ath Party myself. I also was not very religious, and certainly not sectarian. I didn't know much about Sunnis and Alawis, nor did I care to know. But the anti-Sunni discrimination that I saw in the military academy made me rediscover my Sunni identity. I barely prayed prior to joining the military academy, but I became more observant by the time I graduated. I was not happy in the military academy, and I had already spent three years of my life there, and there was no turning back for me. I felt stuck and discriminated against. So I felt the need to get closer to God. I was supposed to go on a training mission in China, and at the last minute, I was replaced by a colleague whose grades were lower than mine, but who was Alawi. The natural backlash is that I had become much more aware of my Sunni identity by the time I left the military academy than [when] I got in. The military academy is a school to learn sectarianism and hatred in Syria.[159]

Second, the Sunni officers said they reacted positively to the popular revolts in Tunisia and Egypt that had preceded the Syrian uprising. They hoped the movements would prove contagious and that the Syrian regime would be next to fall. As confrontations continued unabated in 2012, social pressures urging Sunni officers still in the armed forces to defect became heightened. A colonel who deserted in late 2011 maintained in an interview that the random violence of the Syrian military made being part of it "a source of shame" ('*eib*).[160] My interviewees in Turkey concurred that remaining in the armed forces after the repression began had, indeed, become unbearable to them for moral and social reasons.

It is important to remember that most Sunnis in the Syrian military hail from the countryside, where parochial relations and identification remain strong. The destruction visited upon officers' provincial hometowns (e.g., Idlib, Deir al-Zur, al-Rastan, and Dar'a) made continued loyalty to the regime indistinguishable from the betrayal of local communities, lifelong

---

[159] Interview with Second Lieutenant Ma'mun Sweid (army), Antakya, Turkey (May 12, 2014).
[160] Selvik, "Roots of Fragmentation," 5.

friends, and sometimes close family members.[161] The use of helicopters to bombard civilian neighborhoods in and around Damascus during the spring of 2012, such as al-Ghuta al-Sharqiyya, Mu'azzamiyyat al-Sham, Tishrin, and al-Ghabun, signaled to officers that the future held only increased escalation of violence. Staying the course with the armed forces meant that they approved of the violence unleashed upon civilians, or that they did not abhor it sufficiently to warrant defection – two stances that many officers found dishonorable.[162] And so, the military started bleeding Sunnis who did not want to take part in the killing of Sunni civilians anywhere in Syria, let alone in their own towns and villages. Out of the twenty-four officers I interviewed in Turkey in the summer of 2014, twenty-one stated that the main reason prompting them to defect was the regime's use of violence against the Sunni population in general. Yet most officers also admitted that their decision to break with the regime became more urgent after their own neighborhoods came under fire. The master cleavage (i.e., the Alawi regime vs. Sunni civilians) was paramount to shaping the officers' agency, but parochial considerations overlapped with it.

My interviewees agreed that the sectarian undertone of the conflict unfolding in society at large inevitably had repercussions within the barracks. Tension between Alawi and Sunni officers became more pronounced, while intelligence agencies strengthened their grip over the armed forces. Sunni officers felt more vulnerable than ever and fretted about false denunciations. In short, they lived in mounting fear.[163] They began defecting in the summer of 2011, and continued to do so until 2,500 to 3,000 Sunni officers had left the armed forces.[164] The defections came in waves: they increased in early 2012, peaked between June and September of that year, and stopped abruptly by early 2013. The most important characteristic of Sunni defection was as follows: The officer mutinies never triggered large-scale splintering movements. When officers defected, they left the armed forces alone. Unlike the events that transpired in Libya or Yemen, no entire brigade or company abandoned the Syrian military to join the uprising. Why were Sunni officers unable to prompt splintering movements when they defected? I show below that the regime's coup-proofing tactics accounted for such an outcome.

---

[161] Interview with a captain (Air Defense) who did not wish to be named, Antakya, Turkey (June 5, 2014).

[162] Interview with Lieutenant Colonel Ahmad Hakim (Al-Asad Academy for Military Engineering), Antakya, Turkey (May 8, 2014).

[163] Ibid.

[164] Second Lieutenant 'Abdul-Razzak Tlass is generally considered the first officer to defect from the armed forces in May 2011. A handful of Alawis defected, as well, including a female officer, Colonel Zubeida al-Meeqi, who broke with the regime in October 2012.

How Ethnic Stacking and Counterbalancing Facilitated Repression   Virtually all the interviewees I met in Turkey concurred that the ubiquity of Alawis and the omnipresence of informers in the military posed major hurdles for anyone pondering a break with the regime, and represented an unsurmountable obstacle to massive splintering movements:

Why didn't whole regiments defect? Because even when regiments are led by Sunni officers, they still do not have real authority over them. This is due to the sectarian dynamics of the armed forces. In each regiment or unit, there are multiple centers of power. More precisely, there is an Alawi center facing the few Sunni officers who happen to occupy leadership positions.[165]

In order for, say, a whole brigade to defect, officers must coordinate their action. To do so, they must trust one another. But how could they? How could an officer tell who is an informer and who is not? The simple fact is he cannot. Defections remained confined to the individual level because we faced coordination problems. Splintering on a large scale never happened; it could not have.[166]

Massive splintering never occurred because commanders in the armed forces are not really in charge; decision-making is in the hands of the Military Intelligence. In every unit, there is a security officer whose mission is to keep an eye on the officer corps. More importantly, there are scores of undercover agents who write reports on their comrades and colleagues; they could be ordinary soldiers, noncommissioned officers, or officers. At best, if you know one or two officers who happen to be your lifelong friends, then you can speak freely with them and discuss defection. But you can hardly trust the tens of officers who serve in the same unit as you, let alone the hundreds who serve in your regiment. Add to all this that senior military leaders [who] count are overwhelmingly Alawi.[167]

Sunni officers never enjoyed a true standing in the armed forces vis-à-vis soldiers, let alone Alawi peers. The reason for that is straightforward: soldiers follow those who have real power. When soldiers need a vacation, or to be reassigned into a different unit, or any of those modifications on their conditions that actually matter to them, they know they cannot ask Sunni officers to intervene on their behalf, because they don't have real power and [worry about] being accused of sectarianism. If you were not really leading soldiers when you were still an officer, how do you expect them to follow you when you decide to defect?[168]

These quotes are straightforward and summarize the answers I received when I discussed the dynamics of defection with my interviewees in Turkey. The nexus formed by two important coup-proofing tactics, i.e., ethnic stacking and counterbalancing the military via security agencies,

---

[165] Interview with retired Brigadier General Mohammad Shahime (army), Antakya, Turkey (May 7, 2014).

[166] Interview with Captain Hussam Sabbagh (Air Force), Antakya, Turkey (May 11, 2014).

[167] Interview with Lieutenant Colonel Ahmed 'Abdul-Qader (Al-Asad Academy for Military Engineering), Antakya, Turkey (May 8, 2014).

[168] Interview with Colonel 'Imad al-Din Isma'el (army), Urfa, Turkey (May 20, 2014).

nullified Sunni officers' ability to trigger massive splintering movements. Sunni officers could no more trust soldiers under their command than they could trust Alawi peers due to fear of informants. The few officers who did try to trigger collective defections were typically unable to do so, and 2,000 Sunni officers were imprisoned because they were accused of planning to defect.[169] This failure was not lost on their Sunni colleagues, who knew that their interaction with peers and soldiers alike was closely monitored and refrained from giving their companies orders that they had not received through proper military channels. Put differently, they were unable to lead.

Three additional factors were related to the ethnic stacking that restricted Sunni officers' leeway. First, most of them were not assigned to operational sectors of the military where they had direct authority over a significant number of troops. A series of transmutations accompanying the beginning of the popular protests reshuffled several Sunni officers who did lead infantry brigades into administrative positions in which they had little to no direct contact with soldiers.[170] Second, Alawi field assistants had typically been assigned to Sunnis who had reached senior positions in the armed forces. The closest aides to these officers were the first obstacle to their freedom of action, often making their authority over their companies nominal.[171] Finally, and as a corollary to the above, no Sunni officer emerged prior to the 2011 events as an influential military commander in the armed forces. Junior and mid-ranking officers were under the direct authority of their Alawi superiors. Senior Sunni officers were always fearful of being accused of building a Sunni base of support within the military, and thus refrained from using their standing in the armed forces to ingratiate themselves with their coreligionists in the lower echelons.

Several of my interviewees in Turkey opined that senior Sunni officers were actually harsher toward their coreligionists in lower echelons than Alawis, precisely because the latter were more relaxed, whereas the former felt the constant need to prove they were not trying to build a power

---

[169] One of the earliest attempts to trigger a collective defection occurred in Regiment 90 on the Syro-Israeli border in May 2011. Five Sunni junior officers, led by First Lieutenant Ramy Bitar, hatched a plan to take control of their company and defect to the revolution. The officers were betrayed by a soldier under their command who was affiliated with the Military Intelligence. They remain in prison at the time of this writing. The failure of Bitar and his friends to defect with their company signaled early on to the rest of the officer corps that similar attempts were doomed to fail due to the pervasive presence of informers throughout the armed forces. Interview with Brigadier Yahyia Hajal (Air Force), Antakya, Turkey (June 6, 2014).

[170] Interview with a major (army) who did not wish to be named, Al-Rihanle, Turkey (June 13, 2014).

[171] Ibid.

base. Consequently, when the movement of defections began, no Sunni officer had followers in the armed forces that he could instruct to turn against the regime en masse.[172] Forty years of identity politics under Hafez and Bashar al-Asad, and the omnipresence of a fearsome security apparatus, had long since transformed Sunni officers and soldiers into a leaderless mass in the military. It is interesting to note the extent to which sectarian stacking posed insurmountable obstacles to anti-regime collective action within the officer corps. As of the 1970s, Sunni officers were increasingly kept away from operational positions in the Syrian armed forces, outnumbered, and closely monitored by intelligence agencies and loyalist Alawi colleagues. The officers' resentment of their lot in the military and of their community's ranking in Syrian politics and society did not translate into open rebellion because the regime's coup-proofing system was effective. For all the upheavals caused by the 2011 uprising, it did not fundamentally alter the rules of the game within the armed forces. Sunnis in the officer corps were unable to react to the events as a group. They could either defect alone or stay in the military, but they could not organize their ranks.

All-in-the-family tactics strengthened the regime's ability to survive the 2011 uprising. Table 3.9 in Chapter 3 contains the names of fourteen relatives of Bashar al-Asad, who are all prominent commanders in Syria's military–security complex. It is significant that seven of them were actually sanctioned by the EU for their direct role in violence against civilians throughout the Syrian crisis. These officers include the president's brother, Maher al-Asad (Fourth Armored Division), who, according to the EU, was the "principal overseer of violence against demonstrators." His brother-in-law Asef Shawkat (MID) and first cousins Hafez Makhluf (GID), Iyad Makhluf (Republican Guard), ʿAtef Najib (PSD), Dhu al-Himma Shalish (Presidential Security), and Riad Shalish (Military Housing) were also named. Prominent businessmen Rami Makhluf and Ehab Makhluf, both first cousins of the president, as well as businessman Mohammad Hamsho, Maher al-Asad's brother-in-law, were also sanctioned for funding the regime's violence against civilians.[173] Other members of the ruling families were also involved in repressing demonstrators. These include military officers Zuheir al-Asad and Hilal al-Asad (First

---

[172] A relative exception is Manaf Tlass, the son of the former defense minister Mustafa Tlass, who served until his defection as brigadier general in the Syrian Republican Guard. Tlass had a following among Syrian officers hailing from Rastan, his hometown. However, he and his father were too closely associated with the regime to become widely popular among officers unrelated to them by parochial bonds. Interview with a colonel (Air Force) who did not wish to be named, Antakya, Turkey (July 7, 2014).

[173] See the *Official Journal of the European Union*, Decision 2011/273/CFSP (annex of articles I and IV).

Armored Division), Muhsin Makhluf (Eleventh Armored Division), and Talal Makhluf (Republican Guard), and notorious commanders of loyalist armed gangs (i.e., the *shabbiha*): Fawwaz al-Asad, Mundhir al-Asad, and 'Arin al-Asad. These networks of hardcore loyalists from the al-Asad /Makhluf/Shalish nexus are linked by bonds of clan and sect. They closed rank in response to the uprising, and not one defected, as all feared a day of reckoning, should the regime fall. Theirs was a quintessentially existential conflict. I stated earlier that all-in-the-family tactics contributed to coup-proof the Syrian military, and this proved true. They also played a crucial role in keeping the coercive apparatus loyal and ready to uphold the status quo when the challenge came from the streets, not from regime insiders.

The elite units and security organizations originally created as loyal counterweights to the armed forces also proved useful in quelling the protests. The Fourth Armored Division, in particular, operated as the regime's big stick, literally from the first days of the uprising. The 2011 Syrian revolt began in Dar'a on March 18, following Friday prayer, when thousands marched calling for the release of children who were detained and tortured for painting political graffiti. The authorities responded to demonstrations almost immediately with lethal force. Several brigades from the Fourth Armored Division were dispatched to Dar'a to stamp out demonstrations, and the troops were given shoot-to-kill orders from the get-go. It was not the regular military but the Fourth Armored Division that perpetrated most of the violence there. This, in fact, would turn into a pattern later on, as the division's Regiment 138 slaughtered civilians in Homs, Hama, and Qusayr, while Regiment 41 in Zabadani and Regiment 40 in Nabak (and in other towns on the Lebanese border) committed similar acts.[174] In addition, the division's Regiment 42 crushed the peaceful protests throughout March and May 2011 in Damascus, where the Republican Guard and Special Forces also squelched dissent.

On the other hand, the division was valuable in rendering demographically mixed army units useful. When the uprising began in 2011, the Syrian military numbered around 200,000 soldiers. Most estimates agree that 70 percent of the professional rank and file personnel were Alawi.[175] But Syria's approximately 300,000 conscripts were largely Sunni. Those soldiers posed a permanent threat to military cohesion,

---

[174] See the Orient report on the Fourth Armored Division, November 2, 2013, www.orient-news.net/ar/news_show/1958 (accessed July 17, 2018).

[175] See Stéphane Valter, "Rivalités et complémentarités au sein des forces armées: le facteur confessionnel en Syrie," *Les Champs de Mars* 1, no. 23 (2012): 83. See also Joseph Holliday, "The Struggle for Syria in 2011: An Operational and Regional Analysis," *Middle East Security Report* 2, Institute for the Study of War (December 2011): 9–10.

because they were pervasive in the conventional forces and generally unwilling to repress their coreligionists. To prevent large-scale desertions while at the same time using the much-needed manpower of the regular troops, the regime frequently assigned one company from the division to work with two companies from the regular military – thus creating a battalion under the leadership and close watch of loyalist elements ready to instantly stamp out defection.[176] Thanks to the Fourth Armored Division and other elite units, thousands of conscripts were employed to repress the uprising. Others defected, or were executed or jailed; yet others were put in "functional imprisonment," i.e., confined to their barracks, where they remained largely ineffective.[177] Still, the Syrian example does not corroborate the argument that only volunteer forces can be used to quell uprising simply because a military can be conscripted and ethnically stacked at the same time.

Political security and other intelligence units were also active in the crackdown. Popular anger was originally directed at the former, and demonstrators in Dar'a repeatedly converged upon and burned PSD offices. Soon, however, operatives from the AFID, the MIS, and the GID would compete with the PSD in terms of the level of violence they visited upon demonstrators.[178] Various security organizations played an important role in keeping the regular armed forces cohesive, and worked to squelch military as well as civilian dissent. On the one hand, intelligence agents embedded within the troops were active in spreading rumors that the uprising was a conspiracy against Syria planned by the US and Israel, funded by Saudi Arabia, and executed by local agents. According to this narrative, the Syrian military was duty bound to defend the country against its local and exterior enemies – a message that state media reiterated relentlessly. On the other hand, security officers guaranteed impunity to soldiers, and gave them a free hand to stop the popular protests "by all means necessary." In the words of a defector from the Special Forces,

---

[176] Such tactics explain why the Fourth Armored Division sometimes appeared to be active all over Syria at the same time. Interview with Colonel 'Imad al-Din Isma'el (Air Force), Urfa, Turkey (May 20, 2014). See also Holliday, "The Assad Regime," 13 and 26–27; and Stratfor, "The Use of Mercenaries in Syria's Crackdown," January 12, 2012, https://worldview.stratfor.com/article/use-mercenaries-syrias-crackdown (accessed July 1, 2018).

[177] Yet other conscripts dodged the draft altogether as the conflict escalated.

[178] For a detailed overview of events in Dar'a, see Human Rights Watch, "Syria: We've Never Seen Such Horror, Crimes against Humanity by Syrian Security Forces" (New York: Human Rights Watch, June 2011), especially pp. 3, 11, and 18. See also Jeffrey White, "A Willingness to Kill: Repression in Syria," PolicyWatch 1840, Washington Institute for Near East Policy, August 16, 2011, www.washingtoninsti tute.org/policy-analysis/view/a-willingness-to-kill-repression-in-syria (accessed July 17, 2018).

the Mukhabarat insistently told the troops that the regime opponents were "dogs," and that the soldiers were absolutely free to do with them whatever they wanted without worrying about the consequences. Finally, intelligence operatives made sure soldiers followed orders and shot whoever appeared reluctant to do so by singling out suspicious soldiers to snipers implanted within the different companies or on nearby rooftops. In several testimonies, the Air Force Intelligence appears to be particularly responsible for such extra-judiciary killings, though the Military Intelligence was involved, as well.[179]

A word is due here on the loyalist paramilitaries (i.e., *shabbiha*), which played a huge role in repressing the uprising and perpetrated some of the worst massacres of civilians in Syria. The *shabbiha* arose from tolerated criminal gangs recruiting from the lowest socioeconomic spectrums of society. These networks were operating prior to the beginning of the Syrian conflict, and quickly morphed into militarized sectarian mobs that authorities unleashed upon demonstrators as early as March 2011. All aspects of coup-proofing previously described enabled the creation of such auxiliary forces. First, the *shabbiha* were led by the extended al-Asad, Makhluf, and Shalish families, including military officers and local Mafioso-like bosses in Latakia. All-in-the-family tactics wedded not only the armed forces and the security apparatus to the regime, but the *shabbiha,* as well. Second, wherever Alawis had a significant demographic presence in Syria, the *shabbiha*'s demographic composition was all-Alawi.[180] Consequently, they proved receptive to the narrative of Alawi victimhood and anti-Sunni ideology. In a candid interview, an Alawi member of the *shabbiha* known as Abu Ja'far expressed readiness to kill Sunni women because they gave birth to babies who grow up and take up arms against his community. He said he joined the fray in order to keep power in Alawi hands and fight "those Wahhabi radicals" who were allegedly out to prohibit alcohol in Syria and forcibly veil his wife and daughters. In essence, Abu Ja'far interpreted the uprising and ensuing events as a merciless, all-out final battle between Sunnis and Alawis.[181] Abu Ja'far's assertions are revealing because the "war on Alawis" leitmotiv is actually a fixture of *shabbiha* discourse. Their self-perception included viewing themselves as gallant defenders of a minority under siege who must kill or be killed. That such a worldview and socialization spawned indefectible loyalty to the al-Asads and readiness to commit

---

[179] See Human Rights Watch, "Syria: 'By All Means Necessary!'", 49 and 63–65.
[180] In Syrian regions where Alawi presence was feeble or nonexistent, the regime was sometimes able to mobilize Sunni criminal networks to operate as *shabbiha*. Examples include the notorious Berri clan in Aleppo.
[181] See Macleod and Flamand, "Inside Syria's Shabiha Death Squads."

atrocities against civilians in order to uphold the status quo is unsurprising.[182] Equally understandable is their ability to quickly mobilize the informal network of the Alawi underworld, because they originated from it.

Third, elite units and the security counterbalancing the armed forces beefed up the *shabbiha* and transformed them from loose gangs into organized vigilantes operating under the direct supervision of the Fourth Armored Division and the intelligence units.[183] Air Force Intelligence played a particularly crucial role in monitoring the *shabbiha* from 2012 onward, as they were institutionalized into the officially sanctioned National Defense Force.[184] The skewed demographic composition of the military–security complex and the *shabbiha* facilitated cooperation between the different sides along sectarian lines.

Finally, the corruption game which the regime mastered in order to purchase the loyalty of the military elite was put to use in order to give the *shabbiha* additional incentives to kill on behalf of the loyalist camp. They were already involved in activities such as smuggling, drug-trafficking, and the sale of stolen goods between Syria and Lebanon prior to the uprising. Such undertakings intensified as the regime's need for *shabbiha* manpower made it even less inclined to rein them in. Their militiamen were also given a free hand to loot, steal, and kidnap, in addition to receiving direct cash payments from the authorities. The absolute power and guaranteed impunity they enjoyed meant they could also rape women they fancied, and sometimes kill them afterwards.[185]

How the Political Economy of Loyalty Facilitated Repression   I said earlier that the al-Asad regime transformed its most influential barons

---

[182] See a Reuters' report on the *shabbiha*, July 2, 2012, www.reuters.com/article/us-syria-crisis-shabbiha/syrias-paramilitary-gangs-a-law-unto-themselves-idUSBRE8610 N620120702 (accessed July 21, 2018). See also Stephen Starr, "Shabiha Militias and the Destruction of Syria," *CTC Sentinel* 5, no. 11 (November 2012): 12–14.

[183] The US Department of the Treasury has noted, in this regard, that the *shabbiha* have operated as a "direct-action arm" of Syria's security services, particularly the Air Force Intelligence and Military Intelligence. See the press release "Treasury Sanctions Al-Nusrah Front Leadership in Syria and Militias Supporting the Asad Regime," December 11, 2012, www.treasury.gov/press-center/press-releases/pages/tg1797.aspx (accessed June 7, 2018).

[184] See a report on the Air Force Intelligence Directorate (AFID), prepared by a group of scholars and published by the Toran Center for Strategic Studies on 28 July, 2017, 23, www.torancenter.org/wp-content/uploads/2017/07/إدارة-المخابرات-الجوية..-الذراع-.pdf (accessed June 12, 2018).

[185] See Ruth Sherlock, "Confessions of an Assad 'Shabiha' Loyalist: How I Raped and Killed for £300 a Month," *The Telegraph*, July 14, 2012, www.telegraph.co.uk/news/worldnews/middleeast/syria/9400570/Confessions-of-an-Assad-Shabiha-loyalist-how-I-raped-and-killed-for-300-a-month.html (accessed March 19, 2017).

managing the military–security complex into financial magnates. That these generals stood firm within the loyalist camp in 2011 is self-explanatory: they had no assurance that a prospective post-al-Asad regime would be as generous to them, and every reason to fear retribution for the crimes they perpetrated under al-Asad, including financial corruption. But even generals beyond the immediate circle of the military elite had also benefited from the regime's bounty, and had fewer incentives than younger officers to challenge the status quo. In effect, the overwhelming majority of officers who defected in the wake of the 2011 uprising had previously occupied junior and mid-level positions in the military hierarchy. Only a handful of the estimated 3,000 Sunni officers who defected had previously reached senior ranks in the military.[186] Simply put, generals had more to lose if they deserted than their subordinates in the armed forces. A high-ranking officer candidly told researchers in 2014 that defection would cost him "a good salary, multiple cars, and a beautiful farm." This suggests that even though some senior commanders may have shared the antipathy toward the regime that animated their subordinates, financial and other egoistical concerns kept them on the regime's side.[187]

Furthermore, the uprising and ensuing escalation of violence actually provided senior officers with additional ways to enrich themselves. As previously mentioned, the top brass had long used their influence to reap kickbacks in exchange for allowing conscripts to evade military service. Naturally, the drive to avoid conscription became greater following the 2011 turning point, thus providing senior officers with advantageous financial opportunities. Soldiers also bribed generals to avoid being sent on patrols, or to be assigned to specific areas of Syria, but not others. Occasionally, mid-ranking and junior officers benefitted as well. As checkpoints multiplied throughout the country following the escalation of protests, the officers manning them extracted bribes from civilian travelers inside Syria – especially traders who need to transfer merchandise. Some posts at the entrance of Damascus or Raqqa were eloquently dubbed "the 1 million checkpoint" (*hajez al-maliun*) because they were particularly profitable.[188] Officers also made money selling weapons to

---

[186] See Bou Nassif, "Second-Class," 19.
[187] See Dorothy Ohl, Holger Albrecht, and Kevin Koehler, "For Money or Liberty? The Political Economy of Military Desertion and Rebel Recruitment in the Syrian Civil War," Carnegie Regional Insight, November 24, 2015, https://carnegieendowment .org/2015/11/24/for-money-or-liberty-political-economy-of-military-desertion-and-rebel-recruitment-in-syrian-civil-war-pub-61714 (accessed April 3, 2020).
[188] Khaddour, "Strength in Weakness." See also a report on the commercial activities of the Fourth Armed Division published by *Baladi* website, August 29, 2017, www.baladi-news.com/ar/news/details/22850/ (accessed April 10, 2018).

the opposition, or information about disappeared relatives or the release of prisoners, in exchange for bribes. Two new terms made their way into ordinary Syrian parlance: "The Souk of Sunnis" (*suq al-sunna*) and *ta'fish*. Both refer to a common practice among the *shabbiha* and members of the military–security complex pertaining to stealing furniture from Sunni houses and then selling it at low prices. A lucrative alternative economy tolerated by the regime contributed to wedding the officers closer to the status quo.[189]

With that said, the importance of material incentives in driving military loyalty in Syria should not be overstated. This is particularly true of the lower echelons that benefited far less – if at all – than the top brass from the crisis economy, but faced its most devastating consequences. As operational commanders of the troops in the field, Syrian mid-ranking and junior officers supervised the slaughter of civilians when the uprising was nonviolent. They did the regime's violent bidding on the ground while generals gave orders from afar. Later on, with the escalation of confrontations into war, these same junior officers were far more likely to die than their superiors. And those of them who lived struggled financially in a devastated economy marked by hyperinflation and a severe devaluation of currency. The civil servants – including military personnel – were particularly hard-hit by the economic downturn: prior to the conflict, the average value of their salaries was $200; it shrunk to less than $60 in 2017, while consumer price index rose more than 500 percent.[190] As discussed previously, the bulk of loyalist units in Syria are manned by Alawi officers and their men; and these remained on the regime's side despite the crisis not because of it. Though shared aversions and material self-centered considerations are not mutually exclusive, the former carried far more weight wedding the military lower echelons to the regime, and the loyalist top brass serving it.

Conclusion of the Syrian Case Study

I said previously that promoting the material interests of the top brass can divide the military along generational lines, if money does not trickle down to the mid-ranking and junior officers. I also maintained that

---

[189] Ohl, Halbrecht, and Kohler, "For Money or Liberty." See also Rafia Salemeh, "Sanawat al Ta'fish," *Al-Jumhuriyya*, August 8, 2018, www.aljumhuriya.net/ar/con tent/سنوات-التعفيش (accessed August 13, 2018).

[190] See Raja Abdulrahim, "War-Torn Syria's Battered Economy Marked by Inflation and Poverty," *The Wall Street Journal*, July 29, 2017, www.wsj.com/articles/war-torn-syrias-battered-economy-marked-by-inflation-and-poverty-1501234205 (accessed August 1, 2017).

counterbalancing creates friction capable of alienating conventional troops if the regime favors their praetorian rivals over them. Both dynamics were actually at work in Syria. Inside the military–security complex, the regime's major beneficiaries were generals hailing from families such as the al-Asads, Makhlufs, Shalishs, Kheir-Beiks, and a few others, who secured the biggest fortunes officers made in the last decades. Other top brass were less fortunate, but enjoyed sufficient privileges to be satisfied with their situation overall. In contrast, the mid-ranking and junior officers had been struggling financially since the neoliberal turn became entrenched under Bashar al-Asad. Their situation regressed further after the Syrian economy contracted in the wake of 2011; the real value of their monthly salaries shrunk from $400–$800 to $100–$200.[191]

On the other hand, it was an open secret in Syria that elite units had it better than the regular troops in terms of influence, financial privileges, access to new equipment, and prestige. Such unequal treatment was not lost on the armed forces, and scholars of Syria have long noted the rivalry and friction between the military and the nation's praetorians.[192] The 2011 uprising could have been an occasion for such conflictual undercurrents to boil over, with very dire consequences for the regime, but that never happened. The junior and mid-ranking officers in the regular troops – and especially the elite units and security organizations – upheld the status quo and went to great lengths to defend it, as demonstrations escalated from nonviolence to insurgency and civil war.

Like the Egyptian top brass, Syrian generals were, for the most part, loyalists. Unlike their Egyptian peers, however, the military elite in Syria could instruct their subordinates to quell the uprising through overwhelming violence without fearing a breakdown in discipline, or a non-hierarchical coup. What explains this variation? My answer is straightforward. In Syria, the ruling elite wedded the officer corps ideationally to the status quo, whereas the Egyptian regime did not. To be sure, young Alawi officers in the armed forces were cognizant that their superiors in the military hierarchy, as well as their institutional rivals in elite units and security organizations, benefitted far more from the regime than they ever did. These officers were aware of the pervasive corruption

---

[191] Khaddour, "Strength in Weakness."

[192] See, for instance, Eisenstadt, "Syria's Defense Companies," 11–12; Alasdair Drysdale, "The Succession Question in Syria," *Middle East Journal* 39, no. 2 (Spring 1985): 248; and Selvik, "Roots of Fragmentation," 5. See also CIA document no. RDP85T00314R000200140002-4, "Syria: The Succession Struggle and Rif'at's Prospects," 3, approved for release January 31, 2011, www.cia.gov/library/readin groom/docs/CIA-RDP85T00314R000200140002-4.pdf (accessed June 5, 2018).

around them, simply because the generals-turned-magnates did not bother to hide it. Their sprawling mansions in the Alawi hinterland were only one indicator (among others) of their accumulated riches. But the alternative that the uprising appeared to be promising was the return of Sunni rule, possibly accompanied with retributions against the Alawi community. Everyone in the Alawi power structure rejected this, from the lower echelons of the officer corps to the military top brass, and all the way to Bashar al-Asad and the ruling circle around him. Significantly, even retired Alawi officers who had once supported Salah Jdid and were later imprisoned under Hafez al-Asad, opposed regime breakdown in 2011, though they admitted that some reforms were necessary. As Valter noted, the old Jdidists' sectarian solidarity with the regime trumped their political opposition to it.[193] If these long-standing nemeses of the al-Asad dynasty still found it preferable to the alternatives, then it became a given that other sectors in the Alawi community would do so, as well – even though they paid a hefty price to defend the regime as the endgame was over and conflict escalated into warfare. And so the al-Asads survived the massive peaceful uprising in 2011 just as they prevailed over previous military challenges to their rule. In sum, Hafez and Bashar al-Asad's coup-proofing tactics delivered coup-proofing and more. The same proved true in Libya, though not in Tunisia, as I show next.

---

[193] Valter, "Rivalités et complémentarités," 94–95.

5 How Coup-Proofing Structured Military Response to Protest in Tunisia and Libya

On December 17, 2010, a twenty-six-year-old fruit vendor, Mohammed Bou'azizi, ended his life by self-immolating in Sidi Bouzid, a city in central Tunisia, in protest against poverty and frequent humiliations by local authorities. On the same day, Bou'azizi's family and friends marched to police headquarters to express their outrage. Riots broke out in Sidi Bouzid, and quickly spread to engulf Tunisia. Former Tunisian president Zein al-'Abidin Ben 'Ali authorized the interior ministry to use deadly force in order to crush popular movements, but the protests continued unabated despite the growing death toll.[1]

In the early days of January 2011, the exhausted, overextended police force began to collapse. Meanwhile, the ruling Rassemblement Constitutionnel Démocratique (RCD) failed to marshal counterdemonstrators, and Ben 'Ali ordered the armed forces to restore order on January 7. The military was deployed around embassies and ministries as well as in the streets of major cities, but proved unwilling to open fire on civilians, not even to prevent them from burning police stations. On January 13, two days after the armed forces were deployed in Tunis, the head of presidential security, 'Ali Seriati, was still complaining about the military's neutral stance in the crisis. Seriati warned that the presidential palace would be empty in twenty-four hours absent proactive military support to the regime.[2] By that time, thousands were clamoring for regime change in daily protests all over the country. Only overriding repression could have upheld the status quo, but the Tunisian military lacked the stomach for it. On January 14, Ben 'Ali fled into exile in Saudi Arabia, and the process of democratic transition began in Tunisia. The

---

[1] According to a national commission created in the wake of the Tunisian uprising, 338 Tunisians died, and 2,147 were injured. Some of the deadliest incidents unfolded in the last days of the uprising, on January 8, 9, and 12 in the Kasserine governorate in west-central Tunisia. The police were found guilty of repeatedly opening fire on civilians in situations in which deadly force could not be justified by self-defense.

[2] See "Tunisie: que mijotait Ali Seriati," *Jeune Afrique*, March 28, 2011, www.jeuneafrique.com /192243/politique/tunisie-que-mijotait-ali-seriati (accessed September 5, 2018).

former president had coup-proofed his rule masterfully, and no serious threat to his power had ever originated from the barracks. However, what worked to prevent power seizure by military actors failed to avert regime breakdown when opposition sprung from the streets, as I shall discuss below.

The Tunisian uprising was still ongoing when protests started in neighboring Libya. On February 13, demonstrators in the Libyan towns of Derna and Bani Walid took over neglected housing projects, symbols of unfulfilled government promises to improve the living conditions of the popular classes. On February 15, 2011, a small group of lawyers assembled in front of the courthouse in Benghazi, Libya's second-largest city, in solidarity with a colleague arrested by the authorities. When the police used water cannons to break the mobilization, the lawyers gathered again the following day, only to be met with further violence. The turbulence in Benghazi triggered calls for a "Day of Rage" that spread widely on social media.

On February 17, thousands took to the streets in Benghazi, and the Libyan chapter of the Arab Spring began to unfold. Though Mu'ammar al-Qaddhafi's loyalists opened fire on the protesters, killing 24 of them that day, the popular movement proved unstoppable. By February 20, 233 Libyans had lost their lives despite the nonviolent nature of their undertakings, but the security forces in Benghazi had retreated or defected to the opposition. Protests were simultaneously ongoing in other eastern Libyan towns, including Derna, al-Baida, and Tobruk, but also in the capital, Tripoli, and in the western city of Misrata on the Mediterranean coast. A defiant al-Qaddhafi promised in a speech to "cleanse Libya house to house" of his opponents, while his foreign minister, Musa Kusa, vowed that there would be no Tahrir Square in Libya. As repression continued unabated, the death toll mounted quickly, triggering further defection of military personnel who refused to kill civilians. The armed forces splintered, as some units remained in the loyalist camp, while others joined the opposition.

In March, the peaceful uprising progressively escalated into a full-on insurgency, and Libya plunged into civil war. On October 20, a rebel faction seized and summarily executed al-Qaddhafi, whose troops had been defeated by NATO and the local insurgents. Thus ended al-Qaddhafi's forty-two-year-long rule over Libya.[3] In what follows,

---

[3] For a summary of events during the first weeks of the Libyan uprising, see Christopher S. Chivvis, *Toppling Qaddafi: Libya and the Limits of Liberal Intervention* (New York: Cambridge University Press, 2014), 25–31; and Ethan Chorin, *Exit the Colonel: The Hidden History of the Libyan Revolution* (New York: Public Affairs, 2012), 187–208.

I further ponder Tunisia and Libya, using the same analytical framework developed earlier in this work.

Tunisia

Military conspiracies had been infrequent in Tunisia, and officers generally obedient to civilian authorities. Yet Tunisian autocrats al-Habib Bourguiba and Zein al-'Abidin Ben 'Ali, who ruled with an iron fist after independence, distrusted the armed forces and worried about military interventionism all the same. Bourguiba lost no time coup-proofing his regime immediately after his rise to the presidency in 1957. Ben 'Ali, who seized power in 1987, acted along similar lines. Below, I flesh out the regime-maintenance strategies of both presidents, and ponder the ways in which coup-proofing structured military politics during the decisive events of 2010–2011 in Tunisia.

Coups and Coup-Proofing under Bourguiba

By the time he became president in 1957, Bourguiba had long been at the forefront of his country's struggle to emancipate itself from France. That Bourguiba enjoyed wide popular legitimacy at the time is undeniable, but his position in the first years after independence was not unassailable. On the one hand, he jockeyed for power throughout the 1950s against the other great leader of the independence movement, Saleh Ben Yussef. The latter enjoyed a large following in Tunisia, and was arguably as popular as Bourguiba himself. The Yussefists never gave their allegiance to the postindependence regime in Tunis, and their opposition turned into outright animosity when Bourguiba had the exiled Ben Yussef assassinated in 1961.[4] On the other hand, Bourguiba's modernism earned him the entrenched hostility of Tunisian conservative circles, which rejected secularism as treason to Islam.[5] In addition, Bourguiba recruited his ruling elite largely from the Sahel – on the eastern coast of Tunisia, from which he hailed – and from Tunis, the capital. The southern regions were underrepresented in the postindependence configuration of power, and were largely disenchanted with Bourguiba's regime.

Three additional factors added further strain to the picture. First, Bourguiba's unabashedly pro-Western politics alienated Tunisians who identified with pan-Arab nationalism. This was an important sector of the

---

[4] See al-Safi Sa'id, *Bourguiba, Sira Shebh Muharrama* (Tunis: 'Orabia, 2011), 252–254.
[5] Moncef el-Materi, *De Saint-Cyr au Peleton d'Execution de Bourguiba* (Tunis: Arabesques, 2014), 149.

population. Allegedly, by the end of the 1950s, there were more portraits of Nasser in the streets of Tunis than of Bourguiba himself.[6] Second, the guerrillas who had fought the French during the years of struggle for independence (i.e., the Fellaga) believed themselves the true heroes of Tunisian freedom. Several former Fellaga leaders accused Bourguiba of failing to recognize their sacrifices, and subsequently joined the opposition to his regime.[7] Finally, and perhaps most critically, scores of Tunisian officers turned against him after he led the nascent armed forces into a suicidal confrontation with French troops stationed in the port city of Bizerte in 1961. Politically, the battle served to enhance Bourguiba's prestige in the Arab world as a nationalist leader actively opposed to French colonialism. From a military perspective, however, Bizerte was unwinnable; hundreds of Tunisians perished in its wake, including 302 officers and soldiers.[8] Both civilian opposition and military alienation gave Bourguiba cause for concern at a time when violent overthrow of Arab regimes was pervasive throughout the Middle East. Indeed, he constantly fretted about coup contagion, and was ever suspicious of the armed forces.[9]

In 1958, Tunisia broke its diplomatic relations with Egypt to protest alleged interference in its internal affairs. Bourguiba accused Cairo of dispatching undercover Egyptian officers to his country in order to foment a military coup with Nasserite sympathizers in the Tunisian officer corps. Whether such allegations were factual or not remains unclear to this day, but recriminations between Tunis and Cairo showed that Bourguiba was already fearful of military interventionism only one year after becoming president.[10] A botched putsch in 1962 heightened his qualms about the armed forces. The coup-plotters recruited an army captain in charge of presidential security, instructing him to seize Bourguiba and execute him immediately, should he refuse to abdicate. The fact that officers had planned his demise fueled his anti-militarism, and confirmed his suspicion that the danger of military putsches was real in

---

[6] Noura Boursali, *Bourguiba à l'Epreuve de la Democratie* (Tunis: Samed Editions, 2012), 200.

[7] In retaliation, Bourguiba executed or imprisoned hundreds of Fellaga in the 1950s. Sa'id, *Bourguiba*, 206.

[8] Nicole Grimaud, *La Tunisie à la Recherche de sa Securité* (Paris: Presses Universitaires de France, 1995), 65.

[9] See Audrey Pluta, "Les relations civilo-militaires en Tunisie de l'indépendance a nous jours: l'armée entre soumission au pouvoir civil et nouveau rôle politique" (master's thesis, Institut d'Etudes Politiques, Aix-en-Provence, 2017), 26 and 120.

[10] On the 1958 crisis between Egypt and Tunisia, see the Egyptian daily *al-Yawm al-Sabe'* (October 15, 2016). See also Grimaud, *La Tunisie*, 79.

Tunisia.[11] Two decades later, in 1983, nineteen officers and soldiers in the Tunisian Air Force were accused of plotting against the regime and were struck from the lists because they belonged to Tunisia's underground Islamist movement, Harakat al-Ittijah al-Islami.[12] On November 25, 1987, the authorities announced that a network of Islamist activists spanning the military, police, and National Guard had planned to seize power a few weeks earlier. Bourguiba's prime minister, Zein al-'Abidin Ben 'Ali, was quicker to act, and staged a velvet putsch on November 7 – only one day prior to the Islamists' purported coup.[13] Ben 'Ali's power grab was successful because he enjoyed the active support of the National Guard and the tacit approval of the military top brass.

This review suggests that the image of Tunisian officers as completely "apolitical" under Bourguiba needs to be qualified. To be sure, the armed forces in Tunisia were closer to the republican ideal than any other military in the Arab world, with the possible exception of their Lebanese counterparts. Still, it is certain that Tunisian officers prepared at least one coup and facilitated another under Bourguiba. The latter was aware of the danger the military posed to his rule and crafted a coup-proofing strategy to secure his grip over Tunisia.

First, he wedded the armed forces to his rule ideationally. It is true, of course, that the Tunisian officers had never been forced to join Bourguiba's ruling party, the Neo-Destour, like their counterparts in Syria and Iraq were expected to do under the Ba'ath Party. In fact, he explicitly prevented officers from being affiliated with any party – including his own – and no "political commissar" was ever to serve in the ranks of the Tunisian military. With that said, Bourguiba stood publicly and staunchly for the modernizing values he tried to instill in Tunisia, namely, secularization, economic development, the emancipation of women, and liberalization of social practices. In general, officers who served in the Tunisian military under him shared his aspirations and respected his commitment to achieve them. This was particularly true of the first generations of Tunisian officers formed in Saint-Cyr and other French military schools. Their Francophilia and abhorrence of Islamists mirrored

---

[11] Famously, Bourguiba argued after 1962 that the "genie of the military coup" (jinn al-inqilab) was now out of the bottle in Tunisia. Sa'id, Bourguiba, 282. For a firsthand account of the 1962 plot, see El-Materi, De Saint-Cyr.

[12] Pluta, "Les relations civilo-militaires," 25.

[13] Michel Camau and Vincent Geisser, Le Syndrome Autoritaire: Politique en Tunisie de Bourguiba à Ben Ali "Ben 'Ali, Zein al-'Abidin" (Paris: Presses de Science Po, 2003), 211. According to retired Colonel Munsif Zughlami (army), the Islamists did, indeed, manage to infiltrate the armed forces in 1987, but only a handful of officers and soldiers were involved in the plot. Interview, Tunis (August 6, 2013).

the president's. L. B. Ware correctly pinpoints, in this regard, the "Kemalist ideology" and "tacit agreement" linking the military ideationally to the first president of Tunisia.[14]

It must be noted here that whatever inroads Nasserism and Islamism made in the Tunisian officer corps remained limited. The ideological reference of the 1962 coup plot was pan-Arabist, but no more than ten officers were ever involved. The alienation of these men stemmed from bitterness after the Bizerte debacle as much as from ideological divergences with Bourguiba. Moncef El-Materi, an officer who participated in the failed coup attempt, mentions candidly in his memoirs that Bizerte was the crucial turning point in his perception of the regime (*"Pour moi, il y eut un 'avant Bizerte' et un 'après Bizerte'"*[15]). In the 1970s and 1980s, Tunisia's Islamists had some success recruiting sympathizers into the armed forces. A former director of the Ecole Supérieure de Guerre in Tunisia confirmed that some officers had to be discharged in the 1980s because of their Islamist sympathies.[16] And yet Islamist infiltration, too, was constricted. Overall, Tunisian officers shared the main tenets of Bourguibism, and believed that he stood for a patriotic ideal transcending mere power politics. The incorruptibility of the late president amplified his prestige and credibility. When Bourguiba announced in 1965 that Tunisia's public resources would be allocated primarily to create a robust educational system and foster economic development, his officers believed he was, indeed, dedicated to achieving these goals. To this day, retired officers generally remember Bourguiba as a statesman who served his country well, sent officers to train in prestigious French and American military academies, and respected them despite his anti-militaristic views.[17]

Second, Bourguiba made sure, throughout his tenure, to recruit most officers from the Sahel – especially Sousse and Monastir – as well as Tunis and its surrounding area, including Bizerte and Cape Bon.[18] The southern regions remained deliberately as underrepresented in the officer corps

---

[14] L. B. Ware, "The Role of the Tunisian Military in the Post-Bourguiba Era," *Middle East Journal* 39, no. 1 (Winter 1985): 38.

[15] El-Materi, *De Saint-Cyr*, 29 and 46. See also Boubaker Ben-Kraiem, *Naissance d'une armée nationale, la promotion Bourguiba* (Tunis: Maison d'Edition de Tunis, 2013), 172.

[16] Interview with retired Colonel Major Mukhtar Hishayshi (army), Tunis (July 12, 2013). Note that the colonel major (*'ameed*) rank in Tunisia is the equivalent to brigadier general in other countries.

[17] Interviews with retired Colonels Bashir bin 'Aissa (army) and Lotfi Loghmati (army), Tunis (June 23, 2013). See also Pluta's interviews with several retired Tunisian officers, who all hailed Bourguiba as a clairvoyant statesman who was right to give priority for education and economic development over military spending. "Les relations civilo-militaires," 12.

[18] Ware, "The Role of the Tunisian Military," 38.

as they were among the political elite. In addition, the officers hailed overwhelmingly from the country's urban and educated middle classes, perceived to be the backbone of Bourguiba's modernization project. The first batch of young Tunisians sent to study at Saint-Cyr was actually handpicked by the Neo-Destour. In the words of Camau and Geisser, the cadets were *"enfants du régime."* They all hailed from loyalist milieus, and frequently chose their spouses from such circles. Bourguiba also promoted officers to senior positions on the basis of their loyalty, not professional merit. The former president reckoned that officers sharing the ruling elite's regional and social backgrounds were less likely to threaten his rule.[19] As an institution, the military was never central to his plans for Tunisia. As individuals, however, military officers – and certainly the top brass – had sufficient connections with the power elite to identify and sympathize with the ruling circles. As an additional measure of security, he refused to train Tunisian officers in coup-prone Baghdad and Cairo, and ordered Tunisian cadets to be formed in France, where he hoped they would absorb the principles of civilian supremacy and military subordination to legitimate authorities.[20]

Finally, Bourguiba counterbalanced the armed forces with the National Guard, the police, military intelligence, and the ruling party. When it was founded in 1957, the Guard was part of the Tunisian armed forces, and thus under the control of the ministry of defense. Shortly after independence, Bourguiba severed the Guard from the ministry of defense and placed it under the control of the ministry of interior in order to restrict collaboration (and potentially collusion) between it and the armed forces.[21] After the failed 1962 coup attempt, the Guard was expanded until it numbered 6,000 men – about a third of the armed forces at the time. It was organized along military lines, with a ranking system paralleling that of the armed forces. Bourguiba provided the Guard with advanced military equipment and communications devices that contrasted markedly with the heteroclite, ramshackle weaponry at the disposition of the armed forces. In addition, he ordered the police to report

[19] See Camau and Geisser, *Le Syndrome*, 165 and 169. See also Noureddine Jebnoun, "In the Shadow of Power: Civil-Military Relations and the Tunisian Popular Uprising," *Journal of North African Studies* 19, no. 3 (2014): 299; and Ware, "The Role of the Tunisian Military," 38.

[20] Interview with retired Colonel Major Mohammad Mezughi (army), Tunis (June 5, 2013).

[21] Grimaud, *La Tunisie*, 97. See also Sharan Grewal, "A Quiet Revolution: The Tunisian Military after Ben Ali 'Ben 'Ali, Zein al-'Abidin,'" Carnegie Regional Insight, February 24, 2016, https://carnegieendowment.org/2016/02/24/quiet-revolution-tunisian-military-after-ben-ali-pub-62780 (accessed October 23, 2018). Libyan military threats would eventually force Bourguiba to later allocate more funds for the severely underequipped Tunisian armed forces.

on the armed forces, strengthened the grip of the Military Intelligence over the officer corps, and instructed the Neo-Destour to create a loyalist militia to provide him with an additional security guarantee.[22] These dispositions kept the regime in firm control of the armed forces from the early 1960s until Bourguiba's downfall in 1987.

Coups and Coup-Proofing under Ben 'Ali

Ben 'Ali plotted his 1987 power seizure with the top brass in the military and security establishments.[23] He himself had been an officer in the armed forces and the first director of military security in 1964 before heading the Sûreté Nationale, the main branch of Tunisia's secret police. He then served under Bourguiba as ambassador, minister of interior, and finally prime minister. Throughout his tenure, Ben 'Ali worried that he could lose power the same way he had captured it.[24] It was inevitable, then, that he would be as suspicious of the military as his predecessor had been previously.

Ben 'Ali's anxieties were seemingly corroborated in 1991, when officials at the ministry of interior and leaders of the ruling party – by then called Le Rassemblement Constitutionnel Démocratique (RCD) – convinced him that Islamists had infiltrated the officer corps, and that another coup was brewing. A frightened Ben 'Ali subsequently unleashed the security establishment on the armed forces: 113 officers, 82 NCOs, and 49 soldiers were arrested, and scores of them were tortured in the ministry of interior. These men were eventually released, but they were discharged and banned from traveling or taking civilian jobs. The regime also prevented their colleagues in the military from interacting with them.[25] The Barrakat al-Sahil affair, as the alleged coup attempt came to be known, was for Ben 'Ali what the 1962 military conspiracy was for Bourguiba: confirmation that the armed forces posed a permanent threat to his rule.

---

[22] According to Mezughi, Bourguiba ordered the police to monitor every single movement by military units in the wake of the 1962 coup plot (interview). Bourguiba said in a public speech in December 1962 that officers had dared to conspire because Tunisia was not a police state – and that he intended to strengthen the police to avoid military interventionism in the future. See El-Materi, *De Saint-Cyr*, 113 and 134.

[23] For a firsthand account on the November 7 putsch in 1987, see Rafik Chelly, *Le Syndrome De Carthage des Présidents Habib Bourguiba et Zine El Abidine Ben Ali "Ben 'Ali, Zein al-'Abidin"* (Tunis: Imprimerie Graphique du Centre, 2012), 13–36 (chapter 1).

[24] Interview with Tunisian diplomat Nasr Ben Soltana, Tunis (June 11, 2013); and with Hishayshi.

[25] See Hicham Bou Nassif, "A Military Besieged: The Armed Forces, the Police, and the Party in Ben 'Ali's Tunisia, 1987–2011," *International Journal of Middle East Studies* 47, no. 1 (February 2015): 70–71.

To coup-proof his regime, Ben ʿAli counterbalanced the military just as his predecessor had done. First, the RCD's tentacles were spread all over the country and activated to collect information on civilians and military personnel alike. So efficient was the RCD in this regard that the party may have superseded the ministry of interior as the regime's foremost intelligence-gathering machine.[26] It has frequently been alleged that Ben ʿAli, who served as Tunisian ambassador to Poland in the 1980s, replicated in the RCD the communist methods of control he had learned in Warsaw.[27] Second, Ben ʿAli empowered his old fiefdom in Military Security (MS) even more; my interviewees in Tunis concurred that the true command center in the armed forces after Barrakat al-Sahil became the MS. One anecdote I heard repetitively during interviews with Tunisian officers is very eloquent in this regard: In the wake of shooting drills, the MS expected officers to deliver back empty cartridges equivalent to the number of bullets previously issued to them. The rationale for this practice was straightforward: officers needed to show that they were not secretly storing ammunition that could later be used for subversive purposes.[28] Tunisian officers were also discouraged from interacting socially, and admonished by superiors whenever the MS reported that they had met for dinner, celebrated a holiday, or watched sports together. In the succinct words of one of my interviewees, Ben ʿAli controlled Tunisia with the RCD and the Tunisian armed forces with the MS and other security organizations.[29]

Third, Ben ʿAli strengthened the Presidential Guard (PG), a corps completely independent of the armed forces and under the direct supervision of the presidency. The PG boasted 5,000 competitively selected recruits, a sniper's squad, an autonomous intelligence unit, and enjoyed preferential treatment in terms of equipment and salaries. The service of guardsmen was easier than that of regular troops, because they were stationed near the presidential palace in the capital, whereas the armed forces could be posted anywhere in Tunisia. This was particularly true of the military's armored regiments stationed in the countryside, since

[26] See International Crisis Group, "Tunisie: Lutter Contre L'Impunite, Restaurer la Securite," Middle East and North Africa report no. 129, May 9, 2012, 8–9, www.files.ethz.ch/isn/142694/123-tunisie-lutter-contre-l-impunite-restaurer-la-securite.pdf (accessed June 15, 2016). For an excellent analysis of the RCD's surveillance activities, see also Béatrice Hibou, *The Force of Obedience: The Political Economy of Repression in Tunisia* (Malden, MA: Polity Press, 2011), 93–98.
[27] Jean Pierre Sereni, "Après Ben Ali 'Ben ʿAli, Zein al-ʿAbidin,' quelle police en Tunisie?" *Le Monde Diplomatique*, April 1, 2011, www.monde-diplomatique.fr/carnet/2011-04-01-Tunisie (accessed October 15, 2017).
[28] Interview with Mezughi.
[29] Interview with retired Colonel Boubaker Ben Kraiem (army), Tunis (June 20, 2013).

their presence in the capital was deemed politically threatening.[30] As a sign of presidential favor and trust, only the PG was allowed to deploy around the Ben ʿAli and Trabelsi families in the chic neighborhoods of La Marsa, Carthage, and La Goulette. The PG would also search the personnel of the military and other security organizations protecting the president whenever he visited the provinces.[31] These privileged conditions and elite status generated resentment toward the PG in the armed forces and police alike. The ill-feeling was mutual. According to Seriati, the powerful intelligence czar long in charge of Ben ʿAli's personal security, Presidential Guardsmen distrusted other security organizations, but also one another. They were perpetually on high alert to prevent coups d'état or assassination schemes fomented from within the regime.[32] On the other hand, Ben ʿAli lavished resources on the National Guard, the strength of which stood at 12,000 men. Allegedly, the National Guard received 50 percent more funding than all three sectors of the armed forces combined: the army, navy, and air force.[33]

In addition, Ben ʿAli militarized and expanded the "special" branches of the ministry of interior: the Brigade Antiterrorisme (BAT), the Brigade Nationale d'Intervention Rapide (BNIR), l'Unité Spéciale de la Garde Nationale (USGN), and the Brigade de l'Ordre Publique (BOP). The former president also cultivated a complex security network affiliated with the ministry, including organizations such as the State Security Service (SSS), the General Directorate of National Security (GDNS), the General Directorate of Special Services (GDSS), the General Directorate of Public Security (GDPS), and the General Intelligence Directorate (GID). All of these organizations spied on the military, political opponents, and one another. The SSS and GID were particularly invasive in their handling of the armed forces, even when their meddling in military affairs hampered the troops operationally in dangerous

---

[30] Jebnoun, "In the Shadow of Power," 301–302. The fact that the army was deployed in Tunis on January 12, 2011, broke the tradition of keeping it outside the capital, and revealed the depth of the regime's crisis two days before Ben ʿAli fled from Tunisia.

[31] Michael Makara, "Rethinking Military Behavior during the Arab Spring," *Defense & Security Analysis* 32, no. 3 (2016): 216.

[32] See Zohra Abid, "Tunisie: Les faux vrais aveux de Ali Seriati," *Kapitalis*, March 12, 2012, www.kapitalis.com/politique/8846-tunisie-les-faux-vrais-aveux-de-ali-seriati.html (accessed October 23, 2018). See also International Crisis Group, "Popular Protests in North Africa and the Middle East (IV): Tunisia's Way," Middle East and North Africa report no. 106, April 28, 2011, 1 and 11, www.crisisgroup.org/file/1560/download?token=u5P7yh_T (accessed August 6, 2016).

[33] See Clement Henry and Robert Springborg, "The Tunisian Army: Defending the Beachhead of Democracy in the Arab World," *Huffpost*, January 26, 2011, www.huffingtonpost.com/clement-m-henry/the-tunisian-army-defendi_b_814254.html (accessed August 25, 2018).

situations. Such was the case in December 2006, when the military confronted a jihadist group that had crossed from Algeria. The SSS and GID insisted not only on supervising the military officers actively fighting the jihadists, but also on overseeing the distribution of ammo to the troops, lest it be used later to trigger a mutiny or coup.[34]

There is no agreement with regard to the exact number of personnel in the various police organizations under Ben 'Ali. According to a minister who served in the post-2011 transitional government, all security forces under the control of the ministry of interior (i.e., police, National Guard, and civil defense forces) numbered around 49,000 on the eve of the Tunisian revolution.[35] Other estimates range from 45,000 to 80,000, and even to an improbable 133,000.[36] Regardless of the numbers, it is certain that the omnipresent police became even more intrusive under Ben 'Ali, and felt untouchable throughout his tenure. Policemen could arrest people arbitrarily, and be rude even to military officers without worrying about consequences.[37] The armed forces could only move troops under police supervision. If soldiers were to be transferred from one barrack to another, the bureau of the army's chief of staff needed to inform the ministry of interior beforehand, so the latter could dispatch police informants to monitor troop movements and report to the ministry's operational command room.[38] Inevitably, military officers loathed being under the permanent supervision of the police, and resented the arrogance of its officers. One military officer I interviewed in Tunis complained bitterly:

Being a police officer was something under Ben 'Ali, but being a military officer wasn't much. This was infuriating.[39]

Nor were officers happy to be starved for resources while the budget allocated to the ministry of interior invariably exceeded that of the ministry of defense. They were painfully aware that the opposite used to be true throughout Bourguiba's tenure.[40] On the other hand, Ben 'Ali continued the latter's practice of favoring officers hailing from Tunis and the Sahel. An interviewee who did not wish to be named maintained

[34] Jebnoun, "In the Shadow of Power," 303.
[35] See Querine Hanlon, "Security Sector Reform in Tunisia, a Year after the Jasmine Revolution," United States Institute of Peace, report no. 304, March 2012, 6, www.usip.org/sites/default/files/SR304.pdf (accessed April 5, 2016).
[36] See Hibou, *The Force of Obedience*, 81.
[37] Interview with retired Colonel Major Hasin Bzaniyya (air force), Tunis (July 24, 2013).
[38] Interview with retired Colonel Mohammad Ahmed (army), Tunis (August 7, 2013).
[39] Interview with a retired colonel (air force) who did not wish to be named, Tunis (July 22, 2013).
[40] See Bou Nassif, "A Military Besieged," 74.

that he had personally heard ʿAbd al-ʿAziz Ben Dhia, Ben ʿAli's third defense minister, refusing to sign a list of promotions presented to him for his approval by the Tunisian armed forces' highest authority, the CSA (Conseil Supérieur des Armées), because it did not contain enough people from the Sahel.[41] Other interviewees concurred that Ben ʿAli indeed favored the Sahelians in the officer corps. Such allegations are factual. Sharan Grewal demonstrated in an excellent study covering the background of all senior officers serving in the Tunisian military until 2009 that the ratio of officers hailing from Tunis and the Sahel was 70.8 percent, 67.4 percent, and 73.9 percent, respectively, for colonels, colonel majors, and generals. On average, the odds of promotion for officers hailing from privileged regions were 43 percent higher than for their colleagues originating from the coast. Such favoritism was public knowledge in the military. According to Grewal's study, close to 89 percent of officers he interviewed concurred that Ben ʿAli favored officers hailing from the Sahel in terms of promotion, notably to the rank of general. In the words of retired Colonel Major Mohammad Ahmed:

If you are from Kairouan, Gafsa, or Kef, you are just an average officer. But if you are from the Sahel, you have a big chance of being promoted more quickly.[42]

This practice perpetuated the overrepresentation of the Sahel in senior commandership positions. In contrast, a majority of soldiers and junior officers hailed from the interior, according to a former director general of Military Security who did not wish to be named.[43] On the other hand, after General Mohammad Saʿid al-Kateb retired from his position as chief of staff of the armed forces in 1991, Ben ʿAli did not appoint a replacement. This left the armed forces with three competing senior generals leading the army, navy, and air force, respectively. This type of scheme invariably hinders military effectiveness, but also the capacity to trigger coups. With no one in charge of bringing together the different sectors of the military, the president took it upon himself to make decisions that normally fell under the jurisdiction of the chief of staff. In the words of one retired colonel major:

Ben ʿAli worked directly with the military as if he was the minister of defense! We [senior officers] often sent reports directly to the [presidential palace in] Carthage. This was the old system. It was a personal rule, not a rule by the state.[44]

---

[41] Interview with a retired colonel (army) who did not wish to be named, Tunis (August 15, 2013).
[42] Sharan Grewal, "To Coup or Not to Coup: The Tunisian Military in 2013," paper prepared for the 2016 annual meeting for the Middle East Studies Association, 16.
[43] Grewal, "A Quiet Revolution."   [44] Ibid.

Interestingly, Ben 'Ali also operated as Tunisia's de facto interior minister. He nominated not only the interior ministry's directors, but also its lower-ranking officials. He kept in regular touch with police directors, thus circumventing his own interior ministers, who were only allowed to serve brief tenures lest they develop an independent power base. To a large extent, Ben 'Ali reduced the role of his ministers of defense and interior to a mere façade in order to bring the military and the police under direct presidential control.[45]

While several aspects of Ben 'Ali's coup-proofing system were a continuation of Bourguiba's, the ideational dimension was missing. As mentioned previously, Bourguiba projected an image of an incorruptible father of the nation à la Mustafa Kamal in Turkey. It is interesting to note that even the above-cited Moncef El-Materi, whom Bourguiba jailed for ten years following the failed 1962 putsch, pinpoints in his memoirs the late president's sincere commitment to modernization and the "undeniable successes" of his regime.[46] The truth is, the officer corps was overwhelmingly loyalist in the ideational sense of the term throughout Bourguiba's tenure. This was not to be the case under Ben 'Ali, whose notorious corruption precluded any claim to moral leadership, particularly in the second half of his tenure, when the venality of his clan – especially his wife, Leila, and her brother, Belhassen Trabelsi, dubbed "*Le Parrain*" (i.e., the Godfather) – became a matter of public knowledge.[47] It is important to note in this regard that while civilians were particularly vulnerable to the insatiability of the ruling elite, the armed forces were themselves unshielded from the surrounding rapaciousness. For instance, Ben 'Ali used funds allocated to the military to build a presidential palace in the coastal town of Hammamet, and purchase a $1.2-million yacht, the *Alyssa*. In addition, the former president confiscated real estate belonging to the ministry of defense and transferred it to

---

[45] Derek Lutterbeck, "Tool of Rule: The Tunisian Police under Ben Ali 'Ben 'Ali, Zein al-'Abidin,'" *Journal of North African Studies* 20, no. 5 (2015): 820–821.

[46] El-Materi, *De Saint-Cyr*, 14 and 62.

[47] WikiLeaks revealed that in June 2008, the US embassy in Tunis said, "Whether it's cash, services, land, property, or yes, even your yacht, President Ben 'Ali's family is rumored to covet it and reportedly gets what it wants," thus adding fuel to public disenchantment and disgust. See the US embassy report "Corruption in Tunisia: What's Yours Is Mine," report ID: 08TUNIS679_a, June 23, 2008, https://wikileaks.org/plusd/cables/08TUNIS679_a.html (accessed April 5, 2016). It goes beyond the limits and purpose of this book to investigate the corruption of the Ben 'Ali regime in detail, but two books are particularly instructive in this regard: Nicolas Beau and Catherine Graciet, *La Régente de Carthage, Main Basse Sur La Tunisie* (Paris: La Découverte, 2009); and Nicolas Beau and Jean-Pierre Tuquoi, *Notre Ami Ben 'Ali "Ben 'Ali, Zein al-'Abidin," L'Envers du Miracle Tunisien* (Paris: La Découverte, 2011).

himself, family members, and a handful of senior officers at favorable prices.[48] Money lost this way to venality and fraud – or poured on the military's institutional rivals – kept the armed forces permanently cash-strapped and unable to maintain their equipment or upgrade it. In April 2002, this neglect had tragic consequences: an old helicopter crashed while flying west of Tunis, killing army chief of staff General ʿAbdul-ʿAziz Skik and twelve other officers on board. Tunisia immediately became rife with rumors that Ben ʿAli had arranged the incident to get rid of the popular Skik, but the truth was more prosaic: so underfunded was the military that it could not afford to retire a dated helicopter.[49] Against such a backdrop, it was impossible for Ben ʿAli to cultivate an ideational link with the armed forces, or, for that matter, with the public at large. Ben ʿAli's repeated attempts to frame himself as the genuine heir to his predecessor failed. The former president seemed indifferent or inattentive to the effects of his greed, that of his wife, and the ostentatious corruption of their clan on his credibility as a national leader.

The decadence of the RCD contributed to the moral and ideational decay of the regime. Once a school of civism and a platform for genuine debates about national policies, the ruling party morphed under Ben ʿAli into yet another component of Tunisia's repressive machine. It was clear to Tunisians that RCD members were driven by self-centered considerations, and that the party's days of genuine attachment to public service were gone.[50] Ben ʿAli's inability during his hour of need in 2011 to effectively mobilize the RCD and his coercive apparatus betrays a weakness that was inherently ideational. In the words of Merouan Mekouar, Ben ʿAli's regime suffered from a glaring "ideological vacuity" and lacked the "ideological credibility" that he needed to turn the ruling party and state apparatus against the popular mobilization in 2011. Consequently, the very elements Ben ʿAli called upon to defend his rule cared little about his survival – he had become "indefensible."[51]

---

[48] Grewal, "To Coup or Not to Coup," 13. See also See Pluta's interview with Colonel Amor Ben Romdhane, "Les relations civilo-militaires," 113.

[49] On the Skik affair, see Imad Bahri, "Tunisie: Le vrai faux complot de Ben Ali 'Ben ʿAli, Zein al-ʿAbidin' contre le général Skik," *Kapitalis*, April 23, 2011, www.kapitalis.com/p olitique/3642-tunisie-le-vrai-faux-lcomplotr-de-ben-ali-contre-legeneral-skik.html (accessed September 26, 2018).

[50] Hibou, *The Force of Obedience*, 92.

[51] Merouan Mekouar, "Police Collapse in Authoritarian Regimes: Lessons from Tunisia," *Studies in Conflict and Terrorism* 40, no. 10 (2017): 863. See also Lynch, *The New Arab Wars*, 51.

The 2011 Uprising and the Breakdown of the Ben 'Ali Regime:
Explaining Military Behavior

I have shown previously that the Egyptian military elite had the will, but not the capacity, to save the Mubarak regime in 2011. In Syria, the top brass had both the will and the capacity to defend Bashar al-Asad – and they did. In contrast, the Tunisian generals were not committed to the status quo; and they could not have upheld it anyway even if they had wanted to because their subordinates were unwilling to kill fellow Tunisians to save the regime. In other words, the top brass lacked both the will and the capacity to keep Ben 'Ali in power. The Tunisian officer corps was not a monolithic bloc; regional and generational divergences did create friction among its members. And yet in 2011, officers over-whelmingly agreed upon one thing, irrespective of rank or background: the Tunisian armed forces were not going to use violence to break the popular protests. In effect, that meant military defection – one that ushered in regime collapse and democratic transition in Tunisia.

How Counterbalancing Predetermined the Defection of the Armed Forces Counterbalancing the military under Ben 'Ali was a ruthless affair. The combined forces of the National and Presidential Guards signaled to officers that the regime wielded a credible deterrence com-mitted to the status quo. A military plot to unseat Ben 'Ali was unlikely to succeed. It was also exceptionally risky due to the vigilance of existing surveillance networks. The Barraket al-Sahel affair left a divisive legacy along multiple lines: first, the military became permanently alienated from the presidency, and vice versa; second, the armed forces' rivalry with the police and security apparatus morphed into outright animosity as officers blamed the interior ministry and the RCD for their misfortune; and finally, the chiefs of staff lost credibility with their subordinates because they failed to defend military personnel who were unjustly accused and persecuted. Mohammad al-Hadi Bin Hassine, army chief of staff, was particularly loathed because he had appeared apathetic throughout the whole affair, even though the corps he led bore the brunt of police accusations. Yet Bin Hassine's unpopularity in the army did not affect his tenure. It may have actually contributed to its longevity, because it made him less threatening to Ben 'Ali.[52] As a general rule, the

---

[52] "What Ben 'Ali wanted from the chiefs of staff was absolute obedience. Mohammad al-Hadi Ben Hassine was the army's most sycophantic officer, which is why Ben 'Ali kept him in his position for so long. The chiefs of staff were not popular with the officer corps and the armed forces at large – they didn't want, or try, to be. Ben 'Ali would not have approved of it." Interview with retired Colonel Beshir Bin 'Aissa (army), Tunis (June 23, 2013).

armed forces' chiefs of staff who served under Ben 'Ali were not held in great esteem in the officer corps. The president, it was said, promoted the most uncharismatic, bureaucratically minded, and personally loyal officers, not the most gifted professionally. Rather than armed forces representatives in the regime, the chiefs of staff were considered by many officers to be the regime's delegates to the armed forces.[53] The death of army chief Skik in the 2002 helicopter crash fueled military estrangement. Some officers were convinced that Ben 'Ali had actually conspired to kill the general and his colleagues, who were allegedly suspected of being "insufficiently loyal."[54] Others maintained that the president was indirectly responsible for the tragedy because he had neglected the basic material needs of the armed forces while allocating ever-increasing funding to the interior ministry. Either way, the Skik affair compounded the disaffection of the military institution.

Meanwhile, Tunisia's worsening economic conditions were exerting tremendous pressure on officers and soldiers alike, both of whom hailed overwhelmingly from Tunisia's struggling middle and lower classes, respectively. The corruption and obscene lifestyle of the ruling elite, which had infuriated the public at large, was no less exasperating in the barracks. It is important to remember, in this regard, that the regime's generosity was largely confined to the "ruling families," e.g., those of Ben 'Ali, Trabelsi, Shibub, Mabruk, and El-Materi. To be sure, the chiefs of staff of the army, navy, and air force enjoyed long tenures, and had access to special grants and undeclared yearly allowances made available by the office of the president. Other senior officers in the military and security establishments may also have benefitted from privileged treatment, but their numbers were few, and they were junior partners in the corruption game.[55] Overall, even the military top brass were marginal in the Ben 'Ali regime, and could not aspire to lucrative postretirement civilian positions like their Egyptian counterparts.[56] Consequently, unequal access to regime patronage never divided the Tunisian officer corps generationally. Mid-ranking and junior officers understood that their superiors were no more regime clients than they were themselves.

With that said, other types of intra-military fractures did exist, with rivalries over promotions serving as a case in point. For decades, the

---

[53] Interview with Bzaniyya.

[54] Derek Lutterbeck, "After the Fall: Security Sector Reform in Post-Ben Ali 'Ben 'Ali, Zein al-'Abidin' Tunisia," Arab Reform Initiative (ARI), September 2012, 6, www.arab-reform.net/en/node/592 (accessed June 12, 2018). See also Risa Brooks, "Abandoned at the Palace: Why the Tunisian Military Defected from the Ben Ali Regime in January 2011," *Journal of Strategic Studies* 36, no. 2 (2013): 216.

[55] Interview with Bzaniyya.   [56] Bou Nassif, "A Military Besieged," 76–77.

Bourguiba cohort (1958) had monopolized all commandership positions in the military. For instance, on the eve of the 1987 coup that delivered power to Ben 'Ali, members of the first cohort of the Tunisian armed forces were in control of the commandership of the National Guard (Habib 'Ammar), the commandership of the army's general staff (Yussef Baraket), the directorship of Military Intelligence (Yussef Ben Suleiman), and the general inspectorship of the armed forces (Sa'id al-Kateb). And when General Skik died in 2002, all three chiefs of staff still belonged to that cohort. This created resentment among younger officers, who were eyeing much-desired promotions that were seemingly always out of reach.[57]

Regional frictions represent another example. Until the very end of Ben 'Ali's rule, officers occupying military commandership positions were more likely to hail from the ruling Sahelians, while the interior, especially the extreme south, remained underrepresented in the upper ranks. In addition, there was a pervasive sense in the military that senior officers were being promoted to commandership positions on the basis of political loyalty and servility toward Ben 'Ali, and not according to professional competence. The position of General Rashid 'Ammar, army chief of staff, was particularly tenuous in this regard: most of the interviewees with whom I met concurred that the he had never been a particularly brilliant officer. They maintained that he had been promoted to his exalted position (and kept in it) because he hailed from the Sahel, was obedient to the president, had an intelligence background as former director of the MS, and had gained favor with Leila Ben 'Ali. 'Ammar was not popular with his men and could not have been so, considering his role in Barrakat al-Sahel.[58] How did these dynamics shape military behavior in 2011?

Ben 'Ali had no qualms about shedding Tunisian blood in order to retain power. Upon his orders, the police killed hundreds of civilians before the regime ordered the military to deploy in Tunisian cities. And yet it seems that the former president refrained from instructing the armed forces to repress the uprising. To be sure, early journalistic accounts on the Tunisian uprising suggested that Ben 'Ali had, indeed, ordered the military to open fire upon demonstrators, and that 'Ammar had refused to obey him. 'Ammar himself debunked this version of

---

[57] Interview with retired colonel (army) who did not wish to be named, Tunis (June 24, 2013).

[58] 'Ammar served as head of military disciplinary councils (*majales al-ta'dib*) that struck the victims of Barraket al-Sahel from the lists after they were falsely accused of conspiring against the state (interview with Mezughi).

events, however.[59] And though the officers I met in Tunis were critical of the Ben 'Ali regime, they were all convinced that he had never explicitly ordered 'Ammar to quell the uprising. Why would a president desperate to save his regime and ready to kill his countrymen to do so refrain from instructing the army's chief of staff from repressing a popular rebellion that threatened his hold on power?

The most credible hypothesis is that the former president knew that such orders would not be carried out because the Tunisian armed forces loathed him. It is significant to note, in this regard, that Ben 'Ali deployed the military in the streets of Tunis on January 11, three weeks into the wake of the uprising and only three days before he fled the country. Clearly, Ben 'Ali sustained hope until the last minute that such a measure could be avoided. Nor could the former president have harbored illusions about the extent of the support he could expect from the armed forces, since 'Ammar had told him on January 8 that his men will not open fire on civilians (*L'armée veut bien maintenir l'ordre, pas réprimer*).[60] It is unlikely that Ben 'Ali expected otherwise, considering the history of civil–military relations under his lengthy rule. The armed forces had long written off his regime as dominated by the interior ministry, the RCD, and the ruling families – but not the military. The officers were cognizant of the fact that their president distrusted them, and they felt, in the words of a retired colonel, "constantly insulted" under Ben 'Ali.[61] Resentment was pervasive in the officer corps irrespective of rank and generation. When the troops were deployed in the streets of Tunisian cities during the 2011 turning point, the officers and their men were welcomed as liberators by the population, and fraternized with them immediately.[62] Families took photos in front of army tanks, joined by smiling officers and soldiers associating with civilians they identified as fellow countrymen.

Soon enough, the troops would start collaborating with neighborhood defense committees to reestablish public order in the last days of the uprising.[63] Audrey Pluta notes convincingly that it would have been

---

[59] See a detailed report on the last days of the Ben 'Ali regime, "Tunisie: la véritable histoire du 14 Janvier 2011," *Jeune Afrique*, January 25, 2012, www.jeuneafrique.com/143296/politique/tunisie-la-v-ritable-histoire-du-14-janvier-2011/ (accessed August 11, 2018). Note also that 'Ammar was not sacked or placed under house arrest in the waning days of the Ben 'Ali regime, contrary to news that suggested otherwise.

[60] See Christophe Ayad, "Tunisie: La Révolution en Trois Actes. Carthage, la Chute," *Libération*, February 5, 2011, www.liberation.fr/planete/2011/02/05/carthage-la-chute_712598 (accessed September 11, 2018).

[61] Pluta, "The Role of the Tunisian Military," 8.

[62] See International Crisis Group, "Popular Protests (IV)," 5.

[63] Peter J. Schraeder and Hamadi Redissi, "The Upheavals in Egypt and Tunisia: Ben Ali's Fall," *Journal of Democracy* 22, no. 3 (July 2011): 14.

"unrealistic" for the military commandership to give repression orders without triggering immediate munities in the armed forces.[64] The officers I met in Tunisia were unanimous in their declarations that the military would not have obeyed orders to open fire upon civilians, had the high command issued such a directive. Two leitmotifs were central to the answers pertaining to military behavior in 2011, namely, the officers' identification with the suffering of the Tunisian popular classes, and their loathing of the police:

The mobilization in 2011 was massive. The mid-ranking and junior officers had parents and friends among the protesters. Had the armed forces been ordered to shoot, immediate mutinies would have ensued. I believe this fact weighed directly on the calculus of the military commandership.[65]

It was unthinkable for the armed forces to commit slaughter in order to defend Ben 'Ali, because we serve the state, not a specific ruler. Also, keep in mind that the people in the streets belonged to the lower-middle and popular classes, and these are precisely the social classes that our officers hail from. The mid-ranking and junior officers were particularly disinclined to open fire on the population.[66]

We shed no tears when the people attacked police stations. The police were corrupt, arrogant vis-à-vis the population and the armed forces alike. That the military should kill civilians in order to protect the police was out of the question; whatever happened to the police, they asked for it.[67]

These quotes summarize the essence of the answers I received repeatedly from my interviewees in Tunis, all of whom agreed that military repression was not an option in 2011. Above anything else, the officers I met loathed the interior ministry, and resented what they perceived to be military subjugation to it. In addition, no vision or ideational commitment wedded them to the Ben 'Ali regime. Unlike Bourguiba, the latter did not stand for a genuine patriotic ideal that officers could identify with. And unlike Bashar al-Asad in Syria, Ben 'Ali could not instrumentalize polarized group identities. To be sure, frictions pitting the interior against the Sahel were real in Tunisia. But the 2011 uprising was a cross-class, cross-regional, and cross-partisan national mobilization that engulfed Tunisia. Ben 'Ali could not have framed it as a reactionary movement driven by parochial antagonism or religious fundamentalism. Finally, the officers had no financial stake in regime maintenance – unlike the top brass in Egypt as previously shown. In other words, there were neither shared aversions nor a higher set of beliefs that the former president could

[64] See Pluta, "The Role of the Tunisian Military," 18.   [65] Interview with Mezughi.
[66] Interview with Ben Kraiem.
[67] Interview with a retired colonel major (army) who did not wish to be named, Tunis (July 15, 2013).

have manipulated to unleash soldiers on unarmed civilians.[68] Nor were there specific economic interests that officers could have risked losing, had they allowed regime breakdown. No one was more aware of all the above than the architect of the system himself: Ben ʿAli.

And so, the former president never instructed the top brass to unleash the armed forces on his opponents. In so doing, he avoided the frightful prospect of open military mutiny in the last days of his rule. Yet he connived nonetheless to lure the military into confronting civilians when he ordered troops to remove their distinctive helmets after dispatching them to maintain public order. Without their characteristic helmets, the military units could have been mistaken for National Guardsmen, who wore similar fatigues. Popular ire was directed against the Guard and police forces, which occasionally opened fire in self-defense. Ben ʿAli reckoned that the same scenario could repeat itself should civilians attack soldiers, which would force the military to enter the fray in full force against the protests. ʿAmmar, however, ordered his troops to wear distinctive red military hats and to remain physically separate from the police and Guard, even when deployed in proximity to them.[69] The tactic worked: there are no reports of civilians attacking the armed forces, despite the intensity of popular protests and the sacking and looting of scores of police stations throughout the country. In addition, ʿAmmar issued a telegram to his troops on January 10, forbidding them to open fire under any circumstances unless otherwise commanded by the military high command. Reportedly, on January 13, he warned the leaders of security services that the military would retaliate if agents under their command kept shooting on protesters.[70] And on January 14, he rejected a request from Seriati for the military to install troops in residential areas inhabited by the much-hated Trabelsi.[71] That same day, the chief of staff also refused orders from minister of defense Ridha Grira to move against a police mutiny instigated by Colonel Samir Tarhuni and his men in the Anti-Terrorism Brigade (BAT) who had taken members of the Trabelsi family hostage at Carthage Airport. According to Tarhuni, ʿAmmar actually congratulated him on this action when they met in

---

[68] Brooks, "Abandoned at the Palace," 217. See also Vincent Geisser and Abir Krefa, "L'uniforme ne fait plus le régime, les militaires arabes face aux révolutions," *Revue Internationale Stratégique* 3, no. 83 (2011): 99–101.

[69] Pluta, "Les relations civilo-militaires," 69. During the 1985 uprising in Sudan, the loyalist State Security Organization (SSO) tried the exact same tactic in order to trigger a confrontation between the armed forces and civilian protesters. The result was equally unsuccessful.

[70] Taylor, *Military Responses*, 71.   [71] See "Tunisie: la véritable histoire."

the interior ministry a day later, on January 15.[72] In effect, ʿAmmar committed the military to protect state institutions, but nothing more. From a procedural perspective, this was impeccable legalism, and a strict interpretation of the military's mandate. The armed forces deployed when ordered to do so and stayed within the limits of what their mandate required. Politically, however, neutralism and legalism accounted for defection, for the following reasons: (1) Ben ʿAli wished to remain in power and kept asserting until his last day in office that "the number of dead people matter little, whether it is one thousand Tunisian that are killed or more,"[73] in order to save his rule. (2) After the collapse of the police and the RCD, the military was Ben ʿAli's last potential defense line. To assume that the former president would have hesitated to pit the armed forces against protesters when his survival was on the line is to underestimate his resolve to stay in power even if a bloodbath was required to do so. (3) Ben ʿAli indeed schemed to trigger a confrontation between soldiers and demonstrators, but his tactics were unsuccessful. Simply put, Tunisian officers were unwilling to quell the uprising; that ʿAmmar explicitly told Ben ʿAli as much should not be forgotten when the military politics of the Tunisian uprising are analyzed. The officers knew that merely protecting public facilities would not save the regime, and yet they were reluctant to do more, although the writing was on the wall for Ben ʿAli.

Note that a revisionist reading of the Tunisian events maintains that the military remained loyal to Ben ʿAli, whereas defection occurred within the security forces.[74] As mentioned above, men from the BAT did indeed take hostage members of the Trabelsi clan trying to flee Tunisia – an act that constituted open rebellion against their superiors in the interior ministry. Driven by hatred of the Trabelsis and solidarity with their colleagues, elements from two other elite security units joined the BAT in its defiance of the interior ministry. But the argument that the military remained loyal is unconvincing because it is based on two suggestions: (1)

---

[72] See La rédaction, "Grira Voulait Délivrer les Trabelsi et Tuer Tarhouni," *Réalités*, July 12, 2012, www.realites.com.tn/2012/07/exclusif-nouvelles-revelations-sur-le-14-janvier-grira-voulait-delivrer-les-trablesi-et-tuer-tarhouni (accessed October 9, 2018). See also "Le lieutenant-colonel Samir Tarhouni dévoile les circonstances de l'arrestation des Trabelsi le 14 janvier," *Leaders*, August 8, 2011, www.leaders.com.tn/article/5980-le-lieutenant-colonel-samir-tarhouni-devoile-les-circonstances-de-l-arrestation-des-trabelsi-le-14-janvier (accessed November 7, 2018).
[73] See Jebnoun, "In the Shadow of Power," 306.
[74] See Alejandro Pachon, "Loyalty and Defection: Misunderstanding Civil–Military Relations in Tunisia during the Arab Spring," *The Journal of Strategic Studies* 37, no. 4 (2014): 508–531.

the military, just like the police, used lethal force against the demonstrators when soldiers were ordered to do so; and (2) the protesters had allegedly nothing "to offer the military," which suggests that the latter had few reasons to defect, even though they were not exactly keen on saving Ben ʿAli. Both contentions are dubious for reasons I explain below.

First, the armed forces used lethal force only *after* Ben ʿAli had fled the country. That the military would only reestablish public order forcefully in the wake of the breakdown of Ben ʿAli's regime can hardly be interpreted as a sign of loyalty to him.[75] On the other hand, the uprising was a chance for the military to humiliate its rivals and settle accounts with a much-hated president and his regime. Arguing that the protesters did not have much to give the armed forces ignores the legacy of Barraket al-Sahel and the bitterness of civil–military relations under Ben ʿAli. The revisionist argument makes a distinction between "inaction" and a "more active role" in the context of an endgame scenario, suggesting that when the armed forces avoided the latter, they had, in effect, remained loyal to the powers that be. But when police breakdown leaves the military as the last line of defense shielding a beleaguered autocrat from angry crowds, the armed forces need do no more than confine themselves to the sidelines in order for the regime to crumble. As I argued in Chapter 1, neutralism in these situations is action in itself – one that dooms the status quo to a certain demise. It is understandable, in this regard, why former first lady Leila Ben ʿAli maintained in her memoirs that her husband lost power to a coup that was not "hatched by the interior ministry."[76] The hint at the military's responsibility for Ben ʿAli's downfall is clear. It is equally understandable that the head of presidential security, Seriati, fumed against the armed forces, which he called "sons of bastards" because they fraternized with the population in the streets of Tunis and protected the protesters instead of squelching dissent.[77] Leila Ben ʿAli would have wanted the military to behave in a very different manner toward the population. The same is true of Seriati: the last minister of defense under Ben ʿAli, Ridha Grira, said that Seriati was consistently prodding the military to use violence against protesters without explicitly

---

[75] Between January 15 and 27, seventy-seven civilians were killed in Tunisia: twenty-four by the police, thirty-seven by the military, and sixteen by unidentified actors. For a detailed account on the violence exerted by both the police and military forces during the Tunisian uprising, see Abdelaziz Belkhodja and Tarak Cheikhrouhou, *14 Janvier: L'Enquete* (Tunis: Apollonia, 2013), especially the index, 175–180.

[76] Leila Ben Ali "Ben ʿAli, Zein al-ʿAbidin," *Ma Vérité* (Paris: Edition du Moment, 2012), 45.

[77] See Isabelle Mandraud, "Peut-être on partira, mais on brûlera Tunis," *Le Monde*, January 17, 2011, www.lemonde.fr/afrique/article/2011/01/17/peut-etre-on-partira-mais-on-brulera-tunis_1466502_3212.html (accessed October 8, 2018).

giving orders in this regard because he had no prerogative to do so.[78] Along similar lines, a former adviser to Ben ʿAli who spoke anonymously to the International Crisis Group said that Seriati beckoned army generals to support the regime in tandem with the police and "acted as if he was the generals' general, which the army did not accept."[79] That was enough for breakdown to become inevitable: in endgame scenarios, militaries do not need to march on presidential palaces to remove autocrats from power. Defections do not need to be "hard," like that of Samir Tarhouni and his men, to be considered as such; a velvet form suffices to trigger autocratic downfall. And that was precisely what happened in Tunisia.

Conclusion of the Tunisian Case Study

The military was not central to the founding regime of contemporary Tunisia, but overall, the officers respected the work and legacy of the country's leader, al-Habib Bourguiba. The latter's successor, Zein al-ʿAbidin Ben ʿAli, seized power by way of a coup, and feared losing it the same way. In addition, he lacked the legitimacy that Bourguiba enjoyed, and quickly squandered whatever popular support he had attained as his rule became marred by nepotism and obscene corruption. To remain in power, Ben ʿAli counted on the ruling party, which he transformed into an intelligence network devoid of ideological commitment. He also relied on the interior ministry and the sprawling network of security organizations it controlled. The RCD/interior ministry nexus kept the military at bay, and persecuted regime opponents in both the armed forces and civilian population. However, when three weeks of persistent popular mobilization triggered the collapse of the party and loyalist security networks, Ben ʿAli was unable to count on the military to kill civilians in order to save his rule. Events in neighboring Libya diverged from the Tunisian scenario precisely because civil–military relations in that country had been molded according to another model.

Libya

Al-Qaddhafi was a captain in the military when he staged a successful putsch against King Idris al-Senussi in 1969. He then promoted himself to colonel, and ruled his country with an iron fist till his demise. Though al-Qaddhafi's "radical" regime differed markedly from al-Senussi's, both rulers feared the military and distrusted the officer corps. Unlike his

---

[78] See "Tunisie: que Mijotait."
[79] See International Crisis Group, "Popular Protests (IV)," 11.

predecessor, however, al-Qaddafi proved successful in keeping the armed forces at bay, and plots against him invariably ended in failure. As in other coup-prone countries, civil–military relations in Libya were structured according to the regime's security necessities.[80] I show below that the splintering of the Libyan troops during al-Qaddafi's hour of need in 2011 was a direct result of previously established coup-proofing tactics. The same control methods that served him well against opponents in the officer corps delivered suboptimal results when the challenge to his rule came from popular mobilizations in the streets of Libya.

Coup and Coup-Proofing under King Idris al-Senussi

Libya's independence in 1951 unified the country's west (Tripolitania), east (Cyrenaica), and south (Fezzan) into the United Kingdom of Libya, but fell short of creating a national consciousness superseding parochial regional and tribal identities. The power base of the al-Senussi dynasty was centered in the east, and the ruling elite essentially hailed from Cyrenaica. The Libyan monarch was reluctant to build a professional military, and the armed forces never exceeded 6,500 men throughout his tenure (1951–1969).

The source of the king's suspicion of the military was threefold: first, coups were pervasive in the Arab world in the 1950s and 1960s, and this heightened al-Senussi's fear of contagion. Second, the king understood that his legitimacy was dubious in the west and south. The loyalty of military personnel recruited from these regions was, therefore, questionable. And third, al-Senussi was a moderate, pro-Western politician at a time when nationalism and radical anti-imperialism fired the imagination of enthusiastic officers throughout the Arab world. In order to coup-proof his regime, he recruited military personnel heavily from Cyrenaica, and counterbalanced the armed forces with two paramilitary units manned by 14,000 Bedouins. In September 1969, the king's fears of the armed forces proved warranted – and his coup-proofing system defective. When al-Qaddafi and his associates in the Revolutionary Command Council (RCC) struck, not even the tribal levies of the paramilitary Cyrenaican Defense Force or the officers and soldiers from that

---

[80] The infiltration of the armed forces by Islamists in the early 1990s heightened al-Qaddafi's misgivings vis-à-vis his officers. See Yezid Sayigh, "Militaries, Civilians and the Crisis of the Arab State," *The Monkey Cage*, December 8, 2014, www.washingtonpost.com/news/monkey-cage/wp/2014/12/08/militaries-civilians-and-the-crisis-of-the-arab-state/?utm_term=.ecd8bcfa236f (accessed December 2, 2018).

region defended the monarchy. It was overthrown, and al-Senussi spent the rest of his life in exile.[81]

Coups and Coup-Proofing under al-Qaddhafi

In the weeks immediately following the September 1969 coup, the RCC foiled two military plots led by mid-ranking and junior officers and sacked the army's new chief of staff only days after his appointment.[82] The officer corps was split into a faction loyal to al-Qaddhafi and another led by defense minister Major Adam al-Hawaz and interior minister Major Musa Ahmad. Al-Hawaz and Ahmad plotted a coup, but were arrested along with thirty officers in December 1969. The former was killed in 1984, and the latter remained in jail until 1988.[83]

In 1970, supporters of the al-Senussi dynasty in the armed forces plotted a putsch under the leadership of 'Abdullah al-Senussi, an exiled cousin of King Idris. The conspiracy failed, and al-Qaddhafi purged the officer corps from the remaining sympathizers of the old regime.[84] In 1972, a member of the RCC, Captain Mohammad Abu Bakr al-Muqaryaf, died under mysterious circumstances. Later on, al-Qaddhafi revealed that al-Muqaryaf had been conspiring to overthrow him before his death. It has long been rumored that al-Qaddhafi ordered the latter's assassination.[85]

In 1975, two other members of the RCC, Colonels Bashir Huwadi and 'Umar al-Muhayshi, planned a coup supported by Misrata officers. The conspiracy was uncovered at the last minute, and both colonels were executed in 1977 along with twenty-two junior officers. 'Abdul-Salam Jalloud, an RCC member and Libya's number two until 1995, argued that the 1975 plot was a turning point because al-Qaddhafi had thus far

[81] Lisa Anderson, *The State and Social Transformation in Tunisia and Libya, 1830–1980* (Princeton, NJ: Princeton University Press, 1986), 259. See also Ronald Bruce St John, *Libya: From Colony to Independence* (Oxford: Oneworld Publications, 2008), 125–126.

[82] For an account of these events and the first years of al-Qaddhafi in power, see Mohammad Yusef al-Moqaryaf, *Inqilab al-Qaddhafi, Mu'ammar, al-Toghian al-Thawari wa-'Abqariyyat al-Sufh, September 1969–March 1977* (Oxford: Centre for Libyan Studies, 2018). See also the memoirs of Fathi al-Dib, Gamal Abdul Nasser's envoy to Libya, *Abdul Nasser wa-Thawrat Libya* (Cairo: Dar al-Mustaqbal al-'Arabi, 1986), 39–40.

[83] On the coup attempt led by al-Hawaz and Ahmad, see Al Jazeera's interview with Major General Ahmad al-Hasi, August 11, 2013), www.youtube.com/watch?v=5cfW8NBYU N4 (accessed December 13, 2018).

[84] See an account of Libyan military coups published by *Ra'y al-Yawm*, February 16, 2014.

[85] See a report on the RCC members published by *al-Hayat*, July 26, 1993, www.alhayat.com/article/1874054 (accessed December 9, 2018). See also a report on coups in Libya published by *al-Akhbar*, February 24, 2011, https://al-akhbar.com/Arab/84023 (accessed December 13, 2018).

trusted Misrata officers, and was personally close to al-Muhayshi. The dictator surmised that in the wake of the failed putsch, his kin alone could be trusted, and began actively stacking his armed forces with members from his own clan, the al-Qadhadhifa (around 125,000 of Libya's roughly 6 million).[86] The latter became the regime's ultimate line of defense, but not always. In 1985, it was rumored that al-Qaddhafi's cousin, Hasan Shkal – the commander of the military region of Sirte who hailed from an influential clan in the al-Qadhadhifa tribe – had tried to topple him. Shkal was executed that same year, as were seventy-five officers accused of implication in anti-regime activities.[87]

In 1993, discontented officers from the loyalist Warfalla tribe hatched a coup attempt against al-Qaddhafi, but they, too, failed to overthrow him. Six senior officers involved in the coup were executed in 1997.[88] Two other putsches were foiled in July and August 1996, respectively. Reportedly, the first conspiracy was organized by Colonel Khalifa Haftar, an exiled officer who reemerged as a warlord after 2011. The second involved forty-five officers, including several disgruntled al-Qadhadhifa. The officers who led the conspirators were said to have been executed. These attempts were to be the last military intrigues against al-Qaddhafi until the armed forces fractured in 2011.[89]

Against such a turbulent background, al-Qaddhafi developed a particularly complex coup-proofing system. First, as mentioned previously, he stacked his armed forces with loyal tribal elements, including family members. The al-Qadhadhifa, in particular, secured privileged access to the Libyan military academy, and their presence in the elite units, the air force, and military security was ubiquitous. Al-Qadhadhifa's pervasiveness in regional commanderships was an indicator of their omnipresence in the armed forces: for instance, in 1995, all commanders

---

[86] See Ghassan Charbel, *Fi Khaymat al-Qaddhafi, Mu'ammar, Rifaq al-'Aqid Yakchufun Khabaya 'Ahdih* (Beirut: Riad El-Rayyes Books, 2013), 84–85.

[87] On the Shkal affair and the intra-al-Qadhadhifa struggle for power, see Ahmad al-Safrani, "Sira' al-Qabila wa-Asrar Maqtal Hasan Shkal," *Libya al-Mustaqbal*, August 7, 2009, http://archive.libya-al-mostakbal.org/Articles0809/ahmad_assafrani_070809.html (accessed December 7, 2018).

[88] See Chris Hedges, "Qaddafi Reported to Quash Army Revolt," *The New York Times*, October 23, 1993, www.nytimes.com/1993/10/23/world/qaddafi-reported-to-quash-army-revolt.html (accessed December 2, 2018).

[89] For more information on Libyan coups, see Mansour O. El-Kikhia, *Libya's Qaddafi: The Politics of Contradiction* (Gainesville, FL: University Press of Florida, 1997), 51 and 90; Lisa Anderson, "Libya's Qaddafi: Still in Command?" *Current History* 86 (February 1987): 65; Raymond A. Hinnebusch, "Libya: Personalistic Leadership of a Populist Revolution," in *Political Elites in Arab North Africa, Morocco, Algeria, Tunisia, Libya, and Egypt*, ed. I. William Zartman et al. (New York: Longman, 1982), 204; and Lucy Dean (ed.), *The Middle East and North Africa 2004* (New York: Europa Publications, 2004), 788.

of Libya's military sectors hailed from the al-Qadhadhifa, including Khalifa Hanaish (central region – Sirte), Masud ʿAbdul-Hafiz Ahmad (southern region – Sebha), Misbah ʿAbdul-Hafiz (eastern region – Benghazi), and Ahmad Qaddhaf al-Dam (the coast – Tobruk).[90]

Two allied tribes, the Warfalla (approximately one million) and the Maqarha, were also overrepresented in the officer corps. To be sure, it was convenient to deny the policies of tribal preferential treatment. After all, pan-Arab nationalism had long informed the ideological mantra of the al-Qaddhafi regime. In theory, then, al-Qaddhafi should have been hostile to tribal and regional parochialism as the antithesis of his unionist message. It made sense for the former leader to warn occasionally that "Muʾammar does not belong only to the Qadadfa tribe, but is the son, the father, the cousin, and the uncle of all revolutionaries."[91] Still, the regime's practice disconfirmed its rhetoric, as Table 5.1 shows.

In addition to ethnic stacking, al-Qaddhafi counterbalanced the armed forces. The so-called Revolutionary Committees (RCs) were created in 1977, allegedly to spread the regime's ideological message. In effect, the RCs infiltrated the armed forces and acted as an intelligence unit, overseeing officers and civilians alike. In addition to a large spy network, the RCs boasted a military wing, the praetorian Revolutionary Guards – comprising 3,000 men, mostly al-Qadhadhifa. The regime provided the Guards with helicopters and battle tanks. On various occasions, the Guards and the RCs operated as the death squads responsible for the "liquidation of the enemies of the revolution," both within Libya and abroad. The RCs also guarded ammunition in military barracks in Tripoli and Tobruk. That al-Qaddhafi counted on the RCs in the early 1990s to crush the series of Islamist rebellions in the east suggests that he trusted their loyalty, but not that of the military troops stationed there.[92] Still, the RCs were not the only paramilitary group operating in Libya. Another one was the Islamist Pan-African Legion, composed of mercenaries active in internal and external security operations. The Legion was made up of 1,000 men, but more could quickly be enlisted in times of need.[93] Two other organizations were the Presidential Guard and the Popular Militia, in charge of the security of the al-Qaddhafi family in Tripoli and patrolling the countryside and protecting the infrastructure, respectively. All four paramilitaries operated independently from the armed forces.

[90] El-Kikhia, *Libya's Qaddafi*, 90.   [91] Anderson, *The State*, 67.
[92] Dirk Vandewalle, *A History of Modern Libya* (New York: Cambridge University Press, 2012), 145.
[93] Said Haddad, "The Role of the Libyan Army in the Revolt against Gaddafi's Regime," Al Jazeera Center for Studies, March 16, 2011.

Table 5.1 *Prominent officers under al-Qaddhafi, by tribal and family affiliation*[94]

Name	Position	Family tie with the al-Qaddhafis	Tribal affiliation
Khamis al-Qaddhafi	Commander of the Thirty-Second Reinforced Brigade/ graduate of the Frunze Military Academy in Moscow	al-Qaddhafi's son	al-Qadhadhifa
Mu'tasim al-Qaddhafi, Mu'ammar	National security advisor	al-Qaddhafi's son	al-Qadhadhifa
al-Sa'di al-Qaddhafi, Mu'ammar	Commander of the Ninth Brigade (Special Forces)	al-Qaddhafi's son	al-Qadhadhifa
Ahmad Qaddhaf al-Dam al-Qaddhafi	Commander of the Cyrenaica region/al-Qaddhafi's personal diplomatic envoy	al-Qaddhafi's cousin	al-Qadhadhifa
Sayyid Muhammad Qaddhaf al-Dam al-Qaddhafi	Senior officer in the Military Intelligence	al-Qaddhafi's cousin	al-Qadhadhifa
Khalifa Ehnaish al-Qaddhafi	Commander of armaments and munitions	al-Qaddhafi's cousin	al-Qadhadhifa
Hassan Eshkal al-Qaddhafi[95]	Commander of the central region	al-Qaddhafi's cousin	al-Qadhadhifa

[94] I collected the data in this table from several sources, including Mohammad Makhluf, "Man Hom Rijal al-Khayma al-Ladhin Yudirun al-Nidham al-Libi," *Al-Majalla*, August 23, 1988, 23–26, http://archive.libya-al-mostakbal.org/Archives/mo3aredoon/almajalla1993/almajalla_aug93_libya02.html (accessed November 15, 2018); El-Kikhia, *Libya's Qaddafi*, 151–161; Ali Sariba, "The Role of the Military in the Arab Uprisings: The Case of Tunisia and Libya"(PhD diss., University of Nottingham, 2016), 172–173; and Hanspeter Mattes, "Formal and Informal Authority in Libya since 1969," in *Libya Since 1969: Qadhafi's Revolution Revisited*, ed. Dirk Vanderwalle (New York: Palgrave Macmillan, 2008), 74–76. This list is not exhaustive, nor is it meant to be. Other commanders hailing from the al-Qadhadhifa include Major General al-Barany Ishkal al-Qaddhafi (security units in Tripoli); al-Tuwati al-Mahdi Mansour al-Qaddhafi (officer in the Intelligence Bureau of the Leader, i.e., Maktab Ma'lumat al-Qa'id); al-Majdhoub Saleh al-Qaddhafi (officer in the Intelligence Bureau of the Leader); and Rajab Bouzeid al-Qaddhafi (colonel in the Presidential Guard).

[95] He was especially powerful throughout the 1970s and early 1980s until he was killed in mysterious circumstances in 1984.

Table 5.1 *(cont.)*

Name	Position	Family tie with the al-Qaddhafis	Tribal affiliation
ʿAbdullah al-Senussi	Head of Military Intelligence (also known as the Jamahiriya Security Organization)	Married to al-Qaddhafi 's sister-in-law (al-Senussi's wife is the sister of Safia Farkash, al-Qaddhafi's spouse)	al-Maqarha
Ahmad al-Qaddhafi, Muʿammar al-Qahsi	Army colonel	al-Qaddhafi's son-in-law (husband of ʿAisha al-Qaddhafi)	al-Qadhadhifa
al-Hadi al-Tahir Imbirsh	Commander of the Popular Defense Brigades (Also known as the People's Resistance Forces)	-	al-Maqarha
al-Saʿdi ʿAbdul-Salam	Senior officer in the Presidential Guard	al-Qaddhafi's nephew	al-Qadhadhifa
al-Khuwaildi al-Humaidi	General inspector of the armed forces	Father-in-law of al-Saʿdi al-Qaddhafi, al-Qaddhafi's son	-
Mansur Daw al-Qaddhafi, Muʿammar	Commander of the Presidential Guard (Seventy-Second Armored Battalion)	al-Qaddhafi's first cousin	al-Qadhadhifa
ʿAli al-Rifi al-Sharif	Commander of the air force	-	al-Maqarha
Bushʿraya Farkash	Senior officer in the Military Intelligence	al-Qaddhafi's brother-in-law (Bushʿrya is the brother of Safia Farkash)	al-Baraʿsa
Ahmad Fathallah al-Muqassibi	Head of military reconnaissance	-	al-Maqarha

In parallel to the paramilitary units, al-Qaddhafi developed a sprawling intelligence sector. As mentioned previously, the RCs functioned as the regime's eyes and ears, both in the military and in society at large. Two other organizations did the same. The first was Military Intelligence, or the Jamahiriyya Security Organization, headed by the notorious ʿAbdullah al-Senussi, stacked with the al-Qadhadhifa and flanked with internal and external security branches. The second was the Intelligence Bureau of the Leader (Maktab Maʿlumat al-Qaʾid), created with the help of the East German Stasi and tasked with coordinating the activities of various units in the security sector. The so-called Purification Committees (Lijan al-Tathir) also spied on the armed forces and other security and paramilitary organizations, thereby providing the regime with additional guarantees against political opponents.[96]

Al-Qaddhafi's divide-and-rule tactics also strengthened his grip on the armed forces. In essence, he pitted officers appointed to lead elite military unit stations in Tripoli against their colleagues heading regular troops and deployed in the east. The first group of officers belonged to the regime's inner circle; the second operated on its fringes. The elite units comprised the Thirty-Second (approximately 10,000 men) and Ninth Mechanized Brigades, known, respectively, as the "Khamis Brigade" (in reference to al-Qaddhafi's son Khamis) and "al-Sa'adi Brigade" (in reference to his other son, al-Sa'adi). These were the Special Forces of the Libyan military and, at least on paper, answerable to its chain of command. Men serving in these units were mainly drawn from the al-Qadhadhifa, but also from the Warfalla and the Maqarha.

The Thirty-Second and Ninth Mechanized Brigades were better trained and equipped than the regular troops. For instance, the regime allocated Soviet T-72 tanks manufactured in the 1970s to the elite units, whereas the regular troops were equipped with dated T-55s, introduced in the years following the Second World War. In addition, officers in the regular troops struggled to make ends meet: a Libyan colonel in the regular military made no more than $500 to $600 per month on the eve of the 2011 uprising. Their counterparts in the elite units received better salaries, bonuses from oil rent, and subsidies to buy real estate, cars, fuel, and food. In addition, the regime turned a blind eye toward the corruption of senior officers close to the circles of power in Libya. Meanwhile, the regular troops in the eastern regions lacked basic facilities, and their training was said to be "nonexistent."[97] In essence, then, al-Qaddhafi replicated in the military the policies of preferential treatment of the western region (Tripolitania) over the east (Cyrenaica). Unsurprisingly, the regular army troops felt no special loyalty toward the regime. That recruits serving in the east themselves hailed from that region only compounded their disaffection, because their families and tribes generally harbored ill-feeling toward al-Qaddhafi.[98]

---

[96] Gilbert Achcar, *The People Want: A Radical Exploration of the Arab Spring* (Berkley, CA: University of California Press, 2013), 166; Anderson, "Libya's Qaddafi," 65; and Vandewalle, *A History of Modern Libya*, 147–148.

[97] William Parsons and William Taylor, "Arbiters of Social Unrest: Military Responses to the Arab Spring," report prepared for the US Military Academy (2011), 24–25, https://apps.dtic.mil/dtic/tr/fulltext/u2/a562816.pdf (accessed November 7, 2018).

[98] Ibid. See also Sariba, "The Role of the Military," 251 and 260.

Despite his fiery "anti-imperialist" rhetoric and attempts to present his regime as progressive, ideological legitimacy remained missing from al-Qaddhafi's coup-proofing system. As mentioned above, he cloaked himself in the garb of Nasserism in the first decades of his rule. Unlike Nasser (or Bourguiba), however, his ideational credentials were always dubious. On the one hand, the appeal of Arab nationalism was weakened after the Six-Day War in 1967 and Nasser's death in 1970. In effect, al-Qaddhafi emerged on the Arab scene when his professed beliefs were becoming a spent force. On the other hand, his multiple attempts to unify Libya with other Arab states – e.g., Egypt, Syria, Sudan, Algeria, Tunisia, and Morocco – all ended in failure. And his strident defiance of Western powers isolated Libya and damaged its economic prospects.

Furthermore, many in the eastern parts of the country felt discriminated against in favor of Tripolitania. The brazen corruption of al-Qaddhafi's family fueled popular animosity. All Libyans knew that their country was floating on a reservoir of oil, yet many suffered from unemployment, poor wages, and housing shortages while the president's cronies controlled sectors like energy and telecommunications.[99] Long before the turning point in 2011, al-Qaddhafi's "revolutionary" message was ringing hollow. Most Libyans understood that the so-called state of the masses (jamahiriyya) was a ploy to maintain them in "perpetual political infancy," while "the grown-up business of politics" was restricted to an unaccountable power elite operating behind closed doors.[100] To be sure, tribal solidarity and economic favoritism kept most of the al-Qadhadhifa, Warfalla, and Maqarha on the side of the former leader. But outside such strongholds, regime support was weak or simply nonexistent among soldiers and civilians alike.

Overall, the Libyan armed forces under al-Qaddhafi present a textbook case of a military "coup-proofed to death." On paper, the troops grew from 7,000 in 1969 to 85,000 in 1988. In effect, however, the regime did everything possible to demoralize the soldiers, save for the elite units. First, Libya hadn't had a minister of defense since 1969. Second, conscript recruitment was haphazard and unpredictable. Third, embargos against military shipments imposed by the United States and Europe prevented Libya from acquiring arms throughout the 1980s and most of the 1990s. By the time the sanctions were lifted in 1999, most military

[99] See John Wright, *A History of Libya* (New York: Columbia University Press, 2012), 200–201; Sariba, "The Role of the Military," 168–169; and Ronal Bruce St John, "Redefining the Libyan Revolution: The Changing Ideology of Muammar al-Qaddafi," *The Journal of North African Studies* 13, no. 1 (March 2008): 95.

[100] See Hugh Roberts, "Who Said Gaddafi Had to Go?" *London Review of Books* 33, no. 22 (2011): 8–11.

equipment had become seriously outdated. New weapons purchased from Russia were essentially diverted to the Thirty-Second and Ninth Brigades, while the rest of the troops lagged behind. Military commanders were frequently rotated from one sector to another in order to prevent them from building a loyal following among troops stationed in the regions under their control. Officers were promoted as a function of their tribal background and political loyalties, not professional performance. In essence, the military operated like a social safety net, absorbing thousands of young men from the Libyan lower classes who otherwise could have been unemployed.[101] Unsurprisingly, the troops performed dismally against American airstrikes in April 1986. More embarrassingly, the armed forces were routed in 1987 by the ragtag Chadian military in southern Libya, after which their numbers were slashed. Al-Qaddhafi's control system crippled his troops as a fighting machine, but kept him in power for forty-two years. Because coup-proofing delivered self-preservation, it was maintained for decades until it inevitably molded civil–military relations, and, by extension, the response of the armed forces to the 2011 uprising.

The 2011 Uprising and the Breakdown of al-Qaddhafi's Regime: Explaining Military Behavior

I have shown previously that the Egyptian and Tunisian armed forces remained cohesive during the 2011 uprising. In Syria, thousands of officers and soldiers deserted individually, but no military company or battalion defected as a whole, let alone brigades or divisions. In Libya, the armed forces splintered. The elite units led by Khamis and al-Saʿdi al-Qaddhafi remained loyal and ready to repress civilians in order to defend the status quo. In contrast, the regular troops stationed in Benghazi defected collectively. In effect, the brutality of the regime's response to the nonviolent demonstrations activated intra-military fault lines and triggered the disintegration of the armed forces, which, in turn, hastened the escalation of the conflict into civil war.

How Ethnic Stacking and Divide-and-Rule Predetermined the Splintering of the Armed Forces   In the early years of his rule, al-Qaddhafi claimed to be fighting parochialism in the name of Arab nationalism and the state of the masses (*jamahiriyya*) he intended to build. Al-Qaddhafi

---

[101] Vandewalle, *A History of Modern Libya*, 146.

then spent the following decades using tribal and regional loyalties to consolidate his rule. Stripped from its ideological veneer, his regime represented the political preeminence of western Libya over the east; of Sirte or Bani Walid over other cities and towns; and of the al-Qadhadhifa, Maqarha, and Warfalla over other Libyan tribes.

The al-Qadhadhifa, in particular, had four powerful reasons to defend the status quo. First, they harbored a stronger emotional attachment to the regime due to tribal solidarity with its ruling family. Second, they were the primary recipients of the regime's largesse, and thus had more to lose, should it fall. Third, they had been the backbone of the regime's repression against its enemies, and had collected many blood feuds along the way. The tribe therefore feared a post-al-Qaddhafi hour of reckoning. Finally, the al-Qadhadhifa's feeble demographic weight condemned them to marginalization, should they lose their grip on power. And so they operated as diehard loyalists throughout the fateful events of 2011.

Similarly, the Warfalla and Maqarha remained overwhelmingly in the loyalist camp. Leaders from both tribes who deserted failed to trigger massive defections in their wake.[102] Against this backdrop, it is perhaps unsurprising that the allegiance of the ethnically stacked elite units in the military was unwavering. Writing on the Thirty-Second Brigade, Flaurence Gaube correctly observed that it was "capable of anything" to defend al-Qaddhafi, including executing prisoners and using lethal weaponry against civilians such as cluster bombs and land mines.[103] As mentioned previously, the Libyan uprising began in earnest on February 17, 2011, in Benghazi. Only two days later, on February 19, the Thirty-Second Brigade was dispatched to the city to quell the demonstrations. There is consensus among observers of Libya that the so-called Khamis Brigade used everything it had against protesters, including anti-aircraft guns, mortars, heavy artillery, sniper units, and even helicopter attacks. When Misrata, Libya's third-largest city, joined the uprising, the Brigade shelled it heavily for months, and tried to starve its civilians into submission. The atrocities continued till the end: on August 22, 2011, the

---

[102] These include, most prominently, the previously mentioned 'Abdul-Salam Jallud (Maqarha); Albarrani Shkal (al-Qadhadhifa), a deputy head of the military intelligence who turned rebel informer in May 2011 and was assassinated in May 2012; and Akram al-Warffali, a tribal notable (Warfalla). The latter said in an interview with Al Jazeera in March 2011 that "brother al-Qaddhafi, Mu'ammar" is "no longer a brother," and asked him to leave the country. In the wake of al-Warfalli's interview, there were wide speculations about an imminent Warfalla defection, but it never materialized. See David D. Kirkpatrick, "Tribal Ties, Long Qaddafi's Strength, May Be His Undoing," *The New York Times*, March 14, 2011, www.nytimes.com/2011/03/15/world/africa/15tribes .html (accessed December 15, 2018). See also Wolfram Larcher, "Families, Tribes and Cities in the Libyan Revolution," *Middle East Policy* 18, no. 4 (Winter 2011): 145.

[103] Gaub, "The Libyan Armed Forces," 237.

Brigade summarily executed at least fifty detainees in a warehouse south of Tripoli. By that time, the capital had fallen to the insurgents, and al-Qaddhafi was on the run. Violence no longer had any strategic value, but that didn't prevent the massacre. Around the same time, seventeen additional detainees were also killed by the Brigade in another makeshift prison in Tripoli.[104] It is significant that the elite units never disintegrated, were deployed against protesters in several Libyan cities simultaneously, and fought aggressively against the rebels after the uprising escalated into insurgency. NATO joined the fray in March 2011, but the elite units were still fighting when Tripoli fell in August, five months later. Their resistance continued in Sirte until the end of October, when al-Qaddhafi was killed. Had it not been for the Western strikes, it is possible that the al-Qaddhafi regime's counteroffensive would have been victorious.[105]

In addition to the elite units, two organizations originally created for coup-proofing purposes turned against the demonstrators. First, the Revolutionary Committees (RCs) intervened alongside loyalist forces to crush the uprising. Just as the wrath of the demonstrators in Egypt had been directed at the police, Libyans attacked RCs headquarters as a particularly hated symbol of regime repression and heavy-handedness. Second, the Islamist Pan-African Legion also played a role in repressing the uprising. The Legion's numbers swelled as the regime quickly hired hundreds of foreign mercenaries who had no connection with Libyan society and felt no compunction about slaughtering Libyans in their own country. Several eyewitness accounts converge, arguing that the Legion and its mercenaries were particularly ruthless and more inclined to kill civilians than the armed forces.[106] In contrast to the continued loyalty of military elite units, the regular troops stationed throughout the eastern part of Libya were quick to defect. Some special forces that were not ethnically stacked also refused to suppress the protests. Thus, the so-called Thunderbolt Squad (al-Saʿiqa), dispatched to crush the uprising in Benghazi, actually turned on loyalist troops and expelled them from the city when interior minister ʿAbdul-Fattah Yunis joined the opposition. Had it not been for al-Saʿiqa's readiness to fight against the regime RCs in Benghazi, the city could not have emerged quickly as a rebel bastion.[107]

[104] See the BBC report, "Profile: Khamis Gaddafi," September 4, 2011, www.bbc.com/n ews/world-africa-14723041 (accessed December 15, 2018); and Achcar, *The People Want*, 169.

[105] Derek Lutterbeck, "Arab Uprisings and Armed Forces: Between Openness and Resistance," Geneva Centre for the Democratic Control of Armed (2011), 34, www.ubiquitypress.com/site/books/10.5334/bbm/ (accessed December 5, 2018).

[106] Ibid., 35; and Sariba, "The Role of the Military," 253.

[107] Lutterbeck, "Arab Uprisings," 33.

Even more importantly, however, the army commander in Tobruk, Major General Suleiman Mahmud, defected in February 22, and his units turned against the regime wholesale. The same is true of military forces deployed in the eastern Jabal al-Akhdar.[108] Both Yunis and Mahmud hailed from the northeastern ʿObeidat tribe, the leaders of which publicly withheld their allegiance from the regime in the first days of the protests. Other northeastern tribes such as the al-Baraʿsa and the ʿAwaqir also joined the uprising, and the defection of officers stationed in the eastern parts of Libya followed that of their clans.[109] Some troops stationed in the west defected, as well. For instance, Colonel Hussein Darbuk, an army commander in Zawiya, a city on the coast 45 kilometers away from the capital, Tripoli, defected with most of his troops in late February. Darbuk became the field commander of insurgents in the city, and died fighting loyalist units on March 4.[110] Not all defectors chose to join the insurgents, however; most simply melted into the population. The Libyan armed forces splintered. They were the first to do so in the Arab Spring, though the Yemeni military would soon follow.

Conclusion of the Libyan Case Study

Muʿammar al-Qaddhafi was yet another Arab autocrat who seized power by way of a coup and worried about being overthrown the same way. He ethnically stacked the special units in the armed forces, pitted them against regular troops stationed in the eastern regions, promoted the material interests of his favorite generals, and fostered paramilitary forces and intelligence agencies to counterbalance the military. Like the ethnically stacked troops in Syria (and Bahrain), the privileged units in Libya were ready to kill civilians and defend the regime in 2011. Disenfranchised sectors of the Libyan military were not wedded to al-Qaddhafi by tribal solidarity, however, and did not benefit from his rule economically. When the Libyan uprising clamored for regime change, these sectors defected wholesale, fighting against their military rivals or melting into the population. Libya soon plunged into civil war against a backdrop of implosion within the armed forces. When al-Qaddhafi instrumentalized identity in Libya, he did so to guarantee his political

---

[108] See Ian Black, "Libya: Defections Leave Muammar Gaddafi Isolated in Tripoli Bolthole," *The Guardian*, February 23, 2011, www.theguardian.com/world/2011/feb/2 3/muammar-gaddafi-libya-tripoli-uprising (accessed December 15, 2018).

[109] Larcher, "Families, Tribes and Cities," 144.

[110] Zawiya itself was back in loyalist hands by March 10. On the events in Zawiya, see David D. Kirkpatrick and Kareem Fahim, "Rebels in Libya Gain Power and Defectors," *The New York Times*, February 27, 2011, www.nytimes.com/2011/02/28/world/africa/28un rest.html (accessed December 15, 2018).

survival. His control methods delivered, but the price was dire for the military institution and the population at large. The calamities that befell Libya in 2011 were the direct result of forty-two years of coup-proofing that kept al-Qaddhafi in power while wrecking the armed forces and polarizing society.

Conclusion

The struggle for power in countries plagued by military interventionism is a brutal business. Autocrats threatened by rival elite rarely show or expect mercy in politics. Indeed, they seldom receive it in the wake of successful putsches. Beyond influence and prestige, what is at stake for apprehensive rulers in weakly institutionalized polities is survival in the most elementary sense of the term. That they prioritize coup-proofing over other considerations when civil–military relations are conflictual is predetermined by the ruthless environment that surrounds them. Therefore, the study of military politics in such countries is largely a function of examining putsches and methods employed by rulers to stem their tide. This is a fundamental assertion of the present study. A second argument is as follows: Coup-proofing tactics are path-dependent, and shape civil–military relations in fundamental and durable ways. Such tactics are also variegated. Some are ideational, wedding officers to autocrats via the powerful bonds of identity and/or ideological commitment. Ideational control mechanisms deliver coup-proofing and military readiness to repress civilians when opposition comes from the streets. Other coup-proofing tactics operate differently. They may guarantee the loyalty of only a small coterie of the top brass, overwhelmingly alienate officers regardless of rank, or polarize them into feuding camps. All the above lead to the book's main contention: dissimilar combinations of coup-proofing tactics generate divergent types of civil–military relations; and, by extension, inform the willingness and capacity of officers to uphold autocracy in a wide variety of ways during popular uprisings.

Theoretical Contribution and Implications: Coup-Proofing and Democratization

The contribution of this book belongs to a broad research agenda centered upon the political and military effects of coup-proofing. Scholars of civil–military relations have previously shown that important by-products of coup-proofing go beyond the original purpose of its tactics. For example, James T. Quinlivan argued that the downside of coup-proofing is the failure of militaries to achieve their potential as fighting forces due to a baneful upshot upon the morale and effectiveness of the troops.[1] Caitlin Talmadge has developed this point deftly in her book on the battlefield performance of militaries operating under nondemocratic regimes.[2] Along similar lines, Risa Brooks has shown how Egyptian military ineffectiveness in 1967 was heavily shaped by domestic politics and the civil–military balance of power. This negatively affected key issues such as strategic assessment, appointments in higher echelons of the armed forces, and strategic command and control.[3] For their part, Belkin and Schofer maintain that coup-proofing can potentially lead to heightened risk of international conflict.[4] By contrast, Powell found that coup-proofing reduces the need of autocrats to engage in foreign bullying by strengthening their internal grip. It also reduces the need for diversionary wars and rally-around-the-flag tactics. In addition, autocrats know how ill-prepared their troops are for war. They fear the results of a humiliating defeat abroad, and consequently restrain from adventurism.[5] For his part, Roessler showed that ethnic exclusion/stacking is central to coup-proofing in Africa, and directly related to the heightening of civil wars on the continent.[6] Finally, Brown et al. have argued that coup-proofing is correlated with the development of nuclear, chemical, or biological weapons as well as the search for external alliances as dictators seek to offset the self-induced military weakness of their regimes.[7] Scholars have, thus far, debated coup-proofing repercussions on combat readiness, international conflict, civil wars, foreign policy, and the growth of WMDs. As Kårtveit and Jumbert correctly note, less attention has been paid to the ways in which coup-prevention tactics might affect military behavior in the

---

[1] James T. Quinlivan, "Coup-Proofing: Its Practice and Consequences in the Middle East," *International Security* 24, no. 2 (Autumn 1999): 134.

[2] Talmadge, *The Dictator's Army*.

[3] Risa Brooks, "An Autocracy at War: Explaining Egypt's Military Effectiveness, 1967 and 1973," *Security Studies* 15, no. 3 (2006): 396–430.

[4] Aaron Belkin and Evan Schofer, "Coup Risk, Counterbalancing, and International Conflict," *Security Studies* 14, no. 1 (2005): 140–177.

[5] Jonathan Powell, "Regime Vulnerability and the Diversionary Threat of Force," *Journal of Conflict Resolution* 58, no. 1 (2014): 169–196. See also Powell, "Coups and Conflict."

[6] Philipp Roessler, "The Enemy Within: Personal Rule, Coups, and Civil War in Africa," *World Politics* 63, no. 2 (2011): 300–346.

[7] Cameron S. Brown, Christopher J. Fariss, and R. Blake McMahon, "Recouping after Coup-Proofing: Compromised Military Effective and Strategic Substitution," *International Relations* 42, no. 1 (2016): 1–30.

face of massive popular uprisings;[8] and this is precisely what this book seeks to redress. As previously mentioned, the assertion that armed forces are central to the dynamics of transition and consolidation is an established orthodoxy in the democratization literature. At the same time, the literature on civil–military relations has long shown the centrality of coup-proofing tactics in authoritarian regime survival politics. Yet rarely do reflections on democratization and coup-proofing speak to one other though they can be enriched by cross-fertilization. This book brings them together.

On the other hand, my framework highlights the need to problematize intra-military generational dynamics and to put young officers analytically at the center of transitology. The central dilemma autocrats face during endgames is the following: The agents whose allegiance they need to overpower opponents are not the privileged beneficiaries who reap the greatest advantage from the status quo. Depending on regime subtype, the ruling coalition in dictatorships characteristically includes some or all of the following agents: the autocrat's family members, allied business cartels and media moguls, party apparatchiks, and senior commanders of military and security agencies. But these actors will not suffice to uphold the status quo if popular uprisings reach critical mass and sustain it. In contrast, young military officers who lead soldiers operationally can be formidable allies to autocrats when they remain compliant. To weather endgames, dictators need to convince coercive agents who benefit less – or not at all – from their rule to mete out violence on behalf of those who hold power or have preferential access to it. How strongmen go about achieving such results and whether they are successful in doing so is the acid test of autocratic survivalism. Hence the need to put generational dynamics in the officer corps at the center of the equation, analytically; again, this is precisely what the book does.

It is important here to emphasize a second point that stems directly from the previous one and represents the other side of the same coin: regime opponents shift the correlation of forces decisively in their favor if they peel the lower echelons of the officer corps away from the autocratic order. If the military is ethnically stacked, then in-group officers need guarantees that neither they nor their communities would suffer from

---

[8] Bård Kårtveit and Maria Gabrielsen Jumbert, "Civil–Military Relations in the Middle East: A Literature Review," Chr. Michelin Institute, Working Paper 2014:5, June 2014, 1–24, www.cmi.no/publications/file/5188-civil-military-relations-in-the-middle-east.pdf (accessed January 15, 2015). Exceptions include: Theodore McLauchlin, "Loyalty Strategies and Military Defection in Rebellion," *Comparative Politics* 42, no. 3 (April 2010): 333–350; and Michael Makara, "Coup-Proofing, Military Defection, and the Arab Spring," *Democracy and Security* 9, no. 4 (2013): 334–359.

retributions should the regime fall. In these contexts, the hardliners of the out-group operate paradoxically as the dictator's best friends precisely because they fuel in-group anxieties and compound the opposition's commitment dilemmas. When societies are deeply fractured along identity lines, reaching out to repressive agents and calming their apprehensions is no easy task for the opposition to achieve. It is not an impossible mission either as the process that led to the end of apartheid in South Africa suggests. Then again, the recent findings of Theodore McLauchlin indicate that the military politics of the transition process in South Africa may have been an outlier. When a deliberate and sustained process of ethnic exclusion reifies in-group members as loyalists irrespective of their actual political preferences, it becomes difficult for the autocrat's kinsmen to break the loyalty trap that he set for them.[9] Consequently, when in-group officers believe that the opposition will treat them as enemies for ascriptive reasons they are likely to uphold autocracy. Happy endings are rare in these scenarios precisely because exclusivism narrows the options of loyalists while leaving moderate opponents vulnerable to extremist co-ethnic rivals. In effect, the powers that be and radical opponents operate as objective allies because both push to ethnicize the struggle for change whereas the moderate opposition seeks to de-ethnicize it. Far more attention is needed to understand how these dynamics shape the attitudes of young officers toward the opposition, and by extension, the prospects of authoritarian breakdown. Pollinating the literature on civil–military relations and contentious politics is highly warranted in this regard.

Yet another implication of my argument is this: coup-proofing strategies that include ideational tactics of political control of the armed forces have distinctive dynamics. Quoting Dan Slater:

When trying to understand why elites have come to provide collective political support to an authoritarian regime, we are better guided by an alternative axiom to the notion that people do not bite the hands that feed them – that the *enemy of one's enemy is one's friend*. Understanding elite collective action under dictatorship requires more than "following the money." It requires recognizing how a shared "fear of enemies" can serve as "a means for the achievement of collective ends."[10]

I have shown in this book that ideational coup-proofing generates precisely this common "fear of enemies," which in turn spawns militaries supportive of autocratic bulwarks against popular unrest. As previously

---

[9] Theodore McLauchlin, "The Loyalty Trap: Regime Ethnic Exclusion, Commitment Problems, and Civil War Duration in Syria and Beyond," *Security Studies* 27, no. 2 (2018): 296–317.
[10] Slater, *Ordering Power*, 12. Slater includes mid-level officers in the armed forces (and the police) in his definition of "elites."

argued, promoting top-brass interests may pacify the senior military commandership while simultaneously creating dangerous grudges below. Establishing powerful paramilitaries to counterbalance the armed forces can indeed deter coups but also spurs counterproductive professional jealousies. Playing divide-and-rule may wed one loyalist faction to the regime while alienating another. As long as societal opposition is weak, the chances of skillful autocrats to manage contradictions inherent to their regimes are high. But exogenous chocks of massive uprisings can activate dormant intra-regime frictions unless gaps are bridged ideationally. This is where shared aversions can make the difference between autocratic consolidation or breakdown. Negative partnerships that wed loyalists to the status quo can be ascriptive or ideological. They can also be non-existing: lest we forget, the mere fact that an autocrat is in power does not imply invariably that he enjoys ideational legitimacy. The latter may erode over time; or it can be weak from the get-go. Conversely, it can be vibrant and enduring. The consequences are tremendous either way.

Finally, by pondering the threat environment surrounding dictators in countries with troubled civil–military relations, I highlight the fragility of their position even when at the apex of influence. And by demonstrating the path dependence of coup prevention I pinpoint the limits of autocratic power. Put differently, I debunk perceptions of strongmen so dominant they can choose freely from a menu of coup-proofing tactics. Both factors – i.e., the perilous milieu against which power games unfold and restrictions on the dictator's ability to manage coercive agents – explain why autocrats who appear frightening are characteristically themselves frightened of regime insiders. A keen understanding of the dread this environment generates among the fretful elite is perhaps a better guide to fathoming their choices than assumptions of unshakable confidence and roaring will to power.

Empirical Contribution: The Military in Middle East Politics

I have argued in this book that despite tensions in civil–military relations stemming from the presidential ambitions of Gamal Mubarak, the Egyptian top brass remained firmly loyalist until the last days of the 2011 drama. The fact is, democratic transition in Egypt was not inevitably doomed to fail. Had Islamists and their secular opponents closed ranks against military interventionism despite ideological differences they could have put Egypt on a path toward democratic consolidation. This was a nightmarish scenario for the Egyptian generals who had too much to lose from the fall of the autocratic order and nothing to win personally from democracy. Why, then, didn't the military elite unleash their troops on demonstrators? I maintained that defense minister Field Marshal Hussein Tantawi lacked the capacity, not the will, to save Hosni Mubarak. Specifically, the Supreme Council of the Armed Forces (SCAF) feared that had it ordered subordinates to crush the uprising, insubordination on a large scale would have ensued with devastating consequences for the military and its commandership. But why wasn't the same mechanism at play in Syria? Surely, the Syrian military elite must have reckoned that ordering soldiers to slaughter civilians and shell neighborhoods indiscriminately would lead to military desertions – which it did. In fact, defectors were instrumental in setting up some of the first rebel groups that fought the armed forces after the uprising escalated into insurgency and Syria plunged into civil war. These prospects were easily foreseeable; and yet they were not dissuasive. Why did the Syrian generals lack the inhibitions of their Egyptian peers?

The answer of this book is the following: Ethnic stacking in Syria delivered coup-proofing and more. In other words, it protected the Syrian regime from insiders as well as out-group popular mobilizations. The Syrian top brass figured correctly in 2011 that desertions would remain restricted to Sunni officers and soldiers in the wake of repression. Considering the low ratio of Sunni officers and the marginality of positions they occupied from an operational perspective, defections could not have spiraled out of control into a wide-ranging collapse of military discipline. Indeed, they never did in 1982 when the Syrian armed forces slaughtered perhaps 20,000 Sunnis in a few days of carnage in Hama. Considering also that the Syrian military had become even more Alawitized since Hama, massive rebellion against loyalist generals was even less likely in 2011. Indeed, ethnic stacking implied that Alawis enjoyed an overwhelming majority at all levels of the officer corps in the Syrian military, and among career soldiers as well. Furthermore, the elite praetorian units used to counterbalance the regular military were quasi all-Alawi forces. The same was true of the intelligence sector, particularly the powerful Air Force Intelligence Directorate (AFID). The all-Alawi units could be expected to go all the way in squelching dissent; and the generals could also pair such units with other formations whose loyalty was less certain. These factors gave leverage to the Syrian generals that the SCAF lacked in Egypt. The fundamental contradistinction in this regard is the following: Repression would only cost loyalist top brass the margins of the military in Syria whereas it threatened its very core in Egypt. The defection of Sunni officers and soldiers in Syria could not cripple the armed forces as long as their Alawi spine remained loyalist. In contrast, when a handful of mid-ranking and junior officers joined protesters in Tahrir Square the SCAF dreaded a diffusion effect with far-reaching consequences. Put differently, the SCAF feared that the entire military could disintegrate in 2011 whereas the Alawi commanders of the Syrian armed forces did not. These were very different prospects to consider and they weighted directly on top-brass calculations.

Arab militaries are major players in the contemporary politics of their countries but they have been understudied for decades. Scholarly interest in the politics of Arab officers peaked in the 1960s, and then dwindled.[11] A survey of peer-reviewed journals in the fields of Middle East studies and security studies has highlighted the small number of articles dealing with the Middle Eastern security sector. Most of these articles, incidentally, are about non-Arab states (i.e., Israel and Turkey).[12] Zoltan Barany noted that his colleagues studying the Arab world told him that he was looking for "what does not exist," when he asked them for recommendations on Arab military politics prior to 2011.[13] Beyond the somewhat feeble academic interest in civil–military relations generically, reasons for the scholarly neglect of Arab militaries are threefold. First, academic interest in civil–military relations centers upon coups. Putsches in the Middle East waned as of the 1970s, when Arab autocrats mastered the art of coup-proofing, and scholars subsequently lost interest in studying the seemingly quietest armed forces – in the words of F. Gregory Gause, the stability of Arab regimes led scholars to assume that their militaries were "no longer important."[14] One consequence of this inattention is the following: We know that coups receded in Arab autocracies but we know less about the complexity, evolution, and repercussions of coup-proofing on civil–military relations. Second, the illiberal nature of Arab regimes is not conducive to fieldwork-based academic research, let alone research on the armed forces. Third, Arab officers are reluctant to discuss military affairs with civilians, and are even more hesitant with foreign researchers. Gaining access to sources within the armed forces appears difficult or downright impossible. Ahmed Hashim noticed, for instance, that "it is very difficult to get information out of [the Egyptian] officer corps. They do not welcome

---

[11] Landmark studies from this period include: Vatikiotis, *The Egyptian Army in Politics*; Abdel-Malek, *Egypt*; and J. C. Hurewitz, *Middle East Politics: The Military Dimension* (New York: Praeger, 1969).
[12] Oren Barak and Assaf David, "The Arab Security Sector: A New Research Agenda for a Neglected Topic," *Armed Forces & Society* 36, no. 5 (2010): 804–824.
[13] Barany, *How Armies Respond*, 3.
[14] F. Gregory Gause III, "Why Middle East Studies Missed the Arab Spring: The Myth of Authoritarian Stability," *Foreign Affairs* 90, no. 4 (July/August 2011): 85.

interviews."[15] Sarah Philips refers to information pertaining to the Yemeni military as "shrouded in secrecy ... a point of great contention ... extremely vague ... notoriously inaccurate," and so forth.[16] Nothing in this book disconfirms these observations. Conducting fieldwork on military politics and/or the security sector in the Arab world remains indeed difficult – and sometimes outright dangerous as the Matthew Hedges case has shown again recently.[17] And yet a small group of dedicated researchers has been doing its best since 2011 to investigate Arab militaries. I benefitted from their efforts and hope in turn that this book will contribute to the budding renewal of the field after decades of stagnation.

Future Research

I argued in this book that coup-proofing structures military response to civilian uprisings in different ways. Knowledge is almost never complete and predictions always risky; hence the need for intellectual humility and circumspection. And yet if my insights are correct, we should be able henceforth to make informed extrapolations on how armed forces will react to mass protest by pondering coup prevention and its effects on civil–military relations. To be sure, my study is geographically limited to the Arab world. And yet, coups, coup-proofing, and nonviolent uprisings are far from being specifically Arab phenomena. If my argumentation is accurate, my framework should also be analytically valid outside my region of interest.

On the other hand, if endgames can lead societies to democratic transition, autocratic consolidation, or civil war, and if coup-proofing has a tremendous impact on molding such outcomes, then the question becomes: Why does coup-proofing differ from one regime to another? Clearly, social structure matters. Ethnic stacking, for instance, is only possible in countries where political loyalties break along identity-related fractures and these cannot be contrived out of thin air. Fiscal health matters as well. Other factors may include partisan penetration of the armed forces; or historical legacies stemming from military contribution

---

[15] Hashim, "The Egyptian Military, Part One," 1.

[16] Sarah Philips, *Yemen's Democracy Experiment in Regional Perspective: Patronage and Pluralized Authoritarianism* (New York: Palgrave Macmillan, 2008), 69–71, cited in Zoltan Barany, "Comparing the Arab Revolts: The Role of the Military," *Journal of Democracy* 22, no. 4 (October 2011): 26.

[17] Matthew Hedges, a doctoral student at Durham University, UK, was arrested in the United Arab Emirates in 2018 on espionage charges. He spent seven months in solitary confinement before being pardoned and released in November 2018. Hedges was doing dissertation fieldwork in the UAE on the military–industrial complex in the Gulf.

to state formation and wars of independence. Probing why coup-proofing varies in dictatorships falls beyond the scope of this book but further attention is warranted as per this issue specifically.

Finally, and perhaps most importantly, this book is concerned with military reaction to popular uprisings, and does not study the agency of the armed forces in post-transitional contexts. And yet military politics in nascent democracies are worthy of attention. Two insights are important to keep in mind here. First, democracy is the result of transition from dictatorship, followed by consolidation of the post-authoritarian order. Transition, in other words, is the beginning of the democratization process, but progress can be reversed and autocracy reestablished. Simply put, transition does not guarantee in itself democratic consolidation. Second, no democratizing regime can consolidate absent civilian control of the armed forces. The July 2013 military coup in Egypt is one of the most recent reminders pertaining to the omnipresent military threat to democratizing regimes. But other examples abound in Thailand, Mauritania, Sudan, and elsewhere. All authoritarian breakdowns provide political actors with the prospect of renegotiating civil–military relations under new configurations more amenable to instituting civilian control. In some cases, the momentum is seized. In others, attempts to reform civil–military relations fail and consolidation is subsequently derailed. The original ambition of this book was to study the democratization process holistically, from transition to consolidation – or breakdown. I restricted my curiosity for practical reasons pertaining to economy of space and the time – eight years – it took me to finish this work within its current limitations. But if coup-proofing goes a long way in structuring the military politics of transition, the same may also be true in post-transitional scenarios in which the consolidation of democracy is at stake. This contention warrants future research.

Bibliography

ʿAbdalla, Ahmed. "The Armed Forces and the Democratic Process in Egypt." *Third World Quarterly* 10, no. 4 (October1988): 1452–1465.

ʿAbdalla, Ahmed (ed.). *Al-Jaysh wa-l-Dimoqratiyya fi Masr*. Cairo: Sina li-l-Nashr, 1990.

ʿAbdallah, Mahmud. "Hares Amn … Wazifa bi-la Muʾahhalat." *Al-Badil*, January 12, 2017.

Abdel-Malek, Anouar. *Egypt: Military Society: The Army Regime, the Left, and Social Change under Nasser*. New York: Random House, 1968.

ʿAbdul-ʿAl, Khaled. "Imbriatoriat al-Shorta al-Masriyya al-Iqtisadiyya." *Al-ʿArabi al-Jadid*, December 30, 2016. www.alaraby.co.uk/investigations/201 6/12/29/1-امبراطورية-الشرطة-المصرية. Accessed December 30, 2016.

"Siraʿ al-Jaysh wa-l-Dakhiliyya fi Masr … al-Maʿraka ʿala al-Nufudh." *Al-ʿArabi al-Jadid*, April 15, 2015. www.alaraby.co.uk/investigations/2015/4/1 5/صراع-الجيش-والداخلية-في-مصر-المعركة-على-النفوذ. Accessed March 16, 2016.

ʿAbdul-Aziz, Muhammad, and Youssef Hussein. "The President, the Son, and the Military: The Question of Succession in Egypt." *The Arab Studies Journal* 9/10, no. 2/1 (Fall 2001/Spring 2002): 73–88.

ʿAbdul-Fattah, Abul-Fadl. *Kunto Naʾiban li-Raʾis al-Mukhabarat*. Cairo: Dar al-Shuruq, 2001.

ʿAbdul-Karim, Ahmad. *Hasad Sinin Khasba wa-Thimar Morra, Mudhakkarat Ahmad ʿAbdul-Karim*. Beirut: Bissan, 1994.

Abdulrahim, Raja. "War-Torn Syria's Battered Economy Marked by Inflation and Poverty." *The Wall Street Journal*, July 29, 2017. www.wsj.com/articles/ war-torn-syrias-battered-economy-marked-by-inflation-and-poverty-15012 34205. Accessed August 1, 2017.

Abid, Zohra. "Tunisie. Les faux vrais aveux de Ali Seriati." *Kapitalis*, March 12, 2012. www.kapitalis.com/politique/8846-tunisie-les-faux-vrais-aveux-de-ali -seriati.html. Accessed October 23, 2018.

Abu Basha, Hasan. *Fi al-Amn wa-l-Siasa, Mudhakkarat Hasan Abu Basha*. Cairo: Dar al-Hilal, 1990.

Abu Fakhr, Saqr. *Suria wa-Hutam al-Marakeb al-Mubaʾthara, Hiwar maʿ Nabil al-Shueiri, ʿAflaq wa-l-Baʿath wa-l-Muʾamarat wa-l-ʿAskar*. Beirut: al-Muʾassasa al-ʿArabiyya li-l-Dirasat wa-l-Nashr, 2005.

Abul-Magd, Zeinab. *Militarizing the Nation: The Army, Business, and Revolution in Egypt*. New York: Columbia University Press, 2017.

"Zaman al-Thamaninat al-Jamil: Ayyam Abu Ghazalah." *Al-Manassa*, December 30, 2015. https://almanassa.com/ar/story/664. Accessed January 9, 2016.

"US Military Aid to Egypt Lost Value." *Jadaliyya*, July 25, 2013. www.jadaliyya.com/pages/index/13186/us-military-aid-to-egypt-lost-value#_ed n6. Accessed December 9, 2013.

"The Egyptian Republic of Retired Generals." *Foreign Policy*, May 8, 2012. https://foreignpolicy.com/2012/05/08/the-egyptian-republic-of-retired-gener als. Accessed May 12, 2017.

Abul-Nur, 'Abdul-Muhsen. *Al-Haqiqa 'an Thawrat 23 Yulyu, Mudhakkarat 'Abdul-Muhsen Abul-Nur*. Cairo: al-Hay'a al-Masriyya li-l-Kitab, 2001.

Achcar, Gilbert. *The People Want: A Radical Exploration of the Arab Spring*. Berkley, CA: University of California Press, 2013.

Aguero, Filipe. *Soldiers, Civilians and Democracy: Post-Franco Spain in a Comparative Perspective*. Baltimore, MD: Johns Hopkins University Press, 1995.

al-Atrash, Mansur. *Al-Jil al-Mudan, Sira Dhatiyya*. Beirut: Riad al-Rayes, 2008.

al-Ayubi, Nazih. *Al-Dawla al-Markaziyya fi Masr*. Beirut: Markaz Dirasat al-Wihda al-'Arabiyya, 1989.

al-Baghdadi, 'Abdul-Latif. *Mudhakkarat 'Abdul-Latif al-Baghdadi*, vol. 2. Cairo: Maktab al-Masri al-Hadith, 1977.

al-Baz, Mohammad. *Al-Mushir wa-l-Fariq, al-Malaffat al-Siasiyya li-Tantawi wa-'Annan, Ma'arik al-Ashbah bayna al-Ikhwan wa-l-Jaysh*. Cairo: Kunuz li-l-Tawzi' wa-l-Nashr, 2014.

Al-Mushir, Qissat Su'ud wa-Inhiar Abu Ghazalah. Cairo: Kunuz li-l-Tawzi' wa-l-Nashr, 2007.

al-Bushari, Tareq. *Al-Dimoqratiyya wa-Nizam 23 Yulyu, 1952–1970*. Cairo: Dar al-Shuruq, 2013.

Albrecht, Holger, Aurel Croissant, and Fred H. Lawson (eds.). *Armies and Insurgencies in the Arab Spring*. Philadelphia, PA: University of Pennsylvania Press, 2016.

Albrecht, Holger, and Dorothy Ohl. "Exit, Resistance, Loyalty: Military Behavior during Unrest in Authoritarian Regimes." *Perspectives on Politics* 14, no. 1 (March 2016): 38–52.

Albrecht, Holger, and Dina Bishara. "Back on Horseback: The Military and Political Transformation in Egypt." *Middle East Law and Governance* 3, no. 1–2 (2011): 13–23.

al-Dahamesha, 'Abdallah. *Suria, Mazra'at al-Asad*. Beirut: Dar al-Nawa'ir, 2011.

al-Dib, Fathi. *Abdul Nasser wa-Thawrat Libya*. Cairo: Dar al-Mustaqbal al-'Arabi, 1986.

Alexander, Yonah. "The Politics of Terror." *The Washington Times*, March 11, 1987. www.reaganlibrary.gov/sites/default/files/digitallibrary/smof/publicliaison/green/Box-027/40-219-6927378-027-017-2017.pdf. Accessed June 25, 2018.

al-Finchi, Hanem. "Al-Kashef: Mukalamat Telephone Tahmi Tujjar Mukhaddarat." *Al-Wafd*, April 1, 2011. www.ahram.org.eg/News/857/38/2 16600.aspx. Accessed March 27, 2015.

al-Firzli, Suleiman. *Hurub al-Nasiriyya wa-l-Ba'ath*. Beirut: Naufal, 2016.

al-Gamasy, Mohammad 'Abdul-Ghani. *Mudhakkarat al-Gamasy, Harb October 1973*. San Francisco, CA: Dar Buhuth al-Sharq al-Awsat al-Amirikiyya, 1977.

al-Gawadi, Mohammad. *Qadat al-Shurta al-Masriyya, 1952–2002, Dirasa Tahliliyya wa-Mawsu'at Shakhsiyyat*. Cairo: Madbuli, 2003.

Mudhakkarat Qadat al-'Askariyya al-Masriyya, 1976–1972, fi A'qab al-Naksa. Cairo: Dar al-Khayyal, 2001.

al-Haj 'Ali, Muhannad. "Limadha Yulahiq al-Asad Rijal A'malih." *Al-Modon*, June 1, 2016. www.almodon.com/opinion/2018/6/1/لماذا-يلاحق-الأسد-رجال-أعماله. Accessed June 1, 2018.

al-Haj Salih, Yassin. "The Syrian Shabiha and Their State: Statehood & Participation." Heinrich Böll Stiftung, April 16, 2012. https://lb.boell.org/en/2014/03/03/syrian-shabiha-and-their-state-statehood-participation. Accessed June 18, 2018.

al-Husseini, Dina. "Wuzara' Dakhiliyyat Masr min al-Sadat li-l-Sisi." *Al-Bawaba News*, September 3, 2015. www.albawabhnews.com/1160398. Accessed September 15, 2015.

al-Jundi, Sami. *Al-Ba'ath*. Beirut: Dar al-Nahar, 1969.

'Allam, Fu'ad. *Al-Ikhwan wa-Ana, Min al-Manshiah ila al-Minasah*. Cairo: Akhbar al-Yawm, 1996.

al-Naggar, Ahmad Sayyid. "Madha Yurid al-Gharb min Iqtisad al-Jaysh al-Masri." *Dunia al-Watan*, October 10, 2013. https://pulpit.alwatanvoice.com/content/print/308621.html. Accessed November 27, 2015.

"Iqtisad al-Jaysh bayna al-Tahwil wa-Mantiq Tafkik al-Dawla." *Al-Ahram*, April 12, 2012. www.ahram.org.eg/Archive/866/2012/4/11/4/142891.aspx. Accessed June 10, 2015.

al-Raggal, 'Ali. "Masr: Jihaz al-Dakhiliyya wa-l-Neoliberaliyya." *Al-Safir*, November 10, 2016. http://arabi.assafir.com/Article/5521. Accessed November 10, 2016.

"Al-Tawari' ka-Qanun wa-Ideologia li-l-Hokm fi 'Asr Mubarak." *Al-Safir*, June 2, 2016. http://arabi.assafir.com/Article/25/4984. Accessed June 2, 2016.

"Riwayat Ma Jara fi Masr fi al-Ayyam al-Hasima." *Al-Safir*, April 21, 2016. http://assafir.com/Article/1/489170/RssFeed. Accessed April 21, 2016.

"Alat al-Qatl fi al-Dawla wa-l-Mawja al-Thawriyya al-Qadima." *Al-Safir*, December 31, 2015. http://assafir.com/Article/1/464433/RssFeed. Accessed December 31, 2015.

"Tashaddhi al-Dawla al-Masriyya." *Al-Safir*, October 12, 2015. http://assafir.com/Article/69/461062. Accessed October 12, 2015.

al-Razzaz, Munif. *Al-Tajriba al-Murra*. Beirut: Dar Ghandur li-l-Tiba'a wa-l-Nashr, 1966.

al-Sadat, Anwar. *Al-Bahth 'an al-Dhat, Qissat Hayati*. Cairo: al-Maktab al-Masri al-Hadith, 1979.

al-Safadi, Muta'. *Hizb al-Ba'ath, Ma'sat al-Mawled, Ma'sat al-Nihaya*. Beirut: Dar al-Adab, 1964.

al-Safrani, Ahmad. "Sira' al-Qabila wa-Asrar Maqtal Hasan Shkal." *Libya al-Mustaqbal*, August 7, 2009. http://archive.libya-almostakbal.org/Article s0809/ahmad_assafrani_070809.html. Accessed December 7, 2018.

al-Sayyed, Jalal. *Hezb al-Ba'ath al-'Arabi*. Beirut: Dar al-Nahar, 1973.

al-Sharif, Ashraf. "Kamal al-Din Hussein wa-Wujuh Dawlat Yulu al-Muhafiza." *Mada Masr*, October 1, 2015. www.madamasr.com/ar/opinion/politics. Accessed October 4, 2015.

al-Shazli, Sa'ad al-Din. *Harb October, Mudhakkarat al-Fariq Sa'ad al-Din al-Shazli*. Cairo: Ru'ya li-l-Nashr wa-l-Tawzi', 2011.

al-Wali, Mamduh, and 'Abdul-Nasser, Salemeh. "Tawarrut Ru'assa Amn al-Dawla al-Sabiqayn fi al-Istila' 'ala Aradi." *Al-Ahram*, June 21, 2013. www.ahram.org.eg/News/857/38/216600.aspx. Accessed June 21, 2013.

Anderson, Jack. "Syrians Aiding Heroin Traffic in Bekaa Valley." *The Washington Post*, February 1, 1984. CIA approved for release December 21, 2011, no. RDP90-00965R000100130129-8. www.cia.gov/library/readingroom /docs/CIA-RDP90-00965R000100130129-8.pdf. Accessed May 26, 2018.

"Syrian Factions Challenge Assad for Dominance." *The Washington Post*, July 15, 1983. CIA approved for release April 13, 2012, no. CIA-RDP90 -00965R00010040058-6. www.cia.gov/library/readingroom/docs/CIA-RDP90-00965R000100140058-6.pdf. Accessed May 25, 2018.

Anderson, Lisa. "Libya's Qaddafi: Still in Command?" *Current History* 86 (February 1987): 65–87.

The State and Social Transformation in Tunisia and Libya, 1830–1980. Princeton, NJ: Princeton University Press, 1986.

Aroyan, Nubar. *Diary of a Soldier in the Egyptian Military: A Peek Inside the Egyptian Army*. Bloomington, IN: WestBrow Press, 2012.

Ashour, Omar. "Bullets Beat Ballots: The Arab Uprisings and Civil–Military Relations in Egypt." In *Revisiting the Arab Uprisings: The Politics of a Revolutionary Moment*, edited by Stephane Lacroix and Jean-Pierre Filiu, 45–60. New York: Oxford University Press, 2018.

"Ballots versus Bullets: The Crisis of Civil–Military Relations in Egypt." Brookings, September 3, 2013. www.brookings.edu/articles/ballots-versus-bullets-the-crisis-of-civil-military-relations-in-egypt. Accessed March 20, 2019.

Awad, Marwa. "Special Report: In Egypt's Military, a March for Change." Reuters, April 10, 2012. www.reuters.com/article/us-egypt-army-idUSBRE8390IV20120410. Accessed March 12, 2014.

"Egypt Army Officer Says 15 Others Join Protesters." Reuters, February 11, 2011. www.reuters.com/article/us-egypt-protest-officers/egypt-army-offi cer-says-15-others-join-protesters-idUSTRE71A12V20110211. Accessed June 4, 2013.

"Egypt Army Seeks to Free Tahrir Square for Traffic." Reuters, February 5, 2011. www.reuters.com/article/us-egypt-protests/egypt-army-seeks-to-free-tahrir-square-for-traffic-idUSTRE7141S820110205. Accessed January 5, 2014.

Awad, Marwa, and Dina Zayed. "Army Tries to Limit Cairo Protest Camp Space." Reuters, February 6, 2011. https://uk.reuters.com/article/uk-egypt-

protests-army/army-tries-to-limit-cairo-protest-camp-space-idUKTR
E71527J20110206. Accessed January 16, 2014.

Ayad, Christophe. "Tunisie. La Révolution En Trois Actes. Carthage, la chute."
Libération, February 5, 2011. www.liberation.fr/planete/2011/02/05/carth
age-la-chute_712598. Accessed September 11, 2018.

Bahri, Imad. "Tunisie. Le vrai faux complot de Ben Ali 'Ben 'Ali, Zein al-
'Abidin' contre le général Skik." *Kapitalis*, April 23, 2011. www
.kapitalis.com/politique/3642-tunisie-le-vrai-faux-lcomplotr-de-ben-ali-
contre-legeneral-skik.html. Accessed September 26, 2018.

Baker, Raymond William. *Egypt's Uncertain Revolution under Nasser and Sadat.*
Cambridge, MA: Harvard University Press, 1978.

Balanche, Fabrice. *La région alaouite et le pouvoir syrien.* Paris: Editions Kharthala,
2006.

Bar, Shmuel. "Bashar's Syria: The Regime and Its Strategic Worldview."
Comparative Strategy, no. 25 (2006): 353–345. www.offiziere.ch/wp-
content/uploads/Shmuel_Bar_2.pdf. Accessed May 30, 2018.

Barak, Oren, and Assaf David, "The Arab Security Sector: A New Research
Agenda for a Neglected Topic." *Armed Forces & Society* 36, no. 5 (2010):
804–824.

Barany, Zoltan. *How Armies Respond to Revolutions and Why.* Princeton, NJ:
Princeton University Press, 2016.

"Explaining Military Reponses to Revolutions." Arab Center for Research and
Policy Studies, June 26, 2013. www.dohainstitute.org/en/ResearchAndStu
dies/Pages/Explaining_Military_Responses_to_Revolutions.aspx. Accessed
December 15, 2014.

"Why Most Syrian Officers Remain Loyal to Assad." Arab Center for
Research and Policy Studies, June 17, 2013. www.dohainstitute.org/en/
PoliticalStudies/Pages/Why_Most_Syrian_Officers_Remain_Loyal_to_Ass
ad.aspx. Accessed June 26, 2018.

*The Soldier and the Changing State: Building Democratic Armies in Africa, Asia,
Europe, and the Americas.* Princeton, NJ: Princeton University Press, 2012.

"Comparing the Arab Revolts: The Role of the Military." *Journal of Democracy*
22, no. 4 (October 2011): 24–35.

Democratic Breakdown and the Decline of the Russian Military. Princeton, NJ:
Princeton University Press, 2007.

"Civil–Military Relations in Comparative Perspective: East-Central and
Southeastern Europe." *Political Studies* 41, no. 4 (1993): 594–610.

Barayez, 'Abdul-Fattah. "This Land Is Their Land: Egypt's Military and the
Economy." *Jadaliyya*, January 25, 2016. www.jadaliyya.com/pages/index/2
3671/%E2%80%9Cthis-land-is- their-land%E2%80%9D_egypt%E2%80
%99s-military-and-the. Accessed January 28, 2017.

Bar-Joseph, Uri. *The Angel: The Egyptian Spy Who Saved Israel.* New York:
HarperCollins, 2016.

Barraca, Steven. "Military Coups in the Post-Cold War Era: Pakistan, Ecuador,
and Venezuela." *Third World Quarterly* 28, no. 1 (2007): 137–154.

Barthe, Benjamin. "Ces Oligarques Syriens qui Tiennent à bout de Bras le
Regime Assad." *Le Monde*, May 30, 2014. www.lemonde.fr/international/a

rticle/2014/05/30/ces-oligarques-syriens-qui-tiennent-a-bout-de-bras-le-reg
ime-assad_4429096_3210.html. Accessed May 30, 2018.

Batatu, Hanna. *Syria's Peasantry, the Descendants of Its Lesser Rural Notables, and Their Politics*. Princeton, NJ: Princeton University Press, 1999.

"Some Observations on the Social Roots of Syria's Ruling, Military Group and the Causes for Its Dominance." *Middle East Journal* 35, no. 3 (Summer 1981): 331–344.

BBC News. "Top Yemeni General, Ali Mohsen, Backs Opposition." March 21, 2011. www.bbc.com/news/world-middle-east-12804552. Accessed March 24, 2014.

"Egypt Protests: Curfew Defied in Cairo and Other Cities." January 29, 2011. www.bbc.com/news/world-middle-east-12314799. Accessed May 12, 2013.

Army Officers in Arab Politics and Society. New York: Praeger, 1970.

Beau, Nicolas, and Jean-Pierre Tuquoi. *Notre Ami Ben Ali "Ben 'Ali, Zein al-'Abidin," L'envers du Miracle Tunisien*. Paris: La Découverte, 2011.

Beau, Nicolas, and Catherine Graciet. *La Régente de Carthage, Main Basse Sur La Tunisie*. Paris: La Découverte, 2009.

Beecher, William. "Syrians Are Said to Suspend Terror Role." *Boston Globe*, February 1, 1987. CIA approved for release December 21, 2011, no. CIA-RDP90-00965R000100420001-7. www.cia.gov/library/readingroom/docs/CIA-RDP90-00965R000100420001-7.pdf. Accessed May 28, 2018.

Be'eri, Eliezer. "The Waning of the Military Coup in Arab Politics." *Middle Easter Studies* 18, no. 1 (January 1982): 69–128.

Belkin, Aaron, and Evan Schofer. "Coup Risk, Counterbalancing, and International Conflict." *Security Studies* 14, no. 1 (2005): 140–177.

Bellin, Eva. "The Puzzle of Democratic Divergence in the Arab World: Theory Confronts Experience in Egypt and Tunisia." *Political Science Quarterly* 133, no.3 (Fall 2018): 435–474.

"Reconsidering the Robustness of Authoritarianism in the Middle East: Lessons from the Arab Spring." *Comparative Politics* 44, no. 2 (2012): 127–149.

Belkhodja, Abdelaziz, and Tarak Cheikhrouhou. *14 Janvier, L'Enquete*. Tunis: Apollonia, 2013.

Benadad, Hassan. "Le 'Hirak' Algérien Gagne la Citadelle De L'Armée." *Kiosque 360*, February 18, 2019. http://fr.le360.ma/politique/le-hirak-algerien-gagne-la-citadelle-de-larmee-184362. Accessed March 30, 2019.

Ben, Ali. "Ben 'Ali, Zein al-'Abidin," Leila. *Ma Vérité*. Paris: Edition du Moment, 2012.

Ben-Kraiem, Boubaker. *Naissance d'une armée nationale, la promotion Bourguiba*. Tunis: Maison d'édition de Tunis, 2013.

Berridge, W. J. *Civilian Uprisings in Modern Sudan: The 'Khartoum Springs' of 1964 and 1985*. New York: Bloomsbury Academic, 2015.

Beshara, 'Azmi. *Suria: Darb al-Alam, Muhawala fi al-Tarikh al-Rahin*. Doha: al-Markaz al-'Arabi li-l-Abhath wa-Dirasat al-Siasat, 2013.

Bhalla, Rheva. "Making Sense of the Syrian Uprising." Stratfor, May 5, 2011. https://worldview.stratfor.com/article/making-sense-syrian-crisis-0. Accessed June 20, 2018.

Bienen, Henry (ed.). *The Military Intervenes: Case Studies in Political Development.* New York: Russel Sage Foundation, 1968.

Binnendijk, Anika Locke, and Ivan Marovic. "Power and Persuasion: Nonviolent Strategies to Influence State Security Forces in Serbia(2000) and Ukraine (2004)." *Communist and Post-Communist Studies* 39, no. 3 (2006): 411–429.

Black, Ian. "Libya: Defections Leave Muammar Gaddafi Isolated in Tripoli Bolthole." *The Guardian*, February 23, 2011. www.theguardian.com/world/2011/feb/23/muammar-gaddafi-libya-tripoli-uprising. Accessed December 15, 2018.

Black, Ian, Jack Shenker, and Chris McGreal. "Egypt Set for Mass Protest as Army Rules Out Force." *The Guardian*, January 31, 2011. www .theguardian.com/world/2011/jan/31/egyptian-army-pledges-no-force. Accessed June 15, 2013.

Blair, Edmund, and Samia Nakhoul. "Egypt Protests Topple Mubarak after 18 Days." Reuters, February 10, 2011. www.reuters.com/article/us-egypt/egyp t-protests-topple-mubarak-after-18-days-idUSTRE70O3UW20110211. Accessed November 5, 2014.

Blumenthal, Sidney. "Intel Report and Options: What Really Happened and What Should Happen Now." WikiLeaks, February 12, 2011. https://wiki leaks.org/clinton-emails/emailid/13117. Accessed April 5, 2016.

Borshchevskaya, Anna. "Sponsored Corruption and Neglected Reform in Syria." *Middle East Quarterly* 17, no. 3 (Summer 2010). www.meforum.org/articles/2010/sponsored-corruption-and-neglected-reform-in-syria. Accessed June 1, 2018.

Bou Nassif, Hicham. "Coups and Nascent Democracies: The Military and Egypt's Failed Consolidation." *Democratization* 24, no. 1 (January 2017): 157–174.

"Generals and Autocrats: How Coup-Proofing Predetermined the Military Elite's Behavior in the Arab Spring." *Political Science Quarterly* 130, no. 2 (2015): 245–275.

"A Military Besieged: The Armed Forces, the Police and the Party in Ben Ali's Tunisia, 1987–2011." *International Journal of Middle East Studies* 47, no. 1 (February 2015): 65–87.

"Second-Class: The Grievances of Sunni Officers in the Syrian Armed Forces." *Journal of Strategic Studies* 38, no. 5 (August 2015): 626–649.

"Wedded to Mubarak: The Second Career and Financial Rewards of Egypt's Military Elite from 1981 till 2011." *The Middle East Journal* 67, no. 1 (Winter 2013): 509–530.

Boursali, Noura. *Bourguiba A l'Epreuve De La Democratie.* Tunis: Samed éditions, 2012.

Boyne, Sean. "Assad Purges Security Chiefs to Smooth the Way for Succession." *Jane's Intelligence Review* 11, no. 6 (June 1999): 4.

Bratton, Michael, and Nicolas van de Walle. *Democratic Experiments in Africa: Regime Transitions in Comparative Perspective.* New York: Cambridge University Press, 1997.

Brooks, Risa. "Abandoned at the Palace: Why the Tunisian Military Defected from the Ben Ali 'Ben 'Ali, Zein al-'Abidin' Regime in January 2011." *Journal of Strategic Studies* 36, no. 2 (2013): 205–220.

The Civil–Military Politics of Strategic Assessment. Princeton, NJ: Princeton University Press, 2008.

"An Autocracy at War: Explaining Egypt's Military Effectiveness, 1967 and 1973." *Security Studies* 15, no. 3 (2006): 396–430.

"Political–Military Relations and the Stability of Arab Regimes." Adelphi paper 324, International Institute for Strategic Studies. London: Oxford University Press, 1998.

Brown, Cameron S., Christopher J. Fariss, and R. Blake McMahon. "Recouping after Coup- Proofing: Compromised Military Effective and Strategic Substitution." *International Relations* 42, no. 1 (2016): 1–30.

Brownlee, Jason. "Peace before Freedom: Diplomacy and Repression in Sadat's Egypt." *Political Science Quarterly* 126, no. 4 (Winter 2011): 641–668.

"The Heir Apparency of Gamal Mubarak." *Arab Studies Journal* 15/16, no. 2/1 (Fall 2007/Spring 2008): 36–56.

Bruce, James. "Changes in the Syrian High Command." *Jane's Intelligence Review* 7, no. 3 (1995): 126–128.

Bumiller, Elisabeth. "Egypt Stability Hinges on a Divided Military." *The New York Times*, February 5, 2011. www.nytimes.com/2011/02/06/world/middleeast/06military.html. Accessed February 12, 2015.

Camau, Michel, and Vincent Geisser. *Le Syndrome Autoritaire: Politique en Tunisie de Bourguiba à Ben Ali "Ben 'Ali, Zein al-'Abidin."* Paris: Presses De Science Po, 2003.

Campbell, Kirk S. "Civil–Military Relations and Political Liberalization: A Comparative Study of the Military's Corporateness and Political Values in Egypt, Syria, Turkey, and Pakistan." PhD diss., George Washington University, 2009.

Casey, Nicholas. "Venezuelan Opposition Leader Steps Up Pressure, but Maduro Holds On." *The New York Times*, April 30, 2019. www .nytimes.com/2019/04/30/world/americas/venezuela-guaido-maduro.html? action=click&module=Top%20Stories&pgtype=Homepage.   Accessed April 30, 2019.

Casey, Nicholas, and Anna Vanessa Herrero. "As Maduro's Venezuela Rips Apart, So Does His Military." *The New York Times*, August 8, 2017. www .nytimes.com/2017/08/08/world/americas/nicolas-maduro-venezuela-mili tary.html?smid=fb-share&_r=0. Accessed August 10, 2017.

Cassandra. "The Impending Crisis in Egypt." *Middle East Journal* 49, no. 1 (Winter 1995): 9–27.

Central Intelligence Agency. "Syria: Facing the Economic Constraints of the 1990s." Document RDP90T00100R000500760001-5. Approved for release March 13, 2014. www.cia.gov/library/readingroom/docs/CIA-RDP90T00100R000500760001-5.pdf. Accessed May 28, 2018.

"Syria's Elite Military Unit: Key to Stability and Succession." Document RDP88T00096R000500590001-3. Approved for release January 9, 2012. www .cia.gov/library/readingroom/docs/CIA-RDP88T00096R000500590001-3.pdf. Accessed June 18, 2018.

"Syria: Scenarios of Dramatic Political Change." Document RDP86t01017-r000100770001-5. Approved for release February 15, 2011. www.cia.gov/

library/readingroom/document/cia-rdp86t01017r000100770001-5.   Accessed
June 12, 2018.

"Syria: The Succession Struggle and Rif'at's Prospects." Document
RDP85T00314R000200140002-4. Approved for release January 31, 2011.
www.cia.gov/library/readingroom/docs/CIA-RDP85T00314
R000200140002-4.pdf. Accessed June 5, 2018.

"International Narcotics Development." Document RDP7900912A00180001
0017-2.A. Approved for release May 12, 2009. www.cia.gov/library/readin
groom/docs/CIA-RDP79T00912A001800010017-2.pdf. Accessed May 26,
2018.

"Syria without Assad: Succession Politics." Document RDP80T00634A0001
0052-5. Approved for release May 25, 2006. www.cia.gov/library/readin
groom/docs/CIA-RDP80T00634A000400010052-5.pdf. Accessed May 26,
2018.

"Asad's Domestic Position." Document RDP85T00353R000100270005-
25X1. Approved for release September 29, 2003. www.cia.gov/library/read
ingroom/docs/CIA-RDP85T00353R000100270005-2.pdf. Accessed June 25,
2018.

Chalabi, Ahmad, and Yosri al-Badri. "Al-Dawla Tastarid 178 Malioun Jineih fi
Fasad al-Dakhiliyya." *Egypt Independent*, January 28, 2016. www
.almasryalyoum.com/news/details/882701. Accessed January 28, 2016.

Chandra, Siddharth, and Douglas Anton Kammen. "Generating Reforms and
Reforming Generations: Military Politics in Indonesia's Democratic
Transition and Consolidation." *World Politics* 55, no. 1 (October 2002):
96–136.

Charbel, Ghassan. *Fi Khaymat al-Qaddhafi, Mu'ammar, Rifaq al-'Aqid
Yakchufuun Khabaya 'Ahdih*. Beirut: Riad El-Rayyes Book, 2013.

Chehabi, H. E., and Juan J. Linz. "A Theory of Sultanism 2: Genesis and Demise
of Sultanistic Regimes." In *Sultanistic Regimes*, edited by H. E. Chehabi and
Juan J. Linz, 26–48. Baltimore, MD: Johns Hopkins University Press, 1998.

Chelly, Rafik. *Le Syndrome De Carthage des Présidents Habib Bourguiba et Zine El
Abidine Ben Ali "Ben 'Ali, Zein al-'Abidin."* Tunis: Imprimerie Graphique Du
Centre, 2012.

Chenoweth, Erica, and Maria Stephan. *Why Civil Resistance Works: The Strategic
Logic of Nonviolent Conflict*. New York: Columbia University Press. 2011.

Chivvis, Christopher S. *Toppling Qaddafi: Libya and the Limits of Liberal
Intervention*. New York: Cambridge University Press, 2014.

Chouet, Alain. "Impact of Wielding Power on 'AlawiCohesiveness.'" *Maghreb-
Machrek*, no. 147 (January–March 1995): 5.

Chorin, Ethan. *Exit the Colonel: The Hidden History of The Libyan Revolution*.
New York: PublicAffairs, 2012.

Clement, Henry M., and Robert Springborg. "A Tunisian Solution for Egypt's
Military: Why Egypt's Military Will Not Be Able to Govern." *Foreign Affairs*,
February 21, 2011. www.foreignaffairs.com/articles/tunisia/2011–02-21/tu
nisian-solution-egypt-s-military. Accessed August 7, 2014.

Colton, Timothy J. *Commissars, Commanders, and Civilian Authority: The Structure
of Soviet Military Politics*. Cambridge, MA: Harvard University Press, 1979.

Cook, Steven A. *The Struggle for Egypt: From Nasser to Tahrir Square*. New York: Oxford University Press, 2012.

"Five Things You Need to Know about the Egyptian Armed Forces." Council on Foreign Relations, January 31, 2011. www.cfr.org/blog/five-things-you-need-know-about-egyptian-armed-forces. Accessed February 5, 2019.

Ruling but Not Governing: The Military and Political Development in Egypt, Algeria, and Turkey. Baltimore, MD: Johns Hopkins University Press, 2007.

Cooper, Andrew Scott. *The Fall of Heaven: The Pahlavis and the Final Days of Imperial Iran*. New York: Picador, 2018.

Cooper, Mark N. "The Demilitarization of the Egyptian Cabinet." *International Journal of Middle East Studies* 14, no. 2 (May 1982): 203–225.

Cordesman, Anthony H. "If Mubarak Leaves: The Role of the Egyptian Military." Center for Strategic and International Studies, February 10, 2011. www.csis.org/analysis/if-mubarak-leaves-role-egyptian-military. Accessed May 15, 2014.

"Corruption in Tunisia: What's Yours Is Mine." WikiLeaks, US embassy report ID: 08TUNIS679_a, June 23, 2008. https://wikileaks.org/plusd/cables/08T UNIS679_a.html. Accessed April 5, 2016.

Croissant, Aurel, David Kuehn, and Tanja Eschenauer. "The 'Dictator's Endgame': Explaining Military Behavior in Nonviolent Anti-incumbent Mass Protests." *Democracy and Security* 14, no.2 (2018): 174–199.

Croissant, Aurel, and Tobias Selge. "Should I Stay or Should I Go? Comparing Military (Non-) Cooperation during Authoritarian Regime Crises in the Arab World and Asia." In *Armies and Insurgencies in the Arab Spring*, edited by Holger Albrecht, Aurel Croissant, and Fred H. Lawson, 97–124. Philadelphia, PA: University of Pennsylvania Press, 2016.

Crouch, Harold. *The Army and Politics in Indonesia*. Singapore: Equinox Publishing, 2007.

Dean, Lucy (ed.). *The Middle East and North Africa 2004*. New York: Europa Publications, 2004.

De Atkine, Norvell B. "Why Arabs Lose Wars." *Middle East Quarterly* 6, no. 4 (December 1999). www.meforum.org/441/why-arabs-lose-wars. Accessed September 11, 2014.

De Bruin, Erica. "Preventing Coups- d'état: How Counterbalancing Works." *Journal of Conflict Resolution* 62, no. 7 (March 2017): 1433–1458.

"Coup-Proofing for Dummies: The Benefits of Following the Maliki Playbook." *Foreign Affairs*, July 27, 2014. www.foreignaffairs.com/articles/ir aq/2014-07-27/coup-proofing-dummies. Accessed July 7, 2014.

Debs, Alexander, and Henk E. Goemans. "Regime Type, the Fate of Leaders, and War." *American Political Science Review* 104, no. 3 (August 2010): 430–445.

Decalo, Samuel. *Coups and Army Rule in Africa*. New Haven, CT: Yale University Press, 1990.

Dekmejian, Richard H. "Egypt and Turkey: The Military in the Background." In *Soldiers, Peasants, and Bureaucrats: Civil–Military Relations in Communist and Modernizing Societies*, edited by Roman Kolkowicz and Andrzej Korbonski, 28–51. London: George Allen & Unwin, 1982.

Egypt under Nasir: A Study in Political Dynamics. London: Hodder & Stoughton, 1972.

Demirel, Tanel. "Lessons of Military Regimes and Democracy: The Turkish Case in a Comparative Perspective." *Armed Forces & Society* 31, no. 2 (Winter 2005): 245–271.

Dix, Robert. "The Breakdown of Authoritarian Regimes." *The Western Political Science Quarterly* 35, no. 4 (December 1982): 554–573.

Droz-Vincent, Philippe. "'Prospects for 'Democratic Control of the Armed Forces'? Comparative Insights and Lessons for the Arab World in Transition." *Armed Forces & Society* 40, no. 4 (2014): 696–723.

"From Fighting Formal Wars to Maintaining Civil Peace." *International Journal of Middle East Studies* 43, no. 3 (August 2011): 392–394.

Drysdale, Alasdair. "The Succession Question in Syria." *Middle East Journal* 39, no. 2 (Spring 1985): 246–257.

"Ethnicity in the Syrian Officer Corps: A Conceptualization." *Civilisations* 29, no. 3/4 (1979): 359–374.

"Egyptian Revolution Cost At Least 846 Lives." CBS News, April 19, 2011. www.cbsnews.com/news/egyptian-revolution-cost-at-least-846-lives. Accessed June 15, 2013.

Eisenstadt, Michael. "Who Rules Syria? Bashar al-Asad and the Alawi Barons." Policy Watch, report no. 472. Washington Institute for Near East Policy, June 21, 2000. www.washingtoninstitute.org/policy-analysis/view/who-rules-syria-bashar-al-asad-and-the-alawi-barons. Accessed June 22, 2018.

"Syria's Defense Companies: Profile of a Praetorian Unit." Unpublished paper, 1984.

El-Kikhia, Mansour O. *Libya's Qaddafi: The Politics of Contradiction.* Gainesville, FL: University Press of Florida, 1997.

El-Materi, Moncef. *De Saint-Cyr au Peleton d'Execution de Bourguiba.* Tunis: Arabesques, 2014.

El-Shimy, Yasser. "Unveiling the Gun: Why Praetorian Armies Decide to Rule, the Case of Egypt (2011–2013)." PhD diss., Boston University, 2016.

European Union. *Official Journal of the European Union* 54. Decision 2011/273/CFSP, Annex of articles I and IV, June 24, 2011.

Fadl, Bilal. "Al-Sadat wa-Ma Adraka Ma al-Sadat," part 4. *Al-'Arabi al-Jadid,* December 30, 2015. www.alaraby.co.uk/opinion/2015/12/30/ السادات-وما-أدراك-ما-السادات-4. Accessed January 27, 2016.

Fahmi, Faruq. *I'tirafat Shams Badran wa-Mu'amarat 67.* Cairo: Mu'assasat Amun al-Haditha, 1989.

Farcau, Bruce W. *The Transition to Democracy in Latin America: The Role of the Military.* Westport, CT: Praeger, 1996.

The Coup Tactics in the Seizure of Power. Westport, CT: Praeger, 1994.

Faruq, 'Abdul-Khaleq. *Iqtisadiyyat al-Fasad fi Masr: Kayfa Jara Ifsad Masr wa-l-Masriyyin, 1974–2010.* Cairo: al-Shorooq International Bookshop, 2010.

Judhur al-Fasad al-Idari fi Masr, Bi'at al-'Amal wa-Siasat al-Ujur wa-l-Murattabat fi Masr, 1963–2002. Cairo: Dar al-Shuruq, 2008.

Fawzi, Mohammad. *Al-Nabawi Isma'il wa-Juzur Hadithat al-Minassa.* Cairo: Dar al-Nashr Haitieh, 1991.

Harb al-Sanawat al-Thalath, 1967–1970, Mudhakkarat al-Fariq, Mohammad Fawzi Wazir al-Harbiyya al-Asbaq. Cairo: Dar al-Wihda, 1988.

Feaver, Peter D. *Armed Servants: Agency, Oversight, and Civil–Military Relations.* Cambridge, MA: Harvard University Press, 2003.

Ferris, Jesse. *Nasser's Gamble: How Intervention in Yemen Caused the Six-Day War and the Decline of Egyptian Power.* Princeton, NJ: Princeton University Press, 2013.

Fikri, Amira. *Al-Mushir Mohammad 'Abdul-Halim Abu Ghazalah, Masirat Hayat.* Cairo: Dar al-Jumhuriyya, 2010.

Finer, Samuel E. *The Man on Horseback: The Role of the Military in Politics.* Boulder, CO: Westview Press, 2006.

Fisk, Robert. "As Mubarak Clings On . . . What Now for Egypt." *The Independent,* February 11, 2011. www.independent.co.uk/voices/commentators/fisk/robe rt-fisk-as-mubarak-clings-on-what-now-for-egypt-2211287.html. Accessed June 5, 2013.

Frisch, Hillel. "The Egyptian Army and Egypt's 'Spring.'" *Journal of Strategic Studies* 36, no. 2 (April 2013): 180–204.

"Guns and Butter in the Egyptian Army." *Middle East Review of International Affairs* 5, no. 2 (Summer 2001): 1–12.

Galey, Patrick. "Why the Egyptian Military Fears a Captains' Revolt." *Foreign Policy,* February 16, 2012. http://foreignpolicy.com/2012/02/16/why-the-egyptian-military-fears-a- captains-revolt/. Accessed November 28, 2014.

"Soldiers of Conscience." *Foreign Policy,* January 24, 2011. https://foreignpo licy.com/2012/01/24/soldiers-of-conscience/. Accessed March 15, 2019.

Gallad, Magdi (ed.). *Mushir al-Nasr, Mudhakkarat Ahmad Isma'el, Wazir al-Harbiyya fi Ma'rakat October 1973.* Cairo: Dar Nahdat Masr, 2013.

Gambill, Gary C. "The Political Obstacles to Economic Reform in Syria." *Middle East Intelligence Bulletin* 3, no. 7 (July 2011). www.shrc.org/en/?p=19864. Accessed May 26, 2017.

"Syria after Lebanon: Hooked on Lebanon." *The Middle East Quarterly* 12, no. 4 (Fall 2005). www.meforum.org/articles/2005/syria-after-lebanon-hooked-on-lebanon. Accessed June 22, 2018.

Garside, Juliette, and David Pegg. "Mossack Fonseca Serviced Assad Cousin's Firms Despite Syria Corruption Fears." *The Guardian,* April 5, 2016. www .theguardian.com/news/2016/apr/05/mossack-fonseca-panama-papers-rami -makhlouf-syria-assad-hsbc. Accessed May 29, 2016.

Gaub, Florence. *Guardians of the Arab State: When Militaries Intervene in Politics, from Iraq to Mauritania.* London: Hurst & Company, 2017.

"An Unhappy Marriage: Civil–Military Relations in Post-Saddam Iraq." Carnegie Endowment for International Peace, January 13, 2016. http://car negieendowment.org/2016/01/13/unhappy-marriage-civil-military-relations -in-post-saddam-iraq/im00. Accessed February 20, 2016.

"The Libyan Armed Forces between Coup-Proofing and Repression." *Journal of Strategic Studies* 36, no. 2 (2013): 221–244.

Gause III, F. Gregory. "Why Middle East Studies Missed the Arab Spring: The Myth of Authoritarian Stability." *Foreign Affairs* 90, no.4 (July/August 2011): 81–90.

Geddes, Barbara. "Why Parties and Elections in Authoritarian Regimes?" Unpublished manuscript, University of California, Los Angeles, 2006.

"What Do We Know about Democratization after Twenty Years." *Annual Review of Political Science* 2 (June 1999): 115–144.

Geddes, Barbara, Joseph Wright, and Erica Frantz. "Autocratic Breakdowns and Regime Transitions: A New Data Set." *Perspectives on Politics* 12, no. 2 (June 2014): 313–331.

Geddes, Barbara, Erica Frantz, and Joseph Wright. "Military Rule." *Annual Review of Political Science* 17 (May 2014): 147–162.

Ghadabian, Najib. "The New Asad: Dynamics of Continuity and Change in Syria." *Middle East Journal* 55, no. 4 (Autumn 2001): 624–641.

Gilsinan, Kathy. "How Syria's Uprising Spawned a Jihad." *The Atlantic*, March 16, 2016. www.theatlantic.com/international/archive/2016/03/syria-civil-war-five-years/474006/. Accessed July 11, 2018.

Goemans, Henk E. "Which Way Out? The Manner and Consequences of Losing Office." *Journal of Conflict Resolution* 52, no. 6 (December 2008): 771–794.

Goemans, Henk E., Kristian Skrede Gleditsch, and Giacomo Chiozza. "Introducing Archigos: A Dataset of Political Leaders." *Journal of Peace Research* 46, no. 2 (March 2009): 269–283.

Geisser, Vincent, and Abir Krefa. "L'uniforme ne fait plus le régime, les militaires arabes face aux revolutions." *Revue Internationale Stratégique* 3, no. 83 (2011): 93–102.

Greitens, Sheena Chestnut. *Dictators and Their Secret Police: Coercive Institutions and State Violence*. New York: Cambridge University Press, 2016.

Grewal, Sharan. "A Quiet Revolution: The Tunisian Military after Ben Ali 'Ben ʿAli, Zein al-ʿAbidin.'" Carnegie Regional Insight, February 24, 2016. https://carnegieendowment.org/2016/02/24/quiet-revolution-tunisian-military-after-ben-ali-pub-62780. Accessed October 23, 2018.

"To Coup or Not to Coup: The Tunisian Military in 2013." Paper presented at the 2016 annual meeting for the Middle East Studies Association.

Grieb, Kenneth J. "The Guatemalan Military and the Revolution of 1944." *The Americas* 32, no. 4 (April 1976): 524–543.

Grimaud, Nicole. *La Tunisie a la recherche de sa securité*. Paris: Presses Universitaires de France, 1995.

Gubser, Peter. "Minorities in Power: The Alawites of Syria." In *The Political Role of Minority Groups in the Middle East*, edited by R. D. McLaurin, 37–41. New York: Praeger, 1979.

Gurr, Ted Robert. *Why Men Rebel*. Princeton, NJ: Princeton University Press, 1970.

Haddad, Bassam. *Business Networks in Syria: The Political Economy of Authoritarian Resilience*. Stanford, CA: Stanford University Press, 2012.

"Change and Stasis in Syria: One Step Forward." *Middle East Report* 213, Millennial Middle East: Changing Orders, Shifting Borders (Winter 1999): 23–27.

"The Economic Price of Regime Security: Mistrust, State-Business Networks, and Economic Stagnation in Syria, 1986–2000." PhD diss., Georgetown University, 2002.

Haddad, Said. "The Role of the Libyan Army in the Revolt against Gaddafi's Regime." Al Jazeera Center for Studies, March 16, 2011.

Hammad, 'Abdul-'Azim. "Alladhin idha Hakamu Dawla Afsaduha: Wahm al-Istiqrar wa-l-Injaz fi Dawlat Yulyu." *Mada Masr*, September 2, 2016. https://madamasr.com/ar/2016/09/02/opinion/u/مم-1-وها دوهسافأ-ةلود-اومكحاذإ-نيذلا/الاس. Accessed September 2, 2016.

Al-Thawra al-Ta'iha, Sira' al-Khudha, wa-l-Lihia, wa-l-Midan, Ru'yat Shahid 'Ayan. Cairo: al-Mahrousa, 2013.

Hammad, Jamal. *Asrar Thawrat 23 Yulyu*, vol. 2. Cairo: Dar al-'Ulum, 2011.

"Qissat al-Sira' 'ala al-Sulta bayna Mohammad Neguib wa-'Abdul Nasser." In *Man Yaktob Tarik Thawrat Yulyu, al-Qadiyya wa-l-Shahadat*, edited by Faruq Juaida. Cairo: Dar al-Shuruq, 2009.

Hammuda, 'Adel. *Ightial Ra'is, bi-l-Watha'iq, Asrar Ightial Anwar al-Sadat*. Cairo: Dar Iqra', 1985.

Hamrush, Ahmad. *Thawrat Yulyu*. Cairo: al-Hay'a al-Markaziyya li-l-Kitab, 1992.

Hani Metwalli, Mohammad (Major General). Interview on *Al-Masry al-Yawm*, April 10, 2016. www.almasryalyoum.com/news/details/926329. Accessed April 10, 2016.

Hanlon, Querine. "Security Sector Reform in Tunisia, a Year after the Jasmine Revolution." United States Institute of Peace, report no. 304, March 2012. www.usip.org/sites/default/files/SR304.pdf. Accessed April 5, 2016.

Harb, Imad. "The Egyptian Military in Politics: Disengagement or Accommodation." *Middle East Journal* 57, no. 2 (Spring 2003): 269–290.

Hasan 'Ali, Kamal. *Mashawir al-'Omr fi al-Harb wa-l-Mukhabarat wa-l-Siasa, Asrar wa-Khafaya 70 Aman min 'Omr Masr*. Cairo: Dar al-Shuruq, 1994.

Hasan, Yusuf Fadl. "The Sudanese Revolution of October 1964." *Journal of Modern African Studies* 5, no. 4 (1967): 491–509.

Hashem, Ahmad. "Al-Jaysh wa-l-Dawla fi Masr: Tashabok al-'Askari wa-l-Madani." Al Jazeera Center for Strategic Studies, June 1, 2015. http://studies.aljazeera.net/ar/reports/2015/05/201553111285692330.html. Accessed July 7, 2015.

Hashim, Ahmed S. "'The Man on Horseback': The Role of the Military in the Arab Revolutions and in Their Aftermaths, 2011–2015." *Middle East Perspectives* 7 (October 2015): 1–32. www.researchgate.net/publication/313739034_The_Man_on_Horseback_The_Role_of_the_Military_in_the_Arab_Revolutions_and_in_their_Aftermaths.

"The Egyptian Military, Part Two: From Mubarak Onward." *Middle East Policy Council* 18, no. 4 (Winter 2011). www.mepc.org/egyptian-military-part-two-mubarak-onward. Accessed March 3, 2015.

"The Egyptian Military, Part One: From the Ottomans through Sadat." *Middle East Policy Council* 18, no. 3 (Fall 2011). www.mepc.org/journal/middle-east-policy-archives/egyptian-military-part-one-ottomans-through-sadat. Accessed April 16, 2015.

Hedges, Chris. "Qaddafi Reported to Quash Army Revolt." *The New York Times*, October 23, 1993. www.nytimes.com/1993/10/23/world/qaddafi-reported-to-quash-army-revolt.html. Accessed December 2, 2018.

Heikal, Mohammad Hasanein. *Kharif al-Ghadab, Qissat Bidayat wa-Nihayat 'Asr Anwar al-Sadat.* Cairo: Markaz al-Ahram li-l-Tarjama wa-l-Nashr, 1988.

Heinecken, Lindy. "Discontent within the Ranks? Officers' Attitudes toward Military Employment and Representation – A Four-Country Comparative Study." *Armed Forces & Society* 35, no. 3 (April 2009): 477–500.

Henry, Clement, and Robert Springborg. "The Tunisian Army: Defending the Beachhead of Democracy in the Arab World." *Huffpost*, January 26, 2011. www.huffingtonpost.com/clement-m-henry/the-tunisian-army-defen di_b_814254.html. Accessed August 25, 2018.

Herspring, Dale R., and Ivan Volgyes. *Civil–Military Relations in Communist Systems.* Boulder, CO: Westview Press, 1978.

Hessler, Peter. "Egypt's Failed Revolution." *The New Yorker*, January 2, 2017. www.newyorker.com/magazine/2017/01/02/egypts-failed-revolution. Accessed January 2, 2017.

Hibou, Béatrice. *The Force of Obedience: The Political Economy of Repression in Tunis.* Malden MA: Polity, 2011.

Hill, Evan, and Muhammad Mansour. "Egypt's Army Took Part in Torture and Killings during Revolution, Report Shows." *The Guardian*, April 10, 2013. www.theguardian.com/world/2013/apr/10/egypt-army-torture-killings-revolution. Accessed January 18, 2014.

Hinnebusch, Raymond A. "Understanding Regime Divergence in the Post-uprising Arab State." *Journal of Historical Sociology* 31, no. 1 (2018): 42–43. https://onlinelibrary.wiley.com/doi/pdf/10.1111/johs.12190. Accessed July 3, 2018.

   "Syria: From 'Authoritarian Upgrading' to Revolution." *International Affairs* 88, no. 1 (January 2012): 95–113.

   Egyptian Politics under Sadat: The Post-populist Development of an Authoritarian-Modernizing State. Boulder, CO: Lynne Rienner Publishers, 1988.

   "Libya: Personalistic Leadership of a Populist Revolution." In *Political Elites in Arab North Africa, Morocco, Algeria, Tunisia, Libya, and Egypt*, edited by I. William Zartman, Mark A. Tessler, John P. Entelis, Russel A. Stone, Raymond A. Hinnebusch, and Shahrough Akhavi, 177–222. New York: Longman, 1982.

   "Egypt under Sadat: Elites, Power Structure, and Political Change in a Post-populist State." *Social Problems* 28, no. 4 (April 1981): 442–464.

Hlaing, Kyaw Yin. "Setting Rules for Survival: Why the Burmese Military Regime Survives in an Age of Democratization." *The Pacific Review* 22, no. 3 (July 2009): 271–291.

Holliday, Joseph. "The Assad Regime: From Counterinsurgency to Civil War." *Middle East Security* 8, Institute for the Study of War (March 2013): 7–59.

   "The Struggle for Syria in 2011: An Operational and Regional Analysis." *Middle East Security* 2, Institute for the Study of War (December 2011): 1–29.

Human Rights Watch. "Syria: 'By All Means Necessary!' Individual and Command Responsibility for Crimes Against Humanity in Syria," December 2011. www.hrw.org/sites/default/files/reports/syria1211webw cover_0.pdf. Accessed June 12, 2014.

"Syria: We've Never Seen Such Horror, Crimes against Humanity by Syrian Security Forces." New York: Human Rights Watch, June 2011.

"Egypt: Investigate Arrests of Activists, Journalists." February 9, 2011. www .hrw.org/news/2011/02/09/egypt-investigate-arrests-activists-journalists. Accessed January 12, 2014.

Hunter, Wendy. *Eroding Military Influence in Brazil: Politicians against Soldiers.* Chapel Hill, NC: University of North Carolina Press, 1997.

Huntington, Samuel. *The Third Wave: Democratization in the Late Twentieth Century.* Norman, OK: University of Oklahoma Press, 1991.

The Soldier and the State: The Theory and Politics of Civil–Military Relations. New York: Vintage Books, 1957.

Hurewitz, J. C. *Middle East Politics: The Military Dimension.* New York: Praeger, 1969.

Husni, Mohammad. "Durus Mustafada min al-Tasribat . . . Mujaz Hal al-Dawla al-Masriyya." *Noon Post,* December 6, 2014. www.noonpost.org/content/4 595. Accessed December 10, 2014.

Huweidi, Amine. *Al-Foras al-Daʾiʾa, al-Qararat al-Hasima fi Harbay al-Istinzaf wa-October.* Beirut: al-Sharika al-ʿArabiyya li-l-Tawziʿ wa-l-Nashr, 1992.

Imam, ʿAbdallah. *Al-Fariq Mohammad Fawzi, al-Naksa, al-Istinzaf, al-Sijn.* Cairo: Dar al-Khayyal, 2001.

Salah Nasr Yatadhakkar, al-Thawra, al-Mukhabarat, al-Naksa. Cairo: Dar al-Khayyal, 1999.

Haqiqat al-Sadat. Cairo: Muʾassassat Rose al-Youssef li-l-Sahafa wa-l-Tibaʿa wa-l-Nashr, 1986.

International Crisis Group. "Yemen's Military-Security Reform: Seeds of New Conflict?" Middle East and North Africa report no. 139. April 4, 2013. https://d2071andvip0wj.cloudfront.net/yemens-military-security-reform-seeds-of-new-conflict.pdf. Accessed June 5, 2015.

"Tunisie: Lutter Contre L'Impunite, Restaurer La Securite." Middle East and North Africa report no. 129, May 9, 2012. www.files.ethz.ch/isn/142694/123-tunisie-lutter-contre-l-impunite-restaurer-la-securite.pdf. Accessed June 15, 2016.

"Lost in Transition: The World according to Egypt's SCAF." Middle East and North Africa report no. 121, April 24, 2012. www.crisisgroup.org/middle-east-north-africa/north-africa/egypt/lost-transition-world-according-egypt-s -scaf. Accessed February 5, 2014.

"Popular Protest in North Africa and the Middle East (V): Making Sense of Libya." Middle East and North Africa report no. 107, June 6, 2011. www .crisisgroup.org/middle-east-north-africa/north-africa/libya/popular-protest -north-africa-and-middle-east-v-making-sense-libya. Accessed January 5, 2013.

"Popular Protests in North Africa and the Middle East (IV): Tunisia's Way." Middle East and North Africa report no. 106, April 28, 2011. www .crisisgroup.org/file/1560/download?token=u5P7yh_T. Accessed August 6, 2016.

"Popular Protest in North Africa and throughout the Middle East: Egypt Victorious?" Middle East and North Africa report no. 101, February 24,

2011. https://d2071andvip0wj.cloudfront.net/101-popular-protest-in-north
-africa-and-the-middle-east-I-egypt-victorious.pdf. Accessed March 7,
2015.

Ismail, Salwa. *The Rule of Violence: Subjectivity, Memory and Government in Syria.*
New York: Cambridge University Press, 2018.

"The Egyptian Revolution against the Police." *Social Research* 79, no. 2
(Summer 2012): 435–462.

Janowitz, Morris. *Military Institutions and Coercion in the Developing Nations.*
Chicago, IL: The University of Chicago Press, 1977.

Jebnoun, Noureddine. "In the Shadow of Power: Civil–Military Relations and the
Tunisian Popular Uprising." *Journal of North African Studies* 19, no. 3
(2014): 296–316.

Jenkins, David. *Suharto and His Generals: Indonesian Military Politics, 1975–1983.*
Ithaca, NY: Cornell University Press, 1984.

Kamal, ʿAbdul-Rahman. "130 Alf Jineih Towazaʾ ʿala al-Dubbat wa-l-Umanaʾ
al-Moqarrabin Yawmiyyan . . . wa-Musaʿed al-Wazir li-l-Shuʾun al-Maliyya
Yataqada 7 Malayin Shahriyyan." *Al-Shaʿab*, November 26, 2013. https://
travel-alone.xyz/?ts_id=1. Accessed April 3, 2020.

Kamal, Ashraf. "Al-Fasad Yadrub Diwan ʿAam al-Minia." *Al-Wafd*, February 3,
2016. https://alwafd.news/المنيا-عام-ديوان-برضي-داسفلا-1037107/تاظفاحملا.
Accessed February 3, 2016.

Kamil, Mustafa. "Infirad ʿal-Rijal' Yahki Qissat Awwal Inqilab ʿAskari Islami ʿala
al-Sadat." *Mobtada*, April 3, 2015. www.mobtada.com/news_details.php?I
D=313387. Accessed April 15, 2015.

Kamrava, Mehran. "Military Professionalization and Civil–Military Relations
in the Middle East." *Political Science Quarterly* 115, no. 1 (Spring 2000):
67–92.

Kandil, Hazem. *The Power Triangle: Military, Security, and Politics in Regime
Change.* New York: Oxford University Press, 2016.

"Back on Horse? The Military between Two Revolutions." In *Arab Spring in
Egypt: Revolution and Beyond,* edited by Bahgat Korany and Rabab El-Mahdi,
175–198. Cairo: The American University in Cairo Press, 2012.

Soldiers, Spies, and Statesmen: Egypt's Road to Revolt. New York: Verso Books,
2012.

Kanovsky, Eliyahu. "Syria's Troubled Economic Future." *Middle East Quarterly*
4, no. 2 (June 1997). www.meforum.org/articles/other/syria-s-troubled-
economic-future. Accessed May 29, 2018.

Kårtveit, Bård, and Maria Gabrielsen Jumbert. "Civil–Military Relations in the
Middle East: A Literature Review." Working paper 2014:5, Chr. Michelsen
Institute, June 2014, 1–24. www.cmi.no/publications/file/5188-civil-military
-relations-in-the-middle-east.pdf. Accessed January 15, 2015.

Kechichian, Joseph, and Jeanne Nazimek. "Challenges to the Military in Egypt."
Middle East Policy Council 5, no. 3 (September 1997). www.mepc.org/chal
lenges-military-egypt. Accessed July 12, 2017.

Ketchley, Neil. "The Army and the People Are One Hand! Fraternization and the
25th January Egyptian Revolution." *Comparative Studies in Society and
History* 56, no. 1 (January 2014): 174–175.

Khaddour, Khader. "Strength in Weakness: The Syrian Army's Accidental Resilience." Carnegie Middle East Center: Regional Insight, March 14, 2016. http://carnegie-mec.org/2016/03/14/strength-in-weakness-syrian-army-s-accidental-resilience-pub-62968. Accessed May 29, 2018.

"Assad's Officer Ghetto: Why the Syrian Army Remains Loyal." Carnegie Middle East Center: Regional Insight, November 4, 2015. http://carnegie-mec.org/2015/11/04/assad-s-officer-ghetto-why-syrian-army-remains-loyal-pub-61449. Accessed May 31, 2018.

(writing under the pseudonym ʿAziz Nakkash). "The Alawite Dilemma in Homs: Survival, Solidarity, and the Making of a Community." Friedrich Ebert Stiftung Institute, March 2013, 1–18. http://library.fes.de/pdf-files/iez/09825.pdf. Accessed August 1, 2018.

Khadduri, Majid. "The Role of the Military in Middle East Politics." *The American Political Science Review* 47, no. 2 (June 1953): 511–524.

"The Coup D'État of 1936: A Study in Iraqi Politics." *Middle East Journal* 2, no. 3 (July 1948): 270–292.

Khaled, Kamal. *Rijal ʿAbdul Nasser wa-l-Sadat*. Cairo: Dar al-ʿAdala, 1986.

Khaled, Leila. "Fasad al-Shorta fi Masr ... Khams Turuq li-Isitighlal al-Muwatinin." *Al-ʿArabi al-Jadid*, May 30, 2016. www.alaraby.co.uk/investigations/2016/5/30/فــســاد-الـشـرطـة-فـي-مـصـر-5-طـرق-لـاسـتـغـلـال-الـمـواطنـيـن. Accessed June 1, 2016.

King Hussein of Jordan. *Uneasy Lies the Head: The Autobiography of His Majesty King Hussein I of the Hashemite Kingdom of Jordan*. New York: Random House, 1962.

Kirkpatrick, David D. "The White House and the Strongman." *The New York Times*, July 27, 2018. www.nytimes.com/2018/07/27/sunday-review/obama-egypt-coup-trump.html. Accessed August 16, 2018.

"Tribal Ties, Long Qaddafi's Strength, May Be His Undoing." *The New York Times*, March 14, 2011. www.nytimes.com/2011/03/15/world/africa/15tribes.html. Accessed June 13, 2016.

"Egyptians Say Military Discourages an Open Economy." *The New York Times*, February 17, 2011. www.nytimes.com/2011/02/18/world/middleeast/18military.html. Accessed January 8, 2016.

"Mubarak's Grip On Power Is Shaken." *The New York Times*, January 31, 2011. www.nytimes.com/2011/02/01/world/middleeast/01egypt.html. Accessed on March 5, 2014.

"Mubarak Orders Crackdown, with Revolt Sweeping Egypt." *The New York Times*, January 28, 2011. www.nytimes.com/2011/01/29/world/middleeast/29unrest.html. Accessed March 27, 2014.

Kirkpatrick, David D., and Kareem Fahim. "Rebels in Libya Gain Power and Defectors." *The New York Times*, February 27, 2011. www.nytimes.com/2011/02/28/world/africa/28unrest.html. Accessed December 15, 2018.

"Mubarak's Allies and Foes Clash in Egypt." *The New York Times*, February 2, 2011. www.nytimes.com/2011/02/03/world/middleeast/03egypt.html. Accessed January 18, 2014.

Kirkpatrick, David D., and Mona El-Naggar. "Protest's Old Guard Falls In behind the Young." *The New York Times*, January 30, 2011. www

.nytimes.com/2011/01/31/world/middleeast/31opposition.html.   Accessed
January 15, 2013.

Knights, Michael. "The Military Role in Yemen's Protest: Civil–Military
Relation in the Tribal Republic." *Journal of Strategic Studies* 36, no. 2
(2013): 261–288.

Koehler, Kevin. "Political Militaries in Popular Uprisings: A Comparative
Perspective on the Arab Spring." *International Political Science Review* 38,
no. 3 (2017): 363–377.

"Officers and Regimes: The Historical Origins of Political–Military Relations
in Middle Eastern Republics." In *Armies and Insurgencies in the Arab Spring*,
edited by Holger Albrecht, Aurel Croissant, and Fred H. Lawson, 34–53.
Philadelphia, PA: University of Pennsylvania Press, 2016.

Kormanaev, Anatoly, and Isayen Herrera. "Venezuela's Maduro Cracks Down
on His Own Military in Bid to Retain Power." *The New York Times*,
August 13, 2019. www.nytimes.com/2019/08/13/world/americas/venezuela-
military-maduro.html. Accessed August 13, 2019.

L. S. "Continuing Business by Other Means: Egypt's Military Economy." *Mute*,
May 30, 2014. www.metamute.org/editorial/articles/continuing-business-
other-means-egypts-military-economy. Accessed April 17, 2015.

Lacouture, Jean. *The Demigods: Charismatic Leadership in the Third World*.
New York: Alfred Knopf, 1970.

Lakzani, Alimar, and Roy Gutman. "In Tartous, Syria, Women Wear Black,
Youth Are in Hiding, and Bitterness Grows." *The Nation*, May 15, 2017.
www.thenation.com/article/in-tartous-syria-women-wear-black-youth-are-
in-hiding-and-bitterness-grows/. Accessed July 5, 2018.

Landis, Joshua. "A Great Sorting Out: The Future of Minorities in the Middle
East." Interview by *Al Noor* staff (Spring 2016). www.bcalnoor.org/single-
post/2016/09/03/A-Great-Sorting-Out-The-Future-of-Minorities-in-the-
Middle-East. Accessed July 7, 2017.

"Zahran 'Allush: His Ideology and Beliefs." *Syria Comment*, December 15,
2013. www.joshualandis.com/blog/zahran-alloush/. Accessed July 11, 2018.

Larcher, Wolfram. "Families, Tribes and Cities in the Libyan Revolution."
Middle East Policy 18, no. 4 (Winter 2011): 140–154.

Lee, Terence. *Defect or Defend: Military Responses to Popular Protests in
Authoritarian Asia*. Baltimore, MD: Johns Hopkins University Press, 2015.

"The Armed Forces and Transitions from Authoritarian Rule: Explaining the
Role of the Military in 1986 Philippines and 1998 Indonesia." *Comparative
Political Studies* 42, no. 5 (2009): 640–669.

"Military Cohesion and Regime Maintenance: Explaining the Role of the
Military in 1989 China and 1988 Indonesia." *Armed Forces & Society* 32,
no. 1 (October 2005): 80–104.

Leenders, Reinoud. *Spoils of Truth: Corruption and State-building in Postwar
Lebanon*. Ithaca, NY: Cornell University Press, 2012.

Lewis, Andrew L. "The Revolt of the Admirals." Air Command and Staff
College/Air University, April 1998. www.au.af.mil/au/awc/awcgate/acsc/98-
166.pdf. Accessed June 15, 2014.

Linz, Juan J., and Alfred Stepan. *Problems of Democratic Transition and Consolidation: Southern Europe, South America, and Post-Communist Europe.* Baltimore, MD: Johns Hopkins University Press, 1996.

Lipman, Thomas W. *Egypt after Nasser: Sadat, Peace, and the Mirage of Prosperity.* St. Paul, MN: Paragon House, 1989.

Londregan, John B., and Keith T. Poole. "Poverty, the Coup Trap, and the Seizure of Executive Power." *World Politics* 42, no. 2 (January 1990): 151–183.

Luckham, Robin. "The Military and Democratization in Africa: A Survey of Literature and Issues." *African Studies Review* 37, no. 2 (September 1994): 13–75.

Lund, Aron. "A Voice from the Shadows." *Diwan*, November 25, 2016. https://carnegie-mec.org/diwan/66240. Accessed July 7, 2018.

Lutterbeck, Derek. "Tool of Rule: the Tunisian Police under Ben Ali 'Ben 'Ali, Zein al-'Abidin.'" *Journal of North African Studies* 20, no. 5 (2015): 813–831.
    "Arab Uprisings, Armed Forces, and Civil–Military Relations." *Armed Forces & Society* 39, no. 1 (2013): 28–52.
    "After the Fall: Security Sector Reform in post-Ben Ali 'Ben 'Ali, Zein al-'Abidin' Tunisia." Arab Reform Initiative (ARI), September 2012. www.arab-reform.net/en/node/592. Accessed June 12, 2018.
    "Arab Uprisings and Armed Forces: Between Openness and Resistance." Geneva Center for the Democratic Control of Armed, 2011. www.ubiquitypress.com/site/books/10.5334/bbm/. Accessed December 5, 2018.

Luttwak, Edward. *Coup d'État: A Practical Handbook.* Cambridge, MA: Harvard University Press, 1979.

Lynch, Marc. *The New Arab Wars: Uprisings and Anarchy in the Middle East.* New York: PublicAffairs, 2016.

Macleod, Hugh, and Anna-Sofie Flamand. "Inside Syria's Shabiha Death Squads." *The Star*, June 15, 2012. www.thestar.com/news/world/2012/06/15/inside_syrias_shabiha_death_squads.html. Accessed July 8, 2018.

Makara, Michael. "Rethinking Military Behavior during the Arab Spring." *Defense & Security Analysis* 32, no.3 (2016): 209–223.
    "Coup-Proofing, Military Defection, and the Arab Spring." *Democracy and Security* 9, no. 4 (2013): 334–359.

Makhluf, Mohammad. "Man Hom Rijal al-Khayma al-ladhin Yudirun al-Nidham al-Libi." *Al-Majalla*, August 23, 1988. http://archive.libya-al-mostakbal.org/Archives/mo3aredoon/almajalla1993/almajalla_aug93_libya02.html. Accessed November 15, 2018.

Malbrunot, Georges. "60.000 centurious Alaouites protègent le clan Assad." *Le Figaro*, July 31, 2011. www.lefigaro.fr/international/2011/07/31/01003-20110731ARTFIG00201-60000-centurions-alaouites-protegent-le-clan-assad.php. Accessed July 16, 2016.

Mandraud, Isabell. "Peut-être on partira, mais on brûlera Tunis." *Le Monde*, January 17, 2011. www.lemonde.fr/afrique/article/2011/01/17/peut-etre-on-partira-mais-on-brulera-tunis_1466502_3212.html. Accessed October 8, 2018.

Marroushi, Nadine. "US Expert: Leadership of 'Military Inc.' Is Running Egypt." *Egypt Independent*, October 26, 2011. www.egyptindependent.com /us-expert-leadership-military-inc-running-egypt. Accessed July 22, 2017.

Marshall, Jonathan V. *The Lebanese Connection: Corruption, Civil War, and the International Drug Traffic*. Stanford, CA: Stanford University Press, 2012.

Marshall, Shana. "The Egyptian Armed Forces and the Remaking of an Economic Empire." Carnegie Middle East Center, April 15, 2015. http://carnegie-mec.org /2015/04/15/egyptian-armed-forces-and-remaking-of-economic-empire-pub-5 9726. Accessed April 30, 2015.

Marshall, Shana, and Joshua Stacher. "Egypt's Generals and Transnational Capital." *Middle East Research and Information Project* 262 (Spring 2012). www.merip.org/mer/mer262/egypts-generals-transnational-capital. Accessed June 25, 2015.

Masoud, Tarek. "The Upheavals in Egypt and Tunisia: The Road to (and from) Liberation Square." *Journal of Democracy* 22, no. 3 (July 2011): 20–34.

Mattes, Hanspeter. "Formal and Informal Authority in Libya since 1969." In *Libya Since 1969: Qadhafi's Revolution Revisited*, edited by Dirk Vanderwalle, 74–76. New York: Palgrave Macmillan, 2008.

McAdam, Doug. "Conceptual Origins, Current Problems, Future Directions." In *Comparative Perspectives on Social Movements: Political Opportunities, Mobilizing Structures, and Cultural Framings*, edited by Doug McAdam, John D. McCarthy, and Mayer N. Zald, 23–40. Cambridge: Cambridge University Press, 2008.

McAdam, Doug, John D. McCarthy, and Mayer N. Zald (eds.). *Comparative Perspectives Movements: Political Opportunities, Mobilizing Structures, and Cultural Framings*. Cambridge: Cambridge University Press, 2008.

McCoy, Alfred. *Closer than Brothers: Manhood at the Philippine Military Academy*. New Haven, CT: Yale University Press, 1999.

McLauchlin, Theodore. "Loyalty Strategies and Military Defection in Rebellion." *Comparative Politics* 42, no. 3 (April 2010): 333–350.

"The Loyalty Trap: Regime Ethnic Exclusion, Commitment Problems, and Civil War Duration in Syria and Beyond." *Security Studies* 27, no. 2 (2018): 296–317.

Mekouar, Merouan. "Police Collapse in Authoritarian Regimes: Lessons from Tunisia." *Studies in Conflict and Terrorism* 40, no. 10 (2017): 857–869.

Middle East Insider. "Syria: Narcotics Center of the Middle East." *Middle East Insider Report* 16, no. 38 (1989). www.larouchepub.com/eiw/public/1989/ei rv16n38-19890921/eirv16n38-19890921_032-syria_narcotics_center_ of_the_mi.pdf. Accessed May 7, 2017.

Middle East Watch. *Syria Unmasked: The Suppression of Human Rights by the Asad Regime*. New Haven, CT: Yale University Press, 1991.

Mietzner, Marcus. *Military Politics, Islam, and the State in Indonesia: From Turbulent Transition to Democratic Consolidation*. Singapore: Institute of Southeast Asian Studies, 2009.

Migdal, Joel. *Strong Societies and Weak States: State–Society Relations and State Capabilities in the Third World*. Princeton, NJ: Princeton University Press, 1988.

Mignot, Leïla. "Algérie: Pourquoi l'armée peut changer la donne." *L'Orient Le Jour*, March 9, 2019. www.lorientlejour.com/article/1160857/pour quoi-larmee-peut-changer-la-donne.html?fbclid=IwAR2qsChQtQ1TEOs VoUkJDl8Ea1Q9qbuTfQLsXYBRNKSxc0AL2UyD4xCHcc4. Accessed March 9, 2019.

Moniquet, Claude, and Vanja Luksic. "Armes, drogue, voitures: le traffic Syrien." *L'Express*, May 8, 1987.

Moosa, Matti. *Extremist Shiites: The Ghulat Sects*. New York: Syracuse University Press, 1988.

Mora, Frank O., and Quintan Wiktorowicz. "Economic Reform and the Military: China, Cuba, and Syria in Comparative Perspective." *International Journal of Comparative Sociology* 44, no. 2 (April 2003): 87–128.

Muhieddin, Khaled. *Wa-l-Ana Atakallam*. Cairo: Markaz al-Ahram li-l-Tarjama wa-l-Nashr, 1992.

Munck, Gerardo L., and Richard Snyder. *Passion, Craft, and Method in Comparative Politics*. Baltimore, MD: Johns Hopkins University Press, 2007.

Mustafa, Khalil. *Suqut al-Julan*. Cairo: Dar al-I'tisam, 1980.

Nepstad, Sharon Erickson. *Nonviolent Revolutions: Civil Resistance in the Late 20th Century*. New York: Oxford University Press, 2011.

Nordlinger, Eric A. *Soldiers in Politics: Military Coups and Governments*. Upper Saddle River, NJ: Prentice Hall, 1977.

Nutting, Anthony. *Nasser*. New York: E. P. Dutton, 1972.

O'Donnell, Guillermo, and Philippe Schmitter. *Transitions from Authoritarian Rule: Tentative Conclusions about Uncertain Democracies*. Baltimore, MD: Johns Hopkins University Press, 1986.

Ohl, Dorothy, HolgerAlbrecht, and Kevin Koehler. "For Money or Liberty? The Political Economy of Military Desertion and Rebel Recruitment in the Syrian Civil War." Carnegie Regional Insight, November 24, 2015. https://carne gieendowment.org/2015/11/24/for-money-or-liberty-political-economy-of-military-desertion-and-rebel-recruitment-in-syrian-civil-war-pub-61714. Accessed April 3, 2020.

'Omran, Mohammad. *Tajribati fi al-Thawra*. Beirut: Dar al-Jil li-l-Tab' wa-l-Nashr wa-l-Tawzi', 1970.

'Othman, Hashem. *Tarikh Suria al-Hadith, 'Ahd Hafez al-Asad, 1971–2000*. Beirut: Riad El-Rayyes Books, 2014.

Otis, John. "Veteran President's Rift with Bolivian Military Helped Drive His Early Exit." *The Wall Street Journal*, December 5, 2019. www.wsj.com/arti cles/veteran-presidents-rift-with-bolivian-military-helped-drive-his-early-exit-11575541801. Accessed December 5, 2019.

Ottaway, David B. "Syrian Connection to Terrorism Probed: 'New and Very Disturbing' Evidence." *The Washington Post*, June 1, 1986. CIA approved for release May 4, 2012. www.cia.gov/library/readingroom/docs/CIA-RDP90-00965R000604900038-5.pdf. Accessed May 28, 2018.

Owen, Roger. *The Rise and Fall of Arab Presidents for Life*. Cambridge, MA: Harvard University Press, 2012.

"Military Presidents in Arab States." *The International Journal of Middle East Studies* 43, no. 3 (August 2011): 395–396.

Pachon, Alejandro. "Loyalty and Defection: Misunderstanding Civil–Military Relations in Tunisia during the Arab Spring." *The Journal of Strategic Studies* 37, no. 4 (2014): 508–531.

Parsons, William, and William Taylor. "Arbiters of Social Unrest: Military Responses to the Arab Spring." Report prepared for the US Military Academy (2011). https://apps.dtic.mil/dtic/tr/fulltext/u2/a562816.pdf. Accessed November 7, 2018.

Paul, James A. *Human Rights in Syria: A Middle East Watch Report.* New York: Human Rights Watch, 1990. https://books.google.com/books?id=NxjxWY WnlwC&printsec=frontcover&source=gbs_ge_summary_r&cad=0#v=one page&q&f=false. Accessed August 15, 2017.

Perthes, Volker. *The Political Economy of Syria under Asad.* New York: I.B. Tauris, 1995.

Philips, Christopher. "The World Abetted Asad's Victory in Syria." *The Atlantic,* August 4, 2018. www.theatlantic.com/international/archive/2018/08/assad-victory-syria/566522/. Accessed August 14, 2018.

Philips, Sarah. *Yemen's Democracy Experiment in Regional Perspective: Patronage and Pluralized Authoritarianism.* New York: Palgrave Macmillan, 2008.

Pion-Berlin, David. "Military Relations in Comparative Perspective." In *Armies and Insurgencies in the Arab Spring,* edited by Holger Albrecht, Aurel Croissant, and Fred H. Lawson, 7–33. Philadelphia, PA: University of Pennsylvania Press, 2016.

Pion-Berlin, David, Diego Esparza, and Kevin Grisham. "Staying Quartered: Civilian Uprisings and Military Disobedience in the Twenty-First Century." *Comparative Political Studies* 47, no. 2 (2014): 230–259.

Pion-Berlin, David, and Trinkunas, Harold. "Civilian Praetorianism and Military Shirking during Constitutional Crises in Latin America." *Comparative Politics* 42, no. 4 (July 2010): 395–411.

Pluta, Audrey. "Les relations civilo-militaires en Tunisie de l'indépendance a nous jours: l'armée entre soumission au pouvoir civil et nouveau rôle politique." Master's thesis, Institut d'Etudes Politiques, Aix-en-Provence, 2017.

"Political–Military Relations and the Stability of Arab Regimes." Adelphi Papers 324, International Institute for Strategic Studies. London: Oxford University Press, 1998.

Powell, Jonathan. "Regime Vulnerability and the Diversionary Threat of Force." *Journal of Conflict Resolution* 58, no. 1 (2014): 169–196.

"Coups and Conflict: The Paradox of Coup-Proofing." PhD diss., University of Kentucky, 2012. http://uknowledge.uky.edu/polysci_etds/3/. Accessed March 3, 2016.

Prieur, Denis. "Defend or Defect: Military Roles in Popular Revolts." SSRN, December 15, 2011. http://ssrn.com/abstract=2115062. Accessed September 14, 2014.

"Protests in Egypt and Unrest in Middle East – As It Happened." *The Guardian,* January 25, 2011. www.theguardian.com/global/blog/2011/jan/25/mid dleeast-tunisia. Accessed March 12, 2014.

Prothero, Mitchell. "Beirut Bombshell." *Fortune* on *CNN Money*, May 4, 2006. http://money.cnn.com/2006/05/01/news/international/lebanon_for tune_051506/. Accessed May 30, 2018.

Przeworski, Adam. *Democracy and the Market: Political and Economic Reforms in Eastern Europe and Latin America.* New York: Cambridge University Press, 1991.

Quinlivan, James T. "Coup-Proofing: Its Practice and Consequences in the Middle East." *International Security* 24, no. 2 (Autumn 1999): 131–165.

Rabinovich, Itamar. "The Compact Minorities and the Syrian State, 1918–45." *Journal of Contemporary History* 14, no. 4 (October 1979): 693–712.

Syria under the Ba'ath, 1963–1966: The Army–Party Symbiosis. Jerusalem: Israel University Press, 1972.

Raphaeli, Nimrod. "Egyptian Army's Pervasive Role in National Economy." The Middle East Media Research Institute, Inquiry and Analysis Series no. 1001, July 29, 2013. www.memri.org/reports/egyptian-armys-pervasive-role-national-economy. Accessed April 5, 2015.

Rathmell, Andrew. "Syria's Intelligence Services: Origins and Development." *The Journal of Conflict Studies* 16, no. 2 (1996). https://journals.lib.unb.ca/i ndex.php/jcs/article/view/11815/12636. Accessed June 20, 2018.

Read, Christopher S. "Allegiance: Egypt Security Forces." Master's thesis, Naval Postgraduate School, Monterey, California, 2013. www.dtic.mil/dtic/tr/full text/u2/a620384.pdf. Accessed February 2, 2014.

Rémy, Jean-Philille. "Les manifestants au Sudan appellant désormais à la chute de la junte." *Le Monde*, April 12, 2019. www.lemonde.fr/afrique/article/201 9/04/12/les-manifestants-au-soudan-appellent-desormais-a-la-chute-de-la-junte_5449085_3212.html. Accessed April 12, 2019.

Riveria, Temario. "The Middle Class and Democratization in the Philippines: From the Asian Crisis to the Ouster of Estrada." In *Southeast Asian Middle Classes: Prospects for Social Change and Democratization*, edited by Embong Abdul Rahman, 230–261. Bangi: National University of Malaysia, 2001.

Roberts, David. *The Ba'ath and the Creation of Modern Syria.* London: Routledge, 1987.

Roberts, Hugh. "Who Said Gaddafi Had to Go?" *London Review of Books* 33, no. 22 (2011): 8–18.

Roessler, Philip. "The Enemy Within: Personal Rule, Coups, and Civil War in Africa." *World Politics* 63, no. 2 (April 2011): 300–346.

Roll, Stephan. "Managing Change: How Egypt's Military Leadership Shaped the Transformation." *Mediterranean Politics* 21, no. 1 (October 2015): 23–43.

Rosen, Nir. "Among the Alawites." *London Review of Books* 34, no. 18 (September 2012). www.lrb.co.uk/v34/n18/nir-rosen/among-the-alawites. Accessed July 18, 2018.

Rouquie, Alain. *The Military and the State in Latin America.* Berkley, CA: University of California Press, 1982.

Russell, D. E. H. *Rebellion, Revolution and Armed Force: A Comparative Study of Fifteen Countries with Special Emphasis on Cuba and South Africa.* New York: Academic Press, 1974.

Ryan, Curtis R. "Political Strategies and Regime Survival in Egypt." *Journal of Third World Studies* 18, no. 2 (Fall 2011): 25–46.

Sabra, Hasan. *La'nta Lubnan*. Beirut: Difaf Publishing, 2016.

Suria, Suqut al-'A'ila, 'Awdat al-Watan. Beirut: Arab Scientific Publishers, 2013.

Sabri, Mussa. *Watha'iq Harb October*. Cairo: al-Maktab al-Masri al-Hadith, 1975.

SadeqMahmud., *Hiwar hawla Suria*. London: Dar 'Okaz, 1993.

Sadowski, Yahya M. "Patronage and the Ba'ath: Corruption and Control in Contemporary Syria." *Arab Studies Quarterly* 19, no. 4 (Fall 1987): 445–459.

Saghieh, Hazem. *Al-Ba'ath al-Suri, Tarikh Mujaz*. Beirut: Dar al-Saqi, 2012.

Sa'id, al-Safi. *Bourguiba, Sira Shebh Muharrama*. Tunis: 'Orabia, 2011.

Said, Atef. "The Paradox of Transition to 'Democracy' under Military Rule." *Social Research* 79, no. 2 (Summer 2012): 397–434.

Salemeh, Rafia. "Sanawat al-Ta'fish." *Al-Jumhuriyya*, August 8, 2018. www .aljumhuriya.net/ar/content/سنوات-التعفيش. Accessed August 13, 2018.

Sami, Riad. *Shahed 'ala 'Asr al-Ra'is Mohammad Neguib*. Cairo: al-Maktab al-Masri al-Hadith, 2004.

Sariba, Ali. "The Role of the Military in the Arab Uprisings: The Case of Tunisia and Libya." PhD diss., University of Nottingham, 2016.

Sassoon, Joseph. *Anatomy of Authoritarianism in the Arab Republics*. New York: Cambridge University Press, 2016.

Sayf, Nabil. "Al-Haras al-Jumhuri … Min al-Malik Faruq ila Mursi." *Al-Wafd*, September 12, 2012. https://alwafd.news/ملفات-محلية/263841-الحرس-الجمهوري من-الملك-فاروق-إلي-«مرسي. Accessed July 14, 2014.

Sayigh, Yezid. "Missed Opportunity: The Politics of Police Reform in Egypt and Tunisia." Carnegie Middle East Center, March 7, 2015. http://car negieendowment.org/files/missed_opportunity.pdf. Accessed April 18, 2016.

"Militaries, Civilians and the Crisis of the Arab State." *The Monkey Cage*, December 8, 2014. www.washingtonpost.com/news/monkey-cage/wp/20 14/12/08/militaries-civilians-and-the-crisis-of-the-arab-state/?utm_term= .ecd8bcfa236f. Accessed December 2, 2018.

"Above the State: The Officers' Republic in Egypt." Carnegie Middle East Center, August 1, 2012. http://carnegie-mec.org/2012/08/01/above-state-officers-republic-in-egypt-pub-48972. Accessed November 22, 2017.

"Agencies of Coercion: Armies and Internal Security Forces." *International Journal of Middle East Studies* 43, no. 3 (2011): 403–405.

Schenker, David. "Washington's Limited Influence in Egypt." Washington Institute for Near East Policy, September 15, 2011. www.washingtoninstitute.org/policy-analysis/view/washingtons-limited-influence-in-egypt. Accessed January 15, 2019.

Schmitter, Philippe, and Guillermo O'Donnell. *Tentative Conclusions about Uncertain Democracies*. Baltimore, MD: Johns Hopkins University Press, 1985.

Schraeder, Peter J., and Hamadi Redissi, "The Upheavals in Egypt and Tunisia: Ben Ali's Fall." *Journal of Democracy* 22, no. 3 (July 2011): 5–19.

Scott Cooper, Andrew. *The Fall of Heaven, the Pahlavis and the Final Days of Imperial Iran*. New York: Picador, 2018.

Seale, Patrick. *Asad: The Struggle for the Middle East*. Berkley, CA: University of California Press, 1988.

Selvik, Kjetil. "Roots of Fragmentation: The Army and Regime Survival in Syria." *CMI Insight*, no. 2 (April 2014). www.cmi.no/publications/file/5127-roots-of-fragmentation.pdf. Accessed June 5, 2016.

Semenov, Kiril. "Who Controls Syria? The Al-Assad Family, the Inner Circle, and the Tycoons." Russian International Affairs Council, February 14, 2018. http://russiancouncil.ru/en/analytics-and-comments/analytics/who-controls-syria-the-al-assad-family-the-inner-circle-and-the-tycoons/. Accessed May 29, 2018.

Sereni, Jean Pierre. "Après Ben Ali 'Ben 'Ali, Zein al-'Abidin,' quelle police en Tunisie?" *Le Monde Diplomatique*, April 1, 2011. www.monde-diplomatique.fr/carnet/2011–04-01-Tunisie. Accessed October 15, 2017.

Seurat, Michel (writing as Paul Maler). "La Société Syrienne Contre Son Etat." *Le Monde Diplomatique* (April 1980): 4–5.

Seymour, Martin. "The Dynamics of Power in Syria since the Break with Egypt." *Middle Eastern Studies* 16, no. 1 (January 1970): 35–47.

Sfakianakis, John. "The Whales of the Nile: Networks, Businessmen, and Bureaucrats during the Era of Privatization in Egypt." In *Networks of Privileges in the Middle East*, edited by Steven Heydemann, 77–100. New York: Palgrave Macmillan, 2004.

Shah, Aqil. "Constraining Consolidation: Military Politics and Democracy in Pakistan, 2007–2013." *Democratization* 21, no. 6 (2014): 1007–1033.

Sharaf, Sami. *'Abdul Nasser: Kayfa Hakama Masr*. Cairo: Madbuli al-Saghir, 1996.

——— *Sanawat wa-Ayyam ma' 'Abdul Nasser, Shahadat Sami Sharaf, al-Kitab al-Awwal*. Cairo: al-Maktab al-Masri al-Hadith, 2014.

Shatz, Adam. "Mubarak's Last Breath." *London Review of Books* 32, no. 10 (May 2010). www.lrb.co.uk/v32/n10/adam-shatz/mubaraks-last-breath. Accessed March 2, 2013.

Shehata, Dina. "The Fall of the Pharaoh: How Hosni Mubarak's Reign Came to an End." *Foreign Affairs* 90, no. 3 (May/June 2011): 26–32.

Shenker, Jack. "Egyptian Arms Officer's Diary of a Military life in a Revolution." *The Guardian*, December 28, 2011. www.theguardian.com/world/2011/dec/28/egyptian-military-officers-diary. Accessed November 27, 2014.

Sherlock, Ruth. "Confessions of an Assad 'Shabiha' Loyalist: How I Raped and Killed for £300 a Month." *The Telegraph*, July 14, 2012. www.telegraph.co.uk/news/worldnews/middleeast/syria/9400570/Confessions-of-an-Assad-Shabiha-loyalist-how-I-raped-and-killed-for-300-a-month.html. Accessed March 19, 2017.

Shukr, 'Abdul-Ghaffar. *Al-Tali'a al-'Arabiyya, al-Tanzim al-Qawmi al-Sirri li-Gamal 'Abdul Nasser, 1965–1986*. Beirut: Markaz Dirasat al-Wihada al-'Arabiyya, 2015.

Shukri, Ghali. *Al-Thawra al-Mudada fi Masr*. Cairo: Kitab al-Ahali, 1987.

Singh, Naunihal. *Seizing Power: The Strategic Logic of Military Coups.* Baltimore, MD: Johns Hopkins University Press, 2014.

Sirrs, Owen L. *The Egyptian Intelligence Service: A History of the Mukhabarat, 1910–2009.* London: Routledge, 2010.

Slater, Dan. *Ordering Power: Contentious Politic and Authoritarian Leviathans in Southeast Asia.* Cambridge: Cambridge University Press, 2010.

Soffer, Gad. "The Role of the Officer Class in Syrian Politics and Society." PhD diss., American University, 1968.

Sohn, Jae Souk. "Political Dominance and Political Failure: The Role of the Military in the Republic of Korea." In *The Military Intervenes: Case Studies in Political Development,* edited by Henry Bienen, 103–126. New York: Russel Sage Foundation, 1968.

Soliman, Samer. "The Political Economy of Mubarak's Fall." In *Arab Spring in Egypt: Revolution and Beyond,* edited by Bahgat Korany and Rabab El-Mahdi, 43–62. Cairo: The American University in Cairo Press, 2014.

Springborg, Robert. *Mubarak's Egypt: Fragmentation of the Political Order.* Boulder, CO: Westview, 1989.

Stacher, Joshua. *Adaptable Autocrats: Regime Power in Egypt and Syria.* Stanford, CA: Stanford University Press, 2012.

Starr, Stephen. "Shabiha Militias and the Destruction of Syria." *CTC Sentinel* 5, no. 11 (November 2012): 12–14.

Steavenson, Wendell. *Circling the Square: Stories from the Egyptian Revolution.* New York: HarperCollins, 2015.

———. "On the Square: Were the Egyptian Protesters Right to Trust the Military?" *The New Yorker,* February 21, 2011. www.newyorker.com/magazine/2011/02/2 8/on-the-square-wendell-steavenson. Accessed April 4, 2020.

Stepan, Alfred. *Rethinking Military Politics: Brazil and the Southern Cone.* Princeton, NJ: Princeton University Press, 1988.

St John, Ronald Bruce. *Libya: From Colony to Independence.* Oxford: Oneworld Publications, 2008.

———. "Redefining the Libyan Revolution: The Changing Ideology of Muammar al-Qaddafi." *The Journal of North African Studies* 13, no. 1 (March 2008): 91–106.

Stratfor. "The Use of Mercenaries in Syria's Crackdown." January 12, 2012. https://worldview.stratfor.com/article/use-mercenaries-syrias-crackdown. Accessed July 1, 2018.

Svolik, Milan. *The Politics of Authoritarian Rule.* New York: Cambridge University Press, 2012.

———. "Power Sharing and Leadership Dynamics in Authoritarian Regimes." *American Journal of Political Science* 53, no. 2 (April 2009): 477–494.

Synaps Network. "Picking Up the Pieces: How Syrian Society Has Changed." August 6, 2018. www.synaps.network/picking-up-the-pieces. Accessed August 6, 2018.

Syrian Human Rights Committee. "Report on the Human Rights Situation in Syria over a 20-Year Period, 1979–1999." London, 2001. Released by WikiLeaks. https://wikileaks.org/gifiles/attach/150/150649_SYRIAN%20H UMAN%20RIGHTS%20COMMITTEE.pdf. Accessed April 15, 2018.

Tallaa, Maen. "The Syrian Security Services and the Need for Structural and Functional Change." *Omran for Strategic Studies* (November 2016). http://en .omrandirasat.org/publications/papers/the-syrian-security-services-and-the-need-for-structural-and-functional-change.html. Accessed March 8, 2017.

Talmadge, Caitlin. *The Dictator's Army: Battlefield Effectiveness in Authoritarian Regimes*. Ithaca, NY: Cornell University Press, 2015.

Taylor, Brian. *Politics and the Russian Army: Civil–Military Relations, 1689–2000.* New York: Cambridge University Press, 2003.

Taylor, William C. *Military Responses to the Arab Uprisings and the Future of Civil– Military Relations in the Middle East: Analysis from Egypt, Tunisia, Libya, and Syria.* New York: Palgrave Macmillan, 2014.

Thompson, William. "Organizational Cohesion and Military Coup Outcomes." *Comparative Political Studies* 9, no. 3 (October 1976): 255–276.

"Regime Vulnerability and the Military Coup." *Comparative Politics* 7, no. 4 (July 1975): 459–487.

"The Grievances of Military Coup-Makers." Sage Professional Papers in Comparative Politics, no. 01-047. Beverly Hills, CA: Sage Publications, 1973.

Tlass, Mustafa. *Mer'at Hayati, al-'Aqd al-Thani, 1958–1968.* Damascus: Dar Tlassli-l-Dirasat wa-l-Nashr wa-l-Tawzi', 2006.

Mer'at Hayati, al-'Aqd al-Thaleth, 1968–1978. Damascus: Dar Tlassli-l-Dirasat wa-l-Nashr wa-l-Tawzi', 2003.

Transparency International. "Corruption Perceptions Index 2017." www .transparency.org/country/SYR. Accessed June 1, 2018.

Trinkunas, Harold. *Crafting Civilian Control of the Military in Venezuela: A Comparative Perspective.* Chapel Hill, NC: University of Carolina Press, 2005.

"Crafting Civilian Control in Argentina and Venezuela." In *Civil–Military Relations in Latin America*, edited by David Pion-Berlin, 161–193. Chapel Hill, NC: University of North Carolina Press, 2001.

Trotsky, Leon. *History of the Russian Revolution.* Chicago, IL: Haymarket Books, 2008.

US Department of the Treasury. "Treasury Sanctions Al-Nusrah Front Leadership in Syria and Militias Supporting the Asad Regime." Press release, December 11, 2012. www.treasury.gov/press-center/press-releases/pages/t g1797.aspx. Accessed June 7, 2018.

Valter, Stéphane. "Rivalités et complémentarités au sein des forces armées: le facteur confessionnel en Syrie." *Les Champs de Mars* 1, no. 23 (2012): 79–96.

Van Dam, Nikolaos. *The Struggle for Power in Syria: Politics and Society under Asad and the Ba'th Party.* New York: I.B. Tauris, 1996.

"Sectarian and Regional Factionalism in the Syrian Elite." *Middle East Journal* 32, no. 2 (Spring 1978): 201–210.

Vandewalle, Dirk. *A History of Modern Libya.* New York: Cambridge University Press, 2012.

Vatikiotis, P. J. *The Egyptian Army in Politics: Pattern for New Nations?* Bloomington, IN: Indiana University Press, 1961.

Ware, L. B. "The Role of the Tunisian Military in the Post-Bourguiba Era." *Middle East Journal* 39, no. 1 (Winter 1985): 27–47.

Waterbury, John. *The Egypt of Nasser and Sadat: The Political Economy of Two Regimes.* Princeton, NJ: Princeton University Press, 1983.

Wedeen, Lisa. *Ambiguities of Domination: Politics, Rhetoric, and Symbols in Contemporary Syria.* Chicago, IL: The University of Chicago Press, 2015.

Weeks, Jessica L. P. *Dictators at War and Peace.* Ithaca, NY: Cornell University Press, 2014.

Wege, C. A. "Assad's Legions: The Syrian Intelligence Services." *The International Journal of Intelligence and Counterintelligence* 4, no. 1 (Spring 1990): 91–100.

Weymouth, Lally. "Egyptian Generals Speak about the Revolution, Elections." *The Washington Post,* May 18, 2011. www.washingtonpost.com/world/mid dle-east/egyptian-generals-speak-about-revolution-elections/2011/05/16/A F7AiU6G_story.html?utm_term=.e8a659988cfb. Accessed April 25, 2014.

White, Jeffrey. "A Willingness to Kill: Repression in Syria." PolicyWatch 1840. Washington Institute for Near East Policy, August 16, 2011. www .washingtoninstitute.org/policy-analysis/view/a-willingness-to-kill-repres sion-in-syria. Accessed July 17, 2018.

Wilford, Hugh. *America's Great Game: The CIA's Secret Arabists and the Shaping of the Modern Middle East.* New York: Basic Books, 2013.

Williams, Philip J., and Knut Walter. *Militarization and Demilitarization in El Salvador's Transition to Democracy.* Pittsburgh, PA: University of Pittsburgh Press, 1997.

Woods, Kevin N., Murray Williamson, and Holaday Thomas. "Saddam's War: An Iraqi Military Perspective of the Iraq–Iran War." McNair Paper 70. Washington, DC: National Defense University, 2009.

Wright, John. *A History of Libya.* New York: Columbia University Press, 2012.

Wright, Lawrence. *The Terror Years: From Al-Qaeda to the Islamic State.* New York: Vintage, 2017.

Ya'ari, Ehud. "Sadat's Pyramid of Power." *The Jerusalem Quarterly* 14 (Winter 1980): 113–114.

Yossef, Amr. "Sadat as Supreme Commander." *The Journal of Strategic Studies* 37, no. 4 (2014): 532–555.

Yuness, Sharif. *Nida' al-Sha'b, Tarikh Naqdi li-l-Ideologia al-Nasiriyya.* Cairo: Dar al-Shuruq, 2012.

Yusef al-Moqaryaf, Mohammad. *Inqilab al-Qaddhafi, Mu'ammar, al-Tughian al-Thawari wa-'Abqariyyat al-Sufh, September 1969–March 1977.* Oxford: Centre for Libyan Studies, 2018.

Zargoski, Paul. "Democratic Breakdown in Paraguay and Venezuela: The Shape of Things to Come for Latin America." *Armed Forces & Society* 30, no. 1 (Fall 2003): 87–116.

Zein al-'Abidin, Bashir. *Al-Jaysh wa-l-Siasa fi Suria (1918–2000), Dirasa Naqdiyya.* London: Dar al-Jabia, 2008.

"Malaf al-Fasad fi Suria, al-Halaqa al-Rabi'a: Rumuz al-Fasad, al-Asad." *Majallat al-Sunna,* no. 100 (October 2000). http://sunah.org/main/393-3–ملفات-ملف

الفساد-في-سوريا-الحلقة-الرابعة-رموز-الفساد-آل-أسد.html. Accessed April 25, 2018.

Zénobie. "Syrie: un officier supérieur parle." *Le Monde Diplomatique*, September 7, 2011. www.monde-diplomatique.fr/carnet/2011–09-07-Syrie-un-officier-superieur-parle. Accessed September 7, 2011.

Ziade, Ridwan. *Al-Sulta wa-l-Istikhbarat fi Suria.* Beirut: Riad El-Rayyes Books, 2013.

Zisser, Eyal. "The Syrian Army on the Domestic and External Fronts." In *Armed Forces in the Middle East: Politics and Strategy*, edited by Barry Rubin and Thomas Keaney, 113–129. London: Frank Cass, 2002.

"Appearance and Reality: Syria's Decision-Making Structure." *Middle East Review of International Affairs* (May 1998). www.rubincenter.org/1998/05/zisser-1998–05-05/. Accessed March 7, 2016.

"Decision Making in Asad's Syria." The Washington Institute Policy Focus, research memorandum no. 35 (February 1998).

Index